HOUSE TO HOUSE

Books by Keith Nolan

Operation Buffalo

The Battle for Saigon

Battle for Hue

A Hundred Miles of Bad Road (with Dwight W. Birdwell)

The Magnificent Bastards

House to House

Death Valley

Into Cambodia

Ripcord

Sappers in the Wire

Into Laos

HOUSE TO HOUSE

*Playing the Enemy's Game in Saigon,
May 1968*

KEITH NOLAN

ZENITH PRESS

This edition published by Zenith Press, an imprint of
MBI Publishing Company, Galtier Plaza, Suite 200,
380 Jackson Street, St. Paul, MN, 55101-3885 USA.

Cover by Mandy Iverson
Design by Lynn Dragonette

Cover photograph: Dismounted troops from
Company B of the 2nd Battalion, 47th Mechanized
Infantry, in District 8, Saigon, May 11, 1968.
Courtesy of Ken Pollard

ISBN: 0-7603-2330-5
ISBN-13: 978-0-7603-2330-4

Printed in the United States

For Britt, who's six now

I don't go to reunions. Guess I never wanted to be a soldier. My military experience is a double-edged sword. I'm very proud, yet sad. Being in combat is like a journey into the unknown, and I was able to survive. That's all I can say.

Robert Mark Nauyalis
9th Infantry Division
Vietnam, 1968–1969

CONTENTS

Preface
THE ILLUSION

Doing as his president asked, General William C. Westmoreland, Commander, U.S. Military Assistance Command, Vietnam, addressed a joint session of Congress in November 1967. His message: victory was just around the corner in Vietnam. The response: rapturous applause.

Westmoreland also spread the good news of impending triumph on the television program *Meet the Press* and in an address to the National Press Club. The general said nothing he did not believe; his can-do optimism perfectly served the public-relations campaign being waged by an administration anxious to shore up support for a war which the average voter did not understand and was beginning to question.

President Lyndon B. Johnson was less concerned with the antiwar movement (though he was certainly aggrieved by the chant, "Hey, hey, LBJ, how many kids did you kill today") than the quiet disenchantment spreading throughout Middle America with the war's cost and apparent lack of progress. At the time, U.S. ground combat units had been fighting in South Vietnam for over two and a half years. To a citizen turning on the evening news, the war was an incomprehensible charnel house of body bags, body counts, wailing peasants, and burning hootches. For all the bombs and napalm and all the American boys slogging across rice paddies, nothing seemed to change.

To persuade the people otherwise, President Johnson called his popular field commander home to Washington. Thus, General Westmoreland—resplendent in dress greens, chest covered in ribbons, incapable of self-doubt after so flawless a career—faced the cameras and explained how he had checked and was presently destroying communist aggression in South Vietnam.

"I am absolutely certain," said the general, "that whereas in 1965 the enemy was winning, today he is certainly losing." The government in Saigon had stabilized. The capabilities of its unjustly maligned army were improving. The number of villages under allied control was ever increasing. Most importantly, Hanoi's army, having lost every battle, stood at the brink of defeat. "[T]he enemy's hopes are bankrupt," Westmoreland promised. "In general, he can fight his large forces only at the edges of his sanctuaries [in Laos and Cambodia]. . . . His guerrilla force is declining at a steady rate. Morale problems are developing within his ranks."

And so on.

Prologue
TET

The besieged town was burning. Lieutenant Colonel Anthony P. DeLuca, commander of the relief force, could see the smoke in the distance as his helicopter approached. What was not on fire, he perceived upon drawing nearer, was already flattened and burnt out. The entire town of Ben Tre seemed a smoldering shambles. *Man,* marveled DeLuca, *this looks like a real war zone here.*

DeLuca had been directed to link up with the advisory team headquartered in Ben Tre. When his chopper started to land inside the team's walled compound, the colonel, otherwise enveloped in noise in the open cargo bay, could hear the sharp metallic ticks of bullets piercing aluminum. They were taking hits. There was no indication—no jolts or vibrations—that the helicopter had been damaged, and DeLuca was startled when the pilot abruptly pulled up, breaking off the attempted landing. DeLuca was wearing a flight helmet that plugged into the Huey's communications system, and he asked the pilot, "What's going on? Why didn't we land?"

The pilot said that the tail rotor had been shot up. "We can't hover without it," he explained, "and if we can't hover, we can't land in that courtyard. We're gonna have to take it back to Dong Tam."

A thought struck DeLuca. "If you couldn't land in the courtyard," he asked the pilot, "how are you going to land at Dong Tam?" The pilot intended to land his helicopter like an airplane on Dong Tam's airstrip. Reaching the base, DeLuca braced himself as the Huey slid down the steel runway matting on its skids.

DeLuca returned to Ben Tre aboard another Huey. This time, the helicopter was able to land in the courtyard adjacent the advisory team's operations center without drawing fire. As DeLuca hurriedly exited with his radioman, he saw someone in a helmet and a flak jacket dashing forward and excitedly shouting his name. "Tony! Tony!" DeLuca recognized the face under the steel brim as the man wrapped him in a bear hug. It was Lieutenant Colonel James Dare, a classmate from West Point presently assigned as senior advisor in Ben Tre. The advisory team had been cut off and under fire for almost two days at that point, and Dare sighed with relief as he hugged DeLuca: "Ah, am I glad to see you!"

Ben Tre, a picturesque market town in the backwaters of the delta, is situated on the north bank of a river that shares its name and linked to the fishing village on the opposite shore by a narrow steel bridge. The war came to this tranquil community, and its garrison of militia troops, three and a half hours after midnight on January 31, 1968.

When the attack began, Dare's advisors were in a heightened state of readiness, as were, presumably, the militiamen in their guard posts, thanks to an alert issued that day to all units in South Vietnam warning of possible enemy action during the night. The attack was a profound shock nonetheless. There was no precedent for such an onslaught. The VC—that is, those raggedy-ass Viet Cong in rubber sandals and black peasant garb armed with AK-47s and a few bandoliers of ammunition—waged a war of snipers, mines, and hit-and-run ambushes. They did not launch full-scale attacks on towns and cities. In any event, the alert seemed like another case of higher command crying wolf, for the war always slowed to a virtual standstill during Tet, a holiday of great religious and familial significance that marks the beginning of the lunar new year, which was being riotously celebrated that night throughout Southeast Asia.

Perhaps a thousand guerrilla fighters watched the festivities from the tree lines and rice paddies around Ben Tre, awaiting the mortar barrage that was to signal the attack. Surging forward when the explosions began flashing in the night, the Viet Cong quickly seized the fishing village, as well as Ben Tre's central market and the residential neighborhoods on the east side of town. Resistance was scattered. Like government troops across South Vietnam, at least half of Ben Tre's militiamen were on leave for Tet.

The province chief's villa and the adjacent compound housing Dare's advisory team fronted the river in the southwest corner of town, and came under heavy fire from the south side of the Ben Tre River. The night reverberated with explosions and automatic-weapons fire. The exchange of tracers across the river was almost constant.

When dawn came, there were bodies in the streets and shacks burning along the river. Thousands of terrified civilians streamed out of town as the VC massed at the south end of the steel bridge, intent on storming across and overrunning the advisory compound. They were prevented from doing so by patrol boats and helicopter gunships dispatched by the U.S. Navy.

Throughout the morning and afternoon, the small, fast-moving patrol boats sallied up and down the river, under the bridge and back again, braving a gauntlet of fire to rake the enemy with belt-fed grenade launchers and dual-mounted .50-caliber machine guns. It seemed like there were VC firing from every house in the fishing village. Those occupying the central market launched rocket-propelled grenades (RPG) at the patrol boats from the roof and windows of the impressive two-story complex, each one marked by a contrail of white smoke. In response, the gunships rained salvos of rockets into the marketplace. The Hueys also set the south shore ablaze, blanketing the area in smoke.

The enemy did not retreat. Hoping to preserve the town, corps headquarters at Can Tho—part of the Army of the Republic of Vietnam (ARVN)—had been reluctant to employ heavy firepower to drive out the Viet Cong. Acquiescing to the pleas of the advisors, corps finally authorized the use of artillery. As the battle continued into the night, a twin-engine, fixed-wing AC-47 Spooky gunship droned overhead, jettisoning parachute flares and stitching targets with streams of red minigun tracers as solid as lasers. The enemy returned fire with heavy machine guns. By morning, corps headquarters, having run out of options, was forced to request tactical air support. Jet fighters from the U.S. Air Force began making their runs shortly before noon, flashing in low through the ground fire, dropping napalm and five-hundred pound bombs and demolishing most of what remained of Ben Tre.

As ordered, Lieutenant Colonel DeLuca, having caught a chopper at his battalion base camp, presented himself at the division's forward headquarters at Dong Tam deep in the Mekong Delta late on the morning of February 1.

The whole place was buzzing when DeLuca arrived, and in the absence of more senior officers who were out in their helicopters, it fell to a staff officer, a major, to hastily outline the situation in Ben Tre. Only the province chief's villa and the advisory compound were still in friendly hands, the major explained. DeLuca was to chopper immediately into the compound and make contact with the senior advisor. "What about my battalion?" DeLuca asked.

The major said that air assets were being organized to move the battalion. "Don't worry. We'll send your people in right after you."

Talk about vague orders, mused Tony DeLuca, only three weeks in command of the 3rd Battalion, 39th Infantry of the 9th Division. He had been eager to get his command. Now, hurrying to the airstrip and his first battle, he wondered, *What the hell have I gotten into here?*

Actually, DeLuca wondered what they had all gotten into, for according to the major, enemy attacks had erupted throughout the country during the first morning of Tet. Their phantom foe, emerging from the jungle that hid him and the rural hamlets that sustained him, was engaged in an unprecedented onslaught against the country's urban centers. Over a hundred towns and cities were under assault. The major had ticked off the names of those in the division area. Ben Tre. My Tho. Xuan Loc. Vinh Long. Elements of the division were defending here, counterattacking there, and fighting pitched battles at places long considered untouchable, including Bien Hoa Airbase and the massive logistical facility at Long Binh. Most shockingly, troops from the division were fighting in the streets of Saigon. Everything was touch and go, and DeLuca, taking his seat in the helicopter, had little time to contemplate that the supposedly defeated and demoralized Viet Cong had been able to invade the capital of South Vietnam.

The air strikes had been completed by the time DeLuca reached Ben Tre, but enemy soldiers holding on amid the smoking wreckage had managed to disable and turn away his helicopter. Finally making it in aboard the replacement aircraft, DeLuca considered Dare's effusive greeting a little premature. "Jimmy, don't be too happy yet," DeLuca said when Dare released him. "It's only me, and I don't have any troops with me!"

Dare led DeLuca into the whitewashed French colonial building that housed the advisory team's operations center. Soon, a single-file formation of helicopters came into view, bearing Captain Thomas R. Genetti and Company B. The courtyard in the compound was large enough for the Hueys to land in pairs, with six infantrymen clambering from each. DeLuca expected the worst, but thanks to the gunships flying cover for the insertion, the lift ships took few hits, none serious.

The Hueys returned at length with a second company, and then a third, depositing them on the outskirts of town. DeLuca barely knew Genetti. He had never laid eyes on the other two company commanders. Both had been attached to him from other units, division headquarters being reluctant to pull DeLuca's entire battalion out of its normal area of operations should additional attacks erupt there. Glancing uneasily at the destruction around them, the GIs—better known as grunts in this war—prepared defensive positions in the fading light of dusk in a town that looked like something out of a battlefield newsreel from World War II.

Lieutenant Colonel DeLuca's command group moved with Genetti as Company B advanced on the morning of February 2 toward the steel bridge in the center of town. Suspecting that the enemy had melted away in the face of the relief force, DeLuca had nevertheless made his plans on the assumption that at least a rearguard was still in place. DeLuca instructed his company commanders to proceed with caution and methodically secure each block of demolished houses before proceeding to the next. The need for caution was real. Because battles were raging throughout the country and resources were stretched thin, DeLuca had been forced to inform his company commanders that they would be attacking without benefit of artillery, gunships, or tactical air support.

They encountered sporadic fire on the way to the bridge. At one point, Lieutenant Colonel DeLuca was walking behind Genetti's lead troops when a burst of fire splattered the roadway in front of him. DeLuca darted for cover, with his radioman at his heels. It suddenly occurred to DeLuca that the radioman—who was never farther away from the colonel than the stretch of the radio cord—had marked him as an officer, thus the perfect target for any VC marksman lurking on a roof with an AK-47.

Reaching safety, DeLuca barked at the hapless young radioman to stay as far from him as possible while still being within shouting distance: "Goddamnit, I don't want you right next to me. Get the hell back. If I need you, I'll call for you to move up to me."

After crossing the steel bridge, DeLuca and Major Peter D. Booras, the battalion operations officer, joined Captain Genetti as he sat alongside a demolished house with his own radiomen. According to the plan, Genetti's lead platoon, pushing onward while the rest of Company B regrouped near the south end of the bridge, would soon link up with an ARVN unit that was supposed to have moved into the area from a different direction. At that point, the combined force was to turn and sweep east to west through the burnt-out fishing village along the Ben Tre River.

The lead platoon presently came under heavy fire. In short order, rounds began zipping through the brush around DeLuca and Genetti, whose grunts could not return the fire for fear of hitting the lead platoon. At the prone beside Booras, DeLuca had the radio handset pressed to his ear as he spoke with the brigade commander orbiting overhead in his command ship. DeLuca explained that the ARVN unit that was supposed to have secured the area had failed to materialize. He had one platoon on the verge of being cut off. The fire on his own position was increasing, and he feared that the Viet Cong were maneuvering to encircle all of Bravo Company.

"We're in a bad spot," DeLuca, whose radio call sign was Sandal 6, told the brigade commander. "We're going to head back across the bridge and regroup. Over."

The brigade commander insisted that DeLuca hold his position. Gun-ships were being diverted to help. "Don't give up any ground," the colonel said.

"If we stay here, we're going to take heavy casualties," DeLuca replied. "We're heading back across the bridge. Sandal 6, out."

"Sandal 6, this is Samson 6," cracked the voice of a highly displeased colonel who wanted to get in a dig after such disobedience. "I am the higher headquarters and I will terminate conversations. Over."

"Roger," DeLuca dutifully replied. "Over."

"Roger, out," said the colonel, his point now made.

DeLuca instructed Genetti to get his people moving back toward the bridge. Nobody moved. The grunts were glued to whatever cover they had found as fire continued to crack and whine all around, and they were con-vinced that they would be cut down the instant they exposed themselves.

Not a little uptight himself, DeLuca looked at Booras. "You don't want to die here, do you?" barked DeLuca.

"No fuckin' way," Booras growled defiantly, catching DeLuca's meaning. With that, the two sprang to their feet, shouting the infantry battle cry, "Fol-low me," as they sprinted toward the bridge. It worked. The troops got up and followed.

Reaching the bridge, DeLuca and Booras waved the men across as bul-lets ricocheted off the steel guardrails. Genetti had some of his troops lay down cover fire for their buddies sprinting across the bridge. Not wanting to present the enemy with bunched-up targets, the grunts made good their retreat one or two at a time. DeLuca and Booras brought up the rear. DeLuca was almost to the middle of the bridge when he realized that Booras had stopped short and was standing alone, shouting obscenities at the enemy soldiers as he furiously heaved hand grenades in their direction. DeLuca dashed back and grabbed Booras, pulling him along. "C'mon," DeLuca shouted, "let's get the hell outta here!"

The entire operation had bogged down. Not only had DeLuca's force been repulsed, but one of the attached companies had suffered heavy casu-alties on the other side of Ben Tre. DeLuca's own losses were surprisingly light. Luck had been with them, he realized, when Genetti subsequently reported that at one point during the withdrawal, he had taken cover under the south end of the bridge only to discover a huge mine positioned against the abutments. The enemy had apparently planned to let the relief force enter the fishing village and then drop the bridge behind it, trapping the troops against the river. The mine never exploded, however. Evidently, the demolition cord running to the detonator had been damaged at some point during the battle.

DeLuca went back across the bridge the next day with Company B, but made no contact, the enemy having vanished during the night. Genetti's troops counted five hundred abandoned spider holes and two-man bunkers in a coconut grove near the fishing village that the enemy had used as a staging area.

With the battle over, the people of Ben Tre returned to their shattered homes. "People who have sympathies toward the VC should have seen the refugees streaming [back] into the city," DeLuca wrote his wife. "At least 500 passed through my position with terrible wounds, tears, and lost expressions." Out of a population of thirty-five thousand, "the VC killed 1000 civilians and wounded 2500. . . . In addition, the VC had a list of all key province officials and the locations of their families in Saigon. Assassination teams wiped out these families."

DeLuca's assertion about civilian casualties was correct in the sense that the guerrillas, by making war in a fishing village and sedate market town, could be held morally responsible for all the innocents killed and maimed in the resulting maelstrom. Literally speaking, however, it was the firepower brought to bear in defense of the besieged advisory team that caused most of the civilian casualties. The price paid by those caught in the middle was fearsome. Even the enemy did not suffer as grievously as did the people of Ben Tre. Major Chester L. Brown, U.S. Air Force, who had braved heavy ground fire in a single-engine observation plane to mark targets for the jets, summed up the dilemma when he told Peter Arnett of the Associated Press: "It became necessary to destroy the town to save it."

General Westmoreland confidently declared victory on the first morning of what history would call the Tet Offensive. The assertion sounded fantastic to the reporters with whom he was speaking, especially given the setting for the impromptu press conference. At the time, the theater commander was inspecting the blood-splattered grounds of the U.S. Embassy in Saigon; the enemy sappers who had penetrated the compound had only just been eliminated by MPs and marine security guards. The dead were still sprawled where they had been cut down as Westmoreland robotically asserted that the enemy's plans had gone afoul, his forces sent reeling with heavy casualties, and so on and so forth. It was a disconcerting performance, made even more bizarre by Westmoreland's contention that it was the allies that were on the offensive, not the Viet Cong.

The theater commander would not even allow that he had been taken by surprise. Due to a failure in coordination, the enemy had struck several cities in the northern part of the country a day before the main onslaught. In response, all units had been placed on maximum alert and the traditional holiday truce had been canceled. True enough, but believing his own propaganda about a battered and dispirited enemy, Westmoreland had anticipated a scattering of small attacks designed to disrupt the holiday for propaganda purposes. He had not expected a nationwide conflagration of unprecedented scope and violence with which the communists intended to win the war in one sweeping moment.

Upon receiving the alert in question, Lieutenant Colonel Richard E. George, provost marshal of Saigon—soon to find himself maneuvering three-man MP jeeps against enemy battalions—had expected "the usual terrorist hits on one or more of our billets or activities. There wasn't even the slightest hint that the VC effort would be as massive as it was."

Brigadier General John Chaisson, U.S. Marine Corps, director of the MACV Combat Operations Center in Saigon, spoke candidly to the press: "I'm not the intelligence man. . . but as I read the intelligence, it did not indicate that we were going to have any such massive spread of attacks as this. . . . [T]he Viet Cong surprised us. . . . I've got to give 'em credit for having engineered and planned a very successful offensive, [at least] in its initial phases. It was surprisingly well-coordinated, it was surprisingly intensive. . . ."

With a hundred cities on fire, General Westmoreland, during his remarks at the U.S. Embassy, dismissed the offensive as a diversion for the main blow he predicted would soon fall on the marines at Khe Sanh. The strategic Khe Sanh combat base, located in the remote and mountainous northwest corner of South Vietnam near the Ho Chi Minh Trail in neighboring Laos, had recently been besieged by several North Vietnamese Army (NVA) divisions. Westmoreland predicted a climatic campaign at Khe Sanh and other points along the Demilitarized Zone (DMZ) that would finally finish off the NVA. The theater commander actually had it backward. The hammer never fell at Khe Sanh because the communists had not attacked the cities to divert resources from the northern frontier. Rather, they had surrounded Khe Sanh to draw Westmoreland's attention away from Saigon.

The element of surprise notwithstanding, the enemy's efforts were doomed to failure for no guerrilla force could prevail in open battle against a modern army. Certain enemy commanders had, in fact, argued against the offensive on such grounds. Frontal assaults only played to their foe's strengths, they said. Better to continue bleeding the occupiers of their land with booby traps and ambushes. Time was on their side, as was the land itself. In the jungle, it was the VC and North Vietnamese who initiated most actions. Able to slip away when the tables were turned, the enemy, though sometimes badly hurt, could not be made to sacrifice more men than could be replaced. Thus, it was the communists who controlled the war's rate of attrition, a vexing detail never fully grasped by General Westmoreland, though it sabotaged the entire rationale behind his search-and-destroy strategy, ultimately rendering meaningless the aggressive fighting spirit of American units during those early years of the Vietnam War.

The initial gains won by the enemy through surprise could not be sustained. The communists had expected the government troops to come apart under the weight of the offensive. There were many fine government units, but in the main, the ARVN was apathetic, intimidated, and poorly led. It was an army that had something to fight against but nothing to fight for, given the venality of the various regimes that held power in Saigon. Still, the ARVN performed with stubborn courage when Tet hit. They hung on; they bought time. General Westmoreland and his unit commanders used that time wisely, rolling with the punches and organizing counterattacks that reclaimed most of the enemy-held towns in a matter of days, if not hours. Such was the mobility and overwhelming firepower of the U.S. Army.

The communists believed that the guerrilla fighters, heroes to the rural peasantry, would be greeted as liberators in the cities, sparking a popular uprising against the government. There was no uprising. The people of the cities essentially shut their doors on the guerrillas. Some had those doors broken down. Political cadres who accompanied the enemy's assault units were under orders to eliminate enemies of the revolution. The assassination teams murdered hundreds of men, women, and children. In driving these invaders out, the allies themselves killed thousands of civilians—such was the "collateral damage" from the firepower that kept U.S. casualties relatively low—and turned tens of thousands more into refugees whose neighborhoods had been smashed like crockery by gunships and artillery fire, napalm, and bombs. What happened at Ben Tre happened throughout South Vietnam during Tet.

The carnage reached epic proportions in Hue, former imperial capital of Vietnam and the only objective the communists held onto for any length of time. The enemy had come in force to Hue, a division's worth of VC and NVA regulars who entrenched themselves amid centuries-old battlements and buildings of brick and stone that proved all but impervious to mortar and artillery fire. Air support was hampered by foul weather as three battalions of marines slowly advanced in a grinding house-to-house, block-by-block battle, reinforced by ARVN soldiers who seemed more interested in looting than fighting. Eight-inch howitzers were finally brought forward to support the marines. In addition, elements of the 1st Cavalry Division and the 101st Airborne cut the supply lines running into the city from the A Shau Valley, an enemy bastion in the fog-shrouded mountains west of Hue. The enemy inside Hue was inexorably destroyed, but much of the beautiful and historic city had been reduced to rubble by the time the red flag with the yellow star was finally hauled down on February 24, 1968.

Heavy combat continued throughout the country as General Westmoreland relentlessly pursued the retreating enemy into his rural enclaves. Never before in the war had the communists suffered such punishment. The guerrillas did not crack, and they did recover, but at that moment in the war they were finally as Westmoreland had always described them—defeated, demoralized, and on the defensive—as evidenced by the unprecedented number of prisoners being taken during operations. The theater commander received no accolades, however. Instead, in the midst of the Tet Counteroffensive, it was dryly announced that Westmoreland had been selected to replace the outgoing army chief of staff. He was to assume his new duties that summer. The reassignment was a promotion in name only, giving the impression that Westmoreland was being kicked upstairs for the various failures that had led to the Tet Offensive.

Soon thereafter, on March 31, 1968, President Johnson, looking haggard—his will to continue the war broken by the strength the enemy had shown during Tet—announced a partial bombing halt that he hoped would lead to negotiations with Hanoi. Seated behind his desk in the Oval Office, Johnson concluded his televised address by declaring that in order to devote all his energies to ending the war, he would neither seek nor accept the nomination of his party for another term as president.

With Hanoi quickly agreeing to enter into peace talks, President Johnson, by exhibiting weakness instead of strength, transformed what had been a colossal battlefield disaster for the communists into a decisive psychological victory. It could not have been otherwise. The nation had lost heart for the war, unable to reconcile all the light-at-the-end-of-the-tunnel rhetoric with the scenes of devastation from Saigon and Hue and small towns like Ben Tre.

General Westmoreland blamed the public's loss of faith on the alarmist and overly negative news coverage of the Tet Offensive. The professional officer corps agreed, feeling itself betrayed when Walter Cronkite, the dean of American journalism, declared the war an un-winnable stalemate during a broadcast from Hue. The media was definitely not on the team. On the whole, however, its reporting was more neutral than negative, always paid homage to GI heroism, and tended to reflect, not define, the mood in the United States. Westmoreland was not undone by pessimistic reporting, but by an enemy so determined as to outlast a superpower. It ultimately did not matter to a Middle America that was already dubious about the wisdom of intervening in a civil war on the other side of the world that the cold statistics of Tet and the Tet Counteroffensive (four thousand U.S. and five thousand ARVN soldiers dead against an official body count of nearly sixty-thousand VC and NVA) bespoke great battlefield successes by the allies. No one doubted that the communists had been hurt. Tet had made clear, however, that the enemy, having absorbed every blow thrown at him to that point, still possessed enough manpower to continue fighting for years to come. The price of destroying so resolute and resilient a foe was far beyond anything the American people were willing to bear. Enough young men had already come home in aluminum caskets. It was time to negotiate and get out.

The communists recuperated with alarming speed. Hanoi took advantage of the bombing halt not only to rebuild its infrastructure in North Vietnam—roads, railways, factories, and bridges—but also to pump new life into the guerrillas in the south. Even as diplomatic cables were being exchanged in preparation for the upcoming peace negotiations, enemy supply convoys were rolling and tens of thousands of fresh troops were marching down the Ho Chi Minh Trail. Many of these NVA regulars were assigned as replacements, or "fillers," in Viet Cong units decimated during Tet and the Tet Counteroffensive.

In mid-April 1968, the demoralized colonel serving as political commissar of the 9th Viet Cong Division defected with plans for a "second wave" of attacks against Saigon. The attacks were without military justification and were, in fact, suicidal, given that the enemy had no hope of taking the city. Hanoi's goal was instead political. The attacks were designed to serve as a vivid demonstration to the world that the communists still held the initiative, whatever their losses were during Tet. The second battle for Saigon was timed to begin just days before the opening session of the Paris Peace Talks.

General Westmoreland, anticipating such a strategy, already had numerous screening operations in progress around Saigon. The intelligence windfall provided by the political commissar brought a distinct focus to these efforts; for example, the enemy colonel mapped out the directions from which the various assault units were to strike the capital. As a result, those U.S. and ARVN units securing the approaches to the city, aided by night-flying helicopters equipped with spotlights and miniguns, were able to stop most of the approaching enemy soldiers before they could reach Saigon.

Most but not all. Moving in small groups, enough enemy soldiers were able to slip through the defenses around the city, and heavy fighting flared up again in Saigon on the morning of May 5, 1968. The attack on the capital was the centerpiece of a broader campaign that would be known officially as the May Offensive, or more informally as Tet II or Mini-Tet. The offensive had actually begun five days earlier with several NVA regiments executing a conventional attack across the Demilitarized Zone in the vicinity of Dong Ha.

As fighting erupted in Saigon—and that same morning, the enemy mortared and rocketed a hundred other towns, cities, and military installations—army and marine units on the northern frontier remained locked in terrible battle with the North Vietnamese Army. At the same time, one of the great disasters of the war unfolded as the 2nd NVA Division overran and destroyed the twin Special Forces outposts at Ngog Tavak and Kham Duc on the Laotian border, despite the arrival of marine howitzers and an infantry battalion from the Americal Division. The fury of the offensive did not burn itself out until the end of the second week of May, by which time some eleven hundred GIs and marines had been killed. Most of the casualties were suffered in the defense of Saigon, Dong Ha, Ngog Tavak, and Kham Duc, and during the 1st Cavalry Division's ongoing incursion into the A Shau Valley. It was the highest two-week toll of American dead at any point during the war, worse even than the first two weeks of the Tet Offensive.

Government troops were responsible for Saigon's internal security, and most of the fighting in the capital during Mini-Tet fell to the ARVN. Four battalions from the 9th Division, however, were committed piecemeal-fashion to the southern suburbs of Saigon.

Lieutenant Colonel DeLuca's battalion was among those dispatched to the capital. The enemy had burrowed like termites into several residential neighborhoods. Working in small teams, the guerrillas flitted from house to house through holes knocked in the walls, and they fought until killed or wounded and captured. Having proved they could once again invade Saigon, the communists' only purpose was to cause damage, or rather to have their foe do it for them. DeLuca and his fellow battalion commanders, fighting as any would on an urban battlefield, were forced to play the enemy's game as they once again destroyed a town to save it. All the while, television crews filmed the burning houses, the piteous civilians fleeing the crossfire, and the grunts being hustled out of the wreckage on stretchers or in body bags. The cameras did not lie, and the inevitable destruction of the enemy was duly reported. On the evening news, however, the juxtaposition of the Saigon-under-siege footage with the diplomats sitting down at the conference table in Paris gave exactly the impression that Hanoi wanted. Like Tet, the May Offensive was another tactical victory for the allies that only served to hurt their cause.

It was also, at the grunt level, a fight to remember.

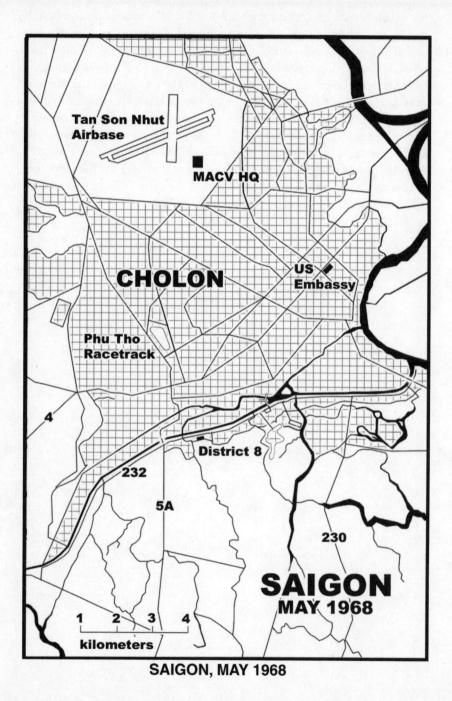

SAIGON, MAY 1968

Part One
FIREFIGHT AT XOM CAU MAT

Chapter 1

The column slowed a bit as it passed through the occasional roadside town or little thatch-roofed hamlet, then picked up speed again during the long, empty stretches, the elevated highway on which it traveled cutting straight as a plumb line across the rice paddies. Distant tree lines paralleled the column's progress. The troops riding atop the personnel carriers—better known as tracks—sweltered in their helmets and flak jackets as they kept a wary eye on the passing scenery. Though casual in posture, those manning the .50-caliber machine gun mounted on the command cupola of each track were ready to reply immediately in case of ambush.

The tropical heat was of more immediate concern, but a remedy was immediately at hand: the cooler full of beer and ice stashed inside every personnel carrier.

Whenever needed, a guy could wipe a cold, wet can of Miller or Falstaff or Carling Black Label across his forehead, then chug it down and toss the empty off into the paddies. These men drinking beer behind their machine guns weren't GIs; they were the bandits of Bandido Charlie (never mind the misspelling), a tough, field-savvy outfit that was really an army unto itself, unencumbered by the petty rules and regulations of the rest of the by-the-book Green Machine.

On paper, if not in spirit, the unit on the highway—Company C, commanded by Captain Edmund B. Scarborough—belonged to the 5th Battalion (Mechanized), 60th Infantry Regiment, 9th Infantry Division. Scarborough's company was divided into three line platoons and a headquarters element, which included one track for the captain and another for the first sergeant, plus a medical track, a maintenance track, and two mortar tracks. Each of the line platoons was authorized four M113 Armored Personnel Carriers, and half a dozen infantrymen sat atop each shoebox-shaped APC.

Though Captain Scarborough commanded a typical mechanized infantry company (less than twenty tracks, little more than a hundred troops ready for duty), Bandido Charlie possessed a raucous pride, a remembrance of past exploits and larger-than-life leaders, all of which made it special in spirit, if not numbers. Each company in the battalion had its own emblem. The Bandidos sported pocket patches featuring a skull grinning malevolently from the center of two crossed cavalry sabers. The design was also stenciled on the front of the tracks, and swallow-tailed cavalry guidons— also decorated with skulls and sabers and officially banned by division headquarters—flapped defiantly from radio antennas, along with the Stars and Stripes and battle flags of the Confederacy.

Captain Scarborough's column had hit the road on short notice from the battalion base camp adjacent to the town of Binh Phuoc. Little time had been required to crank up and get rolling. When lined up in the motor pool between operations, the tracks were always topped off with diesel, the hulls already stacked floor to ceiling with beer, munitions, and other essential supplies. Major Stinson J. Miller, the battalion operations officer, joined Scarborough with several tracks from the battalion command group—model M577s that had higher hulls than the infantry tracks so as to accommodate map boards and additional radios. Rolling through the main gate, the column swung right onto a road that led ten kilometers northwest through the rice paddies to brigade headquarters at Tan An. The drivers of the M113s and M577s stayed in the tread marks of the preceding track in an effort to avoid the mines that were encountered so frequently between Binh Phuoc and Tan An that the route had been dubbed Thunder Road.

As dust swirled in the column's wake, the battalion commander, Lieutenant Colonel Eric F. Antila, flew ahead in a little H23 bubble helicopter to scout Thunder Road for signs of mines and ambushes. No such hazards appeared.

Upon reaching Tan An, Captain Scarborough's column turned northeast onto Highway 4, the main roadway connecting the Mekong Delta with Saigon. The highway, running along the top of an earthen berm in order to remain usable during the rainy season, was wide enough to accommodate the line of personnel carriers even as civilian traffic went by in the opposite lane. The Bandidos could not take such a peaceful scene at face value. Theirs was a war without front lines, a war in which the people they had come to save seemed to be in league with the people they had come to fight. One of their track drivers had recently been killed when the front of his vehicle snagged a wire strung across Thunder Road from one hootch to another inside a hamlet, setting off a cluster of grenades.

There had been other incidents in which mines had been buried in Thunder Road and Highway 4 by guerrillas, who command detonated them from concealed places in the brush and nippa palm, and then slipped away unseen in the resulting chaos. The local villagers never offered warning and never answered questions, even as they fed and sheltered the guerrillas and furnished them information about the Americans. It didn't matter to the troops if that assistance was offered because of intimidation or genuine sympathy for the National Liberation Front; the results were the same either way. For the men of the 5-60th Mech everything outside Binh Phuoc was Indian Country.

Captain Scarborough sat on a small metal seat that had been scrounged up and mounted directly behind the driver's hatch on the left side of his track, the long-barreled .50-cal pointing forward from the command cupola on his right. No one rode inside the tracks because of the threat of mines and rocket-propelled grenades, both of which could easily penetrate the vehicle's aluminum armor. Instead, some of the troopers sat up top on wooden ammunition crates. Others sat shoulder-to-shoulder, two or three abreast, facing forward, on the open cargo hatch cover behind the command cupola of each APC.

Those who had scrounged an extra flak jacket sat on the thick vests to cushion the jolting, engine-roaring ride as the column raced along at thirty-five miles per hour, almost full throttle for a personnel carrier. The tracks could go faster, but it was unwise to do so for a thrown tread at top speed could result in a cart-wheeling crash, with the twelve-ton vehicle upside down or on its side when the dust settled, medevacs and body bags all around. It had happened before.

It was thirty klicks (kilometers) by road—slightly less as the helicopter flies—from Tan An to an intersection just short of the capital where Antila, the column's eye in the sky, instructed Company C to make a right turn from Highway 4 onto Route 232. Whereas the highway continued north before angling northeast into Cholon—the western quarter of the city and home primarily to Chinese immigrants—Route 232 cut northeast for three kilometers to the southwestern tip of Saigon. Company C had fought in Cholon during Tet. This time around, the Bandidos had been tasked to help secure the southernmost edge of Saigon.

Reaching the outskirts of the capital, Scarborough halted the column and said on the radio something to the effect of "all right, people, let's look sharp, let's look professional as we roll into Saigon." The captain wanted everyone alert, weapons at the ready, and he wanted everyone not already wearing a helmet and flak jacket to don his protective gear. He also wanted the column, which had spread out like an accordion during the road march, to tighten back up. "Let's do it right," Scarborough told his troops, and they did; the personnel carriers were uniformly spaced as the company proceeded smartly into town. The narrow street, power lines running along either side, was hemmed in by storefronts and pastel-colored houses and apartments, many of which were two or three stories high. The troops scanned windows and rooftops as the column clattered past. Braced for the worst, they realized that nobody on the crowded street seemed to know there was a war on. It was just an average day in the city, or at least that part of it. Still led by the battalion commander's low-flying helicopter, the column continued toward its first objective, a concrete bridge spanning the river that separated the southern part of the city from Cholon.

So far, so good. . . .

Chapter 2

The legend of the hard-drivin', beer-drinkin', hell-for-leather Bandidos was so renowned that there had been much excited banter as the men mounted up at Binh Phuoc for the road march to Saigon. Almost all the troops, including Captain Scarborough, were relatively green—replacements for casualties suffered during Tet and the Tet Counteroffensive. Company C had been involved in only light and sporadic action since then, and the new guys were anxious to make a mark of their own. One of the replacements, Private First Class Lanny E. Jones, would later recall how "all of us newer guys was kind of jumpin' around, hoppin' up and sayin', 'Man, let's go—let's roll in there and kick some ass.' We had a couple old heads there, and they said, 'You new guys, you don't want to go. Ain't no way you want to go.' We didn't listen to 'em. We didn't know any better, yet. We was ready to roll."

The Bandido Charlie mythos had begun with First Lieutenant Larry A. Garner, a platoon leader in the company when the division was originally deployed to Vietnam in December 1966. To Garner, a handsome mid-westerner with the physique of an athlete and a robust, outgoing persona, the war was the adventure of a lifetime. Garner was going on twenty-seven when he hit the war zone; he was a former divinity student who had since married, fathered two children, served a hitch in the marines, and earned a master's degree in military history. He could converse knowledgeably on any subject, and reportedly had an IQ of 167.

Lieutenant Garner's qualities were such that he was given command of Company C in April 1967, though any number of captains were available. Garner was a singular figure, given his mustache, the red bandanna knotted around his neck, and the .45-caliber pistol worn in a holster on each hip. Preaching that soldiers fought better when they saw themselves as something special and not just cogs in the machine, Garner designed the skull-and-sabers emblem and had their olive-drab personnel carriers painted in a unique camouflage scheme of black and green. Red bandannas soon became ubiquitous among the men. To stand out even more from the crowd, many also donned black berets. "The troops idolized Garner," recalls Charles E. Taylor, then a platoon leader. "He was very charismatic, and had the ability to transcend rank. He was 'Larry' to the general, and he was 'Larry' to the privates."

At the time Garner assumed command, the company was detached to a straight-leg battalion (so called because it relies on leg power to move) at Dong Tam. Having never seen an outfit like Garner's, the battalion commander remarked that the troops looked like a bunch of Mexican *banditos*. Garner liked the sound of that and took to identifying Company C as Bandido Charlie on the radio. Taylor notes that "when the colonel tried to put the hammer down—'You guys are Patron Charlie'—Larry had the strength to say, 'No, we're Bandido Charlie.' Whatever the official call signs might have been, we were always Bandido Charlie."

Garner was an aficionado of George Armstrong Custer and greatly admired the cavalryman's bold charges during the Civil War. He led a charge of his own in May 1967 to relieve a grunt unit that had been ambushed from a tree line and pinned down in a paddy during the Battle of Ap Bac. The Bandidos advanced in a rolling line on the enemy flank, all weapons in action. When reaching the woods that sheltered the ambushers, they clambered off their tracks with war whoops and rebel yells to kill the startled VC in their bunkers with grenades and M16s. Garner was rewarded with the Silver Star. Taylor, who joined the unit shortly thereafter, notes that "Ap Bac was where Bandido Charlie 'arrived.' "

After six months on the line, officers were rotated to the rear for the balance of their one-year combat tours. Captain James D. Johnson, an army chaplain, met Garner shortly before the lieutenant—having actually served eight months in the field—was to turn Company C over to a new captain. "Larry seems to live to have contact with the VC," Johnson writes in his present-tense memoirs.

Garner vented about the division commander's recent order that the Bandidos had to retire their berets and red bandannas (the troops switched to green neckerchiefs that were invisible to senior officers buzzing overhead in their command ships), remove their flags and emblems, and repaint their camouflaged tracks. "Larry feels that the commanding general simply doesn't understand tactics or even simple matters such as how these morale builders play important parts in winning battles," reports Johnson. "I make a mental note that one of two things will happen to Larry if he stays in the army. Either he'll make general because of his intelligence, experience, common sense, and brashness or he'll get kicked out because of the unorthodox way in which he conducts his military business."

After the change of command, Lieutenant Garner went out on one more mission to help orient the new captain to the company's tactics and area of operations. It happened that the Bandidos made contact along Highway 4 during Garner's last day in the field on July 29, 1967, and a medical evacuation (medevac) helicopter took hits while coming in for the wounded. The Huey crash landed some distance away. Unable to reach the area aboard the tracks because the rain-sodden paddies would not support their weight, Garner grabbed the executive officer, first sergeant, and three enlisted men, and raced to the crash site on foot after pronouncing that they were obliged to save the medevac crew even at the cost of their own lives.

Garner forced the Viet Cong back, allowing another helicopter to evacuate the medevac crew; then the team hunkered down around the crippled bird as night fell. The enemy attacked from out of the darkness. Garner was shot through the heart and killed instantly. Two of the enlisted men were also killed and everyone else was wounded before the relief force arrived. "Larry thought he was invincible, that's the sad truth of things," Taylor says in trying to explain Garner's reckless courage. Johnson, moved to tears when he learned that his new friend had been killed, writes that all who knew Garner were stunned by his eleventh-hour death. "Most people felt that Larry was immortal. . . . One bullet has destroyed such thoughts. . . . A legend has been killed. . . ."

The Bandidos, operating as a straight-leg infantry during the rainy season and making heavy contact in the process, did not return to their parent battalion at Binh Phuoc until the monsoon petered out in November 1967.

Lieutenant Colonel William B. Steele, the incumbent battalion commander, was tasked at that time to conduct a spoiling operation in Dong Thap Muoi, or the Plain of Reeds—a vast, forbidding marshland used by the enemy as an infiltration route from their sanctuaries in nearby Cambodia. The incursion got off to a bad start. Company C and the battalion reconnaissance platoon had no sooner disembarked from the helicopters than they realized they were in the middle of an expertly camouflaged base camp. The newest commander of the Company C was immediately wounded; the young lieutenant was shot eight times at point-blank range by a hidden guerrilla. The Bandidos and reconnaissance troops spent the day, the night, and most of the next day trapped in a flooded paddy, completely surrounded, but the artillery, gunships, and tactical air support kept the enemy at bay. The troops, exhausted, muddy, and sopping wet, were finally plucked out by Hueys and ferried to Firebase Cudgel, a temporary position recently established on the edge of the Plain of Reeds to support the operation. The troops anticipated a chance to rest and dry out. That was not to be, however, for the enemy had targeted the trespassers at Cudgel for annihilation.

Captain Thomas Russell, the replacement commander for Company C, placed two platoons along the irrigation canals that defined the north and east sides of the perimeter, where the grunts had good open paddies to their front. His third and fourth platoons dug a line of bunkers in the bamboo and nippa palm on the south side of Cudgel, a more likely avenue of enemy approach. The attached recon platoon, under First Lieutenant Lee B. Alley, crossed the north-south canal running along the west edge of Cudgel by way of a rickety, split-rail footbridge and established a line of five bunkers in the thick vegetation on the other side. The better to catch any sappers—skilled enemy soldiers who sabotaged flares and mines—attempting to penetrate the perimeter.

Having arrived late in the afternoon, neither Russell nor Alley had a chance to clear fields of fire or conduct security patrols before nightfall. As it was, the troops barely had time to deploy claymore mines, dig three-man bunkers—which quickly turned into bathtubs because of the low water table—and reinforce their positions with mud-filled sandbags. Lieutenant Colonel Steele's command group, and the artillery fire-direction center, occupied tents in a patch of sugar cane in the middle of Cudgel. The seven howitzers on site fired from steel platforms, whose corner posts held them just above the waist-deep water of the rice paddies. The platforms had been sling-loaded in under transport helicopters, after which the big, twin-rotor CH-47 Chinooks gingerly set the 105mm howitzers on top of them.

While the troops dug in, enemy scouts among the villagers working the adjacent fields paced off distances and mapped out positions. When darkness fell, the battalion-size assault force departed its staging area in sampans, the entire area being interconnected with streams and canals. Beaching the sampans, the guerrillas made their final approach on foot, led by their scouts. The battle began at two in the morning on November 18 with a torrent of automatic-weapons fire aimed at Company C's positions on the south side of Cudgel. Next, mortar shells began exploding in recon's sector, which was the signal for those guerrillas who had stolen into position on the west side, to begin their own attack. Enemy commanders could be heard shouting orders over the din as the Viet Cong pushed through the heavy brush in squad-sized groups; some of the attackers paused to fire AK-47s, others to unleash spark-trailing RPGs, still others to scream shrill taunts which chilled the blood: "GI, you die! GI, we get you tonight!"

Captain Russell's troops detonated their claymores, heaved fragmentation grenades (frags), and then finally cut loose with M16 and M60 machine guns. Every position that pinpointed itself with a muzzle flash was hit with showers of grenades. Fifteen long minutes passed before Steele could get artillery because the batteries within range were already firing for Firebase Mace, which had been hit by a diversionary force before the main attack on Cudgel. It took even longer to divert gunships from Mace to Cudgel. The pilots eliminated the .51-caliber antiaircraft gun that greeted their arrival; because Cudgel was obscured under a blanket of smoke from the mortar barrage, the pilots then proceeded to strafe the southern perimeter along with the VC.

The first attack was repulsed. When the enemy surged forward again, the troops at the southeast corner of the perimeter—their platoon leader was badly wounded, their platoon sergeant dead, the platoon radioman nearly incoherent—fell back in disorder. Its flank thus exposed, the other platoon on the south perimeter withdrew to the howitzer positions in the middle of Cudgel. As his comrades scrambled back, a badly wounded Bandido named Edward Gallegos hung tough behind his M60, laying down such a sheet of fire as to scatter the pursuing Viet Cong.

On recon's side of the line, Lieutenant Alley, hunkered low in his dugout and splattered with mud from the mortar barrage, met the attack with his CAR15 submachine gun. Lee Alley was to become another battalion legend that night—another Larry Garner—and for that reason, some background is in order. Unlike Garner, Alley was not part of the prewar officer corps of university graduates and West Pointers. Instead, Alley was a college dropout from Laramie, Wyoming, who had been all of twenty when he graduated from Officer Candidate School (OCS). The army needed new lieutenants en masse as the war expanded, and with the sons of privilege angling for deferments and safe spots in the guard, the burden of combat leadership fell mostly on conservative, innately patriotic, lower-middle-class guys—like Alley—who had done well on the military aptitude tests, whatever their lack of formal education. As the candidates poured in, standards at OCS were relaxed and graduation rates improved substantially.

Alley wasn't one of those commissioned without learning how to work a map and compass, but he hardly felt he had mastered the art of war before being shipped to Vietnam. No matter. Sent straight to a line platoon, Alley was selected only a month later to take over the reconnaissance platoon by a battalion commander who recognized raw talent when he saw it. "I was scared to death," recalls Alley, noting recon's ferocious reputation and his own greenness. The recon platoon soon came to revere Alley, however, for his good cheer, common sense, and courage under fire. "Lee was hell on wheels," notes Charles Taylor. "He was absolutely dedicated to his men, and his men knew it, and they'd do anything for him."

It was just that bond which kept the recon platoon together against terrible odds at Cudgel. Lieutenant Alley blasted away with his submachine gun, and his troops detonated their claymores and threw all their frags; the explosions were followed by shrieks of pain, but there was little pause in the incoming fire. Alley finally informed Steele that the enemy was right on top of him, then shouted to his men to fall back to the canal. His intention was to get across the footbridge and reorganize the firing line on the safer side of the water barrier. Alley covered the retreat with his CAR-15.

When it seemed that everyone had pulled back, Lieutenant Alley told one of his radiomen to make his own move for the canal. The radioman was shot in the buttocks as soon as he exited the bunker. Alley hauled him to the canal and then crawled back to his command group. Something exploded, peppering him in the back with little pieces of white-hot metal. Alley's other radioman was seriously wounded in the throat. The fourth member of the command group, a young enlisted man serving as the platoon's artillery spotter, got a bandage around the wound; then in an amazing feat of strength, for the artillery spotter was a small, slightly built kid, he dragged the two-hundred-pound radioman to the canal by the collar of his flak jacket.

Finally rushing to the footbridge himself as the last man out, Alley found that almost everyone in the platoon had been hit at least superficially. Keeping their heads, the able-bodied formed a human chain under the bridge. They gripped the rail with one hand, for the water in the canal was too deep to touch bottom, while passing the seriously wounded with the other. Unable to hang onto both their weapons and their wounded buddies, many of the recon soldiers were forced to drop their M16s, M60s, and M79 grenade launchers into the canal.

Desperate to protect his helpless men, Lieutenant Alley crawled back to his bunker and began sweeping the darkness once again with his CAR-15. The weapon jammed, as it was coated with mud and nicked with shrapnel. Alley grabbed one of the three M16s left behind by his command group. For the first time, he could actually see the VC; they were coming fast through the brush now, coming in for the kill, and he emptied his magazine into the onrushing shadows, temporarily backing them off. Throwing the weapon aside, he dashed to the canal and grabbed an ammo bandolier from one of his troops. He then dove back into his bunker and, came up with another abandoned M16. The mud-clogged weapon blew up in his hands as he fired. He grabbed the third M16, fired all the ammo he had,

then lobbed a grenade at a Viet Cong who suddenly materialized only fifteen feet in front of him. Alley popped his head back up after the blast. His
target was gone, apparently blown backward into the brush.

Alley spotted another dark shape crawling forward on his left. The
enemy soldier raised up to fire an RPG at the gun platforms across the canal,
and then began hurling grenades into the canal itself. Alley cocked back and
threw his last frag at the man, silencing him. Out of ammunition and out
of grenades, he finally got out of there, swimming madly across the canal
to rejoin his platoon, which had made it to the other side thanks to his one-
man stand. "You really don't know what you're going to do until you do it,"
Alley said when interviewed by an army correspondent after being decorated for his actions. "I really don't know why I did some of the things I
did. . . . It may sound funny, but I really wasn't even scared. It didn't scare
me a bit until the next day when I stopped and thought of what I did."

Securing a radio from an artillery position, Alley raised Lieutenant
Colonel Steele, who was greatly relieved, having lost communication with
recon during its withdrawal only to hear Vietnamese voices over one of the
radios that had been left behind. The battalion commander wanted the howitzer crews to fire flechette rounds (beehives) before the enemy could
continue his assault across the canal. Alley hesitated, having come up six
short when he counted heads after climbing out of the canal. *I can shoot
the beehives and hope they don't hit my men,* he thought, though he was not
sure if any of the missing troops were still alive, *or not shoot and take the
chance of the VC overrunning the firebase.*

Lieutenant Alley shouted to fire the beehives, and the howitzer crews,
whose tubes were lowered for direct fire, sent twenty-one of the murderous
flechette rounds shrieking across the canal, knocking the wind out of the
enemy attack.

Three of the missing men had already been killed: two on the bunker
line and the other out on listening post. The other three members of that
cut-off listening post crawled to the canal as the enemy pulled back. When
two were hit by flechettes, their buddy stood up from the bushes, frantically waving his bush hat and screaming at the artillerymen to cease fire.

Lee Alley dove back into the canal to reach his stranded men. He was
joined by Bill Murrey and another cannoneer named Sammy L. Davis, who
had performed with great heroism during the battle. He single-handedly
fired a howitzer whose tires had been set aflame by the direct hit of the rocket
that had injured everyone else in the crew. Unmoored, the 105 had rolled
off the gun platform from the recoil of Davis' fifth round, at which point

he had been wounded by another incoming RPG.

Davis thought to grab an air mattress, and the trio used it to bring the most seriously wounded of the stranded men back across the canal. Alley, Murrey, and Davis made two more trips to rescue the two remaining men. Although they weren't under direct fire—the beehives had done their work—their hearts were in their throats because it would have taken only one lingering guerrilla to shoot them like fish in a barrel.

Lieutenant Alley handled the artillery and gunships on the west side of the firebase, while Captain Russell did the same on the south side. Alley also directed the Spooky that dropped flares and further lit the night with laser-like beams of minigun fire. Tactical air support finally came on station an hour into the battle. Alley, stripped to the waist by then, was so preoccupied adjusting fire that he moved in plain view along the canal with his confiscated radio, heedless of the last shots from the retreating enemy. Someone finally pulled him down by his trouser leg, urging him to take cover and asking what the hell made him think he had an invisible shield around him. Alley just knew; he was, for the moment, invincible.

The attack on the south side of the firebase fell apart under the bombs and napalm. At that time, the Bandidos spotted a dozen enemy soldiers bunched up in what appeared to be a hasty aid station. From farther back, a line of figures, including several female guerrillas, trotted onto the battlefield with litters to help recover their dead and wounded comrades. The grunts took them under fire. The guerrillas nevertheless managed to retreat in good order, leaving behind only five dead to be counted the next morning. Official reports estimated, not unrealistically, that eighty Viet Cong had been killed in the battle for Firebase Cudgel.

Lee Alley and Sammy Davis were both recommended for the Congressional Medal of Honor. Alley had no time to consider what that meant, for no sooner had the smoke cleared at Cudgel than his platoon was out in the paddies again. It was too much, too soon. His nerves were shot. Steele pulled Alley up to the battalion staff to decompress. The war was not over for Alley, however. He would return to the field during Tet as commander of Bandido Charlie.

Chapter 3

U nlike the new guys, First Lieutenant Ronald P. Garver, a Bandido platoon leader, was not exactly eager for battle as Company C prepared to road march from Binh Phuoc to Saigon. He had only rejoined the battalion three weeks earlier, having been badly wounded during the Tet fighting in Cholon. *Hey, didn't we just do this,* Garver thought with an uneasy sense of déjà vu as they mounted up once again to meet the enemy in Saigon.

Basically an unknown quantity at the time of the road march, Lieutenant Garver—who was wiry, blond, and small in stature, as well as a laid-back guy who kept things light—would demonstrate to his new platoon that he had his stuff together during the second go-around in Saigon. "Garver wasn't aggressive by any means," recalls another former lieutenant, "but he was steady, someone with a good head on his shoulders who knew what to do when the shooting started."

Ron Garver grew up in a big farm family living just outside of Ney, Ohio. Quitting his factory job, he enlisted with the draft board breathing down his neck and, after basic and advanced training, was selected for Infantry OCS at Fort Benning, Georgia. He shipped out for Vietnam in November 1967.

Lieutenant Garver, age twenty-three, wanted to serve honorably and get back in one piece to his wife and two baby daughters. He hoped to do both by joining the adjutant general corps. That was not to be, and in January 1968, after two months of staff duty, Garver took over a platoon in Company B. He came under fire his first time out. The company was conducting a roadrunner mission at the time, cruising up and down a designated stretch of Highway 4 all night to deter guerrillas, who used the cover of darkness to plant mines for the morning supply convoys. It was a great way to get ambushed, and sure enough, a rocket-propelled grenade suddenly sizzled out of the darkness to strike the side of Garver's track with a spray of sparks. Fearing secondary explosions, Garver jumped to the road so quickly that his helmet went flying, jerked from his head by the cord stretching from the earphones, which he'd been wearing over his steel pot, and connected to the radio inside the APC.

Garver was lucky. The rocket did little damage, and after the company swept the flanks with .50-cal fire, concentrating on the most obvious target in sight—an isolated clump of hootches along the highway—the area was quickly secured. The hootches were searched. There was a dead boy inside one of them; he was maybe thirteen years old, though it was hard to tell. No one else was there. The boy had a small entrance wound just above his heart. When someone rolled the body over, Garver saw that the machine-gun round had blown half the kid's back away on its way out. There was nothing in the hootch to link the dead boy with the ambush, no way of knowing if the company had killed an innocent bystander or a young guerrilla whose body had been left behind as his comrades disappeared back into the night with their rocket launcher. Welcome to Vietnam.

Two weeks later, the Tet Offensive exploded across Vietnam. On the second day, Companies B and C of the 5-60th Mech were rushed into Cholon, the Chinese section of Saigon, and attached to a battalion from the 199th Light Infantry Brigade. Company B was directed to reconnoiter the area northwest of the battalion command post in the Phu Tho racetrack. The company commander advanced down a narrow city street with two platoons. As mothers pulled their children inside, one little boy ran along the column, shouting a warning: "VC, VC, VC!"

After the lead platoon turned a corner, enemy ambushers suddenly rocketed the second track—it burst into flames—then disabled the company commander's track and the last track in line with a recoilless rifle, neatly preventing Company B from either advancing or withdrawing. Meanwhile AK-47 and RPG fire poured in from the cemetery on the column's right flank and from the windows and rooftops of the buildings on its left. Three men were killed, many more wounded. The company commander, superficially injured, was helped into a building by several troops willing to do the right thing for the new captain, even though they thought he was an incompetent glory hound.

Ordered to reinforce the action, Garver's platoon had only just entered the area when an explosion of unknown origin left the new lieutenant sprawled atop his track with his right arm cut to the bone in one place by shrapnel, a chunk of muscle blown away in another spot, and more skin and muscle ripped from his back just to the left of his spine.

Back at the racetrack, the Bandidos mounted up, cranked up, and were ready to go even before Captain Donald Dick, the highly respected commander of Company C, got the order to move to the aid of Company B. The lead track of the relief column halted behind the last track of the ambushed column—that last personnel carrier hadn't turned the corner into the kill zone—and the men behind the .50-caliber machine guns began blasting away into the sides of the buildings from which the enemy was firing down on Bravo Company.

The drivers stayed with their vehicles to keep the machine gunners supplied with ammunition. The mortar section went into action, too, with tubes pointed almost straight up from the cargo hatches. The rest of the Bandidos dismounted and began dragging Company B's wounded back around the corner. All the while gunships rolled in, one behind the other in a nonstop round-robin that reduced many of the buildings to smoking shells. The firefight lasted an hour before both sides opted to break contact. "It was pretty hot and heavy," recalls John H. Hohman, a former mortar man. "Wayne Parrish was firing the .50, and I was shoveling off the brass with an entrenching tool and cooling down the barrel with an oil-soaked sandbag. We finally had to withdraw because we ran out of ammunition. We fired up everything that we had. We fired all the mortar ammo, and all the machine-gun ammo. We didn't even have pistol ammo left on our track. When we rolled out of there, all I had was a grenade in my hand to toss over the side if we ran into anything."

Lieutenant Garver was loaded aboard a track and medevacked from the grounds of the racetrack after being bandaged, tagged, and hit with morphine. Because the in-country hospitals were overflowing, Garver was sent all the way to Japan. Returning to the battalion two and a half months later, he was reassigned to Company C. Only days before the Bandidos rolled again for Saigon, Garver read in the division newspaper that the hated Company B commander had been awarded the Silver Star for the melee in Cholon. "He didn't do ANYTHING & I mean *ANYTHING*," Garver wrote to his wife in disgust. "He also got a second purple heart that day. He got a scratch on the ear (shrapnel) the night I got a track blown from under me & then a scratch on the neck & minor burns on the day I got hit in [Cholon]. Never even spent one night in the hospital[,] but yet he's got two purple hearts which gets him out of the field. Since then the Army has come out with a new policy. [Two] purple hearts doesn't get you out of the field anymore so I could get hit again & still be a platoon leader. This definitely pisses me off. Let['s] hope it doesn't kill me!"

Following the battle in Cholon, the Bandidos were sent to a temporary firebase named Jaeger that had been established in a rice paddy at the intersection of Highway 4 and a secondary road that led south to Dong Tam.

This was deep guerrilla country where intruders could sense the eyes that tracked their every movement from the shadows. The situation was such that Captain Dick decided one afternoon (it happened to be Valentine's Day) to personally reconnoiter a hamlet through which the Bandidos were supposed to pass that was along the highway near Jaeger. While the rest of the outfit waited in place, a line track started forward, followed by the command track and a mortar track. Unable to maneuver because of the canals running down both sides of the highway, the lead track was forced to halt upon encountering a crater the enemy had dug in the road about a hundred meters inside the hamlet.

The enemy sprang their ambush at that moment from the hootches on the left side of the road. Captain Dick and First Lieutenant William Bausser, his forward observer, were wounded when the first RPG penetrated the side of the command track.

Private First Class Charles A. Stovall, manning the machine gun on the mortar track, opened up on the hootch from which the rocket had been fired. The enemy replied with two more rockets. "They just missed," recalls John Hohman. "We could feel the heat and the sparks go right over our heads." The driver managed to stall the engine at that moment. As the troops clambered off, "we shouted at Stovall that the track was dead and that the next rocket was gonna be right on us," continues Hohman. "We told him to get off the .50, but he kept firing as we climbed down; and then an RPG hit the top of the track and killed him."

The Bandidos from the disabled tracks—including Captain Dick, whose leg was torn and bloody—slid into the canal on the right side of the highway only to come under fire from a Viet Cong concealed in a hootch on that side. Hohman riddled the hootch with a long burst. "The guy stopped firing," notes Hohman, "and we were able to work our way down the canal and get out of there. I remember looking back as we got away and seeing my track sitting on the road on fire."

Lieutenant Colonel Steele tapped Lieutenant Alley, then serving on his staff, to take command of Company C and join Company B at Jaeger. The tracks deployed in a wagon-train circle: Company B on the west side of the perimeter, the Bandidos on the east, a platoon of straight-leg infantry in reserve, and a command group from battalion and a battery of howitzers in the center. The troops digging foxholes between the tracks found the earth so hard-baked that the soil had to be loosened with plastic explosives before it could be turned with an entrenching tool. As no bulldozers were available to push up berms, the personnel carriers sat in the open rice paddy, perfectly exposed from all directions.

As expected, the enemy contested the intrusion, launching a human-wave attack that began at two in the morning on February 25, 1968. Following a noisy feint on the Bandido's side of the circle, the main assault force surged toward Company B from a tree line two-hundred meters away. The troops were ready, having been alerted by motion-detector sensors as the enemy stole into the woods before the attack, and they greeted the onrushing shadows with a scythe of red tracers. The enemy pressed on. "They kept coming over the rice paddy dike, and I kept heaving lead at them," one .50-caliber gunner told the division newspaper. "I must have fired a thousand rounds in the first ten minutes."

Lieutenant Alley had been asleep, wrapped in a poncho and wearing nothing but pants beside his track, when the attack began. Darting up the lowered back ramp of his track, he grabbed a radio handset while shouting at the crew to close the ramp because of all the fire. The engine battery was dead, however. With no power, the ramp would not close. Alley shouted to evacuate the vehicle, and he and his crew were just starting out the back when an RPG slammed into the front of the track. The blast catapulted them onto the ground. Recovering quickly, Alley darted from position to position while still shirtless, with one boot pulled on, the other lost in the explosion, a steel pot on his head, and a .45 in hand. He was trying to get a picture of what was happening even as he encouraged the troops: "Hang in there. You're doing great. Keep up your fire, and we'll all get out of this mess!"

And a mess it was. Captain Daniel R. Schueren, the new but well-regarded commander of Company B, was cut down and killed when he left his bunker and tried to reach a track whose .50-caliber machine gun had gone silent because the gunner had been killed. Specialist Fourth Class William Paul Metzler, the company commander's radioman, managed to drag Schueren's body into a bunker. Meanwhile, a squad of VC penetrated the perimeter in an area where six tracks in a row had been knocked out by RPGs. The enemy headed straight for the artillery inside Jaeger, overrunning at least one of the 155mm howitzer positions.

The enemy squad was eliminated, but not before considerable damage had been wrought. "They killed all our wounded," Specialist Fourth Class Joseph E. Sintoni—a bright, patriotic, young man who had volunteered for combat duty and was part of Company C—wrote in his diary afterward. "The Viet Cong were so high on pot that they would laugh at you as you shot them."

The enemy's lime-green tracers streaked across the surrounded firebase in such torrents that Lieutenant Alley imagined that on any given side the VC couldn't help but be hitting their comrades on the other side. For all the outgoing fire and whatever fratricide the enemy was committing, the rocket-propelled grenades kept shrieking into Jaeger. In addition to the tracks destroyed on Company B's side of the perimeter, three more from Bandido Charlie went up in flames, fuel tanks ablaze and ammunition cooking off inside the hulls. One of Alley's lieutenants was killed in the explosions.

Parachute flares floated down from an orbiting flare-ship, trailing smoke and throwing weird, leaping shadows across the battlefield. Confusion reigned. Metzler made radio contact with the battalion executive officer, the senior man on the base. Metzler told the major that six tracks had been destroyed and the perimeter had been breached. In response, the major said that "he needed accurate information and that I shouldn't exaggerate," Metzler recalls. "I was stunned. The major kept asking to speak to an officer and I kept telling him that there weren't any."

The major was ensconced in one of two command tracks parked back-to-back in the center of the perimeter; both ramps were down, with the red interior lights glowing within the tent that joined the vehicles together as a single stationary unit. Alley stuck his head in the tent at intervals to provide information, not to the major—who seemed preoccupied as he dealt with higher command on the radio—but to First Lieutenant Alec Wade, the Bandido's new but exceptionally skilled artillery forward observer. Ignoring the dud rocket hanging from the hole it had punched in the canvas tenting, Lieutenant Wade juggled radios and controlled both the flare ship and the salvos being fired from every firebase in range. Simultaneously, he personally attended to several wounded GIs who had been dragged inside the high-backed M577s.

Three hours passed as the enemy, no longer charging forward with reckless abandon, methodically closed in dike by dike between flares. Alley finally turned to Wade and said, "Alec, we are in deep shit, man. I think we're gonna get overrun."

"You know, I have this whole place plotted with artillery. Do you think we should call in air bursts on our own position?"

"I think that's our last chance."

"All right," said Wade, "I'll call 'em in."

"Alec, you give me ten minutes because in ten minutes I think I can make it around the perimeter again, and I'll tell everybody to get under anything they can find because we're gonna call in air bursts."

Lieutenant Alley made his way once again around the perimeter, shouting at everyone to take cover. When he returned to the command post, Wade gave the word and the first salvo of time-detonated artillery shells thunderclapped over Jaeger. Metzler and two others with him had missed the word about taking cover, and he remembers how they were "firing like mad from atop the Bravo command track. I shall never forget the moment the first air burst went off over our heads. The sound was paralyzing, and at first we had no idea what had just happened. Shrapnel rained all around us. It's amazing that none of us were hit."

Enemy soldiers could be seen scampering back toward the trees as the air bursts continued. Meanwhile, a relief force of four tracks, piled with straight-leg infantrymen, sped with guns blazing through an ambush the enemy had set up in the roadside hamlet adjacent to Jaeger. "We only got through because the dinks [VC] failed to blow the road," notes John Hohman. The artillery was temporarily shut off to allow the relief force into the firebase. When the tracks halted, Hohman nudged the black grunt sitting beside him and shouted at him to dismount with the rest of the hitchhiking infantrymen. The man didn't move; he was dead, having caught a round in the chest on the way in. The gunships that had recently arrived were engaged by a machine gun positioned across the highway. "There was a steady hail of green tracers going up that kept the gunships at bay," recounts Hohman. In what was essentially the final act of the battle, the crew of Hohman's mortar track placed a salvo on the spot from which the tracers emanated. "We never found out if we hit the crew, but the firing stopped immediately."

Lieutenant Alley would be awarded a Silver Star for his part in the victory at Jaeger, as well as the Distinguished Service Cross for Cudgel. The enemy had indeed been punished at Jaeger. Nearly a hundred bodies were counted around the perimeter, sprawled in a litter of abandoned weapons and grenades, and it was estimated that the Viet Cong had dragged off another fifty dead. Seventy GIs had been wounded, however, and twenty more left the firebase in body bags. Joe Sintoni wrote in his diary that "all descriptions of that night can be summed up in one word, massacre."

Soon after the attack, sniper fire was received from the troublesome hamlet neighboring the firebase. The Bandidos returned fire with a vengeance, their tracers igniting the thatch hootches. The hamlet had harbored the enemy too many times before, "so when we took fire from there again," explains John Hohman, "that was it; we just fired everything up and burnt the place to the ground."

On March 7, 1968, a week after Antila replaced Steele as battalion commander, Company C's maintenance track transported a squad of ARVN from Jaeger to a firebase that had been established farther west on Highway 4.

The track was returning to Jaeger when it encountered a command-detonated mine buried in the unpaved highway. Fortunately, the VC watching the road from a nearby point of concealment (inside a farmer's hootch, as was later learned) touched the mine off a second too soon, so that it exploded in front of the track instead of underneath. The blast left the troopers who'd been sitting on the back deck sprawled along the highway in various states of injury. The track itself went nose first into the crater. "The explosion blew us way up in the air," recalls Jerrold J. Tomlinson. "I thought I was dead." Tomlinson's head was ringing, and his arm was throbbing, the bone being fractured. "I was sort of beat-up all over, but all of a sudden I heard the bullets—the people who had set the mine off were firing at us—so I picked up an M16 and started shooting back."

Lieutenant Alley dispatched one of his platoons to the scene. First Lieutenant Richard D. Bahr, the platoon leader and a good man, due to rotate off the line in a matter of days, rode aboard the lead track. He was within sight of the wrecked maintenance vehicle when the enemy set off another command-detonated mine. This time, their timing was perfect, and the lead track disintegrated in the massive blast. Recalls Tomlinson: "Bodies, parts of bodies, parts of the track all went flying."

Lieutenant Alley arrived moments later with a second reaction force. The action was over by then, the ambushers vanishing after detonating the second mine. The crater from the second blast was ten feet deep, the product of at least five-hundred pounds of explosives. The driver's hatch of Bahr's track, along with the front armor plate and parts of the engine, had been hurled thirty or forty feet into the overgrown rice paddies bordering the highway. The deck had been curled back and ripped away like the lid on a can of sardines. Pieces of scrap metal were scattered throughout the area. The six men who had been on the track were in the same condition. "It was complete carnage," Joe Sintoni recorded in his diary. "I can't describe it except to say I was sick."

Specialist Fifth Class Gary P. Vertrees and his buddy Thomas Beck arrived with the second reaction force. First they noticed the body of a sergeant who'd been behind the .50 of Bahr's track lying on the highway. The dead man was relatively intact, having been launched like a rocket from the command cupola when the mine exploded under him. Vertrees joined the troops policing up the other bodies. When he spotted a flak jacket in the drainage ditch that ran along the highway, he and two GIs he hailed stepped down into the calf-deep water to pull the body out . . . except there was only half a body. When Vertrees grabbed the flak jacket, an arm appeared, then a head, then another arm, and that was it; the man had been cut in half at the waist.

The scene was littered with other horrors, including a foot still laced up in a jungle boot, and a headless, limbless torso which was discovered off by itself in the deep grass covering the rice paddies. The troopers picking up these bloody pieces of their buddies were deeply shaken. In their rage and sorrow and unable to avenge their buddies' deaths, they began pushing and shoving among the villagers congregating on the scene, mumbling that they should mow the bastards down. Worthless gooks. Kill 'em. Waste 'em. It was the least they deserved for playing deaf, dumb, and blind as the guerrillas planted their mines.

The detonation cord from the second mine was found, and a patrol followed it down a paddy dike and into a hootch that sat alone in a spot of brush and trees. In the hootch was a young man garbed in peasant-black, and the patrol escorted him back to Lieutenant Alley. The frightened prisoner jabbered to Alley's interpreter, an ARVN sergeant, that he'd had nothing to do with the ambush. He said that the guerrillas had taken over the hootch in which he lived because it afforded them a safe place from which to monitor the road and trigger the mines. They basically held him hostage, and they were long gone now. If he was a VC, the prisoner pleaded, he would have run away, too. The interpreter told Alley that he believed the young man.

No one else did. Lieutenant Alley was seething and was as determined as the furious troops around him that someone should pay for what had happened. Alley stared at the prisoner. *This lying bastard is probably the one who detonated the mine,* he told himself. He wasn't going to get away with it.

Lieutenant Alley pulled his hunting knife from its sheaf and held it up for the prisoner to see. "I am going to cut you into pieces," he hissed, "and sooner or later one of the pieces I cut off will make you talk."

The prisoner pleaded with the interpreter even as the interpreter continued to beseech Alley that they had captured an innocent man. Alley wasn't listening anymore. "I'm going to start with your ears," he said. His heart was full of pure, liberating hatred, and pulling one of the terrified prisoner's ears away from his head, he sliced half of it off. The interpreter was shrieking now, begging the lieutenant to stop, and the madness suddenly passed from Lee Alley. The lights came back on. Alley's hands began to shake, and he dropped his knife, feeling nauseous and no longer so sure that his bleeding, trembling prisoner wasn't just what he said he was, a rice farmer in the wrong place at the wrong time. Alley called to his medic: "Doc, fix him up, and then get this rotten sonuvabitch piece of shit out of my sight."

The young company commander then instructed his driver to make sure that all the dead were loaded aboard his track. They were his men. He had ordered them to their deaths. He would bring them back. Lieutenant Alley walked to the edge of the road and sat down by himself, with bile in his throat and tears welling in his eyes. "I am very proud of my service," he would later explain, "but that incident has always haunted me. I tried to do everything right over there. I tried to fight a fair fight, and I look back and I think, how could you take your knife and maim somebody? But we had lost so many men and my nerves were so on edge. However I rationalize the incident, it will always be the dark shadow in my memories of Vietnam."

First Lieutenant Merle James "Jim" Sharpe and Company A hastened to Company C's aid and swept the area, finding nothing but more body parts. The cold anger of the moment retained its grip on all involved as the operation continued. Specialist Fourth Class Alan D. Kisling, a member of the forward observer team attached to Company A, accompanied a dismounted patrol that managed to flush a lone sniper from his hiding spot and send him running. The platoon leader grabbed four or five men—Kisling among them—and gave chase, pursuing the guerrilla through the brush and down dikes. Facing another open paddy with no cover, the cornered VC finally threw his AK-47 aside and sank to his knees in a water-filled bomb crater with his hands pressed together in front of his forehead in the Buddhist prayer position. Kisling was at a fever pitch, soaked in sweat from the foot race, and he advanced on the crater with his .45 gripped in his hand and murder in his heart. *Buddy, it's too late to surrender now,* he thought. *I'm blowing this fucker's brains out.* He wavered at the moment of truth, though, unable to shoot a man on his knees begging for mercy. The platoon leader was much firmer in purpose; coming up on Kisling's left, he stopped at the edge of the crater, brought his CAR-15 to his shoulder, pointed the muzzle at the enemy soldier's head, and unhesitatingly pulled the trigger. Scratch one VC.

Joe Sintoni, who didn't have to be there, was killed in action on March 27, 1968, one of twenty Bandidos to die during Tet and the Tet

Counteroffensive. His diary was shipped home with his other personal effects, whereupon his parents and fiancée learned of the hell he had endured in the name of duty. "My best friend was killed last night," Sintoni wrote. "We came [in-country] together. . . . We fought for our lives next to each other, now he is no more. . . . I'm so blue and morose." Other entries from Sintoni's diary blurred together in an elegy of tight-lipped despair, exposing the inner heart of the combat infantryman who knows he has no choice but to soldier on until the law of averages catches up with him. "I am not trying to be a fatalist, but I realize I'll never be able to make one year alive in the field. . . . I realize I may never see the woman or family my heart beats for. I dare not make a friend. . . . All my buddies are either dead or wounded. . . . I really want to go home. . . . Why do I always write of bad things? I guess because things are so terribly bad."

Chapter 4

Lanny Jones was driving the lead track as Captain Scarborough's column rolled into Saigon. Reaching a turn in the road, Jones halted, unable to get past a small car parked at the corner. The street wasn't wide enough for both vehicles. Jones explained the situation as the rest of the column sat idling behind him. The word came back that "we gotta go, push the car out of the way," Jones recounts. "Well, there wasn't no pushin' it. The track was taller and wider than the car, so when I made that corner, I run right up over the side of the car. After everybody else done it, too, there wasn't nothin' left of that little ol' car."

With a map of the capital spread across his lap in his bubble helicopter, Lieutenant Colonel Antila shepherded Scarborough's column to its objective.

Company C was rolling east on Route 232. The roadway paralleled the southern edge of the Kinh Doi, which means Canal Doi in Vietnamese, and was redundantly referred to by Americans as the Kinh Doi Canal. The canal separated Cholon from the narrow, fifteen-kilometer-long string of hamlets constituting the southern fringe of Saigon. The hamlets were not part of the old colonial city. Only three years earlier, the area had been a marshland speckled with miserable shanties. The bogs had since been drained, and schools, markets, and stucco-over-brick housing had been constructed with U.S. aid. The newest part of the city, christened District 8, was crowded but thriving. Warehouses lined the canal, fed by the freighters that anchored in the Kinh Doi after steaming north on the serpentine Saigon River from the South China Sea.

Five kilometers along the east-west canal road, Scarborough's column reached north-south Route 5A that crossed the Kinh Doi from Cholon by way of a concrete bridge before continuing south into the paddy country below Saigon. Route 5A was vital, one of only two major roadways (Highway 4 being the other) by which rice was transported to Saigon from the Mekong Delta.

Having been tasked to secure the Route 5A bridge, Antila directed Scarborough into a field at the intersection of Routes 5A and 232. Alighting from his helicopter, Antila called his officers together to give them the word.

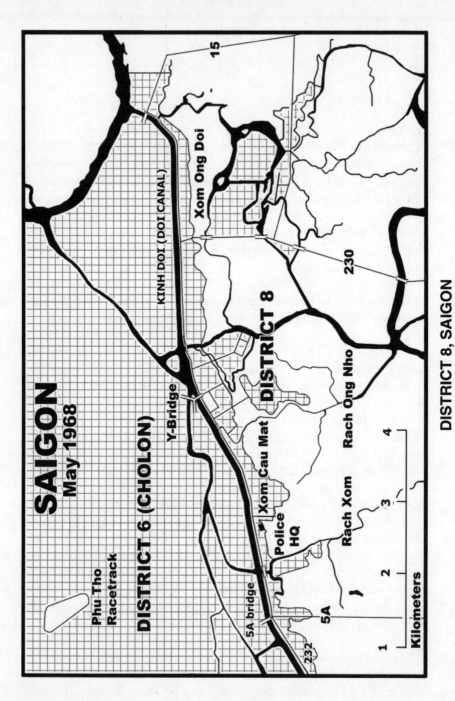

SAIGON
May 1968

Phu Tho Racetrack

DISTRICT 6 (CHOLON)

Y-Bridge

KINH DOI (DOI CANAL)

Xom Ong Doi

15

230

DISTRICT 8

Xom Cau Mat

Police HQ

Rach Ong Nho

Rach Xom

5A bridge

5A

232

1   2   3   4

Kilometers

DISTRICT 8, SAIGON

The enemy's second wave of urban attacks was upon them, he said. Heavy fighting had erupted the day before between the ARVN and VC in Cholon and near the Newport Bridge in eastern Saigon. The morning of May 6, 1968, the enemy had also hit Tan Son Nhut Airbase on the northwest edge of Saigon.

Acting on intelligence that additional enemy units would soon approach the capital from the south, Major General Julian J. Ewell, commanding general of the 9th Division, had directed the 3rd Brigade at Tan An to rush a company from the 5-60th Mech into southern Saigon. It had taken Bandido Charlie less than two hours to reach the capital from Binh Phuoc. Their job now, Antila explained, was to reinforce the government troops defending District 8 and prevent the enemy—should he indeed attack—from crossing the Kinh Doi into Cholon.

Antila quickly decided upon night positions. Captain Scarborough's headquarters and mortars, plus the 3rd Platoon under Lieutenant Garver, were to circle their wagons around the battalion command post in the field near the Route 5A bridge. The 2nd Platoon was to secure the bridge itself. Second Lieutenant Dwight L. Long and the 1st Platoon of Company C were to continue another four kilometers east on the canal road to the Y Bridge, which also spanned the Kinh Doi, and was so named because the three legs extending from the bridge's center looked from the air exactly like its alphabetical namesake.

Leaving the rest of the company behind, Lieutenant Long soon crossed a small bridge that spanned the Rach Xom, a tributary running south from the Kinh Doi. The little hamlet along the tributary was unnamed on Long's map. The platoon next passed the police headquarters for District 8, which faced the canal road between the nameless hamlet and a more substantial built-up area identified as Xom Cau Mat—that is, the village of Cau Mat. Moving on, Long crossed another small bridge, this one spanning a tributary called Rach Ong Nho. Four hundred meters beyond the bridge, a right turn and two lefts brought the tracks around a field and up onto the Y Bridge. Long positioned his three vehicles (the fourth was down for repairs) at the elevated center of the bridge, one facing down each leg. Night soon fell over the city. Some of Long's troops wryly commented that if an attack was expected, it might have been prudent to douse the street lights that blazed along the bridge and illuminated their APCs.

With what appeared to be a major battle brewing, Lieutenant Garver was a little concerned about the quality of his platoon. His men were almost all green replacements. Worse, his platoon sergeant, Bill Bloom (a pseudonym), was no flinty-eyed regular, but a whippet-thin kid who recently graduated from the Noncommissioned Officer (NCO) Candidate School at Fort Benning.

The course had been established the previous summer to make up for all the seasoned Regular Army E5s, E6s, and E7s—sergeant, staff sergeants, and sergeants first class—lost to the war. Many had become casualties; many more had retired early to avoid repeated combat tours or pulled strings to secure desk jobs when sent back to Vietnam. To fill the gap, men like Bloom who exhibited leadership potential in basic and advanced training were asked to volunteer for the NCO academy. Bloom was in the very first class. The school produced E5s. As class honor graduate, Bloom was promoted to E6. He was nineteen at the time, less than a year in uniform. For every instant sergeant who did right by his stripes—and some were naturals, more energetic and devoted to their men than the lifers they replaced—another proved to be in over his head, and as a group they were known derisively as shake 'n' bakes. Bloom and the other graduates of that first class served six months with stateside units to get a little troop time before getting their orders for Vietnam on the eve of the Mini-Tet Offensive.

If the leaders were less seasoned at that point in the war, the troops were less idealistic. The men Larry Garner and Lee Alley led in 1967 might have been draftees, as most grunts were, but they had believed in the war—or at least in the concept of stopping communism—and had assumed they were fighting to win. Tet dampened such enthusiasms. The troops didn't sing "The Ballad of the Green Berets" anymore, but listened to Jimi Hendrix and cried with Eric Burdon and the Animals: "We gotta get out of this place if it's the last thing we ever do!"

Fault lines as deep as those back home appeared in the war zone. Frustrated hawks wanted to nuke Hanoi even as an increasing number of their comrades began to wonder if the hated antiwar movement didn't have a point after all. Many black troops were bitter about fighting a "white man's war," as a wall had gone up between the races—especially in the rear areas—after the assassination of Martin Luther King Jr. The politically inclined argued about Nixon, McCarthy, Humphrey, Wallace, and Bobby Kennedy. Most didn't know what to think anymore, and for many, confusion gave way to apathy. "The American soldier in Vietnam did not give a shit. I mean, he gave less than a shit," to quote a Regular Army E6 who pulled a 1968–1969 tour with the 11th Armored Cavalry Regiment. "You sat there and you just didn't care. Our pilots were practicing crash-landings in a field one day, and I was sitting there killing red ants with a cigarette, you know what I mean?" The only thing that mattered was your unit. "That bond was strong," says the former E6. "You knew that if you were hit, somebody'd come after you, and if you were still alive, chances were you would stay that way because a chopper would come in to pick you up no matter how heavy the fire. In that regard, morale was fantastic, but it was the kind of war where the combat soldiers had more respect for the Viet Cong than the politicians in Washington."

First Lieutenant James M. Simmen of A/5-60th had no qualms about the job at hand; this is from a letter he wrote to his older brother, who was a parish priest:

> You'd be surprised how similar killing is to hunting. I know I'm after souls, but I get all excited when I see a VC, just like when I see a deer. I go ape firing at him. . . . Civilians think such thinking is crazy, but it's no big deal. He runs, you fire. . . . It isn't all that horrifying. When you see a man laughing about it, remember he talks the same way about killing a deer. Of course, revenge has a part in wanting [to kill VC]. . . .

Even aggressive platoon leaders, however, appreciated that minimizing risks had become the name of the game after Tet, as evidenced in Simmen's letter:

> One guy was shooting at my ambush last night. I reported it as heavy contact and got eight barrels of artillery to shoot white phosphorus and high explosives in the wood line. We found a body this morning so the colonel was happy. . . . A friend got killed on an ambush last week. [The colonel] told him to move in the middle of the night. As he drew in all his claymores, Charlie [nickname for VC] hit. Last night they told me to move twice. It'll be a cold day in hell when I move. Thirty minutes later I reported "Moved." The colonel isn't about to come out to see where I am. I'm chicken but not stupid!

Young officers had every reason to bend orders to protect their men. As they saw it, their ARVN allies were too cowardly to fight their own war, and the Vietnamese people cared less about freedom and democracy than making a buck off the Americans. The Vietnamese weren't people to many of the GIs. They were "gooks"—even captains and colonels used this slur—and they always wanted something, whether it be children aggressively begging for smokes and C-rations, or the middle-aged woman, her face shaded under her wide conical hat, holding up a bottle of Pepsi in one hand, a glass of ice in the other, and smiling pleasantly as she overcharged a thirsty GI.

Soda pop was the least of what was for sale. The mamasans also hustled beer, booze, and machine-rolled cigarettes in cellophane-wrapped Salem packages that contained not tobacco, but marijuana. They were usually trailed by ten-year-old pimps ready to sell their fifteen-year-old sisters. Given the money to be made, every city, town, and village had its little tin-roofed shacks where a Vietnamese girl could be found reclining apathetically on an air mattress, naked from the waist down, a poncho liner strung up for privacy as three or four or a dozen GIs waited their turn. "You covered a lot of ground in a mech unit, and, believe me, we knew every place of ill repute between Dong Tam and Lai Khe," jokes John Hohman. Prostitutes even popped up during operations. "I don't care where you went, they would find you," says a former squad leader. "You could be in the deepest, darkest jungle, and you'd heard this *bup-bup-bup-bup* down the trail—and here would come a little Lambretta loaded down with girls."

Troops returning from patrol sometimes smuggled prostitutes into base camp inside their personnel carriers. Once, the guys on Hohman's track rented a girl in Tan An and took her on an overnight security mission to the Ben Luc Bridge. Their platoon sergeant "just turned his head," recalls Hohman, "because he knew it was useless to even waste his time talking to us about some things."

The draftee troopers had little respect, in general, for the handful of Regular Army NCOs in Bandido Charlie. According to rumor, the first sergeant had been caught pilfering valuables from the foot lockers of the company's casualties, in addition to forging the company commander's name to award recommendations he had written for himself to boost his career. Hohman's section leader and platoon sergeant had both fought in Korea and were nice enough guys, but more to the point, many perceived them as over-the-hill lifers concerned less with leading men in combat than staying behind cover. "We tolerated the lifers; that was about it," notes Hohman. "We did what we wanted to, anyway. We knew our jobs, and they weren't going to mess around with a bunch of crazy people."

The draftees had reached something of a collective breaking point by the third year of the ground war. Chilling stories began to circulate about unpopular sergeants, lieutenants, and captains being removed with grenades and accidental discharges that weren't so accidental. Bandido Charlie had an incident of not-so-friendly fire shortly before the road march to Saigon. The squad leader involved was a shake 'n' bake who possessed an abrasive demeanor and did everything according to his training, whatever the counsel of his veterans. Most infuriatingly, he did not lean forward to tap his driver on the helmet to indicate direction changes, as did most track commanders, because the roar of the engine made it difficult to converse, even over the intercom. Instead, the sergeant would arrogantly kick the GI from his seat behind the driver. When the sergeant delivered a particularly head-ringing thump one day, the fed-up driver jerked the track to a halt, informed the squad leader that "someone's gonna shoot your ass if you keep this shit up," then stomped over to the platoon leader's track to deliver an ultimatum: "I'm not gettin' back on that vehicle unless you move Sergeant ——— to another track."

The squad leader did not change his ways with his new crew, however, and during a dismounted sweep, he ended up with his head in the peep sight of an M16. The sergeant's helmet saved his life, and he stumbled pale and shaken back to his track, clutching his steel pot, the back of which had been ripped open by a single shot coming from the wrong direction on an otherwise quiet afternoon.

Lanny Jones, a country boy, recalls an incident more typical in its rough-and-tumble humor of the what-are-they-going-to-do-shave-my-head-and-send-me-to-Vietnam attitude of the troops after Tet. It took place late in his tour after the 5-60th Mech had been switched to the 1st Infantry Division, commonly known as the Big Red One. The Bandidos were securing a firebase when Jones' track was dispatched to base camp for the company's water supply. For all the beer and marijuana around, Jones never saw anyone overdo it during combat operations, "but this is one time that we all got pretty wiped out," he admits. After hitching the water trailer to the track, Jones and the crew spent the afternoon drinking in the base camp's NCO club. "We were in pretty bad shape when we left there," he says. "One of the guys had some cherry bombs, and so here we come back down this dirt road through the jungle, throwing these fireworks out. The company thought we was under fire, and when they got shootin', we thought we was under fire, too."

Rolling into the firebase, Jones had no sooner driven into a defensive position then he backed up, intending to help repel an attack that wasn't really taking place. He put the track into reverse so quickly, however, that his inebriated squad leader fell out of his chair, stepping on Jones' head on his way to the ground and gashing the driver's chin open on the edge of the hatch. In the confusion, Jones backed up over the trailer, destroying it and losing all the water. "We got in a heap of trouble over that. The company commander called us over and said, 'Would you accept an Article 15?' We said, 'Well, no, not really.' He said, 'I think you better, or we're going to go to a court-martial over this.' We said, 'Well, okay,' and he said, 'You're confined to this firebase and you can't go back in to base camp.' I was about ready to get out in another month, so I didn't care."

After five months on the battalion staff, Captain Scarborough assumed command of Company C from Lee Alley only six weeks before the road march to Saigon.

Edmund Scarborough was the son of a retired colonel from a fine Virginia family with a long tradition of military service. A tall, slender, family man of twenty-seven, Scarborough wore horn-rimmed glasses and resembled an accountant rather than a commander of infantry. He was reserved, but well spoken and personable, and obviously possessed of both a fine mind and a deep sense of duty. "He was a wonderful man. There was a lot of substance there," says Jim Sharpe. Antila concurs. "Of all my commands and assignments, Captain Scarborough was the absolute best I ever had, both professionally and personally," the former battalion commander writes. "He would have succeeded in whatever career he might have chosen. He was low key, but still assertive and positive. When orders were being issued, he always asked the most pertinent questions. He was dedicated to doing the job and loyal to his men."

Captain Scarborough might have been new, but his troops were willing to give him the benefit of the doubt. Such was the effect his steady voice had on the radio when the bullets were zipping about, and of the concern he showed when he trooped the line each night to talk with his people. "He was aware of the Bandido Charlie image, and strived to ensure that we maintained it," writes Douglas G. Birge, who admired the captain's professionalism. "Scarborough was a good guy and a good CO [commanding officer]," says Larry D. Miller. "He wasn't one of those officers who just gave orders; when we made patrols, he was right there with us."

Captain Scarborough nevertheless exhibited odd lapses in his field craft. Though most officers prudently wore black-stitch rank insignia, Scarborough sported big silver captain bars on the front of his helmet, unconcerned that by doing so he was practically begging a sniper to shoot him through the head and leave his company leaderless. In addition, instead of keeping his command group spread out when dismounted and letting his radiomen handle the routine traffic (one radioman on the company net, the other on battalion) Scarborough carried a phone in each hand, flanked by his radio-telephone operators. "It was like he didn't trust them to say anything on the radio, so you had this whole cluster of people walking along with radio antennas marking them," recalls Charles Taylor, the company executive officer. "We had arguments about it. I tried to tell him that it wasn't safe to be so conspicuous." Taylor judged the new captain on different grounds than the troops and thus came to different conclusions. "Scarborough had probably been an excellent staff officer, and he needed command time to get his ticket punched, but he didn't have it for commanding troops in the field. He had no command presence. He had to wear those tracks on his helmet to prove he was the commander."

First Lieutenant Frank R. Neild, who had several months in country with another battalion, had recently been reassigned as Company C's forward observer. The artillery spotter quickly grew uneasy about Scarborough. "Career officers vied to get the Bandidos, and it was my understanding that Scarborough pushed for it, too," recalls Neild. "It was a plum position, but you could tell he didn't quite know how to run things when he got out there. He was a nice guy, but green." Once, when ordered to rush to the assistance of another unit, Scarborough puzzled over his map, unsure of his location. Neild broke out his own map to help. Scarborough stiffened and made an unappreciative remark, giving the impression that he feared admitting any fault would weaken his position. "I tried to help him because by that time I was a seasoned officer, but it was hard to give him any advice because I think he was a little unsure of himself. Ultimately, I thought he was quite inadequate as a commander."

Lieutenant Sharpe of Company A liked and respected Scarborough. When Sharpe used the word "gook" in Scarborough's presence, though, "he gave me a sour look, and said, 'They're not gooks, they're civilians.'" Sharpe and Scarborough had words on the subject when a track passing through Binh Phuoc was destroyed and serious casualties incurred during an RPG ambush immediately before Tet. The battalion base camp sat on one side of Binh Phuoc, part of its headquarters on another. "So we went back and forth a lot through town," notes Sharpe, "and came to feel a certain amount of kinship with the townspeople. We were furious with them for not tipping us off to the ambush. I made this remark that we ought to go in and torch the town, and Scarborough got very upset with me. Basically, he was saying that they're civilians, and they're not to be blamed for this, and you can't punish them for it. He had a point. I was speaking from the gut, while he almost had a professorial approach, which I didn't think was appropriate when your guys are getting wiped out. Whether he was right or wrong in the long run, he was definitely out of step with the rest of us regarding the Vietnamese."

***

Lieutenant Colonel Eric Antila hailed from a ranch outside Santa Fe, New Mexico. Drafted just out of high school, he had served as a teenage rifleman with the occupation forces in Korea before his test scores and prowess on the division baseball team earned him a place with the West Point Class of 1951.

Fresh from the academy, Antila served as a junior staff officer at the end of the Korean War. In the years that followed, he earned his jump wings, commanded troops, married the daughter of a colonel, and worked out religiously to stay in peak physical condition. "Eric was very much the arrogant jock type," according to one contemporary. Antila was also something of a scholar, and he finally requested reassignment from the combat arms after service as a nuclear-weapons officer with the North Atlantic Treaty Organization (NATO). "The army was boring," he would later explain. "I figured I could do more than say 'right face, left face.' I was working on my doctorate at the time, and wanted to do medical research in the nuclear field with the army medical corps in Bethesda, Maryland."

The request being denied, Lieutenant Colonel Antila was assigned to Vietnam. He served as the brigade executive officer at Tan An, and was decorated for his actions on the perimeter during Tet, before taking command of the 5-60th Mechanized Infantry. It was immediately apparent to Antila that he had inherited a good battalion from a good commander. According to the junior officers of the battalion, Antila was a worthy replacement for the beloved Steele. "Antila and I got along famously," recalls Jim Sharpe. "I loved the guy. I liked Steele, too. These were good men and great soldiers." Lee Alley agrees: "I was with Antila on a daily basis as a member of his staff, and I thought he was great."

Antila had the reputation of being "a real soldier's commander, very oriented toward the troops," notes another former staff officer named John R. Sweet. Richard F. Neuman, a former platoon leader, is of the opinion that "Antila was the greatest. I felt absolutely confident in his leadership. There was no question that he knew what he was doing tactically." Neuman spent several weeks as Antila's jeep driver and unofficial aide at Binh Phuoc while nursing a broken wrist, and came away very impressed by the battalion commander's intellectual heft. It wasn't every lieutenant colonel of infantry who carried postcards of his favorite Impressionist paintings. "Antila was the colonel," notes Neuman. "He was very much the leader, but if you were respectful, you could have a very easy conversation with him."

For all that, much ill will simmered between the colonel and division headquarters. "A lot of people didn't like my attitude because they were political animals," asserts Antila. In Antila's book, General Ewell was a martinet with a heart of ice and the temper of a bully, he and his clique of favored subordinates were the worst kind of self-aggrandizing careerists. These officers would, in turn, bandy about anecdotes in which Antila played the part of the big-mouthed phony who couldn't cut it in battle. The hierarchy's continuing attempts to strip the battalion of its flags and emblems were a constant source of friction, and tempers flared again when Ewell personally objected to Antila's troops drinking beer in the field. In response, Antila recalls snapping at Ewell: "Either I'm in command, and I'm going to do it my way, or you can relieve me and get somebody in here who'll do it your way."

Antila was not relieved. Instead, Ewell sent him to the 1st Infantry Division when directed that autumn to swap one of his mechanized battalions for a straight-leg unit better suited for the war in the delta. A member of Ewell's clique would later characterize the reassignment as "palming Antila off on the Big Red One." An assistant division commander greeted Antila after his battalion road marched to its new base camp at Lai Khe. Looking over the column, the general asked Antila what the basic load was for his M113s. "Six cases of beer," quipped Antila. Greg Hawkins, a radioman in the battalion command group, recalls that the colonel's remark "probably did not endear him with our new division as they had a standing order of no beer in the field. It sure made us chuckle, though."

Hawkins served under four battalion commanders during his combat tour. "Lieutenant Colonel Antila was the best," he writes. "He was very calm in some pretty stressful situations, and handled supporting fires as good as the best. He was very protective of us. He could be a delight in that he knew we weren't career army people, just draftees doing a lousy job and trying to survive. We were very cavalier in our demeanor, and he was very easy with us, but you always knew that he was The Man."

Hawkins relates how Antila jumped from his chopper to join his recon platoon in a flooded paddy, in which they were pinned down with heavy casualties. "As I heard it, the colonel stood on top of a paddy dike while everyone else was lying down behind the dike so he could better call air and arty on the enemy and arrange helicopter insertions of our companies into blocking positions." When the recon troops urged him to get behind the dike, Antila remarked that he didn't want to get wet. To present a smaller target, he finally sat on the dike, using his helmet for a seat so as not to soak his trousers, all the while continuing to talk on the radio. "Needless to say, the lads in recon liked to talk about how their commander 'doesn't like to get wet, but doesn't seem to give a shit about being shot at.'

"We loved the guy," concludes Hawkins, "and would have followed him anywhere. He had what many officers never find—the ability to lead."

There was something about Antila that neither his officers nor troops were aware of, but which explains, in part, his irreverence, independence, and lack of interest in the politics at division headquarters. He no longer had any career aspirations. "My request for retirement was already signed, delivered, and waiting approval at the Pentagon," explains Antilla. "I sent it from Europe during my NATO duty along with my request to be assigned to a combat unit in Vietnam. I volunteered to fill a moral obligation so I could retire knowing that I had done the best I could. It sounds arrogant," he continues, "and I really don't care, but denied the opportunity to do research at Bethesda, [Maryland,] I didn't see any job at any level in the army—except for commanding a unit in combat—that posed a challenge to me. I wanted to retire and make a contribution in something other than the military. I volunteered for Vietnam before I hung up my suit just for my own peace of mind."

Chapter 5

Specialist Fourth Class Kisling, recently reassigned to Company C's forward observer team, accompanied Lieutenant Neild to the briefing that first night in Saigon. The discussion had a subdued, unhurried quality to it. "It was kind of like, 'yeah, we better move up there and cover the bases,' " recalls Kisling, "versus Tet, when it was like, 'oh shit, the world's coming apart.' "

Lieutenant Neild's team rode with Captain Scarborough, so Kisling climbed aboard the command track some time after dark to grab some sleep. As no one rode in the tracks during the day because of mines, no one slept in them at night lest a rocket shrieked out of the darkness and ignited the ammo inside. Instead, they slept outside on stretchers, or up top like Kisling, who wrapped himself in a poncho liner because of all the mosquitoes. Poncho liners only helped so much. As such, Kisling curled up on the exhaust grille next to the driver's hatch, and in front of the GI who was behind the .50 on watch; when another GI came to change the guard every hour or so, he would start the track to charge the battery, and the exhaust would chase away the mosquitoes. "So you had a brief period there," explains Kisling, "when you weren't being eaten alive."

Unimpressed with Captain Scarborough, Kisling also had his doubts about Lieutenant Neild. Kisling had never met anybody like Neild before. To begin with, the guy was a genius, the son of a Harvard-trained physician who was the town doctor in Geneva, New York. Frank Neild's detour into the front lines of a war he could have avoided was the result of an incident that took place shortly after he'd earned a degree in mathematics from the University of Wisconsin in the summer of 1965.

The incident involved a handful of people with picket signs outside an army recruiting station. It wasn't an ugly encounter. It was early in the war and the Left was still bright and idealistic, but Neild, a lifelong conservative, thought there was something so wrongheaded about picketing the military that he impulsively broke the picket line and walked into the recruiting station. He didn't enlist on the spot, since he was already lined up to do his national service with the Peace Corps. He started thinking, however, that what the country really needed were soldiers, not ambassadors to the Third World. History told him that civilizations didn't survive when their young men weren't willing to risk their lives to defend them. Thus, several months after breaking that picket line, he was standing at attention, one shaved head among many, with a drill sergeant screaming in his face. He soon won his bars at Field Artillery OCS at Fort Sill, Oklahoma.

Lieutenant Neild, age twenty-five, was thin and gangly with a chatty, gee-whiz personality and a tendency to analyze everything to death. Intimidated by Neild's intellect, Kisling tended to shrug him off as just another lieutenant. *So this one's got brains. Big deal,* he thought. Kisling did not really bond with his team leader until he saw him in action in Saigon; then he realized that behind his lopsided grin Frank Neild had the courage of a lion.

Even though it took Kisling some time to appreciate Neild, the lieutenant was impressed with Kisling from the word go. Kisling was full of energy and quick to smile—a pugnacious little guy, standing five-four, thus his nickname Shorty. This tough soldier, who seemed to thrive on the excitement of war, had grown up in the backwoods of Oregon. His father was a logger and his mother was a cook at the logging camp and head honcho on their 136-acre farm. It was hardscrabble all the way. Kisling was a smart but headstrong kid. He didn't do well in school and dropped out to join up at seventeen. He immediately volunteered for Vietnam.

Only eighteen at the time, Kisling was exceptionally aggressive, as much an infantryman as an artillery spotter. Such aggressiveness could cut both ways. Lieutenant Sharpe had twice rebuked Kisling when he was attached to Company A, the first time being after he gunned down a farmer's water buffalo and the company had to pass the hat to pay compensation. Sharpe was under the impression that Kisling had shot the animal for kicks. In Kisling's memory, however, the water buffalo had been charging when he reluctantly opened fire.

More seriously, Kisling called in a fire mission, apparently without authorization, during a subsequent foot patrol in the Jaeger area to clear a path through a booby-trapped tree line; a white phosphorus round that overshot the target landed in a nearby hamlet, destroying several hootches and burning a man to death. "The villagers complained," recalls John A. Holder, a friend of Kisling's in Company A. As a result, the troops on the patrol were sequestered in a schoolhouse "and informed that we were being reprimanded. We were then told to put our statements in writing. We put our heads together and all wrote the same story and never heard anything else about the incident."

Kisling had no sooner joined the Bandidos than he saved an ambushed patrol by calling artillery almost atop their heads and using his .45 to nail a Viet Cong who got too close. Decorated for the action, Kisling also eventually made sergeant for his performance under fire, only to lose his stripes, such were his problems with authority. In the same vein, fed up with garrison duty after rotating stateside, Kisling volunteered to go right back into combat and ended up serving another eighteen months in Vietnam.

Lieutenant Neild's radioman, Private First Class James J. "Lurch" Hewitt (a pseudonym), was big, dumb, and nice—a nineteen-year-old piece of cannon fodder from rural Pennsylvania. He was nicknamed Lurch because of his glazed expression and half-opened mouth. Neild and Kisling found it hard to believe that anyone as slow as Hewitt could have passed the aptitude tests required for military service, and chalked him up as one of McNamara's 100,000, the infamous program by which the services were forced to accept a hundred-thousand substandard recruits per year, the better to protect the sons of the upper class from Vietnam.

Hewitt had started out as a gun bunny in the firing battery to which Neild and Kisling also belonged, but the life of a howitzer crewman was one of monotony and pack-mule labor, and for all the noise, you really didn't even see any action. Bored, he volunteered for a spotter team a month into his tour, joining Neild and Kisling just two weeks before Saigon. He wanted desperately to do a good job as the team radioman, but could not figure out how to adjust frequencies. Kisling was frustrated and impatient with Lurch. Neild tried to coach him, but nothing stuck, and the lieutenant finally went to the battery commander to request that Lurch be replaced with a trooper who actually knew how to operate a radio. Lurch was upset that he had failed as a radioman, but continued to do the best he knew how until his replacement arrived. "Lurch's character was impeccable," notes Neild. "His only problem was that he couldn't think."

One of the mortar tracks had been dispatched to secure the small bridge on the canal road adjacent to the main night position. The crew was joined by several prostitutes escorted by a mamasan. "As soon as they heard the track stop, they were over there soliciting their trade," recalls John Hohman. "We got three or four of 'em. We gave the mamasan ten bucks and they spent the night." The track was parked beside several chopped-down palm trees, "and we were lying on each side of the palm trees with the girls, and we'd switch off, you know. We had a good time!"

The company maintenance team worked into the night, tending to mechanical problems that had popped up during the road march. Finally packing their tool boxes away, Specialist Fifth Class Vertrees popped a few cold ones atop his track. "I drank till I basically passed out," he recalls. It was the only way he could shut down and get some rest before everything cranked up again at dawn. "I don't care if it was day or night, it was just go, go, go all the time over there."

Gary Vertrees hailed from a berry farm outside Tacoma, Washington. He grew up outdoors hunting, having BB gun fights with his buddies, and fiddling with hot rods. He dropped out of high school his senior year and joined the army on his eighteenth birthday. Trained as a heavy vehicle operator, Vertrees was assigned after a year in the States to the transportation element of an armored cavalry squadron in Germany. He hated it. There was constant chicken-shit harassment, old barracks that never got warm when winter came, and NATO alerts that basically amounted to sitting out in the snow and sleet for three days at a time, frozen to the bone. It was garrison duty at its worst. "You had no function," notes Vertrees. Morale was in the dumps.

A guy who joined the unit after service with a transportation battalion in Vietnam soon announced, "This is bullshit." Vertrees asked him what he meant. "Oh, man," the new guy said, "inspections, all this bullshit. In Vietnam, you got none of this crap. You do your job and that's it. Nobody messes with you." The GI said he was going to 10-49 (from the transfer form number) back to Vietnam. Following his lead, Vertrees also put in a transfer for the war zone. "They thought I was nuts," Vertrees recalls, but "I wanted to wear a flak jacket, carry a weapon—kill something. I wanted to be a real soldier."

Vertrees joined the Bandidos two weeks before Tet, shortly before he turned twenty. During his first night at Binh Phuoc (vulgarized by the GIs to "Been Fucked"), a listening post from one of the line platoons came under heavy fire. The motor sergeant asked for volunteers from the maintenance section to join the reaction force. "Everybody goes, 'Yeah, I'm goin', I'm goin'.' I had not a clue what was going on yet, but I said, 'Yeah, I guess I'm going, too.' That's the way the outfit was. It was a kick-ass company. When stuff started, everybody got with the program and did what they had to do."

Vertrees became tight with Jerry Tomlinson and Tom Beck, who had nailed a VC during the Tet fight in Cholon; the two rounds from his .50-cal that went through the midsection literally cut the man in half.

"How'd it feel?" asked Vertrees.

Beck smiled: "Great."

The maintenance track was known as the "deuce track" because of its fender number (every vehicle had one), and the skull on its front armor plate was superimposed over a crossed wrench and screw driver instead of sabers. The deuce track operated more independently than the line tracks. "We could take off whenever we wanted," notes Vertrees. "All we had to do was tell the captain, 'Hey, we gotta go get parts,' and away we'd go. We'd make a beer run. We'd get a requisition form from the orderly room, then we'd haul ass up to Saigon and pull into one of the big supply depots along the river in Cholon. There's something like eighty-six cases of beer on a pallet. They'd bring it out on a forklift. We'd load the beer in the track, haul ass back to Binh Phuoc, unload forty cases in our hootch by the motor pool, then take the rest out to the platoons in the field."

It wasn't a bad war on those days. If Vertrees wasn't driving or taking a turn behind the .50, he might lean back in the seat behind the driver's hatch, relaxing with a cold beer and a cigar as the rice paddies rolled past, the deuce track's little "Fuck Communism" flag flapping from a radio antenna. It was a strange trip, made even more surreal on occasion by a bit of smoke. "I was pretty stupid when I first got over there. I had no idea what marijuana even looked like," recalls Vertrees, who was less a hippie than a blue-collar, beer-and-fast-cars guy, his hair combed straight back. It wasn't long, however, before one of the guys offered him a pipe packed with pot, "and after that, I pretty much found out what it did."

The maintenance troops didn't have it as bad as those in the line platoons. They didn't ride point and didn't go out on ambushes and listening posts. Vertrees was twice injured nonetheless, once by mortar shrapnel at Binh Phuoc, and again when the track he was driving was totaled by a mine on Thunder Road. His nose was broken in the second incident. All things considered, the war was not the cinematic adventure for which he had volunteered. Out on the road, away from officers, the guys on the deuce track could vent their frustrations in ways those in the more tightly controlled line platoons could not. "We used to go down the road and shoot at people. We never killed anybody because we would have got in deep crap, but we'd take a '79 and blow a round out in them rice paddies, and, holy cow, you'd see them gooks just bail. We didn't aim to hurt 'em, we just wanted to scare 'em—just to have fun, you know. Most of 'em were VC sympathizers anyway. It was like, 'hey, take this—we've been gettin' enough of it.'"

As the troops battened down for the night, Major Miller collared one of his assistant operations officers, Lieutenant Sweet, who had recently moved to the battalion staff after six months as a platoon leader, and told him that he would be serving as liaison officer with the local police detachment. The police, armed with hand-me-down carbines and BARs (Browning Automatic Rifles), were manning positions throughout the district in anticipation of trouble that night. Sweet was to keep Miller apprised of their activities and relay any requests they might have for reinforcements or fire support.

Captain Phant, the district police chief, picked up Sweet and his radioman in a jeep and drove them to his home inside the square-shaped police compound on the west side of Xom Cau Mat. The house was small but neat and clean, white stucco with a tile roof like the other buildings in the compound. Sweet and his radioman, Special Fourth Class Gary Rogers, sat on the floor with Phant, his wife, and their four charming young children, eating a late dinner of rice and vegetables and fish eyes for dessert. It was almost midnight by the time Sweet and Rogers turned in for the night in a spare room.

Four hours later, Captain Phant, who had a radio in his house, was shouting at everyone to wake up because the Y Bridge was under attack. Phant jumped behind the wheel of his jeep and sped east on the canal road, with Sweet in the passenger seat and Rogers in back with the radio. They began passing civilians moving in the opposite direction, fleeing the muffled gunfire that could heard farther down the road, leaving the trio in the jeep to hope that they weren't driving into an ambush.

The gunfire directed at Lieutenant Long's platoon from Bandido Charlie on the Y Bridge had begun at 3:45 a.m. on May 7, 1968. At the same time, an enemy mortar crew shelled Cholon, eighty rounds in all, from the nippa palm and rice paddies just south of town. Captain Phant parked his jeep at the south end of the bridge and, after checking with his guards there, proceeded on foot with Sweet and Rogers past Long's personnel carriers and down the northeast leg of the bridge. The guards in the sandbagged post at that end were under heavy fire from the Cholon side of the Kinh Doi. "We tried to get 'em back," recounts Sweet. "Everybody was firing. Everybody was rippin' at that point. You had AK fire coming from all over. The whole sky was lit up over that side of the city." The guards began pulling back. One tumbled to the pavement, wounded. Phant, Sweet, and Rogers started toward the man, then ducked against the guardrails as a sniper zeroed in on them. "We never did figure out where he was," notes Sweet, "but you could hear the rounds ricocheting off the bridge. The wounded guy managed to get back on his own."

The enemy on the north side of the canal ceased fire. There had been reports of additional infiltrators on the south side, however, and the ARVN soldiers who arrived from Cholon moved across the bridge; sporadic bursts of gunfire echoed through the night as the government troops moved down streets and alleys in search of the Viet Cong. Another flare-up of heavy fire (mortars and automatic weapons) began at approximately

4:30 a.m. as more teams of guerrillas hit a power plant and another of the isolated police outposts in District 8.

A pair of helicopter gunships fell upon the muzzle flashes blinking around the police outpost and disrupted the attack. One of the gunships was a Huey outfitted with rockets and machine guns. The other was a newer, sleeker AH-1G Cobra with tube-shaped rocket pods under stubby wings, an electric-powered minigun, and a belt-fed grenade launcher in the chin turret.

At approximately 5:00 a.m., an RPG was launched from the second-story window of a house on the south side of the Kinh Doi. Lieutenant Long and his troops watched as the rocket and its trailing sparks arched toward the track positioned on the south leg. Missing it, the rocket slammed into the guardrail and detonated on impact. There was another flash from the window, another dazzling comet trail of sparks. The second rocket flashed over the heads of the men on the bridge, then plopped harmlessly into the canal. By then, Long had readied a one-shot, over-the-shoulder 66mm light-antitank-weapon (LAW) and sent the rocket flashing toward the Viet Cong.

The rocket missed the target. Others followed the lieutenant's lead, however, including Sergeant Dawin G. "Buddy" Gault—a shake 'n' bake squad leader with less than a month in the field—who popped off an M79 round; it was the first he had ever fired in anger. Incredibly, the round sailed right through the window at which Gault had aimed in the semi-darkness at a range of over a hundred meters. The explosion set off a chain reaction of self-destructing RPGs, the window pulsing in the dark with flashes. Although Gault had neatly destroyed the RPG team—or at least, stopped any further attempts to rocket the bridge—he never thought much of the lucky shot, the medal he won for it, nor the write-up the incident received on the front page of the division newspaper. "It was not a big deal," says Gault. "We were being shot at and all I wanted to do was duck and shoot back to keep the gooks from getting to me."

The enemy hit the police compound on the west side of Xom Cau Mat at about half-past five, moving out of the tree lines and across the grass-covered paddies to the south. The outnumbered policemen with their obsolete carbines didn't have the heart to hold their ground against the multitude of figures who rushed at them from out of the predawn gloom with AK-47s held at their waists and RPG launchers over their shoulders.

As the police began to bug out, two gunships appeared and caught the enemy a mere thirty meters from the perimeter berm. The guerrillas fell back into the trees. Encouraged, the policemen reoccupied their positions.

Lieutenant Colonel Antila directed Captain Scarborough to dispatch the 2nd Platoon, Company C, to the police compound from its present position on the Route 5A bridge. Gary Vertrees watched "Charlie Two" roll past on the canal road. Groups of civilians were also on the road, carrying bags and bundles as they fled the battle area. Vertrees took photos of the civilians and the wheeling gunships in the dim light before realizing that long rounds from the fight for the police headquarters were pinging off his APC.

Dawn was breaking hazy and hot over the city as Charlie Two made a right turn into the police compound from the canal road. Rolling past the whitewashed barracks, the platoon came under fire upon reaching the south side of the compound as thirty or forty VC soldiers rushed forward in another attempt to overrun their objective. The gunships must have peeled away to refuel and rearm, for it is hard to imagine that the enemy would have otherwise risked another assault across the open paddies. The troops jumped from their tracks, and taking cover behind the buildings or at the prone along the south berm, they opened fire on the advancing Viet Cong. The guerrillas must have been shocked to be greeted by such a wall of fire. They had only moved out of their staging areas after nightfall, using the cover of darkness to move upriver in sampans. Given the inadequacy of the enemy's communications system, the commander of the assault force was more than likely unaware that U.S. reinforcements had beaten him to Saigon.

The result: a company of Viet Cong was pinned down in an open paddy by the Bandidos of the 5-60th Mech, 9th Infantry Division.

When Charlie Two reported that it was under heavy fire, Antila sent Scarborough in with Lieutenant Garver and Charlie One. Garver's platoon was turning into the compound when a half-dozen policemen rushed past. "I'll never forget," says Garver. "As soon as we got there, they *di-di-mau'd*"—which roughly translates to mean that the Vietnamese ran like hell, thus leaving the battle to the GIs.

Scarborough told Garver to take up positions on the west side of the compound while his own command track rolled up to Charlie Two's ongoing action along the south berm. The driver stopped near the other personnel carriers sitting in the center courtyard, "and everyone just un-assed the track as fast as they could and headed for cover," recalls Alan Kisling. "There was a hellacious firefight going on."

Lieutenant Neild and radioman Hewitt dashed for a row of white buildings facing the paddy. Enemy soldiers were popping up to fire from behind a dike not more than a hundred meters away. The air seemed electrified with fire. It was a breathless moment, but Neild and Hewitt reached the last building in the row and stood with their backs against it, safe from the enemy to the front. Private First Class Richard G. Heater, one of the captain's radiomen, had not been so lucky; catching a round in the leg, he had gone down in a heap in front of the command track and cried out for help.

To reach the wounded man, Neild would have to step back into the line of fire, and it seemed impossible that he could survive the AK-47 rounds cracking past the wall that shielded him. He hesitated. He didn't have to do anything. It wasn't his job; he was the forward observer. Nobody would notice his inaction. *You've got two choices*, he found himself thinking. *You either go out and get that guy, or you can call yourself a coward for the rest of your life.*

Wanting all the help he could get, Lieutenant Neild grabbed his big, hulking radioman, saying "Come on, Lurch!" Together they sprinted to Heater, grabbed his web gear, and dragged him to cover like a sack of oats. The medic who soon appeared thumped a morphine syrette into Heater, and when Neild next glanced in his direction, the young radioman was smiling and feeling no pain. His face glowed, as much from the morphine as from the indescribable sensation of realizing that he was still alive and would be loaded on a medevac at the first opportunity. The bullets were still buzzing, but *his* war was over.

Ducking inside a building, Kisling joined several troopers who were firing from a back window. Heads and shoulders kept appearing along the dike as individual enemy soldiers rose up to fire. Kisling had never before seen the enemy pinned down. The VC soldiers were usually better than that. They were the ambushers; they did not stumble into traps themselves. These guys, however, were truly up against it. Their only cover was the dike, and the only way out was across wide open ground under direct fire.

Everyone knew it was all over when a gunship streaked into view over the paddy. The shark-bodied Cobra wheeled around, then made several passes down the row of enemy soldiers behind the dike, minigun blazing at four-thousand rounds a minute. It was a slaughter. "When that Cobra arrived, I remember looking out at the enemy, and thinking, 'Man, you got the shaft on this one,' " says Kisling. "The pilot lined up on that dike just like a train on a track, and he went right down it and just tore 'em apart."

There was no denying the vindictive gratification of the moment. There were other emotions, too. "I have to give the little people credit," Kisling reflects. "They fought hard and hung on until completely overwhelmed by firepower. To this day, part of me feels sorry for those guys. You can imagine what it must have been like lying there and looking up and seeing that thing coming at you and knowing what was going to happen. You know, command decisions are made on both sides and the guy at the bottom pays the price, and that's what happened to those guys in the paddy. Somebody above them made a mistake, and they paid for it."

Chapter 6

Lieutenant Garver's four tracks formed a firing line along the western berm of the police compound. Even as the troops clambered off, an RPG came sizzling in their direction from across the paddies to their front. The explosion wounded several men who had just jumped to the ground.

The rocket had come from the nearby nameless hamlet. The platoon commenced firing into the tin-roofed, tree-shrouded hamlet. There was nothing to focus on, and in short order, the troops couldn't even hear the incoming fire over the sustained roar of their own M16, M60, and .50-caliber machine guns.

As the firing tapered off in the wake of the gunship runs, Garver recalls being joined by Captain Scarborough. Fifteen or twenty figures appeared then, walking toward the canal road on a dike that ran due north from the nameless hamlet. They didn't appear to be carrying weapons. Most, in fact, were women and children. There were also men in the line, however, and assuming they were VC trying to slip away with the civilians, a .50 gunner opened up from his APC.

Scarborough shouted to cease fire, that there were women and children in the way. Lieutenant Garver moved to where Scarborough was standing behind a track. Thinking only of protecting his men, Garver reasoned that to let the enemy escape was to invite further action and thus further casualties. Garver stated as forcefully as he could that, yes, there were women and children, but every third or fourth person out there was a *man*. Who did the captain think had been shooting at them?

Garver recalls Captain Scarborough staring at the distant figures for a few long seconds, then giving the command to open fire. Millard R. Goodwin recalls that at the time he didn't know who gave the order, but confirms that he joined in with his M79 when the platoon commenced firing at the unidentified people on the dike. "We mowed 'em down," Garver recounts in his matter-of-fact way. "They didn't even act like they tried to get down behind the dike. They just walked until we hit 'em. Like shooting ducks at a fair midway."

Given the paranoia of combat, it never entered Garver's mind that the people on the dike—including the men—might have been civilians trying to flee the area during the lull in the battle. Instead, it would strike him when he thought about the incident afterward that if the women and children were not combatants themselves—always a possibility in a guerrilla war—then the Viet Cong had ruthlessly used people from the hamlet as human shields in an attempt to cover their withdrawal. "The incident was not discussed at any time with anybody," Garver writes. "As an act of war, it probably didn't affect any of us at the time—our own survival was what mattered above anything else—but it probably did affect all of us at some point after returning to The World."

When veterans of the battalion heard Garver's account years later, comments fell into two categories. From former company commander Jim Sharpe: "I said to myself, boy, Scarborough sure changed. You don't take casualties to heart as much when you're a staff officer. It's a different matter when you're the commander and it's your guys who are hurt, and your responsibility lies with them and not the civilians caught in the middle."

Doug Birge, however, could not believe that Scarborough, who rebuked troops for calling the Vietnamese "gooks," would turn around and order women and children to be fired upon, even in the heat of a confusing combat situation. "He knew the book and went by it. The book did not include shooting civilians." Birge is convinced that Garver, not Scarborough, gave the order to open fire, unmoved by the argument that if Garver meant to distort history to protect himself, he would have put weapons in the hands of the people on the dike, or would have simply remained silent about an incident that only a handful of infantrymen knew about until he discussed it with an outsider. The Scarborough that Birge served under "saw the Vietnamese as human and wanted them treated with dignity. He wouldn't have hesitated to bring charges against someone who wounded or killed civilians."

There was a twist to the tragedy: unbeknownst to the Bandidos, the people of District 8 were not the opportunists and VC sympathizers they took all Vietnamese to be, but anticommunist Catholics who had fled the north after the defeat of the French fourteen years earlier. Originally resettled in the delta, these refugees had since been encouraged to migrate into the marshland slums across the Kinh Doi from Cholon. The area was controlled at the time by communist cadre whose grip was such that they could hold open meetings without fear of interference from government troops. In 1965, the New Life Construction Project—an organization of community leaders funded through the U.S. Embassy and backed up by the paramilitary National Police—recruited cadre of their own among high-school and university students. The organization began doing good works in the district, including working alongside the people to repair roads, dig irrigation canals, and build schools, markets, clinics, and cooperatives to raise hogs and chickens. Shops opened, and housing began to go up that was middle-class by Vietnamese standards.

The New Life Construction Project also collected information about the VC in their midst. Many within the VC cadre were captured, and the rest disappeared. There was not a single report of enemy activity in the district through all of 1967, by which time the area had become a showcase for civic action and nation building, a mandatory stop for politicians jetting in from Washington for a firsthand look at the war. When the area came under attack during Tet, the people knew exactly which buildings had been occupied by the Viet Cong and pinpointed them for the counterattacking ARVN. The residents not only hated the communists but were loyal to Saigon and even grateful in their proud way to the United States of America.

The guerrillas could not have chosen a better community to use as a human shield between themselves and the U.S. Army.

Lieutenant Colonel Antila and his artillery liaison officer, First Lieutenant Tommy R. Franks, were presently picked up in an observation helicopter, leaving Major Miller to run things at the command post. Scarborough reported that he had five badly wounded men. They were soon medevacked aboard a Huey.

In response to reports of enemy activity in the adjacent hamlet, Captain Scarborough's troops remounted their tracks and started across the field between the police compound and Xom Cau Mat. The tracks halted along a paddy dike, then turned left on line to face the hamlet. As enemy fire snapped past from the little tin-roofed buildings just to the front (it was now half-past eight), the Bandidos jumped from their personnel carriers, took up positions along the dike, and began returning fire against the unseen Viet Cong.

Back at the command post, Gary Vertrees took a call that one of the line tracks was down with engine trouble. He hollered to his buddies to load up, then clambered into the driver's hatch of the deuce track, donned a radio helmet, and cranked the track up. Upon reaching Scarborough's position, Vertrees requested that the guys on the stalled track signal as he drove down the rear of the firing line. No signal was seen, so Vertrees turned around upon reaching the last vehicle. He was just starting back up the row when something exploded with such force that he thought the track was going to tip over on its side. Badly shaken, it took Vertrees a moment to realize that his track hadn't been hit by enemy fire. Rather, the deuce track had happened to pass behind an APC mounted with a 106mm recoilless rifle—

a weapon with a ferocious back-blast—at the exact moment the gunner punched off another round into Xom Cau Mat.

Exasperated, Vertrees got on the radio again and demanded that whoever needed help had better start waving and shouting, at which point somebody finally did. The maintenance team tried to jump-start the stalled track with a cable run from their own track, with enemy fire ricocheting off both vehicles all the while. The jump-start did not work. "The hell with it," Vertrees said. "Let's just pull it apart and put new batteries in." The new batteries did the trick. The old batteries were supposed to be returned to the motor pool, and Jerry Tomlinson was dutifully lugging them to the deuce track when he heard the sudden crack-crack-crack of bullets slicing past his head. Tomlinson dumped the government property in the paddy as he sprinted for cover. "Once bullets crack, you know they've already gone by," he explains, "but it's enough to scare the hell out of you. I dropped the batteries in the mud. They're probably still there."

The deuce track joined the firing line. Vertrees climbed into the command cupola behind the .50, and exposed from the waist up because few tracks in the battalion had gun shields, he opened up on the buildings into which the other tracks were already firing. The bark and concussion of each round was considerable, and when firing on automatic, the smoke and muzzle blast at the end of the long barrel blurred the gunner's vision. Vertrees quickly emptied the attached ammunition box. "You go through those cans pretty quick when it's hot and heavy like that," notes Tomlinson, who acted as assistant gunner, retrieving additional thirty-pound, hundred-round boxes from under the benches inside the hull. "During a firefight, you went on autopilot," recalls Vertrees. "You just go blank and do whatever has to be done. Everything happens fast, but in slow motion, and you don't remember half of it afterwards."

The recoilless rifle kept booming, manned by Specialist Fourth Class Clyde W. "Whitey" Whitehead (his name has been changed), a big Georgia redneck who loved the war so much he was on his second tour in Vietnam. He sported a tattoo of the Road Runner on each breast with the words "beep-beep."

Despite the machine-gun and recoilless-rifle fire, a team of dismounted troopers, who attempted to slip into the factory at the south end of the hamlet, were deterred by heavy fire. Antila ordered Scarborough to break off the attack and hold in place until he could bring Lieutenant Sharpe and Company A up from the Ben Luc Bridge. After reaching the capital, Company A was to turn off the canal road and push north to south down the main street of Xom Cau Mat. Company C would block any attempt to withdraw to the west, an ARVN ranger company would do the same on the east side of the hamlet, and helicopter gunships would screen the open ground to the south of Xom Cau Mat.

The gunships prepped the hamlet with rockets. Fires raged, and black smoke boiled skyward. The bodies of two-dozen guerrillas killed by the Cobra in front of the police compound were sprawled behind Company C's firing line. During a lull in the action, soldiers searched the bodies for souvenirs and items that might interest the battalion intelligence officer. A lone wounded survivor was discovered among the bodies and quickly whisked to the battalion command post aboard the deuce track. "I had my .45 screwed in his ear the whole way back," notes Vertrees, who was taking no chances. Though the prisoner had lived through the battle, Vertrees doubted that the man would survive the interrogation awaiting him at the hands of the ARVN and Vietnamese National Police.

Other Bandidos, meanwhile, took snapshots of their dead enemies. The bodies were in bad shape, some literally chewed to pieces by the minigun fire that had cut through the enemy soldiers like a chainsaw as they huddled helplessly against the paddy dike. Alan Kisling had been there too long to be bothered; he sat on the dike beside an eviscerated Viet Cong and proceeded to wolf down a C-ration can of barbecued beef. Hewitt was sitting there, too, and probably in a state of shock from his brutal baptism of fire, he stared at Kisling with a how-can-you-do-that expression. *What the hell, I'm hungry,* thought Kisling, irritated by Lurch's look. Then poor Lurch leaned over and puked his guts out. Kisling grimaced at the perfectly incompetent radioman as if to say, *C'mon, buddy, get your shit together!*

Captain Phant received a call that one of his patrols was pinned down. Speeding to the scene in his jeep, Phant pulled to the side of the road when he saw his men. Along with liaison officer Sweet and radioman Gary Rogers, he joined a half-dozen policemen crouching along a wall. One of their comrades lay in the street, having been shot—it was quickly explained—from the two-story house which dominated the intersection. The snipers were obviously waiting for somebody to attempt to reach the wounded policeman so they could gun down the would-be rescuer in turn. Nobody was making a move. Nobody even dared to shoot back at that point.

"Hey, sir, what are we gonna do?" asked Rogers, who Lieutenant Sweet knew as a nice kid and a good soldier who would do whatever was asked of him, including an attempt to rescue the wounded policeman. Captain Phant spurred his men into providing cover fire as Sweet and Rogers dashed into the intersection to haul the wounded man back to the wall. As far as Sweet could tell, the cover fire had worked. He didn't think the enemy had fired a single shot, though it was hard to tell in all the commotion.

Major Miller informed Sweet that a team of gunships had been scrambled to support the police. When the team arrived, Lieutenant Sweet made radio contact with the flight leader, popped a smoke grenade to mark his position, then ducked behind the wall as the gunships dove in and unleashed rockets two at a time into the target. When they banked away, Phant had several of his men move in on the house from the flanks while the others lay down suppressive fire. Sweet and Rogers opened up with their M16s. The VC had disappeared, though, probably scuttling out the back door and down an alley as soon as the gunships had arrived. Sweet waved down a U.S. Army ambulance that appeared on the street. The medics quickly loaded the wounded policeman on a litter and, slamming the double doors closed, continued on their way, presumably headed for the 3rd Field Hospital near Tan Son Nhut Airbase.

At some point that morning, Lieutenant Long was instructed to rejoin the main body of Company C from his present position on the Y Bridge.

With two months in the field at the time, Lieutenant Long was greatly admired by his Bandidos. He was a mature, self-assured man, a college graduate who, as his men would remember it, had been teaching school when his draft notice arrived. Long listened to his veterans. He made the right decisions in combat. He also possessed a finely developed wit. A photograph of Lieutenant Long in Saigon, taken by Doug Birge, the platoon medic, revealed a dashing individual with glasses and—his helmet in his hands—a shock of reddish-brown hair. He sported a green neckerchief tied like a choker around his throat and a necklace with a tiger claw at the end, and was clean-shaven except for a slight mustache and a half-moon of stubble around his chin. He wore a tight, confident smile. His blue and silver combat infantryman badge was pinned over his heart, and a skull-and-sabers pocket patch hung from the bottom button of his breast pocket. His revolver rested against his hip in a cowboy holster.

"Lieutenant Long truly cared about his men," Birge writes. "He never lost his composure and never showed fear. The shit would be coming in hot and heavy, and you would be scared to death, but then you'd look at this guy, and his expression would be such that you just knew you were going to be okay. He had brass balls. He was by far the best officer I ever served with in Vietnam."

Lieutenant Long's three tracks drove down the south leg of the bridge, then made two right turns to get around the hundred-square-meter field below the elevated span. The lead track was approaching the intersection with the canal road when AK-47s started cracking from a split-level house, which had two stories in the front half, three in the back, and faced the northwest corner of the field. The rockets fired during the night at the Y Bridge had come from the split-level house or one of its neighbors.

Disembarking the tracks as the gunners returned fire, Lieutenant Long and some of his troops climbed over fences and moved between houses to outflank the ambush. Enemy soldiers began firing from other buildings, and at one point, Long's group sprinted one at a time across a side street down which an unseen sniper was firing. The first few men made it across unscathed. Private First Class Samuel E. Marr, a grenadier, dashed next into the sniper's sights, and had almost reached the safe side of the street when a round struck the heel of his jungle boot. Another took him in the side in the next instant, and spun around by the impact he crashed to the pavement, crying out that he was hit. Before the sniper could finish his work, Larry Miller, who had taken Marr under his wing when the two originally joined the company as replacements, ran out to grab Marr's web gear and drag his buddy out of harm's way.

Doc Birge shouted at the guys to cover him, then darted to where Miller had pulled Marr. The medic checked Marr for injuries. There was no blood, no obvious wounds. Marr said his hip hurt, however, and pulled his shirt up, revealing a black-and-blue bruise the size of a flattened basketball. Upon closer examination, Birge noticed that the round that struck Marr had first punched through one end of the LAW slung over his shoulder, missing the warhead inside the fiberglass tube by a fraction of an inch. The round had then been further slowed down by Marr's pistol belt, which was studded cowboy-style with bullets, before ripping through the leather .45-caliber pistol holster itself and ricocheting off his hip.

As the melee continued, Lieutenant Long was scratched across his neck by a spray of little pieces of metal, apparently when a nearby sheet of tin was riddled by AK-47 fire. Before the platoon suffered any serious casualties, Long passed the word to pull back to the tracks and requested gunships to work over the split-level house. Sergeant Gault stepped out from behind a building and fired his M79 grenade launcher down the street to cover his squad's withdrawal. He hadn't looked around the corner before firing, however, and didn't realize there was a utility pole just a few feet away, blocking his shot. "The round ricocheted back and landed at my feet," recounts Gault. The 40mm shell did not explode, designed as they were to spin-arm only after traveling ten meters in order "to keep fools like me from killing themselves. I just looked at the round lying there. I knew how close I had just come to being killed, but it didn't really register. In a firefight, you are pumping and don't think about what just happened or might have happened. The fact that you're still alive is enough."

Private First Class Jearold L. Harper was firing the machine gun on a track parked on a side street while his buddy, Private First Class Harry C. Wagner, sat on the left side of the cargo hatch behind the commander's hatch, manning a second .50-cal that had been welded on the right side. Harper could see an occasional muzzle flash in the windows of the split-level house to their right and, as he was quickly running out of ammo from returning fire, he called over his shoulder to Wagner for more. Wagner did not produce the ammo, and Harper realized that Wagner was not even firing anymore. Expecting the worst, he jerked around to find his buddy leaning over to speak with two reporters who stood behind the track, holding up their microphones to the GI. As relieved as he was angry, Harper shouted, "Wagner, you asshole!" just as an RPG flashed from the split-level house and sailed just over their heads to explode behind the APC.

There were journalists all over the area. One of them, George Severson of CBS News, positioned his film crew to the rear of Harper's track. Two days later, people back home watched as Harper and Wagner, wearing helmets and flak jackets (Wagner was shirtless under his armored vest, his arms gleaming with sweat), methodically blasted away with their .50s. The white tracers seemed to extend three feet from the barrels as they zipped straight as arrows through the leafy trees between the track and the split-level house. The side of the building facing the track became pocked with raggedy black entrance holes, and a cloud of dust formed on the other side of the house from the exit of all the rounds.

Severson narrated the scene:

> The armored personnel carriers have been standing off and blasting Viet Cong positions with .50-caliber machine gun fire. The Americans finally called in helicopter gunships. The sleek Cobras and lumbering Hueys rained deadly salvos of rockets and minigun fire down on the houses. Civilians were warned to get out before the strike, but many are still in there. The aircraft may have gotten some of the Viet Cong, but they're still returning fire. . . .

Captain Phant had authorized the use of gunships after arriving on the scene in his jeep. It was a decision he hesitated to make, for many of his policemen lived with their families in this very neighborhood. Severson's cameraman filmed the gunships as they came in low over the warehouses on the east side of the field below the Y Bridge. By then, Lieutenant Long had backed his tracks up to the road on the south side, near the warehouses and catercorner to the split-level house.

The camera focused on two GIs who seemed terribly casual under the circumstances, standing in the open behind their personnel carrier. With their backs to the camera, one had the butt of his M79 resting against his hip. They looked up as a gunship began its run. One rocket flashed from its pod, followed a moment later by a second rocket. The two GIs turned their heads toward the split-level house. The first rocket scored a direct hit against the side of the building. The second slammed into the flat roof. Both exploded with clouds of gray-black smoke, so close that the two GIs winced a bit, ducking their heads, one rubbing his ear for a quick moment as they side-stepped almost indifferently to the safe side of their APC.

An old papasan suddenly appeared, carrying a blood-splattered child in his arms as he hurried across the street toward the personnel carriers. Another gunship was rolling in at that moment, but broke off as Lieutenant Long explained the situation on the radio even as his troops frantically waved the pilot away. Doc Birge courageously rushed to the old man, scooped up the child in his arms, and darted back behind the cover of his track. The papasan was crying pitifully, and Birge broke his own rules by using the supplies packed in his aid bag—which were for his buddies, not the gooks—to bandage the child and administer morphine. "The child had numerous shrapnel wounds and had lost quite a bit of blood," recalls Birge. "It would be a miracle if he survived."

Either the rockets or the enemy started fires at the embattled corner. It was a windy day, and the flames quickly spread across the canal road to the buildings between it and the Kinh Doi. In response, a fire engine and a red jeep-ambulance arrived from Cholon. Three firemen sat in the jeep, and in the bed of the fire engine stood another half-dozen, all outfitted in old-fashioned silver firefighter helmets, black raincoats over khaki trousers, and knee-high black boots. The jeep was forced to stop when it neared Long's tracks, as the enemy opened fire again from the split-level house, ignoring the vehicle's oversized Red Cross flag. The fires thus burned out of control. Captain Phant later learned that the wives of two of his policemen had died amid the smoke and flame. Four children also perished. In addition, a twelve-man squad of policemen, rushing to the scene in a troop truck, was ambushed and wiped out to the last man after crossing the second little bridge on the canal road between Xom Cau Mat and the Y Bridge.

When the gunships banked off, Lieutenant Long led a second maneuver around the flank of the split-level house. Muzzle flashes continued to wink infuriatingly from the smoking, shot-to-hell building. In return, Sam Marr fired M79 rounds from a window of the house into which Long's team had slipped. Long rested a LAW over his shoulder, shouted "Clear!" to warn the others away from the back-blast, and then squeezed the firing button. "The back-blast deafened us and blew out most of the windows in the building we were in," writes Doug Birge. "I don't know if the lieutenant hit what he was aiming at, but the enemy fire stopped. Incidentally, Lieutenant Long absolutely loved the LAW. He always had one or two with him, and fired them as often as he could. Because of this, the platoon called him The Lawman."

Severson's report on CBS News continued:

> As the Viet Cong pull back, the civilians move out; at first a trickle, then a stream of terror-stricken humanity pours across the bridge. They carry a few pitiful belongings, their children and old people on their backs—thousands of them crowding into downtown Saigon, only a few of them knowing where they would sleep tonight or find food. Their only concern at the moment is to escape from the death and destruction that has engulfed their homes. . . .

Lanny Jones trained his M16 at the passing civilians, lest one turn out to be a guerrilla with a grenade up his sleeve. Jerry Harper would remark that though few non-combatants had been seen during the action itself, "the buildings we'd been firing into were full of civilians. They came flooding out after the VC *di-di-mau*'d. It was terrible, just terrible. But what could you do?"

One of the warehouses on the east side of the field was used as an aid station. Inside, Severson's cameraman filmed an ARVN soldier in sweat-soaked fatigues bending over a man lying upon a stretcher on the concrete floor. A white bandage was wrapped around his head, another on his left shoulder, and yet a third around his left leg above the knee where the trouser has been split open. After more bandages were wrapped around the man's right arm, he was carried to the jeep-ambulance, the sides of his stretcher folding tightly against him. Outside, the camera fixed on another South Vietnamese soldier who rushed toward the lens, a teenage boy on his back. As they went past, the camera turned with them to reveal that the boy's white shirt was soaked red from his shoulder blades down. His face was impassive and streaked with blood, with his cheek resting against the back of his rescuer's helmet.

The cameraman also filmed the rush to the bridge. Several women went past the camera, each pressed against the back of the one to her front. Clinging to each other, they hastened past barbed wire and across the mud puddles between the buildings. Next, the cameraman took up a position on the bridge itself, facing south. Waves of people came toward him, filling the bridge from guardrail to guardrail. They proceeded at a brisk pace, almost jogging. As more and more people crowded onto the bridge, the pace slowed. Behind the slow-moving mass, the houses built on stilts over the canal burned red, with greasy black smoke pouring from the flames. Most of those coming across the bridge were women and children. A young woman rushed past the camera, holding against her shoulder her bare-bottomed baby with a piece of cloth draped over the child's head to protect it from the sun. One man, his shirt hanging open, had a *chogi* pole over his shoulder, a bundle at each end. Some people walked alongside their bicycles, and a women in a conical hat snaked her way through the crowd on a moped. A mother pushed along a two-wheeled cart, in which were three children and a dog. One of the little boy turned to smile at the camera.

Unable to break through, Lieutenant Long's platoon pulled back onto the Y Bridge. Long called Birge over to assist another wounded child. As Birge worked on the child, whose injuries were not fatal, he glanced up and realized a half-dozen news cameras were filming his every move. Jerry Harper lay down against a guardrail and, ignoring the refugees streaming past just inches away, went out hard with his head on his helmet. When he came out of his coma, his buddy Wagner told him that a photographer had taken several shots of him as he slept on the concrete, the perfect picture of a battle-exhausted American GI.

George Severson concluded his report:

> One difference between this fighting and the Tet Offensive seems to be that the enemy this time has no illusions about capturing Saigon. The object of the exercise this time seems to be to cause as much damage and suffering as possible, and in this, as you can see here, they are succeeding admirably.

Chapter 7

"Well, they've been running us ragged trying to thwart the expected second offensive of the V.C.," Lieutenant Sharpe of Company A had written home at the beginning of the month. "We've been going here, there, and everywhere trying to establish contact with the enemy, but so far the results have been negative." Sharpe assumed that they had once again been operating on erroneous intelligence. He had no way of knowing that the guerrillas were indeed planning to strike, and had avoided battle as they marshaled their forces for the attack on Saigon. As such, he intended no irony when he informed his family on the eve of Mini-Tet that "things are beginning to slow down now[.]"

First Lieutenant Jim Sharpe, a boyish-looking young man of twenty-three with thick glasses, ruddy skin, rust-colored hair, and definitely on the short side, had become a combat officer by default. The quiet, thoughtful son of a poor coal-mining family was studying for a career in education at Pennsylvania State University, when he signed up for advanced Reserved Officer Training Corps. He had only done so because he had needed the forty-dollar-a-month stipend and had believed the recruiter who told him that the dirty little guerrilla war, which he was reading about in the papers, would be over by the time he pinned on his bars.

The recruiter had been wrong. Commissioned in the middle of a full-blown war, Jim Sharpe attempted to avoid the battlefield when filling out his branch-selection wish list. There were three spaces on the form, at least one of which, according to regulations, had to be filled in with a combat-arms selection. Putting the combat-arms selection at the bottom of the list, Sharpe requested assignment to the legal, ordnance, or armor branch, and much to his dismay was soon on his way to the armor school at Fort Knox, Kentucky. When Sharpe protested that he was near-sighted and asked what would happen if he lost his eyeglasses in a firefight, the army obligingly issued him five extra pairs before shipping him to the 5-60th Mech of the 9th Infantry Division.

Lieutenant Sharpe had originally assumed command of Company A on Christmas Day 1967, after five months as a platoon leader and staff officer. The company had a poor reputation. It was the battalion's lame duck, having been led of late by one captain who never left base camp and was reassigned for this failure of nerve. The next captain wasn't there long enough to do anything but get his platoons into firefights with each other before a boobytrap sent him out on a medevac with the bodies of his dead radio-telephone operators.

Once on the line, it didn't matter that Sharpe didn't want to be there. The only choice an honorable man had at such a point was to do the best job he could, and in doing so, Jim Sharpe got Company A going in the right direction again. "Lieutenant Sharpe was a good leader," recalls former platoon leader Rick Neuman. "He knew what he was doing, and he was very low-key and matter-of-fact about things. He was like the rest of us. The attitude was 'get in, get it over with.' None of us were about to run off and charge any windmills."

Lieutenant Sharpe had been with Company A for four months when Antila told him that he could turn over his command at any time because his required field-time was completed, and move up to battalion staff. Sharpe delayed leaving his company for some two weeks. Antila finally presented him with a fait accompli: Sharpe's designated replacement, Captain Jerry Dean Dobbs (a pseudonym), was waiting for Company A when it returned briefly to Binh Phuoc on May 6, 1968. Dobbs was to take over in three days after Sharpe brought him up to speed.

Jim Sharpe outlined some of the reasons why he had not jumped at the chance to get off the line in his letters to his twin brother Bill, who was to become a helicopter pilot and follow him to Vietnam. To begin with, there was the satisfying challenge of commanding men in combat, and the pride in the occasional kudos he had received from his experienced soldiers for a job well done. "I have mixed feelings about leaving A Co.," Sharpe wrote. "I know the fellows real well, and feel close to them. I have had a lot of good times, and know I'd have more. Yet, the danger is always present . . . I hate to leave, yet I'll be glad to leave."

There was more. For Lieutenant Sharpe and Company A, the VC had been an elusive, quicksilver foe who was everywhere and nowhere in a hostile, sullen landscape of canals, shimmering paddies, nippa palm, and sunbaked hootches. The guerrillas never showed their faces; they preferred hit-and-run tactics; and they were never where intelligence said they would be. Jim Sharpe had lost five men and over eighty were wounded, mostly to mines, boobytraps, mortar attacks, and friendly fire. In return, Company A had accounted for but a handful of enemy, one or two, here and there. "We weren't seeing a lot of action. Four months I had that company and we were never engaged in heavy combat."

Frustrated, Sharpe informed his brother "that the U.S. *cannot* achieve a military victory in Vietnam solely on the basis of its military might."

Sharpe thought that only government forces, backed up by American firepower, could beat the Viet Cong. It was, after all, their land, their people.

I have seen good ARVN soldiers get information out of civilians that U.S. soldiers could never get, and find cleverly concealed caches that U.S. soldiers normally walk over. He finds draft dodgers, potential V.C., and bona-fide V.C. where U.S. troops would release the same because they had what is considered to be valid identification.

Sharpe also outlined how the civilian population was crucial to victory, though he could see no way to bring them around:

The average Vietnamese civilian rolls with the punches: he's a V.C. sympathizer when the V.C. are around, and friend of the government when [U.S. and ARVN] troops are near. But the V.C. get better use out of him because they invoke the emotion of fear in the civilian much better than Allied troops do. When U.S. troops question a civilian through the use of an interpreter, the stock answer given is that nothing was seen or heard. They say nothing because they know no harm will come to them. But when a VC asks for information or for the use of a son to move war materials, the VC receive 100% cooperation.

Much was left unsaid in these analytical letters. Sharpe did not tell his brother that he had become so determined to avenge his company's losses that he had promised three-day passes to any trooper who had personally killed a VC. Nor did he mention an incident in which one of his night patrols took fire, and he led a dismounted assault in return, such was his desire to close with the enemy. "I just said, 'The hell with it, let's go,'" recalls Sharpe, who was embarrassed when Antila mistook his anger for audacity and wrote him up for the Silver Star. "We just abandoned all caution and pushed into the woods. We didn't get anybody. It was dark as hell, and they slipped away."

Nor did Sharpe write home that in an attempt to avoid further casualties he had, on dismounted sweeps, taken to grabbing the nearest rice farmer and forcing him to lead the way on the premise that if anyone knew where the boobytraps were, it was the villagers. "We never lost a single civilian,"

Sharpe would reflect with bitter irony. "Isn't that remarkable?" Sharpe notes that his interpreter, Sergeant Nguyen Van Nhan, "would step in whenever I got carried away interrogating civilians. Nhan was one of them, and he had a restraining influence on me. He sort of kept us at bay. He didn't care for the fact that we put civilians on point, but I told him that wasn't negotiable. I said, 'I realize there's the Geneva Convention that prohibits this, but I'm sorry, we're doing it.' "

From having tried to avoid serving in a combat unit when originally commissioned, the bloodlust had built up in Jim Sharpe to the point that he hesitated to leave the field "because I needed to kill some Charlies, quite frankly. I wanted to make up for the people we had lost." Sharpe was conflicted between wanting to finish his tour in relative safety at battalion headquarters and wanting to stay with his company long enough to score some payback. In short, he didn't feel like he had yet done the job for which he had trained. "We hadn't made a dent," he says. "You go out in the morning and pound the paddies all day and come back with one less guy. Three days later, you're back humping the *same* territory, and you lose another guy, and you have absolutely nothing to show for it. The frustration of not being able to requite our losses was so excruciating that I thought I was losing my sense of reason. I really thought I was losing my marbles. The desire to kill Charlies had become an obsession with me."

One of Lieutenant Sharpe's platoons had spent the night on the Ben Luc Bridge outside Tan An, while another guarded the nearby Thu Thua bridge. His third platoon had previously been detached to another unit. The ambush patrols came in at first light, and the company was "piddling and puddling around as usual," Sharpe later wrote to his brother, "when we suddenly were given the word to move as fast as possible by the most direct route to Saigon."

Lieutenant Sharpe joined First Lieutenant Grant S. Buehrig's platoon at the Ben Luc Bridge, with the company commander's replacement-in-training, Captain Dobbs, sitting beside him atop the command track. No one was quite sure what to make of Dobbs. Introducing himself to the company the day before, Dobbs—chubby, balding, and old for his rank—had sounded not only unsure of himself but also a bit dim.

Having hastily mounted up, Lieutenant Buehrig and the 3rd Platoon of Company A, accompanied by Sharpe and Dobbs, departed the Ben Luc Bridge at about 9:30 a.m. on May 7, 1968. Grant Buehrig, age twenty-four, was a doctor's son from a farming community in central Illinois who had been drafted upon graduating from college. New to the platoon, he had impressed his people, who described him as an officer who knew his business, led from the front (the platoon leader's track was, in fact, the point vehicle), and "treated us right," as Mark D. Fenton recalls. "He took care of us, and wouldn't ask anybody to do anything he wasn't willing to do himself."

Lieutenant Neuman and the 1st Platoon of Company A joined the rear of the column from the Thu Thua bridge. Rick Neuman, age twenty-three, had grown up poor with his divorced, working mother in Mankato, Minnesota. Running out of funds for college during his sophomore year, he dropped out and was then immediately drafted. He was serious and taciturn and a seasoned platoon leader who had already been wounded three times during his four months in the field. He believed in the creed they preached at OCS: Keep your head about you and do your job, and everything will come out okay.

Absent the detached platoon, Lieutenant Sharpe had only nine tracks on the road and a grand total of fifty-eight GIs. They were all basically in the dark about why they were rushing to Saigon. "I thought it was just another typical trip for some security thing," says Grant Buehrig. "No alarm bells were going off. I had no thought whatever that we were going into a pitched battle."

Specialist Fourth Class Holder, a team leader in Buehrig's platoon, would later recall: "The troops were always the last to know anything about any operation. We were hyped because we thought we were going to be escorting another supply convoy, and that meant that we would have some goof-off time in Saigon."

Morale was good in Company A. There was little bravado, though, despite the "Ass Kicking Alpha" flags that were decorated with a big cartoon boot and flew from some of the tracks. "No one wanted to be there, and there was a perpetual background noise of bitchin' and gripin'," notes Buehrig. The troops were fixated on their rotation date, and their attitude, explains Leslie F. Koenig, was that "We're here and we're gonna watch out for each other. We're gonna do what we have to do. I wouldn't call it gung-ho, but if one of your buddies got in trouble, you were there. Other than that, we weren't about to do anything stupid."

Grant Buehrig would muse that "when you're talking about morale in that kind of situation, it was not a flag-waving-motherhood-and-apple-pie kind of morale. It was not high-minded." Theirs was a thankless task, for they were heroes to no one, and their only reward at the end of another hard day was to open a beer while sitting on a dike with a can of C-rations. "When you think about what everybody went through, I'd say morale was incredible," adds Buehrig. "The guys did whatever was asked of them, and they did it professionally, with equanimity, and sometimes with real bravery. I was proud to be with them."

It took an hour to reach the capital. Nearing the city limits, Sharpe made contact with Lieutenant Colonel Antila, who radioed corrections from his helicopter when Buehrig, unsure if he had reached the right intersection, overshot the turn from Highway 4 onto Route 232. The rest of the column stopped while an embarrassed Buehrig backed his tracks up. Sharpe had a quick conference with Major Miller upon reaching the battalion command post. Then a sergeant in Company A put the word out over the radio before the column continued on toward the columns of smoke rising to the east: "This is a definite contact mission. Be prepared for a long, hard fight."

The tracks followed the canal road to the top of the main road cutting south through Xom Cau Mat. Calling a halt, Sharpe established a staging area in a small clearing among the warehouses facing the Kinh Doi on the north side of Route 232. "As we were unloading from our vehicles, we were told to make sure that we were carrying extra ammo and grenades and our LAWs," recalls John Holder, who realized then "that this might not just be another routine day."

Lieutenant Sharpe's orders were to sweep north to south down the main street of Xom Cau Mat, clearing the buildings to either side until reaching the factory at the end of the hamlet, a distance of approximately five-hundred meters. Swampy rice paddies were visible beyond the factory. There was only a single block of buildings on the west side of the dirt street, and Sharpe had been informed that Company C was on line in the paddies beyond. Meanwhile, the ARVN rangers rushed in from Cholon had assumed blocking positions in the warren of houses and side streets on the east side of Xom Cau Mat.

Private First Class Ronnie T. Everidge, a machine gunner in Buehrig's platoon, glanced into the police compound as they formed up for the attack. There, he saw several uniformed troops playing cards in the shade of a tree with glasses on the table—a tableau of South Vietnamese apathy. "Look at that shit," a GI beside Everidge spat. "What are we doin', goin' down the street, lookin' for action—and these guys are sittin' there, doin' nothing'! It's *their* country!"

Lieutenant Buehrig's platoon was still in the lead as the attack began. Only the drivers and gunners remained on the tracks. The rest of the troops were dismounted on either side of the road, with the lead squad well ahead of the lead vehicle. Sharpe would write to his brother, "We began our search uneventfully; civilians were busy working around their homes in the area we were sweeping so we figured there were no Charlies."

It was never determined how many Viet Cong were waiting at the end of the street for Alpha Company. After the battle, thirteen sampans would be found beached along the Rach Xom, which flowed through the nameless village and was one of several waterways that allowed the enemy to move in close to the capital from their staging areas in the countryside. Each sampan was big enough for thirty passengers, meaning that maybe four-hundred troops—a full battalion by enemy standards—might have infiltrated the area during the night. Given the enemy's various objectives, only part of the assault force would have taken up positions in Xom Cau Mat. "Nobody but the VC know how many enemy troops were involved in the battle," Antila writes. "Based on the volume of fire at times, it was a sizable force. Sizable means what? Damned if I know. One man with an AK-47 and a lot of ammunition can seem like a major force to a squad on the ground."

Sergeant Cedell Raggs, whose squad had the point, was tough but fair and cool under fire. He was something of a showman and good company during a night of drinking and poker in the barracks—in other words, a natural leader. "The only person I had more respect for than Sergeant Raggs was my father," recalls Mark Fenton. "He was a good friend to everybody. He looked after everybody and took care of us. There wasn't a guy in that platoon that wouldn't have followed him anywhere in combat."

Raggs' men expected him to go regular. He actually got out at the end of his enlistment, and became a reverend in the African Methodist Episcopal Church in his hometown of Greenwood, Mississippi. In reality, Raggs had never possessed the lifer requirement of putting the mission over his men. "Raggs was in charge, but he was one of us, too," explains Howard A. Ossen. "His primary concern was our safety. Instead of going out at night and doing something stupid, he would generally find the most defensible place to set up an ambush, which was not necessarily the place where you were going to find the enemy. He was willing to bend an order a little bit to be safe, and that translated to fewer casualties."

Sergeant Raggs had put John Holder's team in the lead, and Holder—a tall, aggressive soldier who was a quarter Pequot Indian and from Pawcatuck, Connecticut—had taken the point himself. Holder was backed up by Privates First Class Les Koenig and Howard Ossen, a draftee who had gambled that this college degree would keep him in the rear but now found himself on a street in Saigon, a machine gun in his hands and belts of ammunition slung over his shoulders and across his chest.

Holder kicked open the front door of the first house and charged inside. Nobody was home. Kicking in a few more doors, Holder joked to Koenig and Ossen that he felt like he was in a Word War II movie with John Wayne. Not exactly. The point team was a little surprised to see George Savini (his real name is not used here), one of the wilder, more immature members of the squad, carry a large stereo system from one of the houses they had cleared and load it into an APC.*

Holder had progressed most of the way down the street before turning right onto a side street where two teenage boys lay dead in a drainage ditch. Holder flipped the selector switch on his rifle to full automatic, and hadn't taken but a couple more steps when someone darted across an alleyway between two of the buildings. He shouted at the figure to halt: *"Dung lai!"* In response, the slats on a boarded-up window flew into the street from a house up ahead to the right, and he realized that he was staring into the muzzle of a machine gun on a bipod with a drum magazine. Holder and the enemy gunner opened fire simultaneously. "It was like a six-gun shoot-out in Dodge City," recalls Holder. "I finally hit the gunner in the chest with my M16."

Holder quickly swapped magazines and continued blasting away. "It seemed as though fire was coming from everywhere," he recounts. "I stood in the middle of the street, firing back, and watched enemy soldiers run back and forth from building to building, trying to reposition or get away."

Lieutenant Sharpe was walking along with Buehrig's people when the battle began precisely at noon; the company commander later wrote his brother: "Suddenly, there were no civilians about, nothing but stillness. Seconds later an unknown force of V.C. opened up on us with rockets, [Soviet-made RPD-56 light] machine guns, and [AK-47] rifles. Their aim was accurate as they were only 20 meters from some of our positions. . . ."

Amid the pandemonium, Private First Class Dalton H. McWaters, a new guy in Sergeant Raggs' squad, was heard hollering for a medic. McWaters, an eighteen-year-old from Mulberry, Florida, had enlisted and was eager to fight. Less than a month in the field, he'd already made good on his declaration that he wanted to shoot somebody, and had just returned from a three-day pass for killing a VC. Now, McWaters—"a brave little guy," to

---

*The stolen stereo system rode around in the personnel carrier until A/5-60th returned to Binh Phuoc. "The stereo resided in our barracks then," notes Koenig, "until one day Savini went on a bender and took a machete to it."

quote Buehrig—was sprawled in a small hole next to one of the buildings on the main street, a gunshot wound in his chest and a chunk of his back blown away from the exit of the round. He had been hit by one of the first bursts of enemy fire. There was no way to get to him, nothing to do but shout to the wounded man to hold on while pouring fire back at the Viet Cong.

Lieutenant Sharpe described the return fire in his letter home:

> Despite the fact that we were in [the enemy's] killing zone and had been taken by surprise, the men in most instances fought the firing with an intense volume of their own [fire]. . . . We moved our tracks up and unloaded on Charlie with cal 50 machinegun. . . . Due to the buildings on both sides of the street, we could only bring 2 or 3 APCs up at a time. . . .

Lieutenant Buehrig, in his first major action, was stunned by the explosion of fire. "We were moving down the street," he recalls, "and, God Almighty, just all of a sudden, the enemy was shooting. I wasn't afraid—I was dumbstruck by the chaos. The noise and confusion, it wasn't anything that I expected."

Lieutenant Buehrig bounced from individual to individual, group to group, urging everyone to keep up their fire and keep moving forward, pausing at intervals to fire his own M16, too. Some of Buehrig's troops played turtle behind the tracks, but most were up against walls, returning fire. Others kicked in doors in an attempt to flush the enemy out. The dismounted riflemen pushed forward, ignoring an old man who lay paralyzed with fear under a straw mat and a mortally-wounded boy of three or four crying terribly on the side of the road. All the while, the gunners on the tracks "tried to suppress the enemy fire, indiscriminately raking the houses on either side with the .50s," recounts Buehrig. "We were bringing a lot of firepower to bear, but I never had the impression that we were facing a concentrated volume of fire from any one area." Trying to make sense of it later, Buehrig concludes that they'd been up against little groups that fired only a few bursts from one position before darting into another building. "I think I might have gotten one fleeting glimpse of an enemy soldier during the whole battle."

Private First Class Everidge, age twenty, was a newly married, bright, innocent, straight-arrow country boy from Harmony, North Carolina. He was walking alongside his track, nicknamed "Pussy Galore," when "all of a sudden, we were taking fire and returning fire. I got down behind my '60, then moved off to the side. There was a barrel or something. I got sort of behind that. I was firin', but I kept wonderin' what I was firin' at. I didn't see anybody."

Sergeant Clifford E. Shields was a twenty-year-old married man from Magnolia, Alabama. A lean, laconic construction-worker-turned-draftee-turned-instant-NCO, Shields had the squad in line behind Cedell Raggs. The squad leader, having dismounted from Pussy Galore, had been walking down the right side of the street with his men when the enemy opened up. In short order, something hit the door frame behind which Shields had taken cover, and a fragment of wood or metal sliced the skin above his eye. Shields thought he was badly hurt, but then realized that he only appeared to be bleeding badly because of all the sweat washing the blood down his face. Shields wiped his eyes clear and started blasting with his M16. "You can imagine a company of people with automatic weapons, everybody shooting at the same time," he recalls. "It was at the point you couldn't tell who was shooting at what."

John Holder didn't know he'd gotten so far out front until he glanced rearward between bursts and realized that Koenig, Ossen, and everyone else were nowhere to be seen. Not sure what to do, Holder continued firing until his M16 jammed; then he lunged behind a fence in front of one of the houses. Crouched low, he was trying to clear the jam when a line of machine-gun rounds stitched a path along the side of the house just inches from his head. A chip of something hit him behind the ear, fooling him into imagining he was seriously wounded. There was a lull in the fire. Holder tried to dart back up the side street, but the shooting from friend and foe alike picked up again, and he spun around to take cover.

Private First Class Robert Mark Nauyalis manned the machine gun on Pussy Galore. He hesitated when the rounds began zipping all around; being a brand-new replacement, he was not sure what to do in the absence of any definable targets. Private First Class Larry A. Lamonica, the driver, propped himself up in his hatch, and cut loose with an M60. Realizing that Nauyalis was not firing, Lamonica calmly called to the new guy to start blasting the houses on their right. With that, Mark Nauyalis—a middle-class kid from Baltimore County, Maryland, who had been working in an office during the day and going to college at night when drafted—swung the .50-caliber machine gun about and commenced firing.

While Lamonica and Nauyalis were stitching the buildings to their right, a figure appeared from the side street to their left-front and stepped from behind the corner to level a RPG at the track directly in front of Pussy Galore. The track commander, Sergeant Carvin L. Simmons, was also firing his .50 to the right, but his driver saw the rocket pointed at them an instant before it was fired, and he leaped straight up from his hatch and dashed across the deck, trying to get away. The driver's reflexes saved him from serious injury, as he only caught a piece of shrapnel in the foot when the RPG slammed into the side of the track. The explosion punched a quarter-sized hole in the armor at the center of a whorl of shrapnel gouges, and sprayed the interior of the personnel carrier with molten metal that ignited everything it touched.

Simmons slumped in his hatch, stunned by the blast. Lieutenant Buehrig ran over with one of his riflemen, and together they pulled Simmons to safety, even as the driver limped back up the street as fast as he could go with his injured foot. "He was actually laughing because he knew he was going home," recalls Rick Neuman. "He was out of there. He was happy."

Lieutenant Sharpe had been standing on the right side of the street, just forward of the track hit by the rocket. The blast knocked him to his knees. He felt incredibly weak. There was a burning sensation in his back and his right arm hung limp at his side. When he tried to raise it, pain shot through him. Sharpe's radiomen must have shouted for a medic because one quickly appeared, dashing forward through the enemy fire. The medic informed Sharpe upon removing his shirt that he had an ugly puncture wound just above his right shoulder blade. Later, Sharpe found out that his scapula had been fractured, but at the time, the medic couldn't tell how serious the wound was. Worried about internal bleeding, the medic recommended that the lieutenant should move back to the staging area to be medevacked.

Sharpe was concerned about how badly he might be hurt and wished that he'd been wearing his flak jacket, but he felt that he had no choice but to stay. After the medic secured Sharpe's useless arm in a sling, the lieutenant took his radio handset back up in his good hand and continued to direct the battle as best he could. Making contact with Antila, he requested that the Cobras he could see overhead be put to use, and he instructed Buehrig and Neuman to pop smoke to mark their positions for the gunships. From Sharpe's tone of voice, Antila had no idea that the young company commander had been wounded, and Sharpe never thought to report that fact. "I didn't see the point of it," he would later explain. "What the shit."

Nauyalis shouted that he was running out of ammo. Lamonica disappeared inside the vehicle to get more. Flames were roaring now from the track to their front, and Nauyalis swung his .50 around in case the VC stepped back around the corner with another RPG. It would have been a smart move, except for the fact that it placed the muzzle of the machine gun directly over the driver's hatch. Nauyalis cut loose with nine or ten rounds just as Lamonica reappeared with a can of ammunition. The concussion of the muzzle blast blew Lamonica back down inside the driver's compartment, leaving his eardrums feeling as if they had been pierced with an ice pick.

Head ringing, Lamonica passed the thirty-pound can of ammo to Nauyalis, who reloaded and resumed firing. Lamonica suddenly pointed to their left, and Nauyalis turned to see fifteen to twenty ARVN soldiers, who had gotten a little too close for comfort, running back up a side street and away from the battle. Moments later, as Nauyalis continued firing the .50, a shrill metallic roar erupted in the sky behind him, and he looked up to see a Cobra making a gun run parallel to the roadway, minigun blazing in its chin turret. The expended shell casings streaming from the minigun by the hundreds looked to Nauyalis like a giant cloud of insects. The gunship flashed past so low that he could see the look of tight-mouthed fear on the face of the gunner seated in front of the pilot in the narrow cockpit. "When the Cobra banked away, all this hot brass came rolling down out of the sky," recalls Ronnie Everidge, who had taken cover behind Pussy Galore. "I had never given a thought as to what happened to all the brass when they fired those miniguns. Well, I found out. It was sort of a shock to have that stuff fall out of the sky on you. Several more gunships made passes. They were coming from behind us and shooting up the buildings in front of us as we hunkered down there behind the APC."

Les Koenig and Howard Ossen were flattened behind two ceramic jugs, positioned against a wall to catch rainwater, and were unable to return fire for all the rounds showering them with dust and plaster. Thinking the company would soon push forward, they were stunned to see a track go up in flames, halting everyone else. They huddled in mute terror as the Cobras streaked past so low as to rattle the rooftops with their miniguns whirring, expended brass splattering around them. There was no doubt that one of the gunships would soon walk a burst right through their hiding place. They had to get out but did not—could not—move, for to edge away from their cover was to put themselves into the sights of an AK-47.

***

Lieutenant Neuman was talking on the radio when his medic bolted for Buehrig's platoon. Neuman tried to stop him, but he was distracted with the radio and the medic was out of reach before he could grab him. He had heard someone shouting for help, and had taken off to answer the call. The medic, Specialist Fourth Class Harry G. Koyl, was a twenty-two-year-old conscientious objector who refused to carry a weapon. He had only just been attached to the platoon from the battalion aid station, replacing Neuman's regular medic, who had taken ill. Neuman had given the man explicit instructions: "I know you haven't been in the field before, so you just stay behind me and don't go anywhere unless I *tell* you to go. If someone gets hit, don't go running up there 'cause you're just gonna get shot, too. The guys will bring the wounded back. That's their job. You take care of the wounded when they get back. That's *your* job."

In short order, Koyl came stumbling back wounded, helped along by the rifleman to either side. Lieutenant Neuman angrily relieved Koyl of his aid bag and handed it to his radioman. "Okay, get your ass back up the road to the staging area," Neuman barked at Koyl. "You're no good to us now that you're hurt."

Unbeknownst to Neuman, Harry Koyl—shrugging off orders again, such was his desire to help the casualties—secured some bandages from somewhere and, along with another GI, tried to reach Dalton McWaters. The grievously wounded kid was still stuck in his hole up front with the lead squad, screaming for help that wasn't coming because a rescue attempt at that point would have been tantamount to suicide. Sergeant Shields watched in amazement as Koyl and his equally intrepid buddy kicked down a flimsy fence between two buildings on a side street so to move forward without exposing themselves. McWaters, however, was up against the front of the next building, and as soon as Koyl and the other GI slipped around the corner to reach him, AK-47 fire began ringing out with a renewed fury. Koyl ducked to his knees next to McWaters and pitched forward then, with a bullet in his brain and a bandage clutched in his hand. McWaters stopped screaming, apparently killed by the same burst that nailed Koyl. The other GI scrambled back. "Somebody ought to give that medic a lot of praise," says Shields, who had no idea who the man was, "because he was not scared. He ran to help somebody, and he got it, too. I saw it happen. I was looking right at him."

Lieutenant Sharpe ordered the company's recoilless-rifle track to the front of the column, hoping to silence the enemy with a volley of canister rounds. The gunner, working fast under heavy fire, somehow got the first round jammed in the breach, rendering the weapon useless. The gunner was struggling to remove the round when he was suddenly shot through the neck. Tumbling to the street, he was hauled to cover by the nearest rifleman. "We never got a round off," recalls Sharpe. "I mean, what a screwed-up mess."

Lieutenant Neuman moved forward along his line of tracks, rifle in one hand, radio handset in the other, and his radioman trailing a few steps behind. Passing in front of an alley, they suddenly came under fire from someone hidden behind a fence that stretched across the narrow passageway. Neuman and his radioman instinctively dropped flat—something had landed a stunning blow against the platoon leader's left forearm—and riddled the fence with their M16s. Several dismounted riflemen threw some bursts of their own down the alley. Taking stock, Neuman saw that a round had grazed a little furrow in his skin and muscle, exposing both bones in his forearm. Pumping with adrenaline and feeling no pain, he pulled the bandage from his first-aid pouch and handed it to his radioman, who wrapped the wound for him. Not sure if he could operate his M16 one-handed, Neuman threw the weapon inside his track and pulled his .45-caliber pistol from its holster.

The attack had completely lost momentum by then. The sight of the track melting down on the road gave everyone pause, as did the gunships. "No one wanted to get in front of those sons of bitches," notes Buehrig. "We'd already had enough friendly fire incidents in previous operations."

Lieutenant Sharpe decided to pull back and regroup. Shouting into his radio handset to make himself heard, Sharpe asked Buehrig and Neuman if they had all their men. "Negative," said Buehrig. The bodies of Koyl and McWaters lay out of reach, and three other men—Holder, Koenig, and Ossen—were missing. "I decided to pull back anyway," Sharpe explained in his letter home, "believing that we'd sustain more useless casualties looking for these people."

The word was passed, and the .50 gunners poured it on as Sergeant Raggs' troops leapfrogged back in small groups, covering each other with more fire. Mark Fenton took rocket shrapnel in his ass as he scrambled rearward. Sergeant Shields might have caught a piece of the same RPG; all he knew was that he was at the prone, firing downrange, when it suddenly felt like somebody had kicked him in the back with all his might. "I kept firing," recalls Shields. "There were so many people wounded and so much confusion, you didn't stop for a little thing like that."

The drivers put their personnel carriers in reverse and backed up the street in stops and starts. Larry Lamonica had no sooner made it to the staging area, when he and Mark Nauyalis were ordered to go back in and pick up several dismounted troops; apparently they were pinned down on the wrong side of the burning track. After rolling back into the now-deserted battle area, Lamonica bypassed the burning track and stopped for two GIs who hastily clambered onto the deck next to Nauyalis. One had been clearheaded enough to climb atop the burning track first, detach the .50 from its mount, and throw the machine gun into the flaming hull so the enemy could not put it to use. It was hard to tell if they were under fire at that point. Taking no chances, Nauyalis opened fire with his M16 after expending all the .50 ammo he had on hand. When he dropped into the hull to get more machine-gun ammunition, he saw that a third cut-off soldier had scrambled inside along with several civilians—including a frantic-eyed woman in her thirties or forties. No one else in need of rescue appeared, so Lamonica once again headed up the street to the relative safety of the staging area along the Kinh Doi.

The firefight had lasted about twenty minutes.

Chapter 8

Back at the staging area, Lieutenant Sharpe made radio contact with Antila. "The colonel wanted to bring in artillery and air strikes on the objective after he learned we had had to pull back," Sharpe noted in his post-battle letter, "but I told him I didn't want them until after I got the [three missing men] out."

As the troops reorganized, Sharpe grabbed Buehrig by the front of his shirt with his good hand. The ruddy-faced company commander was at a fever pitch. "We gotta get back in there," he exclaimed. "We gotta get back in there!"

Sharpe spotted five black-pajamed Viet Cong soldiers sprinting down the main street, heading for the rice paddies behind the hamlet. "We opened up on 'em," he recalls. "I would've cheered if they'd gone down, but we didn't hit a damn one. Not a damn one. It was so frustrating."

Sharpe assumed that the entire enemy force was in flight, having never seen the enemy fight it out before, and immediately gave the word to mount up and attack. Wobbly from the heat and his wounds, Sharpe had to be helped aboard his track. There were still numerous VC soldiers in position, however, and the APCs rolled right back into another hornet's nest of fire. Sharpe caught a little fleck of shrapnel in his stomach. Lieutenant Buehrig was knocked off his personnel carrier by the near-miss explosion of an RPG, and landed in some construction material piled along the side of the road. Getting up, he realized a hot fragment had gone through the side of his boot, cutting deeply into the fleshy part of the sole of his foot. He was struck by the complete randomness of the injury. "I didn't have my flak jacket on and that thing could have just as easily gone through my heart or some other vital organ and killed me," Buehrig muses. "I was gimpin' around there because I couldn't put much weight on that foot, but I wasn't seriously wounded. I was very lucky."

Sharpe immediately pulled his people back to the staging area again and requested a medevac for the worst of his wounded. Deciding it was no use to look for the missing troopers, he told Antila to go ahead and bring in the arty and tac air. Banking in low, a forward air controller in a single-propeller OV-1 Birddog marked targets with white-phosphorus rockets. Next,

A-37 Dragonflies—small, relatively slow-moving jets perfect for close air support—flashed north to south over the rooftops. Using the main street as a guide and the burning track—which was in full flame now with ammo streaking skyward from the cargo hatch like Roman candles—as a reference point, the pilots released their bombs into the south end of Xom Cau Mat.

Tucked behind the water jugs, Les Koenig and Howard Ossen looked up as the first jet screamed past, releasing a bomb that seemed to nosedive straight for them. They were dead, they thought. The bomb, however, hurtled past into the houses to their front. The explosion was shattering. Knowing they wouldn't survive the air strike, Koenig and Ossen frantically crawled rearward through the little courtyards in front of the houses, apparently drawing no AK-47 fire from an equally numbed enemy. Finally reaching the staging area, the weary, dehydrated pair chugged down several beers from the ice-filled mermite can inside their track. "It sounds weird to be drinking beer in combat," says Koenig, "but we didn't even feel it."

The third missing man, John Holder, also escaped, deciding that if he could not go back on the side street along which he was pinned, he might as well go forward. The dirt path came to a dead end in a wet rice paddy, across which some boards had been made into a footbridge. Out of choices, Holder decided to go for it and fully expecting to take one in the back, dashed down the street and across the footbridge, the boards breaking under his weight. Holder spotted a line of personnel carriers and held his M16 over his head, anxious not be killed in a case of mistaken identity as he approached Bandido Charlie.

From his helicopter, Lieutenant Colonel Antila coordinated the support fires, for which he was awarded the Silver Star. The iconoclastic Antila thought the medal a farce. "I might have gotten a Bronze Star at best had I been a battalion commander in World War II, but they were medal-happy in Vietnam."

True enough, but Antila's presence during the battle was a distinct positive, however inflated his reward. Greg Hawkins has never forgotten a radio conversation between Antila and a company commander (apparently Sharpe), in which the colonel said, "You get those kids backed up and buttoned up and we'll put arty in there. I don't want any of my kids hurt." "Well, that certainly endeared him to us kids," notes Hawkins. "Lieutenant Colonel Antila had the bubble shot out of the H13 he was using during Mini-Tet," Hawkins adds; afterward, "the artillery lieutenant [Lieutenant Franks] that was with him said [to the personnel at the command post], 'I was ready to shit myself with the wind hitting me in the face when the colonel leaned over and [nonchalantly] yelled in my ear, "Gee, this makes me nervous." ' Nothing bothered the guy."

Artillery plastered the objective after the air strikes, and some of the machine gunners in the staging area fired downrange into the smoke and dust. In return, the enemy fired a rocket that hit the top floor of a house at least a hundred feet short of the tracks. Sergeant Willie H. Holmes, the mortar section leader, promptly fired a 90mm recoilless rifle into the area from which the rocket appeared to have originated. Howard Ossen was firing the .50-cal on a track when "another RPG went off somewhere and I took shrapnel in my hands. I saw some blood on my hands, but I didn't do anything about it at the time. It wasn't bad."

Les Koenig was also wounded somewhere in there. "All I know," he recalls, "is that I looked down and noticed that I had a couple little pieces of shrapnel in my chest. They were just under the skin, barely drawing blood."

Lieutenant Sharpe gave the word to saddle up for a third attack into Xom Cau Mat. Buehrig's platoon sergeant, the quietly professional and highly respected Sergeant First Class Charles Baker—a thirty-six-year-old black man from Louisiana and a veteran of Korea—was walloped in the kneecap as he sat atop his track, waiting to advance, and was shortly removed aboard a medevac. Officially, Baker had been wounded by enemy fire, though it was just as likely that he'd caught a stray piece of shrapnel from a last U.S. artillery shell before the prepatory fires were lifted. "Who knows where it came from," muses Koenig. "Stuff was flying all over."

Company A started forward around two in the afternoon. Lieutenant Buehrig discovered one of his M60 gunners—a new man—was lingering to the rear, apparently intent on letting the third attack proceed without him. Buehrig didn't blame the guy, but he couldn't let something like that pass. "We're movin' out," he barked, pushing the reluctant GI forward. "Get off your ass—you gotta get up there!" The machine gunner wasn't alone in his attitude. Buehrig's own radioman declared that he didn't want to go back down that street. "I need you. It's critical that you stay by me," Buehrig said to the radioman, another good kid momentarily overcome by fear. Buehrig cajoled the radioman back into action with a promise he hoped wouldn't turn out to be a lie: "You do this one more time and you won't have to do it again. We're gonna get it over with right here. This is the last time we're gonna have to do this."

Lieutenant Sharpe—back on his feet thanks to a few cold ones—joined the third attack with his CAR-15 slung over his good shoulder and a Budweiser in hand, trailed by a network cameraman. The tracks crept cautiously down the debris-strewn street, dismounted troops securing the houses to either side. The south half of the hamlet was in ruins. Walls and roofs had been blown away, exposing interior rooms. Other houses had been completely flattened.

Lieutenant Neuman was gratified when he found two dead guerrillas sprawled behind the fence that he and his radioman had riddled with fire during the first assault. Neuman took a pistol—the mark of an enemy officer—from one of the bodies. The lead track, Sergeant Shields' Pussy Galore, rolled past the personnel carrier that had been rocketed and left behind. The hulk sat dead on the road, leaking smoke, with its interior incinerated and the sides slightly bulged from the trapped heat. Checking the houses, Shields' men found several more dead enemy soldiers and a number of civilians (women included) who had been slain in the crossfire. They also found McWaters, dead in his hole, and Koyl, who lay on his side against a bullet-pocked building, dusted with plaster; they paused to drape ponchos over the bodies. Sporadic gunfire accompanied the advance because, playing it safe, some of the guys would "cut loose with a few rounds after kicking in a door," notes Ronnie Everidge, "and see if anybody came out or returned fire or whatever."

Sergeant Shields saw some of his men pitch grenades at second-floor windows, only to have to dive for cover when the frags bounced off the walls or landed on the roofs and came rolling back. One GI lobbed a grenade onto a thatch roof. It dropped down into the front room at the same time the man's team rushed through the front door. "Needless to say," Shields notes dryly, "it didn't take long for them to come back out the door."

Lieutenant Buehrig, bursting into a house with one of his squad leaders, found himself face-to-face with a Vietnamese man. He was a civilian by all appearances, but the squad leader fell upon him, beating him to the ground. The man cowered under the blows, terrified. "I think the sergeant would have killed him," says Buehrig. "He was really angry. I got between them. I just said, 'Let's get out of here,' and we did." Buehrig would never know if the sergeant thought he was beating to death a civilian or a guerrilla in mufti, or if he even cared who the man was in the heat of the moment. "A lot of guys didn't make any distinction between the civilians and the enemy, frankly," notes Buehrig who, in trying to explain the incident, could only say that the sergeant was a good man caught up in a bad situation. "This was the third go through. The guys were all scared, angry, frustrated. The intensity of it all is hard to explain. Things were burning, we didn't know what to expect. The enemy and the civilians looked the same, basically dressed the same. It was hard to make a distinction between them, especially when a moment's hesitation could get you killed."

The lead track reached the factory at the end of the street without drawing a shot, then turned left onto a side street. The first house on the right was partially demolished. Sergeant Shields led the way inside, followed by Private First Class William E. Grothaus. Entering the second room of the house, Shields realized an enemy soldier in black shirt and black shorts was sitting on the floor behind a bed. Shields threw his M16 to his shoulder and was a fraction of a second from squeezing the trigger when it registered that the VC had raised his arms in surrender. The man was blind, his burned eyes open but blank. His AK-47 leaned against the wall, a rag over the muzzle.

At that moment, another VC opened up with an AK-47 from inside the house. Shields was dumbstruck, but he and Grothaus weren't the target. Instead, the hidden guerrilla had fired at the soldiers who had just stepped into the front room of the house behind their squad leader.

One of those men was Ronnie Everidge. Seeing Shields and Grothaus slip into the house and followed, in turn, by the squad radioman and a rifleman, Everidge had been unconcerned as he approached the doorway, being the last of the five dismounted men in the squad. Kicking the damaged door all the way open, he'd noticed in the front room a table lying on its side with a piece of tin from the roof leaning against the front of it. Holding his M60 across his waist with two belts of extra ammo crisscrossed around his torso, Everidge stepped inside and that's when the hidden guerrilla opened fire. Putting his burst through the table and tin, he missed the radioman in the front room, but hit the rifleman and machine gunner Everidge.

Stunned, not even sure what had happened, Everidge found himself back outside, lying on his left side, his machine gun across his chest. *Well, this is not right,* he thought groggily when he saw that the fingers of his left hand were at his elbow, pointing toward his shoulder. Although it barely hurt, his left forearm had been shattered about three inches above the wrist, so that his forearm was actually bent against itself, with a jagged bone sticking out from the wound.

Sergeant Shields grabbed the blind guerrilla by his hair and jerked him to his feet, then stood rooted for a confused moment with Grothaus, unsure how to proceed without getting fired up by the unseen VC. Actually, help was on the way. As Everidge wrestled the strap of his machine gun over his head to get the weapon off his chest, several soldiers rushed past him and on through the open door. Altogether, five men from Sergeant Raggs' squad—Fenton, Koenig, Ossen, Savini, and Specialist Fourth Class Robert

A. Lynn—charged into the front room of the house, weapons ready, not sure what to expect. The rifleman, who had been shot in the gut and was sprawled on the floor, managed to point down the hall to the back of the house. While turning, Howard Ossen caught a flash of movement, realized there was an enemy soldier ducking down in a little hole not fifteen feet away, and frantically opened fire with his M16.

As Ossen hurriedly changed magazines, Mark Fenton cut loose down the hall and Koenig, Lynn, and Savini hauled the wounded rifleman outside. Ossen went to one side of the hallway entrance, Fenton the other. Ossen pulled the pin on a grenade, let the spoon fly, and leaned around the corner to pitch it down the hall; he was so close that he couldn't miss the hole at the end. Ossen and Fenton dropped flat. *What the hell's this little plaster wall going to stop,* Ossen wondered, with flashbacks of basic training reeling in his head. In basic, they threw grenades as far as they could, not just a few feet, and had a concrete barricade for cover. Fenton was thinking the same thing, but they came through unscathed when the grenade exploded. Fenton lobbed a second grenade, just to make sure they had eliminated the diehard VC.

Feeling no pain, Ronnie Everidge pushed his broken forearm back into place with his good hand, then squeezed tight around the wound so his hand would not flop against his elbow again. The body of the guerrilla who had shot him was dragged outside and dumped in the dirt. The man had taken a crippling leg wound earlier in the battle, evidenced by his one trouser leg that was black with dried blood. Unable to join his comrades as they pulled back, he had chosen to go down fighting—another example of why the GIs hate of their foe was tempered with respect for the bravery of individual Viet Cong.

Everidge and the gut-shot rifleman were rushed back to the staging area aboard Pussy Galore. Because Everidge wouldn't let go, the medic wrapped his right hand and left forearm together with gauze as he lay on a stretcher, and then secured a bandage around the whole mess. The medic kept working, cutting away bloody fatigues and breaking out more bandages, and Everidge—confused for he hadn't felt any other wounds—looked to see that he had also been shot just above his navel, as well as through the right thigh. Yet another round had grazed his shin. Hundreds of little splinters of wood and steel from the table and tin, through which the rounds had ripped, were embedded just under the skin around his wounds. Ronnie Everidge called for a canteen. The medic apologetically said he couldn't have any water because of the stomach wound. Hang on, he was told. A medevac was on the way.

As Shields pulled the prisoner outside, Sergeant Nhan, the company interpreter, went berserk when he saw the stumbling stick figure in black, and rushed over, waving a cocked .45 and screaming in Vietnamese. He wanted the prisoner. "The way he was acting, he may have shot me, so I shoved the VC at him," recounts Shields. Nhan knocked the prisoner to his knees and pressed the pistol to his head as he kept screaming. If Nhan was asking questions, the VC apparently provided the right answers "since the interpreter didn't blow his brains out, but instead put his pistol away and stalked off."

Getting the prisoner back to his feet, Shields walked the blind man to the staging area through a gauntlet of GIs who wanted to execute the VC. As the prisoner squatted amid the troops hustling by with ammunition and the medics treating Everidge and the gut-shot rifleman, "somebody'd walk by there and punch him every now and then," recalls Shields. "He got hit two or three times. Hey, we'd lost a lot of people. It's a wonder somebody didn't shoot him. I wouldn't have stopped them. If I'd been in a different frame of mind that day, I'd of done it myself."

Several troops grabbed the prisoner, who was as lifeless as a rag doll, and threw him up on the exhaust grille of one of the tracks. The exhaust wasn't hot enough to sizzle flesh, but it was suffocating. "GIs are mean, I can tell you," admits Shields. Someone finally jerked the prisoner off the track and he ended up on his back in the dirt, dazed and staring at the sky with sightless eyes. Nauyalis recalls that a personnel carrier pulled up to the prisoner, and one of the guys on board motioned that they wanted to run him over. No one got out of the way or otherwise responded, apparently not angry enough to want to commit murder in so brutal a manner. Mercifully, the prisoner finally passed out.

Lieutenant Sharpe had finally gotten his big contact, but he was ambiguous about the results, writing his brother that although the company recovered several AK-47s, an RPD light machine gun, and two RPG launchers, there were "only 8 dead V.C.—a real disappointment as I had hoped for a big kill." For that, two more of his men had been killed, eighteen more seriously wounded. Sharpe was satisfied, however, to have "carried out our mission of driving the V.C. out of the city in our sector. When the fires had smoldered [out] and the bodies [had been] counted, Co. A held the battlefield."

Chapter 9

L ieutenant Sharpe stood over the unconscious prisoner, seething and with his finger on the trigger of his CAR-15. "I was going to kill him. After four months of frustration, it was like I finally had one in my sights, and I was going to take out all that frustration and just assassinate him right there. But I couldn't do it. I remember thinking, if I kill him and he had some useful information, then I would be responsible for killing some of our own boys. I let him go. I just walked away."

Captain Dobbs approached Lieutenant Buehrig. "You're not leaving?" he asked desperately. "You're not leaving, are you?"

"Yes, sir," said Buehrig. "I'm supposed to be dusted off here."

The green captain, who had spent the battle in the staging area, was panic-stricken at the idea of being left in charge after Sharpe, Buehrig, and Neuman were medevacked. Later, there would be talk to the effect that Captain Dobbs actually broke down in tears, huddled inside an APC.

At the medevac's approach, one of the medics went to mark the landing zone. The smoke grenade was defective, however, and it blew up in the medic's hand when he pulled the pin, leaving him splattered with blood and red dye, his thumb dangling by a bit of skin. *Goddamnit,* thought Buehrig. *Of all the ridiculous things!* The medic, stunned, stood staring at his maimed hand until somebody rushed to him. Somebody else popped another smoke grenade, then brought the medevac in with hand signals. Ronnie Everidge and the gut-shot rifleman were loaded aboard on stretchers. The injured medic stepped up into the cargo bay, holding his hastily bandaged hand. Buehrig and Neuman followed him. Sharpe hesitated a moment, then climbed aboard, finally coming to terms with the fact that the war was over for him and he was no longer the commanding officer of Alpha Company.

The medevac was a blur for Everidge. He didn't come back into focus until a medic cut away the bandages, as he lay on a gurney in a hospital triage area, and pulled his right hand away from his shattered left forearm. The wound began to hurt terribly. Morphine must have been administered because the next thing Everidge knew, he was waking up after surgery, with his arm in a plaster cast and wire sutures sticking from his stomach and right leg. His wedding band was taped to one shoulder, and the bullet that had been removed from his stomach was taped to the other. As bad as it was, it could have been worse. As he lay in the post-operation ward of the 3rd Field Hospital, Everidge was informed that the bullet in his stomach had clipped one of the ammo belts slung over his shoulders. Instead of zipping into his spine, the front of the bullet had split and the slug had turned sideways, losing its momentum after hitting the belt and going no deeper than the outer lining of his stomach. Ronnie Everidge was so relieved not to be paralyzed that he made a promise to himself, then and there, to live the best life he could when he got back home to his wife and family.

Gunships had swooped in during Sharpe's final attack on enemy soldiers who were trying to escape by swimming the river that separated Xom Cau Mat from the rice paddies to the south. Antila directed Captain Scarborough to dispatch a dismounted element to intercept the retreating guerrillas, and Lieutenant Garver hurried to the river with two squads of Bandidos. The point team crossed the river (at about three in the afternoon), cut an opening in the fence running along the top of the steep embankment on the other side, and started through, only to come under AK-47 fire from a small muddy hump to the immediate front that was covered with brush and nippa palm.

Two members of the point team were hit. Private First Class John E. Marrs was chest deep in the water behind them, sheltered by the embankment. "This one sergeant jumped up there, and he was going to throw a grenade," recalls Marrs, "but the VC shot him in the chest, where he had a bunch of concussion grenades hanging on his web gear. One of 'em exploded against his chest. The sergeant came crawlin' back, and said, 'There's a bunker over there,' so I started laying down fire in that direction with my M60."

Lieutenant Garver requested gunship support. Meanwhile, hearing shouts that they had casualties across the river, Alan Kisling—the artillery spotter had tagged along with the patrol—impulsively charged forward. "I just snapped. It had been a long day, and I was getting a little tired of this shit," he remembers. Running, slipping, and crawling through the mud, Kisling collected fragmentation grenades along the way from some of the soldiers he passed. He had at least six frags stuffed in the cargo pockets of his trousers by the time he reached the river. He dropped his rifle and web gear, tossed aside his helmet, and dog-paddled across the river as quickly as he could, slipping under a couple times and pushing off the bottom. "I'm five-four, so it doesn't take much water to put me under," jokes Kisling. "My immediate thought was that I am going to fucking drown with all these grenades in my pockets!"

The point team was huddled against the embankment. Looking over the top, Kisling spotted two mud bunkers amid the brush and nippa palm. He heaved grenades at the nearest bunker until he got one inside, then he scrambled forward to lob the rest of his frags into the second bunker. In the heat of the moment, Kisling was unaware of the role played by Sam Marr. "Somebody got close enough to throw a grenade in the hole," recounts Marr, who did not know Kisling; when the frag exploded, "this Viet Cong came up with his back to me, and I vividly remember firing my machine gun up and down his back."

Out of grenades, Kisling dragged one of the wounded soldiers into the river. Overwrought from the heat and adrenaline, he felt as if he were moving in a dream. Fortunately, Specialist Fourth Class James G. Bianco, the platoon medic, came splashing to Kisling's aid while Private First Class Thomas R. Clemmer, one of Garver's best, covered the rescue with his own barrage of grenades. The wounded were quickly evacuated aboard a gunship, at which point Garver got the entire patrol across the river, set up his machine guns to provide cover fire, and then led his men on an assault over the rise and down into the wood line on the other side. The troops fired from the hip as they charged. No one fired back. "We found a dead VC in one bunker," notes Garver. "If there were other enemy soldiers in the bunkers, they escaped into the trees."

Lieutenant Garver's patrol rejoined Company C. Soon thereafter, as dusk approached, Major Miller—who had taken Antila's place in the observation helicopter—saw a throng of civilians moving north along the main street of Xom Cau Mat. Miller directed Scarborough to stop the group and check identification cards to ensure there were no guerrillas attempting to slip away in the guise of civilians. The Bandidos deployed along a barbed-wire fence on the west edge of the hamlet, whereupon Garver's platoon dismounted and cut its way through.

The platoon advanced toward the road in a skirmish line. A satchel charge suddenly exploded, and snipers opened fire from a little cinder-block building. Lieutenant Garver was burned on his left arm, though he didn't know by what. Three of his men were also hit, including Private First Class James F. Harrier, who was knocked off his feet, having taken a through-and-through gunshot wound in his leg from an AK-47.

John Hohman was jumping over the fence when the satchel charge exploded, and rushing for cover, he collided with a Korean reporter who was standing up to take a picture. Hohman cursed the reporter for an idiot and shouted at him to get out of the way as he shoved past. Terrified civilians were screaming. Shots were cracking overhead. In response, Whitey Whitehead, the war lover on his second tour, opened fire with the .50-caliber machine gun on his recoilless rifle track. According to Hohman, Whitey was a sadistic, kill-crazy bastard, assuredly destined for prison if he ever made it back to The World. "I don't know if he did it intentionally, or if he accidentally brought his fire too low," states Hohman, "but he started firing into the crowd on the road. He shot up a Lambretta with a bunch of civilians in the back. I saw the tracers hit the gas tank. The explosion blew the front half of the Lambretta off and killed the guy who was driving."

The firefight was over in moments. The gunship pilots converging on the scene could see the enemy soldiers dashing away from building to building, then lost track of them in the maze of rooftops and alleyways. Dismounted troops began sweeping the road, which was now deserted, the civilians having fled the scene. Hohman spied a baby girl lying on her stomach near the burning Lambretta, her buttocks sliced open. He paused, sickened, then saw that the child was still breathing. He called to his section sergeant, "Hey, this kid's still alive!"

The section sergeant, a lifer E6 who had also fought in Korea, kept walking and shouted back over his shoulder, "Leave her—it's war."

It happened that a gunship had landed in a nearby field to evacuate Garver's casualties, so Hohman scooped up the infant and sprinted to the Huey. The door gunner tried to wave him off, shouting "No civilians!" The wounded GIs were already on board, and the chopper was ready to lift off, but Hohman's blood was up, and he furiously shouted back over the roar of the engine, "She's goin'! You can deal with this when you get back and sort it all out—but she's goin'!" Hohman put the child on the floor of the cargo bay, far enough inside so she wouldn't roll out. Just to make sure the door gunner understood just how serious this pissed-off Bandido was, he locked eyes with him and warned, "I better not see anything fallin' from this chopper when you take off! You won't be hard to find if I do!" The door gunner nodded. The chopper lifted off. Hohman followed it with his eyes until it disappeared from view, then ran to catch up with the rest of his fellow Bandidos.

Lieutenant Colonel Antila placed Captain Dobbs and Company A in the paddies southwest of Xom Cau Mat for the night. Captain Scarborough and most of Company C assumed positions on the southeast side in coordination with the ARVN rangers. Lieutenant Long's platoon, unable to break through on the canal road, remained on the Y Bridge. Long was reinforced by the scout platoon of the 247th Mechanized Infantry, which had rushed to the scene from the division headquarters at Camp Bearcat northeast of Saigon.

Antila's battalion had suffered two killed-in-action (KIA), plus twenty-eight wounded-in-action (WIA) soldiers who required medical evacuation; another twenty men had relatively minor injuries that were treated in the field. In exchange, nineteen AK-47s had been captured, along with an RPD light machine gun and five RPG launchers. The 5-60th Mechanized Infantry had probably killed forty or fifty Viet Cong. That was not the number trumpeted in the division newspaper and various after-action reports. Two hundred and thirteen was the official body count for the first day of the battle for District 8.

The figure was ludicrous. Whoever created it, however, was merely acting in the highest tradition of the game of body-count inflation practiced by virtually all units. For the sake of professional survival, battalion and brigade commanders tended to provide their superiors with the kind of numbers that MACV wanted in order to prove that the war was being won. Those commanders who did not pad their body counts risked a career-damaging efficiency report; a scrupulously honest officer inevitably suffered in comparison with his peers who accepted that a certain level of manipulation was required when reporting enemy casualties. Had those up the chain of command wanted the truth, they would not have accepted numbers so obviously detached from reality.

Body counts were so important that the imaginary pile of communist corpses were divided up between all the units involved. Supporting elements like artillery and tactical air were given an adequate number for their tote boards, but the big numbers went to C/5-60th with thirty-five VC, A/5-60th with eighty VC, and the supporting gunships of the 7th Squadron, 1st Cavalry, with another fifty-eight VC.

To those combat soldiers at the bottom, the whole thing was a bitter joke, an exercise in phony glory. "We got eight of 'em," says Jim Sharpe. "That was it. If my company was credited with a body count of eighty, well, they made up seventy-two of 'em, I can tell you that."

Even if the numbers were fake, the valor displayed during the action had been real enough. It was liberally rewarded, as was the army's policy in Vietnam. Lieutenant Sharpe received the Silver Star for the night attack in the Jaeger area, as well as the Distinguished Service Cross for retaining command, although wounded, until the end of his company's battle in Saigon. Sharpe has never quite accepted that he had rightfully earned such prestigious decorations. "I was as surprised as anybody when I got them," he says. "I've always thought that Antila over-medalled me."

Lieutenant Colonel Antila and Captain Scarborough won the Silver Star, as did Lieutenants Long and Neuman. Lieutenant Buehrig was pinned with the Bronze Star, Lieutenant Garver an Army Commendation Medal. Lieutenant Sweet and his radioman, Gary Rogers, both received the Bronze Star, as well as some garish decoration from the Vietnamese National Police.

Sergeant Raggs was awarded the Silver Star; Sergeants Baker, Gault, Shields, and Simmons the Bronze Star. John Holder was pinned with the Silver Star, while the five men—Fenton, Koenig, Lynn, Ossen, and Savini—involved in the rescuing of Ronnie Everidge, received Bronze Stars. Tom Clemmer was also decorated with the Bronze Star. Most of the awards were presented in a mass ceremony shortly after the battle. Alan Kisling was one of those standing in the ranks, cited for knocking out the enemy bunker along the river south of Xom Cau Mat. "I never thought anything about the incident," he writes, "until some general pinned a Silver Star on me. When I read the citation, it was like they were talking about somebody else."

Captain Dobbs trooped Company A's lines at dusk, not knowing what to say to the begrimed and weary infantrymen except that they should police up their personnel carriers, which were littered with expended brass and links, empty ammunition boxes, and assorted battle junk. The troops gathered behind Sergeant Raggs' track looked at Dobbs with hostile disbelief. It barely registered that this character was their new company commander, and some of them made rebellious comments. Dobbs bristled. To defuse the situation, Raggs—the acting platoon leader—tried to explain that his men were wrung out and grieving the loss of Dalton McWaters. Dobbs had no time for such excuses and threatened to court-martial the sergeant if he did not follow orders. That did it. "The next thing we knew, the new captain was staring down the barrel of Raggs' M16," recounts Les Koenig. Dobbs' face drained. He hesitated, then turned away and disappeared. "It dawned on him real quick," says Mark Fenton, "that Raggs was going to pull the trigger if he kept up with his bullshit."

Along with ammunition, the resupply that was choppered into Captain Scarborough's position before nightfall included mermite cans of hot food, several of which were loaded into the deuce track to be delivered to Lieutenant Long's cut-off platoon on the Y Bridge. Rolling down the canal road, the track stopped in front of the small bridge spanning the Rach Ong Nho, the tributary running south from the Kinh Doi. Water sprayed across the bridge from a broken water main.

Gary Vertrees, up behind the .50, thought they had reached the bridge in question. Making radio contact with Long's platoon, he asked where they were exactly. The answer: "We're sittin' on the bridge."

"You can't be sittin' on the bridge. *We're* sittin' on the bridge."

"We're on the *Y Bridge*. What bridge are you on?"

"I don't know, but there's water shootin' across it out of a pipe."

"Christ Almighty, we couldn't even get close to that bridge when we tried to get back to the company. That area in there is hotter 'n hell."

The GI explained that after crossing the little bridge the deuce track would have to continue another three-hundred meters on the canal road, then make a right turn, a left turn, and another left to get around the field at the south end of the Y Bridge. "You gotta be shittin' me," Vertrees blurted, concerned they might get lost. "I can't even see another bridge from where we're sittin'."

"If you come through," the GI said, "watch the rooftops and the windows. Watch everything. It's hotter 'n hell through there."

Anxious about being out in unknown territory with darkness closing in, Vertrees asked the other guys what they wanted to do. The consensus was, "Let's go for it," so Vertrees got on the vehicle intercom with Jerry Tomlinson in the driver's hatch: "Put the hammer down and haul ass. Don't stop for nothin'."

Tomlinson put it in gear, and off they went. Vertrees raised the .50 so he could instantly fire should a figure appear on a rooftop with an RPG. Lucky for him that he did so, because a loose wire was hanging across the road, and instead of catching Vertrees in the throat, the wire snagged the machine-gun barrel, pushing it straight up as the track kept right on going. The wire got hooked on the pivot, and Vertrees was frantically trying to push it off with his foot when it finally snapped and whipped away. The buildings along the road were shot up and burned out. Some were still on fire. The area was eerily deserted. Unaware of the ambush of the police earlier that afternoon, Vertrees was shocked when they rumbled past the deuce-and-a-half sitting on the side of the street, bodies piled in the back, hanging over the railing and sprawled on the roadway. *Holy shit,* he thought, getting a little freaked. *This is like a scene out of* Combat!

The deuce track finally reached the Y Bridge. There were reporters on the scene, and a camera crew filmed the track as it rolled up the south leg of the bridge. Vertrees wanted to spend the night with Long's platoon rather than risk a return trip, but Captain Scarborough denied the request. So after the mermite cans were unloaded, the deuce track headed back past the same bodies and the same burning buildings, and Vertrees braced once more behind the .50 as he scanned the rooftops. The only Vietnamese people to appear, however, were civilians recovering belongings from their wrecked homes. Several were crossing the street with a chest-of-drawers, which they dropped to scramble out of the way when the track suddenly appeared, coming their way and stopping for nothing. Tomlinson tried to swerve around the chest-of-drawers, but accidentally clipped it with the back end of the track, smashing the furniture to pieces. Reaching the company without further incident, Vertrees was amused to see some of the guy's packing cases of soda or beer out of an abandoned streetfront store. He raised his camera and took a photo.

Part Two
SAIGON COMMANDOS

Chapter 10

Lieutenant Stan Sirmans, U.S. Navy, caught a resupply Huey out of Vinh Binh and, upon reaching the airfield at Tra Vinh, climbed next into a single-engine passenger plane bound for Tan Son Nhut. An advisor stationed deep in the delta with a patrol boat unit, Sirmans was on his way north to attend the 9th Division's orientation course at Camp Bearcat.

During the flight, Sirmans struck up a conversation with another advisor, an army captain who was also on his way to Saigon. The advisor mentioned that he had a friend at MACV Headquarters who lived with several other captains in a rented villa in Cholon. As it happened to be a Saturday, there was going to be a party in the villa that night, and the army advisor asked Sirmans if he wanted to crash there before continuing on for Bearcat. Sirmans' answer: "Hell, yes!"

The captain from headquarters was waiting for his buddy at Tan Son Nhut. It was raining heavily, so the captain kept the tarp up on his jeep and headed straight for his villa instead of taking Sirmans on the customary tour of Saigon. There was a wall around the villa and a lock on the front gate to keep the jeep from being stolen.

Sirmans took a nap in one of the bedrooms. When he awoke in the late afternoon, music was playing and the rest of the group was gathered around a portable bar in the living room. The bar was stocked with whiskey, soda, beer, and—most amazingly to someone posted at the far end of the supply line—cans of pretzels, potato chips, and mixed nuts. Sirmans had several bourbon-and-Cokes. Come dinner time, a call was made and two Vietnamese women from an establishment across the street arrived with a take-out order of shrimp and rice. The food was free. Sirmans got the impression that in exchange for meals, the staff officers took money from the women at other times and purchased items for them at the Post Exchange. Everything was so underpriced on military bases that these entrepreneurs could make a killing reselling the U.S. goods on the black market.

Sirmans realized that the relationship with the people across the street was not merely commercial. The two women who brought the food stayed for the meal, and when it was time to turn in, they paired off with two of the staff officers and disappeared into adjacent bedrooms. More girls could surely have been rustled up for a price, but Sirmans was a married man. Well into his cups anyway, he was more than content with getting a good night's sleep on a real bed in an air-conditioned room. Though thankful to his amiable hosts, Sirmans could only marvel at the difference between what a tour in Vietnam meant to those with combat assignments and those who, by string-pulling or the luck of the draw, ended up as Saigon commandos.

Major John H. Manley arrived in the capital that same Saturday after an eighteen-hour flight that had begun at Travis Air Force Base in California. An electronics and computer expert, Manley was to head a team being formed at 7th Air Force Headquarters at Tan Son Nhut Airbase to develop a quicker combat-reporting system for the air war in Southeast Asia.

Weary from the flight, Manley, with his duffel bag in hand and wearing wrinkled khakis and a blue forage cap, was met by two early arrivals from his team inside the terminal at Tan Son Nhut. He ended up spending most of the day standing in lines, signing forms, and converting his currency to military scrip. Manley was issued a .38 pistol and eight rounds of ammunition, then directed onto the olive-drab army bus with mesh-covered windows that would transport him to a U.S. Air Force Bachelor Officers' Quarters in Cholon.

Pulling out the main gate of Tan Son Nhut, the bus proceeded down Plantation Road, then turned onto a muddy side street in what looked to Manley like a slum neighborhood. There was an army bachelor officers' quarters at the corner. The bus rolled past two blocks of shacks, then stopped in front of the air force bachelor officers' quarter, which was the last building on the street and featured a sign that identified the ugly, flat-roofed, three-story concrete structure as Horne Hall. Major Manley, thoroughly exhausted and soaked in sweat from the tropical heat, trudged inside past the billet's security force: two middle-aged Chinese Nung mercenaries with old carbines who sat in a sandbagged guard post at the front door of Horne Hall.

At dusk, Manley could see flashes from an air strike going in just beyond the city limits. Flares were dropped that night over Saigon.

Manley had no idea that an attack was expected.

The attack began at four in the morning on May 5, 1968, with a mortar barrage directed at the Newport Bridge—a long concrete span on the east side of the city by which Route 316 crossed the Saigon River in the direction of Long Binh. The Vietnamese Marines defending the bridge exchanged fire with an enemy force in the buildings on the east side of the river.

There was a similar flare-up at the Binh Loi Bridge at the northeast corner of Saigon, with a general barrage of mortar rounds and rockets aimed at the city center. Also, a mortar attack ensued on the power plant and water-filtration facility southeast of the city, which had been secured in anticipation of the offensive by a battalion from the Big Red One. Sappers, who meant to blow up the national television station using a Renault taxi stuffed with five-hundred pounds of explosives, mistakenly set off their bomb in front of an adjacent dormitory belonging to Saigon University. The explosion brought down the roof and front wall of the dormitory, crushing numerous students to death as they slept.

The enemy hit Cholon the hardest. Beforehand, guerrillas had penetrated the ring around the city by hiding under building materials in the beds of trucks entering the area, disguising themselves as merchants and government soldiers, or using forged identity cards at the checkpoints. There, in the slums where the Chinese immigrants lived, the guerrillas emerged from the safe houses owned by the communist underground and formed into squads, platoons, and companies at various rally points. Propaganda teams moved with the fighting units, distributing leaflets and calling through loudspeakers to the people to join the forces of the National Liberation Front. There was no popular welcome for the invaders, however, only a mass exodus of frightened and confused people from the neighborhoods occupied by the Viet Cong.

Stan Sirmans awoke through an alcohol fog to the sound of excited chatter outside his bedroom door. Surprised, he realized that it was still dark outside. One of the staff officer's girlfriends suddenly burst in and, whispering frantically in broken English, said that there were VC soldiers in the street outside. Sirmans bolted to the window. He couldn't see anybody but could hear shouting in Vietnamese that sounded as if coming from a megaphone.

"They look for you," the girlfriend explained. "Tell people they get reward to show where Americans are."

There was a quick conference in the living room. Sirmans and the army advisor each had a .45-caliber pistol and a single magazine of ammunition. The staff officers managed to come up with one pistol and an M16.

One of the officers got through by phone to MACV Headquarters and reported the situation to a duty officer who was logging similar calls from other support troops billeted in Cholon. They were told that they would have to sweat it out until friendly troops could perform a rescue. Outnumbered and outgunned, Sirmans' group hoped to remain undetected and decided to open fire only if the Viet Cong actually came over the wall around the villa.

In another part of town, Major Manley—awakened during the night by explosions—went to the roof of Horne Hall at first light with several other air force officers to see what the hell was going on. One of the officers blurted that there were troops dashing down the road in front of the building, and assuming the worst, most of the group retreated inside. Manley figured the troops were probably ARVN and moved to the walled-in edge of the roof for a closer look. He noticed the long curved magazine of the automatic weapon being carried by one of the soldiers below; then he realized that he was looking at a Viet Cong carrying an AK-47 at the same time the guerrilla noticed the face peering down at him. The enemy soldier immediately shouldered his weapon and opened fire. Bullets thumped into the concrete wall in front of Manley. Others buzzed past his head. Dropping flat, he crawled to the door leading back downstairs.

The situation stabilized for Sirmans' group when two MP jeeps pulled up outside the villa almost as soon as the sun came up. When Lieutenant Sirmans explained his circumstances, one of the MPs volunteered to drive him to the Naval Advisory Group Headquarters on the Saigon River; from there, he could catch the regularly scheduled army bus running to Bien Hoa, Long Binh, and Bearcat. The buses were still running despite the battle. *Weird,* thought Sirmans, *but that's Vietnam.*

In the chaos of the first morning of the offensive, Baron Hasso Rudt von Collenberg, who was driving to the West German embassy where he served as first secretary, was stopped at one of the roadblocks the enemy had thrown up in Cholon. The diplomatic plates on the car meant nothing to the Viet Cong soldiers training their AK-47s at von Collenberg. The guerrillas probably thought they had captured a high-ranking military or CIA officer when they pulled the luckless diplomat from the car, blindfolded him, forced him to his knees on the side of the road, and shot him in the back of the head.

With the war's next big story exploding on its doorstep, the press corps in the capital was scrambling at first light to cover the hot spots.

Specialist Fourth Class John S. Olson parked his jeep on the Newport Bridge. The young combat photographer from the *Pacific Stars & Stripes* was renowned for his shot of wounded marines piled on a tank in Hue. Olson and his partner, Specialist Fifth Class Bruce McIlhaney, who was on loan from the information office of the 9th Division, took cover behind a tank as they got their bearings. Many other media types—including a Japanese film crew—were on hand, but the battle for this key bridge seemed all but over. The mixed bag of MPs, ARVN, Vietnamese Marines, and Canh Sats (police officers better known as White Mice for the color of their uniform blouses) on the bridge were firing at random intervals into the housing on the east side of the river. Enemy guns had winked over there during the night, but if the Viet Cong soldiers were still in position, none were firing now. Nothing could be seen moving through the tropical morning mist rising from the river.

Civilians took advantage of the lull to scamper across the bridge from the embattled housing area. One of the MPs began picking up the children among the refugees and carrying them to safety. The children looked terrified when suddenly scooped off their feet by this big black GI. At one point, a U.S. Army supply truck came barreling out of the mist. Pedal to the metal, weaving around civilians and other obstacles, the driver did not notice that the main gun of the tank on the bridge was trained across the road. The driver crashed right into the gun tube, smashing his windshield and bending the frame of his cab. Nobody was hurt, and the truck drove on.

Olson got McIlhaney's attention and pointed: Brigadier General Nguyen Ngoc Loan, chief of the Vietnamese National Police, had just arrived at the Newport Bridge. The diminutive general was armed with his favorite CAR-15 and otherwise dressed for battle, with his flak jacket pulled over a camouflage suit and a net-covered steel helmet that was too big for him sitting low on his head. An entourage of aides and bodyguards trailed behind him. Soon pronouncing himself satisfied with the situation at the bridge, Loan headed next to an adjacent neighborhood along the river where a small group of guerrillas in a two-story schoolhouse was in a stand-off with the Canh Sats. Loan was news and Olson took off after him like a bloodhound, with McIlhaney in tow. There was no telling what the general might do for the benefit of their cameras.

General Loan, of course, had made himself infamous when, during the Tet fighting in Cholon, he unholstered his snub-nosed .38 and, in the presence of photographers and camera crews, casually executed a VC officer wearing shorts and a checkered shirt who had just been captured by Vietnamese Marines. The uproar was immediate. The antiwar movement seized upon the moment-of-death photo—Loan with his pistol to the head of the bound and helpless prisoner—as a symbol of the depravity of the Saigon regime. It certainly was that, though Loan's detractors might have acknowledged that the general only did for the enemy officer what that officer would have done for him had the situation been reversed. Those who believed in the war railed that Loan had simply executed a terrorist who wore no uniform and made war on civilians. None of the hawks seemed to appreciate that Loan—however brave and ruthlessly efficient in rooting out the communist underground in the capital—was also a giggling sadist and political henchman up to his elbows in graft, corruption, and narcotics smuggling, and someone who never lost an opportunity to make a dollar off the Americans.

Most of those moving down the alley that led to the enemy-held schoolhouse leapfrogged from one spot of cover to another. Not Loan. The general strode straight ahead as if invincible. A tall, bareheaded MP kneeling behind cover up ahead shouted that the VC in the schoolhouse had that part of the alley covered from a second-floor balcony. Loan continued forward. To cover the general, the tall MP tossed his Kodak Instamatic camera to a buddy. "Make sure my wife gets this," he intoned; then he stood up and walked down the alley on stiff legs, firing his M16 from the hip.

Two enemy positions were identified to Loan. The general had his entourage take them under fire from a gated courtyard between two shacks, then launched a one-man assault on the schoolhouse, blazing away with his CAR-15 as he rushed headlong down the alley. Loan stopped in midstride when a guerrilla popped up on a nearby rooftop, and he managed to take one step back toward cover when he was suddenly cut down by the unexpected figure with the AK-47.

Christian Simone-Pietri, a French photographer with *Pix,* was pinned down in the alley with Loan. The enemy lobbed a hand grenade which landed next to the photographer's head. He stared at it, knowing he would be killed when it exploded, but knowing, too, that if he rolled away he would be shot by the rooftop sniper. Miraculously, the grenade sputtered out without exploding.

Most of Loan's entourage had turned and run. Two or three loyal aides frantically sprayed the area with covering fire while Specialist Fourth Class Robert L. Scott, the powerfully built, black MP from the bridge, dashed into the alleyway and dragged Loan back to the courtyard. He had no idea at the time that he had just saved the life of a famous general and also unaware, in the rush, that he had been nipped in the leg by shrapnel. Scott emptied several magazines in the direction of the rooftop sniper, then shouldered his M16 and drew a bead on the spot; he squeezed the trigger when the guerrilla popped up with another grenade in hand, and the man recoiled from sight, obviously hit.

General Loan was sprawled on his back, his helmet gone and his flak jacket stripped away by his horror-stricken aides; one shoulder was peppered with shrapnel, and blood was pouring from a gunshot wound in his right thigh. The femoral artery had been severed. Loan grimaced in pain while Olson shot pictures from as close as he could focus his Nikon. Simone-Pietri offered a camera strap for use as a tourniquet.

The enemy fired a rocket-propelled grenade from the schoolhouse. The ferocious orange explosion sent several Canh Sats running in terror. One of their fellows was made of braver stuff and, stepping repeatedly from his cover, kept putting bursts down the alley with an M3 grease gun. The back of the officer's shirt suddenly puffed out from the exit of a bullet, and he turned, his mouth screwed up in pain, to McIlhaney, who was positioned just behind him with his camera. Blood soaked the front of the Canh Sat's shirt. His legs crumpled beneath him and he fell in a heap. Somebody dragged him back into the courtyard, and as they went to work on him, his breathing became labored, bubbles of blood frothed up around the entrance wound, and a crimson stain with orange bits of lung tissue spread across the ground like spilled paint.

Something thumped into the courtyard at that moment. Olson didn't see what it was, but instinctively shouted, "Grenade!" which gave everyone a precious second to dive for cover. When the grenade exploded, Olson caught a piece of shrapnel in his shin, and Simone-Pietri caught one above his eye. McIlhaney felt as if he'd been kicked in the testicles, for the tender area was, in fact, peppered with fragments. He lurched unsteadily for a place to hide, concussed, ears leaking fluid, forearms bleeding, and limping without realizing that there was a chunk of metal lodged in his heel.

The MPs shouted that it was time to get out. Scott handed his rifle to McIlhaney, then hefted little, limp General Loan over his shoulder. Unable to retreat down the fire-swept alley, he instead slid into the canal running behind the row of shanties that faced the alleyway. The canal, chest deep, was really an open sewer, gray and reeking; the back end of each shanty was positioned over the scummy water on stilts. Olson, whose cameras went under, damaging the film, sloshed past Scott and took the point, armed only with a revolver. The general's remaining aides, several MPs, and finally McIlhaney all followed behind Scott; McIlhaney safeguarded the rear with his borrowed M16.

Moving under the back end of the shanties, Scott struggled through the high water with the thick sewer mud at the bottom of the canal sucking at his boots and the general a dead weight on his back. Finally reaching the end of the canal, Olson and Scott shouted at the people in the room above them to open the hole in the floor through which waste and garbage were dumped. The hole opened. Scott stuck his head through to find himself staring down the barrel of the rifle in the hands of a nervous ARVN. The situation was quickly sorted out, and Loan was lifted through the hole. The rest followed one at a time, while McIlhaney scanned the area for enemy pursuers until his turn finally came. Outside in the street, Scott— grimacing with exhaustion, his uniform soaking wet and plastered against him—pushed through a gauntlet of photographers and television cameras to the ambulance that finally rushed Loan out of the battle area.

Loan survived his ordeal, though the surgeries required to save his leg reduced the limb to a stick with a brace, thus ending his days as a commander.

Scott, Olson, and McIlhaney were all decorated for rescuing Loan.

Looking for his own piece of the war that morning, John Cantwell of *Time* magazine was at the wheel of a flat-faced, low-slung jeep known as a "Mini-Moke." Four other reporters rode along. Michael Y. Birch was in the front-passenger seat. Frank Palmos sat behind Cantwell, his left leg hanging over the side of the overcrowded vehicle. Bruce S. Piggott was squeezed in the middle between Palmos and Ronald B. Laramy. Cantwell, Birch, Palmos, and Piggott were Australian and Laramy was an Englishman. None had much field time, and casually turned out in sports shirts and slacks, they looked less like war correspondents than what they really still were: erudite young adventurers exploring the Orient.

Initially finding nothing of interest, the reporters were heartened when two gunships appeared and began rocketing a housing area to their left. Meaning to track down the target, Cantwell turned onto a side street and headed into a crowded slum area west of the Phu Tho racetrack in Cholon. "Moving the other way was a strong current of refugees carrying babies and household goods, anything they could carry on their backs and in push-carts," Palmos would write in a story filed that night. "We were the only people going in the other direction. . . . All the way along the road, people were saying, 'Viet Cong, VC, VC, VC.' "

More experienced hands might have thought better of continuing on after passing the end of the line of refugees. Cantwell decided to keep going, and in doing so, he drove some minutes later into a group of Viet Cong. The guerrillas stood on both sides of the road, one with a submachine gun, the others with AK-47s. Cantwell swerved to the left, hit the brakes, and tried to shift into reverse to get away from the roadblock, at which point the startled guerrillas, apparently under the impression that a group of enemy officers was trying to make a getaway, opened fire, riddling the Mini-Moke. According to Palmos' subsequent story, he jumped from the vehicle and dropped into a sprawl on the road, playing dead. When the shooting stopped, Palmos wrote that he peered up from under his arm and saw someone, who he thought was Cantwell, lying on his back beside the little jeep. Laramy was still in the backseat. He appeared dead, head thrown back, mouth open. Birch and Piggott had also been shot and were sprawled on the road behind the Mini-Moke.

Palmos heard someone barking orders in Vietnamese. The man giving the orders wore boots and tiger-stripes, while the other guerrillas were outfitted in khakis and sandals. He advanced with his arm extended, pistol trained on the shooting victims. The initial blast of fire had probably been the result of a case of mistaken identity. The communists had no reason to harm foreign journalists and had never deliberately targeted them before. What happened next, however, was cold-blooded murder. By Palmos' account, Birch pleaded, *"Bao chi, bao chi"* (the Vietnamese phrase for reporter), but the guerrilla commander either did not believe him or hated all white men, for in response, he snorted his own sarcastic, *"Bao chi,"* and pumped two bullets into Michael Birch. Palmos watched in abject terror as the man with the pistol walked around to the back of the jeep and stood over John Cantwell, who had already absorbed a dozen hits, but was still moving. The guerrilla commander took deliberate aim and squeezed off three shots. "The first one hit below the body, skipped over the body and missed my head by a fraction of an inch," wrote Palmos. "I heard it zing. I could have been dead from the ricochet. One of the next two bullets entered the body lying there. The body tightened up, then relaxed."

Palmos chanced another glance from under his arm and saw the guerrilla commander pushing his pistol back into his belt. The other enemy soldier in sight had lowered the muzzle of his submachine gun. It was now or never. Palmos had his left foot under his body as if in a starting position for sprinting, and he abruptly sprang to his feet and took off back down the side street. "I had about 100 feet to run and I ran a football dash, zigging and zagging," Palmos wrote. "The AK-47 and the [submachine gun] opened up on me, but they were lousy shots. They hit poles and advertising signs in front of me."

Palmos made it around a corner. The firing stopped, but then to his horror he heard the slap-slap-slap of the guerrilla commander's boots, and realized that the man was following in hot pursuit. Palmos ran frantically on and caught up with the tail end of the refugee column. Seeing that many of the men were shirtless in the heat, he ripped his own shirt off and splashed mud on himself to conceal his white skin. "I crouched over because I was a good foot taller than most of those people. I thought at the time that I would still be caught because the VC commander appeared, firing shots over the refugees' heads to get them to stop me. But not one of those refugees helped the Viet Cong."

Palmos shuffled to safety with the refugees.

No more than an hour and a half later, Palmos was telling his story to Wallace Terry, one of the few black reporters of the day, and a young army-officer-turned-journalist named Zalin B. "Zip" Grant. Palmos sat at a desk in the villa rented by *Time* for its staff, sipping whiskey from a paper cup he held with trembling hands while he described the massacre of his mates. There were, he said, no survivors. Terry and Grant exchanged skeptical glances, wondering how Palmos could be so sure given the confusion and terror of the moment. For all they knew, their colleagues—and Terry was particularly close to Cantwell—were really lying wounded in the alley, bleeding to death. Determined to effect a rescue if there was still time, Terry and Grant set off for Cholon.

It took them most of the day to reach the scene. They originally enlisted a Chinese photographer who knew his way around Cholon as their driver, but the man became unnerved at the eerily deserted streets and turned back after dropping them off at a police precinct headquarters. Walking in a crouch for the occasional shot whistling by, the pair approached a clutch of policemen sitting on the sidewalk. The policemen politely offered the reporters a seat and some tea.

Terry and Grant were led into the office of the precinct commander, a lieutenant colonel who was just then sitting down to an elaborate breakfast in flak jacket and full battle gear. Grant cursed the man in both English and Vietnamese for being so blasé while the communists overran his precinct. The colonel responded with cheerful aplomb, and soon Terry and Grant were heading for the ambush site in the colonel's jeep, an armored car leading the way. They didn't make it that time either, though, because the colonel also had second thoughts. "This is too dangerous," he said, calling the expedition to a halt. The colonel handed Grant his pump shotgun. "You can have my gun. Good luck!"

Frustrated, Grant flagged down a little Renault taxi and offered the driver ten dollars for every block he would take them, an amazing amount of money to a Vietnamese taxi driver. The driver made it two blocks before the sound of automatic-weapons fire had him pulling over and waving his passengers out of the cab. "No amount of money is worth this," he explained. Terry and Grant began walking down the street past ARVN rangers who were tucked into doorways. The rangers smiled at the reporters. They weren't budging themselves.

The two reporters finally reached a point where there were no more government troops in sight. Grant shook his head. "This is impossible," he whispered. "The VC are everywhere. It would be suicidal."

Returning to the office, the two reporters regrouped then sat down for a surrealistic restaurant lunch with Terry's wife who had recently arrived in country for what was supposed to have been a quiet holiday visit. Terry said good-bye to his wife, then he and Grant headed into no-man's-land once again to find their friends. This time armed with carbines provided by a U.S. Army ordnance disposal team cleaning up dud rockets in the area, Terry and Grant finally made it all the way to the bullet-riddled Mini-Moke on that deserted side street in Cholon. There was no one to save. Every one of their colleagues was dead. Their bodies were caked with blood and covered with flies. "I [was] too overwhelmed to cry," Terry would later write. Grant waved Terry away from the bodies, worried about booby traps. They walked back up the road to the ordnance team. After driving the reporters back to the scene, a gutsy sergeant checked the Mini-Moke for booby traps, pulling the bodies apart in the process. Terry gently raised John Cantwell by his shoulders to load him into the Mini-Moke. "This is no time for a show of reverence," snapped Grant. "We've got to toss them in there and get out of here as fast as we can!"

The four bodies were quickly laid across the back of the vehicle, a grotesque stack with necks and arms already frozen in unnatural postures of death. Before Terry and Grant could climb aboard and peel out, thirty or forty young men in black pajamas suddenly appeared, trotting down the street. In formation, four abreast, they were apparently guerrilla infiltrators who had not yet been issued their weapons. They glared at the black man and the white man as they passed, their faces masks of pure hatred.

"Let's get the hell out of here," Grant barked, "before we get it, too!"

Later, when Terry walked into the "five o'clock follies" (the daily press briefing), the room burst into applause. "I look[ed] to see who is coming in behind me, but there [was] no one there. The applause [was] for me. And for Zip. And, I will always feel, for our four comrades who died doing their job."

Chapter 11

When the offensive began, Lieutenant General Fred C. Weyand, commander of II Field Force Vietnam—the corps responsible for securing the Cambodian border and protecting the capital—dispatched his two-star deputy, John H. Hay, to the Capital Military District headquarters in Cholon. General Hay was to coordinate the actions of all U.S. units involved in the defense of Saigon, and he immediately deployed the 199th Light Infantry Brigade ("Redcatchers") in a protective arc across the rice paddies just west of Saigon. It was a fortuitous move; the communists had meant to reinforce the attack with several extra battalions. The reinforcements never reached the city limits, however, running instead into the Redcatchers. As a result, the relative handful of Viet Cong already in Cholon were left to their fate. They carried on with diehard determination, even launching an attack on Tan Son Nhut Airbase on the northwest side of Cholon on the second day of the offensive.

Lieutenant Colonel Billy Jack Carter commanded the 377th Security Police Squadron, 7th Air Force, which manned the perimeter defenses at Tan Son Nhut. Carter and most of his men were veterans of the Tet Offensive.

Attacking in regimental strength, the enemy had breached the western perimeter during the first morning of Tet, intent on destroying the aircraft lined up in revetments along the flight line, blowing up the bomb- and fuel-storage bunkers on the north side of the base, and wreaking havoc among the virtually defenseless support personnel billeted on the south side of Tan Son Nhut. None of these things happened because a thin line of heroic security police managed to stop the enemy at the edge of the flight line, pinning the guerrillas down until daylight when the 3-4th Cavalry, 25th Division, arrived to demolish the assault force from behind. The army general who subsequently arrived to take charge of the area paid tribute to Carter by referring to his squadron as the 377th Light Infantry Brigade. The airmen themselves proudly adopted the motto "Proven In Combat."

Three weeks after the ground attack, the enemy rained sixty 122mm rockets on the air base. More barrages followed, resulting in considerable casualties and damage, towers of black smoke rising from blazing fuel tanks.

If the base was not exactly under siege, the tension was definitely mounting, and Carter's troops devoted much energy to strengthening their positions around the twenty-three-mile perimeter of Tan Son Nhut. In addition, higher command reinforced the 377th Security Police Squadron with elements from the 821st Combat Security Police Squadron.

When Mini-Tet finally came the enemy tried to penetrate that part of the perimeter called the Delta Sector, which extended from the main gate at the southern tip of the base to the ARVN airborne headquarters at the southwest corner. Two fences divided by a perimeter road marked the edge of Delta Sector. On the civilian side of the line, a major thoroughfare named Republic Avenue paralleled the perimeter road. The housing in the area included several seedy blocks along a side street known alternately as 100-P Alley, because a girl could be bought there for a mere hundred piaster, or Soul Alley because of all the black servicemen among the deserters living underground in that part of Cholon. A memorial park—rectangular in shape and carpeted with row upon row of simple white military headstones—sat in neglected silence among the bars, brothels, and apartment complexes that had become its neighbors. This was the French cemetery. "There was a legend," recalls former airman Johnny A. Martin, "that when the French pulled out following the First Indochina War, they left an empty grave in the cemetery for the first American who would die in Vietnam."

Technical Sergeant Curtis McNitt of the 377th Security Police Squadron supervised the midnight-to-six shift along Delta Sector. As it happened, McNitt's shift would be the one on duty at the time of the attack. "McNitt was a no-nonsense kind of sergeant," according to Martin. "He was very serious about the fact that our lives and the lives of the support personnel on the base depended on how well we did our jobs."

The forty airmen assigned to McNitt's shift manned three observation towers and nine bunkers, in addition to crewing two gun jeeps. Additional positions along the perimeter were manned by troops from the Vietnamese Air Force, which had its own transport and fighter squadrons at Tan Son Nhut. Three of McNitt's bunkers were concrete pillboxes built by the French. The other six were steel shipping containers known as conexes—gunports cut out of the room-sized boxes with an acetylene torch. "Sergeant McNitt knew how to weld," notes Martin, and "could often be seen wearing a face shield as he welded quarter-inch steel plates to the conexes." Two plates were affixed to each side with enough space between them to accommodate a wall of sandbags. McNitt also welded runway matting at an angle over each gunport—the sergeant "claimed that this made it practically impossible for a bullet to enter the bunker unless fired from just outside," notes Martin—then the entire conex "would be surrounded with two more layers of sandbags," and "a small sandbagged sniper position would be built on the roof with a stairway of sandbags to get up there. We all spent a lot of time both on and off duty filling and stacking sandbags, which helped all of us in Delta Sector to really get to know each other and Sergeant McNitt. It added to the camaraderie and pride we felt for Delta Sector."

Each perimeter bunker was manned by two or three airmen armed with M16s and .38 Smith and Wesson revolvers. Each team also had an M60 and, in many cases, an M79 grenade launcher. In addition, McNitt scrounged up cases of LAWs from the supply depots at Long Binh. "He also got his hands on field telephones and wiring so that we could link all the Delta Sector bunkers for back-up communications even if our battery-powered portable radios went dead," notes Martin. "We knew that the enemy could remain undetected until he was right on top of us because of the houses along the perimeter. As a result, we worked to know exactly who was supposed to be out there at night so we'd recognize anybody suspicious, and we always maintained a keen observation of our surroundings. Some of us would even walk the civilian side of the perimeter by day while off-duty just to see what was there and look for weak spots in our defenses." By the time of the second attack, concludes Martin, "we felt like we were ready for just about anything. Sergeant McNitt had seen to that."

Following the first day of fighting during Mini-Tet, McNitt told his men at their midnight guardmount that the ARVN and VC were locked in heavy combat in the vicinity of the Phu Tho racetrack in Cholon. "Gentlemen," McNitt announced, "this is going to be *our* fight before it is over."

Most of the young airmen donning helmets and flak jackets and moving out to their posts hoped he was right. It was time to put their preparations to the test. During the night, McNitt pulled up in his jeep to each position in Delta Sector to tell his keyed-up troops to keep their eyes open for any movement in the housing along Republic Avenue. Though ammunition was already plentiful at each bunker, McNitt passed out even more. The shift supervisor clearly relished the idea of battle, and his men joked: "You know, if they really are coming, wouldn't it be ironic if the first shot got Sergeant McNitt?"

The enemy fired ten rockets at the air base just before the scheduled guard change at six in the morning on May 6, 1968. The distant launch flashes were spotted by those security policemen posted in observation towers with binoculars and radios, and air raid sirens were wailing even before the rockets began exploding inside the base. The only casualties were several hapless civilians who operated one of the many concession stands at Tan Son Nhut.

The security policemen on the perimeter could hear muffled gunfire as the VC shot up some of the bachelor officers' quarters and bachelor enlisted quarters along Plantation Road, which ran south through Cholon from the main gate of Tan Son Nhut. Five troops were killed, including a young enlisted man passing through on a Honda motorcycle on his way to his duty station. An MP jeep patrol was pinned down upon responding to the attack. The reaction team that arrived to reinforce the situation was headed by Staff Sergeant Jimmy Bedgood of C Company, 52nd Infantry, a security-guard company made up of combat infantry veterans that was attached to the 716th Military Police Battalion. The reaction team provided the cover fire that allowed the jeep patrol to get out of harm's way. In the process, an RPG slammed into the reaction team's jeep, wounding several GIs and killing Bedgood, a twenty-one-year-old wild Georgia boy who was already on his third tour in Vietnam, having previously humped the bush as a grunt with the Big Red One and the 9th Infantry Division.

First Lieutenant Melvin G. Grover was on duty at Central Security Control, the command post for the 377th Security Police Squadron. "When the rockets hit, the radio went crazy and people were talking over one another all over the net," recalls Grover. One of the security policemen manning Bunker 7, an old French pillbox outside the perimeter fence in Delta Sector, repeatedly attempted to transmit a message to Central Security Control. Grover finally requested silence on the net, then "asked the Delta unit to repeat the message. The man on the radio called in over the background noise of his partner's machine gun that they were being attacked by ground forces through the French cemetery."

Technical Sergeant McNitt made radio contact with the airman in Bunker 7, who confirmed—in a voice that was loud and clear and warbling with an overload of adrenaline—that he had personally seen a squad of men, clad in black pajamas and armed with automatic weapons, cross the street in front of his position and disappear into the adjacent houses.

McNitt, who was behind the wheel of his own jeep, sped to the scene— or more precisely, to the parking lot of a postal unit situated along the perimeter fence near Bunker 7. The security policeman positioned atop a nearby water tower had also reported enemy movement and was firing into the housing along Republic Avenue. Sergeant Holcolm, the assistant shift supervisor, joined in with the M60 mounted on McNitt's jeep, while

Pfc. John H. Hohman of the 5-60th Mechanized Infantry, 9th Infantry Division. *Courtesy of John H. Hohman*

Pfc. Mark Nauyalis of the 5-60th Mechanized Infantry during the Battle for District 8, Saigon, May 1968. *Courtesy of Mark Nauyalis*

Sp5 James Fitzpatrick, combat
photographer, during the fighting
in Saigon, May 1968. *Courtesy of
Ken Pollard*

1st Lt. Richard F. Neuman of the 5-60th Mechanized Infantry receives the Silver
Star and Purple Heart for his role in the firefight in the hamlet of Xom Cau Mat
in District 8, Saigon on May 7, 1968. *Courtesy of Richard F. Neuman*

Armored personnel carriers from Company C of the 5-60th Mechanized Infantry (in rice paddies at bottom of photo) fire into Xom Cau Mat on May 7, 1968. *9th Division photo courtesy of Anthony P. DeLuca*

Radioman from the 5-60th Mechanized Infantry during the Xom Cau Mat action of May 7, 1968. *9th Division photo courtesy of Anthony P. DeLuca*

The pagoda which served as the command post of the 3-39th Infantry during the Battle for District 8, Saigon, May 1968. *Courtesy of Jack A. Brunet*

Lt. Col. Anthony P. DeLuca (left, wearing sunglasses) and Maj. Peter D. Booras, commander and operations officer, respectively, of the 3-39th Infantry, 9th Infantry Division. *Courtesy of Anthony P. DeLuca*

Lt. Col. DeLuca (right) congratulates 1st Lt. Hildebrando Madrigal (middle, wearing bush hat), leader of the reconnaissance platoon of the 3-39th Infantry. *Courtesy of Hildebrando Madrigal*

Lt. Col. DeLuca (center, holding map) briefs Maj. Gen. Julian J. Ewell, Commanding General, 9th Infantry Division, during the Battle for District 8, Saigon, May 1968. Maj. Booras looks on from the right. *9th Division photo courtesy of Anthony P. DeLuca*

Machine gunner from Company B of the 2-47th Mechanized Infantry, 9th Infantry Division. District 8, Saigon. May 1968. *Courtesy of Ken Pollard*

Armored personnel carriers of the 2-47th Mechanized Infantry in District 8, Saigon. *Courtesy of Ken Pollard*

A casualty from the 2-47th Mechanized Infantry is helped to a medevac point after the fighting in District 8, Saigon, on May 9, 1968. *Courtesy of Russell E. Vibberts*

Wounded GIs at a medevac point in District 8, Saigon. *9th Division photo courtesy of Anthony P. DeLuca*

Sp4 Bruce R. Isenhoff of the 2-47th
Mechanized Infantry. *Courtesy of
Bruce R. Isenhoff*

1st Lt. Lee B. Alley of the 5-60th Mechanized Infantry being awarded the
Distinguished Service Cross. *Courtesy of Lee B. Alley*

McNitt himself and the third member of the team, Airman First Class Renato P. "Ron" DellaPorta, took cover behind little flatbed tugs (linked together to haul mail bags) and opened fire through the fence line. McNitt had an M16, and DellaPorta had an M16 modified with a grenade launcher under the barrel—known as an XM148. "We could see glimpses of them moving between the houses," recalls DellaPorta. "We could see tracers and smoke rising from their firing positions. It wasn't a heated battle. There would be a couple of bursts, a dead period, a couple more bursts—that sort of thing. They were doing most of the firing. They probably had a better view of us than we had of them."

Johnny Martin and Airman Wood, his partner in Bunker 9, could hear McNitt's team exchanging fire with the enemy down the line to their left. When their next-door neighbor on that side, Bunker 8, opened up with an M60, "we strained our eyes, but could not see what they were shooting at," recalls Martin. "I called them on the field telephone, and the airman who answered said that there were enemy soldiers in and around the houses next to the French cemetery." Civilians were streaming along Republic Avenue by then, moving away from the cemetery. "I remember telling Wood that we needed to watch them real close to make sure no VC were infiltrating with them," continues Martin. "I also got Bunker 8 back on the field phone to make sure they weren't shooting at the civilians fleeing the scene. The airman in Bunker 8 said that he could see the civilians on the road—and that the people he was shooting at were carrying weapons."

Martin and Wood held their fire until three armed guerrillas finally came into view as they moved between two of the houses at the edge of the cemetery. They knelt down to do something, and Martin, having sighted in on the group, squeezed off several quick shots with his M16. "I don't know if I hit any of them, but I did see the dust fly from the side of the house where my shots hit. They went low and disappeared behind an old wooden fence next to the houses. I had walked along that fence before and knew that it was old and flimsy and held together by wire. I continued to fire low along the fence, knowing that it didn't offer any real protection. I fired until the magazine was empty. Bunker 8 was also raking the fence with M60 fire.

"The civilians," Martin notes, "continued to parade by between us and the enemy, oblivious to the gunfire."

Sergeant Frank Bracken was the driver for a jeep-mounted alert team dispatched to reinforce Delta Sector. The going was slow. Given the sprawling size of the installation and the fact that the all-clear siren had sounded after the rocket attack, the general base population was unaware that a ground attack was taking place. For most, it was just the beginning of another day, as trucks and buses transported thousands of support personnel to their duty stations. "The traffic wasn't bumper to bumper," recalls Bracken, "but it was heavy enough to slow us down considerably. Finally, in frustration, I turned on the fender-mounted red light, and the base police got us through the more crowded intersections. We needed to move. We were determined that we weren't going to lose any bunkers like we did during Tet."

Not all the support troops were so detached. Sergeant David E. Koopman, a jet-engine mechanic with the 460th Field Maintenance Squadron, was billeted on the top floor of one of the barracks along the south perimeter. He had just turned in from working the night shift when the rockets began exploding. Everyone scrambled for the door. Koopman gathered his fatigues, boots, helmet, and flak jacket, all of which were neatly arranged atop his locker for a quick grab in case of emergency. Then he dashed down the outside stairwell and into the sandbagged conex that served as the rocket-protection bunker for the men assigned to his barracks. Koopman hastily dressed, waiting for the all-clear siren. He was startled to hear occasional shots and bursts of automatic-weapons fire and, after the all clear was announced by radio and siren, joined those anxious airmen who were gathering at the arms locker between two barracks.

Even as an occasional stray shot thumped into the wooden barracks, the airman with the key to the arms locker tried to explain that he could not release the weapons without the express permission of the base commander. "We're drawin' fire," someone shouted. "Hand 'em out before we all get killed!"

"Make it quick," someone else snarled, "or we'll kick the crap out of you and just take 'em."

That was enough to change the young airman's mind. He unlocked the conex and hurriedly passed out the M16s and a single magazine of ammunition per weapon. The mob broke up as each man darted off to find what cover he could. No officers were present. No one was giving orders, and no one really knew what the hell they were doing.

Sergeant Koopman and Sergeant Jerald E. Fish took shelter behind a cement monument, which was as big as an elephant, and had once belonged to the Vietnamese but was now just inside the boundaries of Tan Son Nhut Airbase. More energized than scared, Koopman wanted a shot at the enemy. Unable to see much from behind the monument, he turned to Fish and pointed at the big slabs of cement that had broken off the structure. The two pushed the slabs together to form a barricade that they quickly realized offered scant protection from any sniper on a roof. Koopman blurted that they had better get out of there before they got shot and darted back behind the monument.

Fish had just gotten up to follow when a single shot rang out, and the next thing he knew, he was on his back behind the barricade, eyes squeezed shut, the piss and vinegar instantly knocked out of him. He realized he had been shot in the right shoulder at the edge of his flak jacket. Hardly able to catch his breath because the bullet had pierced his right lung, Fish weakly called for a medic until he remembered that there were no medics attached to the unit. Realizing his cries might only panic some of the other guys and get them shot, too, he shut up. Koopman crawled to Fish. Another airman produced a bandage, but simply laid the dressing over the almost bloodless hole in Fish's shoulder, apparently unsure how to secure it without causing his buddy more pain. *To hell with it,* Fish thought, too weak to tell the man that the bandage needed to be taped down to seal the sucking chest wound. Fish kept his eyes closed so as to avoid looking at those looking at him and wished the ordeal over. Surprisingly, two medics from the base dispensary suddenly appeared with a stretcher and, braving the continuing sniper fire, dashed to the monument. They rolled Fish on the stretcher. Before they took off with him to the ambulance in which they had arrived, Fish opened his eyes and mumbled to Koopman, "What a dumb thing to do, getting shot like this."

Heavy automatic-weapons fire began splattering the monument and barracks, and Koopman was suddenly terrified with his realization that this was no game, they were going to die. He prepared himself, however, to face the guerrillas he thought would soon be darting toward the perimeter fence. There wasn't much he could do with the single magazine locked and loaded in his M16, but he thought that if they could hold the VC at the fence line long enough, maybe someone who knew what he was doing would arrive to save the day.

Some of the airmen squeezed off shots during lulls in the incoming fire. One emptied at least half his magazine in a single burst, and Koopman, who was holding his fire until he actually saw something, barked at the airman to stop wasting ammo. The panic-stricken kid turned to Koopman with tears in his eyes and blurted, "But they're shooting at me!"

Koopman could have cheered when an A1E Skyraider from the Vietnamese Air Force swooped into view, then dived toward the houses on the other side of Republic Avenue and pulled up sharply after releasing a bomb from each wing. Koopman watched the bombs plummet toward the rooftops, ducking down and covering his head only at the last moment. The ground seemed to rise up and slam him in the face at the impact, dirt and debris raining down moments later. While a Huey gunship made a strafing run down the line of houses, an army jeep pulled up on the sidewalk behind the barracks. The MP manning the jeep's pole-mounted M60 began laying a sheet of fire through the perimeter fence, giving further pause to the Viet Cong.

The alert team slowed by the base traffic finally rendezvoused with Technical Sergeant McNitt in the mailroom parking lot, and Frank Bracken took up a firing position with his buddy Ron DellaPorta. Meaning to conserve ammunition in case of a frontal assault, Bracken squeezed off single shots at the occasional muzzle flash to his front. When the alert team got the word to reinforce another position that was under fire, Bracken traded his XM148 for DellaPorta's jammed one, and got back behind the wheel of his jeep.

The drive to the new position was interrupted by a barrage of mortar shells lobbed almost straight up from behind the houses on the other side of the fence line. Bracken jerked to a stop on the side of the perimeter road, and the members of his alert team scrambled for cover in the roadside ditches. There were already a number of GIs huddled there, their outdated M14 rifles identifying them as the army support troops attached to the 377th Security Police Squadron in the event of a ground attack. When Bracken looked up in the wake of a particularly close, head-rattling explosion, he saw that several of the cooks and clerk typists had been wounded. One held his bloody hands against his lower stomach, which had been sliced open by shrapnel. No further injuries were discovered when the man's flak jacket was unzipped, and Bracken took some comfort in the realization that the protective gear they wore might just work.

The enemy also mortared the parking lot where McNitt, Holcolm, and DellaPorta were positioned. Holcolm was superficially wounded in the face. Soon thereafter, DellaPorta noticed someone moving on the roof of one of the two-story buildings facing the perimeter. The man popped into view just before each incoming round to point something—a flag on a long stick, it seemed—at different points on the base. When the man slashed the flag down, another round would go down the tube set up somewhere behind the houses. DellaPorta thought he had spotted an enemy forward observer and pointed the figure out to McNitt, who got on the horn to request confirmation that there were no ARVN to their front. Confirmation was received several minutes later. McNitt then requested permission to fire on the individual. When permission was granted, DellaPorta kneeled beside the jeep with the barrel of his borrowed XM148 resting on the bumper, stock snug against his shoulder, and the man with the flag squared in his sights. DellaPorta squeezed the trigger once, twice, then the man jerked out of sight, the flag flying from his hand. "And that was it," recalls DellaPorta, who was awarded the Bronze Star for his marksmanship. "No more mortars."

Even as the enemy attack waned, Martin and Wood barely missed getting shot when a single round suddenly snapped through one of the holes in the runway matting welded across their gunport. The round hit the back wall of the conex. "We both just looked at each other in silence for a moment," recalls Martin, "and then cursed McNitt's bulletproof bunker."

Chapter 12

Lieutenant Colonel Carter had organized a heavy-weapons section in the 377th Security Police Squadron after Tet. First Lieutenant Gerald E. Ingalsbe presently led one of the section's recoilless-rifle teams outside the perimeter to support the counterattack being organized by security personnel from the Vietnamese Air Force.

Technical Sergeant McNitt parked his jeep beside a personnel carrier from the heavy-weapons section that had halted along the fence line opposite the French cemetery. There were any number of enemy soldiers ensconced among the white headstones, and the airman behind the machine gun on the track methodically eliminated those he could see. "He was literally chopping away at the gravestones to get to the VC hiding behind them," recalls DellaPorta. "We were all firing into the cemetery, but the gunner was in a better position to see where they were. We were at ground level. He was up on top of an APC."

Colonel Luu Kim Cuong of the Vietnamese Air Force took personal control of the counterattack on the French cemetery. To prepare the way, Cuong—commander of both an air wing and the tactical zone around the airbase—climbed aboard an obsolete M24 Chaffee tank positioned as a pillbox along the perimeter fence. Standing on the back deck, he opened fire with the .50-caliber machine gun mounted atop the little turret. Specialists Fifth Class James Fitzpatrick and C. Ken Pollard, combat photographers with the 221st Signal Company of the 1st Signal Brigade, focused their cameras on this fighting colonel. Cuong was photogenically suited up in crisp camouflage fatigues, black gloves, polished jungle boots, and a mint-condition flak jacket. Goggles were strapped across the front of his net-covered helmet. An aide stood beside him on the back deck, keeping the ammo coming as the colonel blazed away. Skyraiders roared over the tank to drop their bombs, and clouds of smoke mushroomed up from the houses along Republic Avenue.

The order was given to advance into the cemetery. Fitzpatrick and Pollard followed the Vietnamese Air Force troops over a low wall and photographed them as they fanned out among the headstones, carbines at the ready. There was a sudden flurry of AK-47 fire from one of the houses on the other side of the cemetery, and the security personnel scrambled back in relative disorder, seeking cover.

One of their captains ran out front, urging the men forward, and was shot in the chest just short of the first row of headstones. Pollard hunkered down in a cement drainage ditch with several of the security troops, a smashed-up house at their back. Although the wounded captain—who was lying on his side and impassively staring back at the camera as Pollard snapped shots—wasn't far away, no one wanted to be the first to dart into the sniper's sights to reach him.

Pollard saw a bespectacled young guy, clad in an olive-drab undershirt and having neither weapon nor equipment, appear from out of nowhere and crawl to the wounded captain. Lying on his back, the guy rolled the captain onto him so that they were face to face as he began wiggling back with his elbows and feet, staying low under the fire. Several Vietnamese Air Force personnel finally scrambled to help, pulling the captain into the cement drainage ditch. Fitzpatrick and Pollard helped move the man back over the cemetery wall atop a piece of scrap plywood. When the situation calmed down, Pollard asked the guy in the undershirt for his name, rank, hometown, and unit, and recorded in his notebook that the individual who had performed so bravely under fire was an air force mailman.

Sergeant Joe Skalamera of Philadelphia, Pennsylvania, a member of the 1500th Detachment, Air Postal Squadron, had been driving his mail truck along the perimeter road when he saw what was happening and rushed over to do what he could to help. Pollard bumped into Skalamera again after the battle, and the mailman, who should have gotten a medal for his initiative, lightheartedly told him that he had been reprimanded by his commanding officer for jeopardizing himself and his truck in a combat action that was outside his area of responsibility.

Cuong rallied his troops, leading a squad past the headstones and toward the houses from which the automatic-weapons fire had been received. While Cuong urged his men to move faster, an incoming mortar shell exploded nearby. Diving for cover, Pollard looked up to see another mortar shell explode directly in front of Colonel Cuong, almost between his feet, cutting him in half at the waist and sending his torso—minus his head and an arm—cartwheeling past, as if in slow motion.

As the firing continued, Pollard glanced at the perimeter and was startled to see large numbers of airmen crowding the back staircases of the barracks along the fence line. Many still wore the bright white undershirts and boxer shorts they had been sleeping in when the attack began. "They were just leaning against the railing, watching the battle," recalls Pollard. "They could have easily been shot. They were support troops. They didn't know any better."

Airman First Class Charles Beatie of the 377th Security Police Squadron had taken up a position in a ditch near one of the conex bunkers. "We had several snipers in the buildings in front of us. They never did fire at us, but they would show up in a second-story or attic window to fire on the ARVN moving through the cemetery, keeping them pinned down. The ARVN couldn't see where the shots were coming from, but we could." Given the language barrier and the different frequencies on which units were operating, Beatie's group was unable to inform the soldiers across the road about the location of the Viet Cong. "It was very frustrating having to sit there and watch it all," recalls Beatie. "We made call after call to CSC [Central Security Control], asking for permission to fire, but because there were 'friendly forces' between us and the target, permission was denied. We just sat there, unable to do what we had been trained to do because a bunch of guys in a dark room in the middle of the base didn't think we could hit a sniper at twenty yards with an M16."

In anticipation of the offensive, John Olson had constructed a last-stand bunker on the roof of the villa adjacent to the airbase in which military correspondents were billeted. If the VC blasted their way inside, Olson planned to keep the invaders at bay with his stockpile of grenades and M16 magazines and the claymores he had trained on the door to the roof.

It was not the enemy who came calling, however, but Charles R. Eggleston of United Press International. Eggleston rang the bell to the villa from the entry gate. When let inside, he asked as casually as a neighbor who needed sugar, "Do you guys have any grenades I can borrow?"

Olson produced two frags from his stockpile, then Eggleston, already armed with a hot little Swedish K submachine gun, said that he was going to join the battle in the nearby French cemetery. "It's payback time," he intoned, meaning that he intended to bag a few VC in retaliation for the slaughter of the four journalists that had occurred the day before in Cholon.

Eggleston was a "strange, death-charged kid," according to the writer Michael Herr. Eggleston had, in fact, been twice decorated for valor while serving as a U.S. Navy correspondent in Vietnam, and twice wounded while photographing the Tet Offensive for United Press International.

Charlie Eggleston—war lover—thanked Olson for the frags, then started off toward the French cemetery.

Shortly thereafter, Olson decided to join the battle as well. Numerous reporters, in fact, flocked to the firefight in the French cemetery, including Co Rentmeester of *Life* magazine and freelance photographer Art Greenspon. The pair photographed a prisoner being hustled rearward, then ducked into a concrete drainage trench bordering another plot of headstones, from which South Vietnamese soldiers were bobbing up to fire carbines and M16s. There were more friendly troops in sight atop a two-story building at the end of the trench. A small house next to the two-story building was still occupied by the enemy, however, and a burst of AK-47 fire suddenly tore down the concrete trench. One of the rounds shattered both the telephoto lens of Rentmeester's Nikon and his left hand, before exiting to strike Greenspon in the face, lodging under one eye with such a wallop as to blacken both. John Olson, just arriving on the scene, happened upon Rentmeester and Greenspon as they staggered back under fire. Olson helped them to cover, then removed his belt and fashioned a tourniquet for Rentmeester.

Roger Norum of United Press International Radio hooked up with an ARVN unit fighting its way through an enemy-occupied neighborhood east of the French cemetery. "Rows of buildings are burning up," Norum said into his tape recorder (which picked up the sound of chickens cackling in the background) while he crouched behind an ambulance in a roadside ditch. "Another reporter says they spotted some VC across the road in a building." Several ARVN appeared with a bound young man who had been shot in the back. "The VC suspect looks like he isn't any older than four-teen or fifteen years old, but again I'm told that Vietnamese ages are rather deceiving."

The ARVN called on the guerrillas holed up in a building to surrender, "and they're answering with fire," Norum shouted into his microphone. "They're firing back! This is a little bit too much for me!" The reporter finally ducked into a small house with an aluminum roof. "I can hear mortar rounds going off in the background."

Norum asked a government soldier why they didn't flush the diehard enemy out with grenades. The ARVN answered in heavily accented Eng-lish: "I don't know, uh, the Vietnam army don't like blow the house, you know."

Norum watched incredulously as a U.S. Army supply convoy loaded with mortar shells barreled through the ongoing battle, headed northwest on Republic Avenue. "[T]he VC are firing! This is really weird!"

Civilian fire engines appeared to battle blazes caused by the fighting even as the convoy continued past. Norum paused, startled to see an unidentified figure with a rifle step out from behind the building he was in, and was relieved to recognize that the man was an ARVN. "The trucks are still going by us, and the dust is blowing up all around. One would think that they would hold up this convoy until the Viet Cong are secure in this area, or put down completely. But they're zooming past, going by about thirty or forty miles an hour, and I guess they feel they stand a pretty chance—a good chance of getting through. The wind has shifted the other way now, and it's a welcome relief, blowing the dirt in the other direction. The clouds of smoke [are] rising three-, four-hundred feet in about four different spots here. . . ."

Moving out after the convoy passed, Norum spotted Eggleston on the other side of the road, walking nonchalantly toward the French cemetery. "Charlie!" Norum called excitedly, glad to see a friendly face. Dashing across the road to join his buddy, Norum blurted, "Don't you duck, Charlie?" Eggleston shrugged. Norum admonished his colleague for his casual attitude: "There's no point in inviting it!" Then he held out his microphone and asked, "What do you make of all this, Charlie?"

"It's just about good for a laugh."

Norum and Eggleston joined some South Korean soldiers guarding a radio station on Republic Avenue, then watched another hundred-truck U.S. Army supply convoy thunder past. "This is a little bit more action than I bargained for," Norum said calmly into his microphone, as he and Eggleston continued on toward the French cemetery with a group of ARVN. Norum was breathing hard, and there were long pauses on his tape as he gulped for air: "Miserably hot, miserably hot in the flames and fire. . . . Preceding very, very cautiously now. . . ."

Eggleston darted ahead into a small building. "Is it all right, Charlie?" Norum called after him. Eggleston signaled to come on. "Charlie has just given me the okay," Norum narrated into his microphone as he started forward. "We're right in the middle of a burning village area. Flames all around. Smell the burnt, burnt smell of plastic. It looks like we're inside a little blacksmith shop here."

The firing suddenly picked up again. The ARVN began shouting and returning fire. Though Norum's tape of the battle provides no definitive answer, Eggleston probably opened up with his Swedish K. There would be talk to that effect among Eggleston's colleagues after the battle.

The enemy began firing rocket-propelled grenades. "Eight or nine of us in here," Norum said to his tape recorder. "The heat is just dripping, just dripping." There was a pause, then more shouts and gunfire. Norum tried to joke, "Do you have a match? It's Marlboro Country, huh? Do you have a pencil on you, Charlie? I lost mine."

More shots. "It's coming from behind us, isn't it?"

"Yeah," said Eggleston.

"Or somewhere over to the side."

The blacksmith shop had become a shooting gallery. Norum's narration became decidedly unnerved, but someone else on the tape, probably Eggleston, can be heard saying, "Woo!" like the whole thing was more exciting than scary.

A round struck next to Norum, who blurted, "Was that a bullet?"

"Yeah!" Eggleston answered, almost laughing.

"Jeez," Norum said, giggling nervously, "that was." Sounding like he was going to hyperventilate, he exclaimed, "that must not have been more than a foot away!"

Eggleston must have smiled wickedly because Norum, regaining his composure, can be heard barking on the tape, "It's not funny!" Norum began speaking calmly into his microphone again: "For some reason, I want to stay at this corner and not move anywhere."

There is a pause in the tape, then the sound of a shot and the thump of a falling body. "Oh, no!" Norum blurted, horrified. "No! Charlie's been shot." Norum's voice fell to a near whisper: "Charlie's been killed."

Norum tried to go on, breathing hard, his sentences breaking apart: "Oh my God, blood is streaming out of his nose and mouth. He's got it right in the head. Ah, Jesus—I saw him stand out in this alleyway."

More a soldier again at that moment than a civilian photographer, Charles Eggleston was armed and probably participating in the firefight when shot in the head by an enemy sniper. He was twenty-two years old when killed in the 100-P Alley neighborhood outside Tan Son Nhut Airbase. Colleagues were surprised and touched to later learn that their buddy, the war lover, had willed everything he owned to a Vietnamese orphanage.

At about noon, a battalion of ARVN paratroopers landed at Tan Son Nhut from Bien Hoa Airbase. The reinforcements immediately joined the battle for the French cemetery.

At some point in the chaos, Jim Fitzpatrick and Ken Pollard wound up with two government soldiers in an alley that ran between a row of two-story buildings and the outer wall of the French cemetery. The combat photographers drew fire whenever they tried to look over the wall. Not sure what else to do, Pollard slung his cameras, unholstered his .45, and slipped through a back door into one of the two-story buildings. As his eyes adjusted to the dark, he could see an interior door leading to a hallway. He started forward, then doubled back, for his sixth sense was screaming that there were enemy soldiers inside the house. Stepping back into the alley, Pollard crouched to the left of the back door and, getting Fitzpatrick's attention, indicated the presence of Viet Cong.

With that, the pair began a prudent retreat down the alley. Moments later, one of the government soldiers peered through the window of the house. He began excitedly shouting to the other ARVN. "As they moved to the open door, a burst of AK-47 fire ripped into them," recounts Pollard. "One fell backwards, dead, and the other turned and ran past me with his arm bleeding."

Pollard snapped a quick, blurry photograph of the wounded ARVN, then continued down to the end of the alley, only to realize when he stopped that he'd gotten separated from Fitzpatrick. Fitzpatrick had made a left at the dead end onto a driveway that led to one of the gated cemetery entrances. In the confusion, Pollard had made a right into another alleyway that cut through the row of two-story buildings to the main street that the buildings faced.

Ducking inside one of the buildings, Pollard peered from the front door and, seeing no one, started down the street. Catching sight of somebody moving inside a nearby building, he took off like a sprinter across the street and dove into a shallow, muddy depression in the tall grass between that side of the street and a ten-foot high wall. Automatic-weapons fire bit at the dirt around him. "I played dead for awhile, and then crawled backwards," Pollard recalls. "More fire. Played dead again. Crawled backward again. Fire hit all around me again. An M79 round missed my head by inches and exploded behind me."

The minutes ticked by as Pollard played possum, then to his relief, he heard voices in English. He moved his head slowly, unsure if he was still in somebody's sights, and saw two Americans (one white, one black) walking blithely down the street in his direction and carrying M16s. Pollard's first instinct was to shout at them to get down, but perplexed by how the pair could have walked from the same area from which he had been drawing fire, he remained motionless in his ditch as they walked past. He could make no sense of their appearance. Had the enemy snipers turned their attention elsewhere as two of the dumbest, luckiest support troops ever to play war happened to come along, or—was it even possible—were they a couple of Soul Alley deserters who had reached some sort of accommodation with the Viet Cong?

A team of gunships strafed the row of buildings, but thankfully, the door gunners took no notice of Pollard. Jim Fitzpatrick, meanwhile, spent thirty or forty minutes bellowing for Pollard from behind the cemetery wall. Finally venturing out into no-man's land, Fitzpatrick saw a lump in the grass strip that turned out to be Pollard's flak jacket. Hearing Fitzpatrick, Pollard turned to see his buddy standing in the open, jumped up, and ran toward him, shouting to get down. The snipers opened fire again. Fitzpatrick dove into the tall grass between the road and the ten-foot wall, then jerked violently. Pollard called to him, asking if he'd been hit. He hadn't. Instead, he had been burned by a downed power line. Pollard brushed the wire with his arm as they crawled for better cover and got a muscle-twitching jolt of his own.

Fitzpatrick and Pollard were tucked behind a telephone pole when a trio of guerrillas burst from a burning building into view and raced down the road in their direction, armed with AK-47s. "I yelled at Jim that our .45s wouldn't do us much good and would just give us away," notes Pollard. "The three VC were like something out of a horror film. They were barefoot and wearing only black shorts, and were covered head to toe in black soot. The only thing you could see were their eyes, and you could see the desperation in them. One enemy strategy was to start a fire and move with the flames toward our forces. This strategy had misfired for these three VC."

The figures disappeared into one of the houses near Fitzpatrick and Pollard, who then crawled on through the moist, muddy grass. They lay there for a moment, trying to figure out when they should make their break back across the road. Fitzpatrick went first; the enemy opened fire again as soon as he sprang to his feet. He felt like he was running in slow motion as he struggled through the tall grass and crossed the open road; the air around him filled with the buzzing sound of passing bullets. Fitzpatrick made it to cover unscathed. Pollard waited until the firing died down, then darted across the road himself.

Finally reaching the cemetery, the two sat among the headstones, trying to catch their breath before walking back to Tan Son Nhut. Back inside the safety of the perimeter, Fitzpatrick and Pollard—numb and wrung out, with their leg muscles shaking as the adrenaline drained from their systems—found themselves standing in line with a number of airmen at the snack bar near the base swimming pool. The airmen were unarmed, like all good support troops, and their uniforms were clean and pressed. They glanced at the two grimy, sweat-soaked apparitions in their midst with curiosity, but seemed nervous about starting a conversation. Fitzpatrick and Pollard placed their order, found a table, and proceeded to devour their hamburgers and milk shakes; their cameras and equipment were strewn across the tabletop and the muffled sound of gunfire drifted in from beyond the wire. The scene was surreal, as if they had almost been killed in some weird dream only to step through a portal that took them from Vietnam to a base back in the United States. "The airmen looked at us with amazement," notes Pollard. "To them, it was just another day at their job."

Riding to the rescue, an armored cavalry squadron, the 3-4th Cav, rolled through the north gate of Tan Son Nhut. Some of the tanks and tracks took up positions between the security police bunkers. The rest headed for an enemy-held village on the west edge of Cholon. The VC had dug in deep among the houses, however, and the initial attack was repulsed, one tank having been destroyed and seven other vehicles damaged by RPGs.

General Hay arranged to have the 1-5th Mechanized Infantry, also from the 25th Division, conduct a night move to Tan Son Nhut. During that same night of May 6–7, howitzer tubes were lowered for pointblank fire as the enemy tried to fight his way into Cholon through the 199th Light Infantry Brigade.

Mostly for reasons of image, MACV wanted the South Vietnamese to fight and win the battle for Saigon on their own. Deploying American combat units within the city limits would only seem to confirm the communist line about a desperate regime unable to protect its people. With the government forces in the area fully committed, however, General Hay was forced to pick up the phone on May 6 when intelligence indicated that even more guerrilla battalions were headed for the capital—this time from the south—and have the 5-60th Mechanized Infantry, 9th Division, dispatch a company into District 8.

The predawn attack on the 5-60th Mech coincided with sniper fire and a rain of rockets at Tan Son Nhut. The enemy attempted to launch another attack from the French cemetery at first light on May 7, but the ARVN paratroopers and rangers who had poured into the area shot the life out of the attack. The government troops then spent the day collecting weapons and documents, counting bodies inside the smashed houses, and policing up dazed Viet Cong.

There were many battles taking place at once. While the paratroopers and rangers mopped up outside the airbase, the 1st of the 5th Mech and the 3-4th Cavalry tried to retake the village west of Cholon. Tear gas was employed, but the enemy refused to be dislodged. The village was finally flattened under a deluge of bombs and napalm, artillery shells and gunships rockets, before being secured on the afternoon of May 8. The enemy tried to push a full regiment into the city from the north on May 9, but ARVN paratroopers turned the enemy back after two days of fighting. The 199th Light Infantry Brigade, meanwhile, did battle with smaller Viet Cong units that pressed on toward Saigon from the west until finally abandoning the effort on May 12.

Major Manley, the air force computer expert, had spent the day of the big attack on the airbase trapped in Horne Hall. The notes Manley made on his pocket calendar could speak for many of the men stranded during the first days of the offensive in the various bachelor officers' quarters and bachelor enlisted quarters along Plantation Road:

> Fighting intense all around BOQ [bachelor officers' quarters]— especially between Horne Hall and TSN [Tan Son Nhut]. Cut off all day, phones dead, BOQ hit by small arms fire + shrapnel, no casualties, close to me 3 times, A1E, F4, Huey + F8 air attacks as close as 1 block away, many blocks burned out, ate C rations, heard TSN hit by 19 mortars/rockets—not too good[.]

Records indicate that a guerrilla presented himself at BOQ 1 on Plantation Road that day to surrender.

Major Manley's notes for May 7 read as follow:

> Trapped in BOQ by action all day. . . . TSN hit by 10 rockets— fighting became intense in block next to BOQ—Air strikes within 300 yards by Hueys and A1Es—release point for bomb directly over our BOQ—started huge fires, evacuated BOQ for several hours (under fire—both VC guns and actual fire)—ARVN killed several VC 4 buildings away. . . .

The situation in the area seemed to have been secured by May 8, for Manley wrote on his calendar "sniping only." The air force officers were able to walk down their muddy side road to Plantation Road where they caught a military bus to Tan Son Nhut. From that day forward, Major Manley commuted to the base during the day, to get his team of computer experts up and running, and returned to Horne Hall at dusk, even as battles still raged in other parts of Cholon and the rockets continued to fall on Tan Son Nhut.

A sampling from Manley's pocket calendar:

[May 11] Rockets into Saigon again—several hit at 0615 in crowds [of civilians]—over 130 casualties [reported on the Armed Forces Radio].

[May 12] 0400—5 rockets near Horne Hall—0415—10+ on TSN—Hit C130s and Helicopter—one in Enlisted Billeting area— 3 seriously wounded USA[,] 3 VNAF killed—bunch wounded.

[May 13] Normal workday—Roommate [sic] of Capt Votipka shot in front of quarters + killed—Votipka moved on base—

[May 14] 0615 B52s bombed outside of Saigon, seemed like a rolling earthquake struck town. . . .

The fighting never reached old colonial Saigon, but the ARVN and Vietnamese National Police were still digging out pockets of diehard guerrillas in Cholon until May 16. The operation was supported by U.S. gunships and Vietnamese Air Force Skyraiders, and many blocks in the vicinity of the Phu Tho racetrack were gutted. "[W]e all lived beyond the edge," English war photographer Tim Page wrote of covering the fighting in Saigon during Mini-Tet. "A fully fledged, no-holds-barred, living-colour war raged no further [sic] than a 200-piaster [taxi] ride away . . . Photographically it was a turkey shoot."

The battle had it all. There were fleeing civilians, burning homes, rice-paddy grunts fighting house-to-house, and a crowd of people—mostly children—staring impassively at a pair of dead liberation fighters laid out on a rain-slick road by Vietnamese Marines. The press corps recorded all the pandemonium and pain with an unblinking eye. One day, the cameras focused on a boy whose eyes were filled with tears and his mouth twisted in grief as he looked into the truck bed in which his blood-splattered, mortally wounded sister lay on a woven mat, the accidental victim of a gunship strike.

On another day, approximately twenty-five correspondents covering the fighting near the Y Bridge gathered around a pickup truck that had stopped at some barbed-wire while evacuating a badly wounded ARVN. "All the photographers leaned in for pictures, [and] there was a television camera above him," wrote Michael Herr, uneasy at the voyeurism involved in the profession of truth-telling. "[The wounded soldier] opened his eyes briefly a few times and looked back at us. The first time, he tried to smile (the Vietnamese did that when they were embarrassed by the nearness of foreigners), then it left him. I'm sure that he didn't even see us the last time he looked, but we all knew what it was that he'd seen just before that."

What that young soldier had seen was his own death being turned into a vignette for the evening news.

After a day spent under fire in the streets, the press corps would gather for dinner and drinks on the roof of the Caravelle Hotel. Entertainment was provided by the air strikes being conducted to support the 9th Division units fighting across the Kinh Doi in southern Saigon. "There were dozens of us up there, like aristocrats viewing Borodino from the heights," wrote Herr. While white-jacketed waiters circulated among the crowd, photographers gathered at the railing, cameras at the ready and miniskirted girlfriends standing by their sides with binoculars. One evening, after the jet fighters had whined off with their bomb racks empty and smoke boiling from the enemy-occupied neighborhood that had been targeted, a pretty French girl exclaimed, "Those bombs, some show. *Pas mal,* not bad. Those Americans are really something. Incredible."

The grunts across the Kinh Doi would have agreed.

Part Three

STREET FIGHTING MEN

Chapter 13

Lieutenant Colonel DeLuca received an alert at nine in the morning on May 7 to be ready to deploy to Saigon with two rifle companies and a jump command group from his battalion headquarters.

At the time, DeLuca was headquartered at Rach Kien, a dot on the map located in the rice paddies fifteen kilometers southwest of the capital. His rifle companies were flung across the map. Two platoons of Captain Robert A. Stuart's Company A were securing an artillery battery at an old French fort located eighteen kilometers southeast of Rach Kien and on the Saigon River. With picturesque concrete battlements, steel turrets hung with sleeping bats, and a rust-coated naval gun from another war, the fort had been built at the turn of the century to protect Saigon from any invaders moving up the Saigon River from the South China Sea.

Captain Thomas R. Genetti and Company B (minus a platoon at base camp, but reinforced with Company A's detached platoon) secured a rice-processing facility in An Nhut Tan, a hamlet eight kilometers southwest of Rach Kien. Like the French Fort, the only way into An Nhut Tan was by water or air, and both Alpha and Bravo Companies were resupplied by helicopter.

Captain James D. Latham and Company C were attached to another battalion and not immediately available for the operation in Saigon.

DeLuca's company commanders had been running something of a nine-to-five war from their patrol camps. Therefore, the moment was not without drama when DeLuca instructed Stuart and Genetti to be ready to launch into Saigon. Little preparation was required. Helicopter assaults were routine. The troops traveled light in any event, wearing only steel pots, web gear, ammunition bandoliers, and three day's worth of C-rations slung over a shoulder in a stretched-out sock. The word to go was shortly received, and the two available platoons from Company A were choppered from the French Fort to the southwestern tip of Saigon. Company B's two available platoons were inserted twenty minutes later. The landings were unopposed, a misleading indicator of what was waiting in Saigon for the 3rd Battalion, 39th Infantry Regiment.

***

A contemporary once described DeLuca as "an absolutely straight shooter, as close to a selfless professional as I've known in the service."

Anthony P. DeLuca, the son of Sicilian immigrants, hailed from Jersey City, New Jersey. His father was a tailor, his mother a homemaker. Educated in a Jesuit high school, DeLuca graduated from West Point in 1953, and served a 1959–1961 tour as a captain with Military Assistance Advisory Group, Vietnam. The war simmered at such a low boil in those early days that officers brought their families with them; as a result, DeLuca's wife and children narrowly missed becoming casualties when trigger-happy ARVN soldiers shot up their quarters in Saigon during an unsuccessful coup against President Ngo Dinh Diem.

DeLuca returned to Vietnam in August 1967 as a brigade executive officer in the Big Red One. The wind blasting through DeLuca's helicopter exacerbated an injury he suffered—the shattering of the pigment in his right eye during a handball match—just before going overseas. Thus, he was evacuated within three months to Camp Zama, Japan. He underwent corrective surgery, but the operation was less than a success and left him with one good eye, a medical profile, and a ticket home. "For an infantry lieutenant colonel with a war going on, that was not good news," notes DeLuca. "I prevailed on the medical people to send me back. They checked the regulations, and noted that they prohibited my return to the war zone because I couldn't fire a rifle or drive a jeep. When I protested that I was a lieutenant colonel and didn't have to do either, they changed my profile to a temporary one and cleared me to return to Vietnam."

Consigned to a desk job because of his profile, DeLuca enlisted the assistance of a former superior, Lieutenant General Bruce Palmer, Deputy Commander, U.S. Army, Vietnam. Palmer, in turn, contacted Major General G. G. O'Connor, a comrade from the academy and World War II presently commanding the 9th Infantry Division—the Old Reliables. DeLuca had also served under O'Connor during a previous assignment; he must have made a good impression because O'Connor agreed to give DeLuca a battalion in his Old Reliables. Tony DeLuca, his blind eye concealed behind sunglasses, took command of the 3rd Battalion, 39th Infantry Regiment, on January 12, 1968.

Less than three weeks later, Tet exploded across the country, and DeLuca and his operations officer, Major Booras, went into battle alongside Captain Genetti and Company B in Ben Tre. DeLuca, Booras, and Genetti had all joined the unit within days of each other; and after their collective baptism of fire, DeLuca would be decorated with the Silver Star, Booras and Genetti the Bronze Star.

Tony DeLuca was a believer, and his battalion's objective—to win the hearts and minds of the people of Rach Kien—was enlightened compared to the search-and-destroy operations conducted by most. In addition to employing many of the civilians as laundresses, hootch maids, and the like, the battalion was heavily involved in civic action, providing medical care, for example, and bringing in engineers to build schools and markets. "I believe the 3rd of the 39th treated the civilians better than any other battalion in the division," says former medic Jack A. Brunet. "We knew 'em. We trusted 'em. We practically lived with 'em."

DeLuca's primary mission was stalking the Viet Cong in the paddy-and-tree-line country around Rach Kien, An Nhut Tan, and the French Fort. DeLuca was ably supported by his executive officer, Major John W. Gheen, and Pete Booras, his operations officer—a tactless, overbearing, but brilliant and fearless bull-in-a-china-shop type who was obviously and emotionally devoted to the troops and the battalion. At the company level, Latham and Stuart were good, thought DeLuca, and Genetti was great. Tom Genetti, the product of a military family, had the attitude, says DeLuca, of a "thoroughbred horse wanting to break from the starting gate."

In turn, former subordinates describe Tony DeLuca as a model battalion commander; they speak of him as being demonstrative and affectionate ("He's an Italian!" jokes Genetti, who shares the same ancestry) as well as a cool head who made the right decisions in combat. "DeLuca had the full support of every swingin' dick in the battalion," recalls former lieutenant George Franklin Humphreys II, who commanded DeLuca's support company at Rach Kien. "He had a very strong, reassuring command style, one that made you want to follow his orders. At the same time, he was very affable and easy to approach with ideas and suggestions. He was also self-effacing, not the least embarrassed to laugh at himself."

H. D. Johnson, first sergeant of Company A, notes that "an important principle of leadership is: know your men and look out for their welfare. DeLuca kept that principle at the top of his priorities. DeLuca seemed to me to speak softly but carry a big stick. He was an outstanding battalion commander."

DeLuca did his best to get out in the mud with his grunts. "Pete Booras and Colonel DeLuca went with us on one overnight mission," remembers Genetti. "It's great for the troops to see that the people in charge are doing the same thing they're asking you to do." Necessity dictated that DeLuca supervise most operations from his command ship. Even then, he did it right. "You hear so much about the helicopters being stacked up and senior officers trying to lead companies," notes Genetti; in contrast, "DeLuca let you know that you were in charge of your company and that he was there to provide you the support you needed to get the job done. He didn't say, 'Do this, do that.' Instead, he would say, 'Hey, Tom, this is how the situation looks to me in the air, but you're the guy on the ground; it's your decision. Tell me what you need. I'm here to help.' "

DeLuca, Gheen, Booras, and Genetti were West Pointers, while the troops were mostly draftees. "I met all replacements and gave them a standard talk," recalls DeLuca. "It was along the lines that I knew they probably didn't want to be there and that they might want to argue the merits of the war, but that there were bad guys out there who would be trying to kill them. I told them that my job was to accomplish our assigned missions and to return as many of them safely home as possible." The troops responded smartly if not enthusiastically. "I think they realized that we were not going to do stupid things that would cost them their lives unnecessarily," explains DeLuca. "We were out on operations almost every day and I was always amazed at how these soldiers could go on and on so professionally. You would have thought they were all regulars."

General O'Connor, his tour completed, was replaced—and this was to have profound effects on DeLuca—by Major General Julian J. Ewell, graduate of the West Point Class of 1939 and a storied hero of World War II.

The son of a career officer, Ewell was a little more than a year out of the academy when he volunteered for the 501st Parachute Infantry Battalion, the army's first tactical airborne unit. Soon to be expanded into a regiment, the battalion formed the nucleus for the 101st Airborne Division. Promotions came fast for talented officers during the war; Ewell—caustic, severe, iconoclastic, and fearless—was only twenty-eight years old when he pinned on his silver oak leaves and took command of a battalion that parachuted into Normandy on D-Day and Holland during Operation Market Garden. Ewell was twice awarded the Silver Star and assumed command of the regiment when his colonel was killed by shell fire during the push toward the Rhine after the fighting in Holland.

Ewell's regiment held like a rock when the panzers advanced on Bastogne during the Battle of the Bulge. According to legend, Ewell personally knocked out two Tiger tanks with a bazooka. Whatever the truth of that, Ewell commanded the 501st Parachute Infantry Regiment brilliantly at Bastogne, winning the Distinguished Service Cross, only to be seriously wounded during the counterattack against the retreating Nazis.

Ewell graduated from Command and General Staff College and the U.S. Army War College after recuperating from his injuries. After being promoted to full colonel, he commanded a regiment in the 2nd Infantry Division during the closing days of the Korean War. Ewell spent the next four years as a regimental commander and assistant commandant of cadets at West Point. Several prestigious Pentagon assignments followed, plus service as an assistant division commander and chief of staff of a corps, during which time Ewell became known for the charm he exhibited in the company of his superiors and the ruthlessness with which he dealt with lesser mortals.

General Ewell took over the Old Reliables in late February 1968. As it happened, Colonel George C. Benson had only just earlier assumed command of the 3rd Brigade, 9th Infantry Division, to which DeLuca's battalion was attached. Like DeLuca, Benson was a street kid of humble origins—he grew up in Philadelphia, his dad a mail carrier—who had made it to West Point. Benson was Class of 1945, and missing the big war, finally won his combat infantryman's badge with the 40th Infantry Division in Korea in 1952. Though an infantryman for most of his career, Benson was actually known in the army for the diplomatic skills he acquired during two tours with the U.S. Embassy in Indonesia. Benson, who stood six-foot-three and had the physique of a grizzly bear, was also popular among his peers as a jovial and jocular Irishman.

DeLuca wrote of Ewell and Benson in his letters to his wife:

February 25, 1968:
The new general looks a little bit cold, and I hear that he has his fair haired boys here or on orders [mostly fellow members of the so-called Airborne Club]. That means he'll be looking for the slightest reason for relieving people [and replacing them with his own], so it will be a tough period. I'll just have to work twice as hard.

February 29, 1968:
Col Benson (Brigade CO) was by today and told of his meeting with the new CG. He said that I was being charitable when I referred to the new CG as "cold." He's evidently coming in with the attitude that everything is wrong, and no one is doing their job; doesn't understand why we're so decentralized or why we have so much freedom of action. We may be heading for another 1st Division situation with its overcontrol from the top. God forbid!

March 15, 1968:
Col Benson visited today. . . . He is a real character—everything you tell him[,] he says "okay, Tone!" Pete Booras was saying that some night I'll call Col Benson and say that we've been overrun and I'm the

lone survivor and they're storming the gate, and Col Benson will say "okay, Tone!!"

March 20, 1968:

This afternoon Col Benson dropped by and said that . . . the general was starting to get some appreciation of what a tough job we have—unlike a unit that is all together and operating on one mission. Gen Ewell was amazed at how we were able to pull our units back together for an operation. He said it took genius in planning. He'd flip if he saw us in action!! I get the [helicopters] in the air, tell the companies how many there are, they get in formation, we join up in the air, and off we go. It may not look good but it works.

Like DeLuca, Benson was a believer in civic action over body counts and a commander who tried not to oversupervise his subordinates. The rapport between the two was such that, playing off their ethnic backgrounds, Benson would refer to himself on the radio as Shamrock 6 and DeLuca as Pizza 6. "Benson was a real gentleman," says DeLuca, "but tough in his own way."

Whatever Benson's battalion commanders thought, and all gave the colonel high marks, Ewell remained singularly unimpressed. Deluca related the resulting tension in a letter, dated April 10, 1968:

I saw Col Benson today and had a chat with him. The general really has the pressure on him and he is worried. It looks as though the general is stacking the book against him so he can [relieve him and] put in one of his fair-haireds. If that happens it will be a crime. We can't ask for a better Brigade Commander. Gen Ewell expects miracles and if intelligence says that VC are out there, we are expected to snap our fingers and make them appear. It doesn't work that way.

Dismissive of Benson, Ewell instead extolled Colonel Henry E. "Hank" Emerson, West Point Class of '47—platoon leader and company commander in the Korean War, battalion commander during a previous tour in Vietnam—as the ideal brigade commander in the Old Reliables. Emerson, a tall, rangy, hard-drinking bachelor, had originally made his name as one of the army's premier warriors during that first 1965–1966 tour while commanding a battalion from the 1st Brigade, 101st Airborne Division in the Central Highlands.

Long a student of guerrilla warfare, Emerson had put into practice with his battalion several innovative tactical ideas that were eventually adopted throughout the theater. Emerson's tactical skills were matched by his personal courage, but it was the man's larger-than-life persona that earned him fame. Emerson was profane and excitable—hyperkinetic really—with a booming voice and a singular ability to fire soldiers with a lust for battle. Emerson packed a six-shooter in a cowboy holster; his call sign was Gunfighter. In his zeal to inspire aggressiveness, he had gone so far as to distribute razor-sharp hatchets to his command during his first tour and rename it the Hatchet Battalion. Taking the cue, Emerson's gung-ho paratroopers began decapitating the guerrillas they killed so to strike terror in the VC. Emerson's abilities were such that he not only retained command during the ensuing investigations and bad press, but also won redeeming headlines some months later when his battalion and that of his friend and rival David H. Hackworth destroyed an enemy regiment at Dak To.

Ewell specifically recruited the Gunfighter to command the 1st Brigade of the 9th Infantry Division. "George Benson was a good, solid infantry officer, but not spectacular, not flamboyant, and the contrast with Hank Emerson really stacked the deck against him in General Ewell's eyes," according to former assistant division commander William A. Knowlton. Emerson was the epitome of a fighting colonel, using his command ship like a low-flying scout ship when not down in the mud with his troops. "Hank was not only aggressive, imaginative, and possessed of a real battlefield touch," says Knowlton, "he also had great luck." Once, when Emerson was shot down, his chopper crashed atop a hidden arms cache. On another occasion, Emerson noticed a clump of bushes that looked like a likely hiding place. "He swooped down and threw a smoke grenade into the bushes," recounts Knowlton. Thinking they had been marked for artillery fire, "out came a group of enemy soldiers in uniform with helmets, web gear, weapons, etc. Hank had located an NVA unit."

For those operating in Emerson's shadow, the war went on. On the morning of April 13, DeLuca received an alert to check out several areas where motion sensors had detected movement during the night. "[W]e dropped troops all over the place," DeLuca noted in a letter home. Contact was not made until late in the afternoon. DeLuca landed with one of his companies before his command ship was forced to depart at dusk, and he spent the night in a rice paddy. "This morning we continued the attack and finally came home tonight. It was a fairly good operation—18 VC killed and others seen being dragged off at a cost to us of 3 minor wounded and 1 serious wounded—also one pilot shot in the arm."

DeLuca's letter concluded:

> [The operation proceeded at] a fast and furious pace and the big-
> wigs stayed out of my hair. Gen [Morgan G.] Roseborough [the
> assistant division commander responsible for supervising the 3d
> Brigade, 9th Infantry Division] called me a couple times just for a
> report[,] though. They seemed surprised when I moved my CP onto
> the ground with the troops for the night, but with three rifle compa-
> nies there, that's where I belonged.
>
> Col Benson was pleased. He showed up at my field CP this morn-
> ing with a button that he made—sort of like an Avis button. It said
> WOPS IS TOPS—and he wore it today and showed it off to every-
> one. He is really great to work for. The generals criticize him because
> he doesn't butt in. He stands right up to them[,] though—he told
> Gen Roseborough that "I can help Tone the best by being at my CP
> and making sure he gets the artillery and air support that he needs."
> And we had it. All night long artillery surrounded us and it sounded
> terrific.

Heavy contact was again made six days later near Rach Kien, resulting
in a body count of twenty-four and an award of the Distinguished Flying
Cross for DeLuca. No praise was forthcoming from General Ewell after these
highly successful operations nor, as it happened, any others that the 3rd of
the 39th Infantry fought under DeLuca. Ewell had found Benson's battalion commanders as wanting as their colonel, and DeLuca soldiered through
his tour with something of a Damocles sword over his head. "I used to laugh
to myself when you used to talk about getting relieved," Captain Genetti
wrote to DeLuca shortly after leaving Vietnam, "as I have never served under
a finer commander."

Ewell refrained from relieving either DeLuca or Benson, aware perhaps
that the former had the favor of General Palmer and the latter was something of a protégé of General Weyand at II Field Force. The division
commander instead showed his displeasure by being curt with Benson to
the point of rudeness and finding only fault when visiting the line battalions in this unfavored brigade. DeLuca had acid in his pen as he vented in
his letters to his wife, relating how the attitude of Ewell and his nakedly
ambitious, medal-hungry clique was that:

> [T]he troops are not to be considered; they're things to be worked
> to death. . . . Col Benson hit it on the head when he said that we have

too many "careerists" and not enough "professional soldiers." . . . I'll
continue commanding the battalion in my way and if that isn't
according to the approved method then they can have the battalion—
but God help the men.

No other division commander emerged from the war with a reputation
as controversial as General Ewell's. To his admirers, Ewell was a tough
taskmaster who got the job done. Under Ewell, the pace of operations in
the division accelerated from methodical to relentlessly aggressive. Ewell
made the enemy pay and then pay again. He might not have patted subordinates on the back, but those who served him well were rewarded with
chestfuls of medals—like Gunfighter Emerson, who collected *two* Distinguished Service Crosses—and the kind of efficiency reports which would
lead to eagles and stars of their own.

To the general's detractors, and they remain legion, Ewell was a bully
with odd mannerisms and a vicious tongue, much given to humiliating staff
officers during the evening briefing at division headquarters. He was also a
ruthless practitioner of military politics who badgered his field commanders into reporting fantastic body counts that made the counterfeit numbers
coming from other divisions look reasonable by comparison. The Ewell of
this description seems almost satanic—a pinch-faced, rail-thin self-promoter
devoid of compassion (even for his own troops) who scorned the concept
of winning hearts and minds, made coldblooded comments about killing
a hundred a day every day, and seemed unconcerned that the night-flying
gunships he sent ranging over the most populated area of the country bagged
not only guerrillas but also many farmers and fisherman who broke curfew
to tend to their fields and boats. Ewell's prosecution of the war was considered so merciless that reporters and junior officers began referring to the
division commander as the "Butcher of the Delta."

As the peace negotiations approached, DeLuca's battalion began uncovering weapons caches as it scoured its area of operations for signs of the
enemy. "They are still expecting an attack on Saigon," DeLuca wrote home,
"and our mission is to intercept the VC before they get there—or at least
as they withdraw."

When the offensive began, DeLuca was alerted that Can Giuoc, ten
kilometers south of Saigon, had been hit by the Viet Cong. In response,
Captain Genetti and Company B were picked up at An Nhut Tan on
May 6, 1968 and inserted outside Can Giuoc. Moving through rice
paddies, under a broiling sun, waist-deep in mud, Bravo Company was

approaching an island of dry land slightly elevated from the surrounding fields when the point element came under fire. Genetti took cover with his radiomen in a cemetery. The troops, strung out in the open, ducked behind the paddy dikes as fire snapped past from camouflaged bunkers dug amid the vegetation at the edge of the little island. DeLuca was soon overhead in his command-and-control Huey.

Genetti worked the island with gunships, then brought in a medevac for his casualties. The troops advanced into the nippa palm only to come under more fire from additional bunkers. Genetti had his Tiger Scouts—enemy defectors now serving the allies as guides and interpreters—call to the VC to surrender. The enemy answered with AK-47 fire. DeLuca inserted Company A to support Bravo Company. Genetti, meanwhile, called in artillery and then air strikes that rained dirt clods upon the troops hunkered down in the paddies. "[T]he enemy was still there and it promised to be a real all night battle," DeLuca wrote home. DeLuca was under orders, however, to return his companies to their patrol bases by dark so they would be available, if needed, to reinforce the fighting in Saigon. "It hurt to leave the area without getting the VC," noted DeLuca. Genetti balked at being extracted. Instead, he insisted on a chance to roll up the enemy's flank with a fire-and-maneuver assault. DeLuca agreed. "It was a beautiful piece of work—just like in the movies," wrote DeLuca. "The infantrymen closed on the bunkers and gobbled them up one at a time. It cost the VC 26 killed and ten weapons captured at a cost to us of five wounded. We're sure that there were more VC casualties and weapons in the bombed out areas that we weren't able to search out. We had to extract in the dark as it was—all in all, it was a good day's work."

Companies A and B went into Saigon the next afternoon.

Chapter 14

In addition to DeLuca's battalion, Colonel Benson also alerted the 6-31st Infantry to dispatch elements to Saigon. These troops were not veterans and had only been in the war zone a month. Five months before that, their battalion had not even existed. A rugged baptism of fire awaited these green troops in the streets of Saigon.

Captain Philip L. Eckman, a thirty-year-old career officer much admired by his men for his maturity, judgment, and expert fieldcraft, had assumed command of Company B, 6th Battalion, 31st Infantry when the battalion was originally activated in a parade-ground ceremony at Fort Lewis, Washington, on November 18, 1967. The battalion was raised expressly to fight in Vietnam.

The battalion commander was a genial lieutenant colonel named Joseph H. Schmalhorst. He was a good organizer and terrific with people—his sense of humor helped—but had never seen combat and was not considered exceptionally tactical. Fortunately, Schmalhorst's company commanders were all veterans of Vietnam and recent graduates of the Infantry Officers Career Course at Fort Benning. "We were full of piss and vinegar," jokes Eckman, an airborne ranger who had been an ARVN advisor in the Mekong Delta. "Schmalhorst was a laidback kind of guy," adds Eckman, "but he had it together. I had the utmost confidence in him. The colonel said, 'Boy, I don't know if I'm blessed or what to have such a qualified bunch of company commanders,' and he gave us a tremendous amount of freedom in training our units. He was very supportive."

In addition to the company commanders, some of the first sergeants, platoon sergeants, and even a few squad leaders had also served combat tours, "and this imbued us with a certain aura of authenticity," notes Eckman. "People listened to us." They needed to. The lieutenants taking over the newly formed platoons in the newly formed companies of this newly formed battalion were brand-new OCS graduates; the enlisted men who filled those platoons were mostly draftees just out of basic training, the standard mix of black, brown, and working-class white with a few token middleclass kids, as well as a liberal representation of problem children and order-following cannonfodder from the ranks of McNamara's 100,000.

The new battalion had something special going for it, however. To bring the unit to full strength, troops who had expected to proceed to various service and support schools after basic training were suddenly assigned as infantrymen, test scores and the promises of recruiting sergeants be damned. Prospective mechanics, engineers, and clerks, even a trooper selected for military intelligence and another for the military academy (West Point) preparatory school, were dragooned into the 6-31st Infantry. These men were mostly in their early twenties and better educated than the average grunt; one company claimed a private with a doctorate and two more with master's degrees while about a third of the remaining riflemen either had bachelor's degrees or were only a year or two from earning one.

Captain Eckman and his fellow company commanders spent the winter shepherding their tenderfoots through advanced infantry training in the cold, rainy forests of Fort Lewis. Even if it seemed absurd to seize a mock Vietnamese village in the snow, the miserable living conditions in the field at least had a bonding effect on the battalion. "The lieutenants and sergeants had a chance to gain the confidence of their troops," recalls Eckman, "and I had a chance to see what my people were made of. For the most part, I had outstanding people." Many of the better-educated troopers were certainly bitter about ending up as riflemen and could get a little rebellious at times. When Schmalhorst pitched a tent in the field—a luxury forbidden the troops—unknown persons burned down the colonel's home away from home with an illumination round from a grenade launcher. For all that, the college boys generally took their training seriously, the better to survive the war in one piece. The result, says Eckman, was that "they gradually turned into extraordinarily capable soldiers."

Because new units in a war zone were famous for accidental casualties, special emphasis was placed on weapons safety. The troops carried their rifles at all times in training, just as they would in Vietnam, "and if I caught you traipsing around with your safety off, you got ten pushups," says Eckman. "I purposefully left my safety off sometimes, and you damn well better catch me and give me ten pushups, too." There were many other lessons to absorb. Eckman crosstrained his troops on their crew-served weapons, preaching that each man had to be able to perform beyond his assigned job in case of casualties. For the same reason, he taught both his lieutenants and his enlisted men how to call in supporting fire. "One day, I decided to turn the company over to one of the lieutenants," recounts Eckman, "because I thought these platoon leaders had not really paid attention when I'd issued the training order for the day, and were expecting me to just lead them out there. That's wrong. You have got to listen to what's going on because you may be the next company commander should I get killed or wounded." In the end, Eckman thought the battalion better prepared than those units that had led the way into the war zone three years earlier. "They'd also trained together, but they hadn't trained specifically for Vietnam."

Captain William J. Owen, another company commander in the new battalion, was second-generation army. His father had been wounded and decorated several times while a lieutenant with the Big Red One during World War II. Recalled to active duty, he had served with the occupation forces in Japan before joining the 2nd Infantry Division in Korea. He was killed in action while commanding a rifle company in the summer of 1951, and posthumously awarded the Distinguished Service Cross. "My father set my course in life," reflects Owen. "As a youngster, the only thing I wanted to be was a soldier."

Owen and his older brother grew up with their widowed mother, who did her best to raise them right on a small army survivor's pension in a poor coal-mining region in eastern Pennsylvania. Following his dream, Bill Owen entered the military academy at age seventeen. He completed parachute and ranger training after graduating with the Class of 1963, then reported to the 1st Brigade, 101st Airborne Division at Fort Campbell, Kentucky. "I was delighted when our brigade was alerted for movement to Vietnam in the spring of 1965," he recalls. Owen served as a platoon leader, company commander, and staff officer during his combat tour then, after being promoted to captain, joined the 10th Special Forces Group in Bad Tölz, Germany. "For the next eighteen months," he notes cryptically, "I carried out special operations in Europe and the Middle East."

In addition to the normal confusion inherent in building a new unit, there was an undertow of bitterness among the men when Captain Owen took over Company C. "Many of the guys had enlisted for specific MOSs [military occupational specialties] and felt that the army had screwed them out of their enlistment guarantees," notes Ralph A. "Al" Olson. "We also lacked for career leadership. The only career NCOs in the company were the first sergeant, mess sergeant, supply sergeant, and platoon sergeants. I don't recall any of these old army types as having impressed us. Our lieutenants were as least as young and green as the troops. They did not by appearance inspire confidence. Largely, we were green kids trying to lead other green kids. We lacked experience, we lacked training, and we lacked leadership."

Enter Captain Owen. "I'll never forget his initial meeting with the company," notes Al Olson. "We were seated in a large room. He walked in and somebody called us to attention in the traditional military fashion. Owen immediately put us at ease." Word was already out that the captain was a West Pointer. His uniform was starched and creased, and he wore the combat infantryman's badge and jump wings over his left pocket. He wore a ranger tab, too, plus insignia from the Special Forces and a Screaming Eagles combat patch from his tour with the 101st Airborne. "Owen wouldn't have had to say a word to get our attention," notes Olson. "He looked like the real thing. He looked like business. We were primed and ready for somebody that knew what the hell they were doing."

Captain Owen explained in no uncertain terms that they were going overseas. "He never said the word 'Vietnam,' " recounts Olson, "but when he was finished everybody knew we were going to experience combat. We knew we were going to train hard. We knew we were going to be the best company in the battalion."

At the end of the briefing, Captain Owen said, "All I ask is that you give me six months. Give me your best for six months, then if you don't want to be with me, I'll get you out of the company." The meeting was over. Owen walked from the room, paused, looked back, and said, "Training starts right now."

"In less than ten minutes, our morale had gone up," notes Olson. "We knew we had a leader. We were all going to give him his six months."

By the time the battalion deployed to the war zone, Captain Owen had become a virtual father figure to many of the GIs in Charlie Company. "He dealt easily and fairly with all of his people," remembers David P. Wilson, then company executive officer and the only career man among the lieutenants. "We all looked up to him and appreciated his knowledge and expertise."

Though a handful of soldiers had tried unsuccessfully to avoid the deployment through a variety of shams, Al Olson's attitude was more typical of the soldiers of Charlie Company. Olson had broken his ankle playing basketball during the two-week leave granted to the troops before the battalion departed the United States; a sympathetic doctor at the base hospital told Olson he could get the young sergeant out of the battalion on a medical hold. "He was offering an opportunity to remain on post with only a chance that I would later be sent overseas," Olson says. "I declined the offer. This wasn't bravado, this was logic. I figured if I was going, I wanted to be with the guys I knew and had trained with. I also wanted to be in Owen's company. The night before shipment, one of the guys helped me cut the cast off my ankle with a bayonet. I was afraid they wouldn't let me go if I was still hobbled with a cast. We stuffed my swollen ankle in a size-larger boot and I limped on the plane that was taking us to Vietnam."

***

Lieutenant Colonel Schmalhorst and the advance party, which included his sergeant major and all the company commanders, departed on March 31, 1968, and landed at Chu Lai in the northern part of South Vietnam in preparation for joining the Americal Division. The decision was made at the eleventh hour to assign the 6-31st Infantry to the 9th Division instead. After trading shoulder patches, Schmalhorst's team flew to Tan Son Nhut to greet the troops, the bulk of whom arrived aboard transport planes on April 5. The GIs, carrying their duffel bags, filed down the gangways in helmets and web gear and were issued their weapons—minus ammunition—from the cargo bays before they left the tarmac.

The battalion was then trucked to Camp Bearcat, the division base camp near from Long Binh, where the new GIs spent a restless week getting acclimatized to the heat and humidity, attending mind-numbing briefings, playing cards, and breaking up arguments between troops whose nerves were on edge as they awaited their baptism of fire. Many also listened to news reports of the violent rage sweeping through black communities back home following the recent assassination of Martin Luther King Jr.

The battalion was introduced to the war in steps. By the second week, the companies were running platoon patrols and squad-sized night ambushes in the vicinity of Bearcat. The area around the base camp was sparsely populated and relatively secure, a good place for a new unit to put its training into practice. Captain Owen adopted a suitably aggressive call sign for his company, Charlie Hunter, but for all the élan and good, solid training, the company seemed jinxed during those early days in the war zone. The battalion's first casualty, in fact, was from Charlie Hunter Company. The man accidentally shot himself in the hand on April 19, following the battalion's first air assault and an inconclusive contact with several Viet Cong armed with AK-47s and a captured M79.

Six days later, Charlie Hunter was traveling in column through dense jungle when the point element discovered fresh tracks along a narrow footpath in the course of a recon-in-force operation about ten klicks south of Camp Bearcat. Captain Owen dispatched Second Lieutenant Kerry May and the 1st Platoon in hot pursuit with a warning to stay off the footpath. The warning was ignored, the troops not yet appreciating the dangers of following a trail. Ten minutes and several hundred meters later, an unseen party of guerrillas detonated a mine in the platoon's face, instantly killing Privates First Class Donald R. Hanna and William Rauber. Eight others were wounded, including Lieutenant May and his platoon sergeant, and, most critically, Staff Sergeant George H. Schroeder, one of the few squad leaders in the company who was a Regular Army NCO.

Captain Owen ordered Second Lieutenant Charles William "Bill" Gale and the 3rd Platoon to maneuver around Kerry May's platoon and assault the Viet Cong. Gale was a scrawny young guy with thick glasses and a near-constant expression of befuddlement—"the most unlikely looking combat leader you've ever seen," to quote Owen—who had been both determined to do well and manifestly unsure of himself during the training period at Fort Lewis. Gale's troops were convinced their gawky lieutenant was going to be a disaster once they got to Vietnam. "Luckily for us, we were wrong," notes Al Olson. "Bill Gale turned out just fine. He had guts. Many would describe him as being crazy-brave. Perhaps he was trying to prove himself. Maybe he was just living up to the training he received at Officer Candidate School. Whatever it was, he was a classic follow-me leader."

The enemy withdrew in the face of Lieutenant Gale's assault, and Charlie Hunter found itself in possession of a base camp that lay at the end of the trail that the point platoon had been following. "During our search of the camp, we discovered that as the VC left, they had opened several small cages containing bamboo vipers," notes Owen. "Several of the bunkers were teeming with these lovely little creatures."

Owen moved his people east as dusk approached, not wanting to remain overnight with poisonous snakes slithering about and in a position that the enemy knew like the back of his hand. The company's casualties were laboriously carried along in poncho litters. It took an hour to find a place where the wounded could be winched up to a hovering medevac through a hole in the jungle canopy. George Schroeder died after being evacuated. The medevac did not take out the bodies of Don Hanna and Bill Rauber, and they were carried on through the jungle until the company stumbled upon an open area where it set up its night defensive positions. "It was a long and restless night," recalls Owen. "The men now had no doubt that this was a deadly affair, especially with two of their own lying in the middle of our perimeter, wrapped in ponchos. We finally got the dead evacuated early the next morning. We had been bloodied. But we had learned some lessons that would carry us through some of the tough times ahead."

Schmalhorst's battalion departed Camp Bearcat on April 27 and convoyed to Smoke, a muddy, miserable little firebase located adjacent to a roadside hamlet seven kilometers below the southwestern tip of Saigon. Attached to Benson's brigade, Schmalhorst joined the spoiling operation being conducted to disrupt the expected offensive against the capital. The pace was exhausting, the results negligible. The guerrillas melted away whenever the helicopters clattered in, leaving only snipers to harass from a distance. Instead of producing body counts, the 6-31st Infantry lost men to accidents and boobytraps.

On May 4, Captain Owen and Charlie Hunter Company were air assaulted into an area immediately south of Saigon. In the process of fording a river, one of Lieutenant Gale's men, Specialist Fourth Class Richard M. Campbell, was swept under and away. The hapless rifleman drowned, weighted down as he was with ammunition bandoliers, grenades, canteens, and other equipment. Gale's platoon spent most of the afternoon trying to locate the body. When Owen alerted Gale that choppers were inbound to pick up the company for insertion into another location where higher command hoped the enemy might be found, he had a difficult time getting the platoon leader to abandon the search of the river banks. "Gale argued with me on the radio, but finally relented. The airmobile insertions continued until we finally returned to Firebase Smoke late that day. The results weren't satisfying. There had been only minimal contact, and we had lost one of our own and hadn't recovered his body. I'm happy to report that the body was later recovered by another unit, but at the time I had a very dejected 3rd Platoon."

The enemy who had so successfully eluded detection mortared Smoke before dawn on May 5 at the onset of the Mini-Tet Offensive. The barrage resulted in eight wounded and the death of Specialist Fourth Class Arnold L. Stewart of Company D, which was responsible for perimeter security at Firebase Smoke. During the night of May 5–6, Company A, under the command of Captain Channing M. Greene, was set up along the Kinh Doi several kilometers beyond the southwestern tip of Saigon. At nearly three in the morning, fire was received from the far side of the canal that wounded one man and killed a young black private named Bobby Ray Childs. The wounded man was hit by a dud M79 round which still had flesh stuck to it when found later. Greene originally thought his company had been shot up by overly excited ARVN manning other positions along the canal, but a patrol dispatched at daylight to investigate the area where the fire had originated found expended brass from an AK-47.

Lieutenant Colonel DeLuca was up in his command ship when the air assault into Saigon began at three in the afternoon on May 7. Captain Stuart's two platoons from Company A, 3rd Battalion, 39th Infantry Regiment, and Captain Genetti's two platoons from Company B were inserted at the southwestern tip of the capital, but had only begun to search the houses there when word came to fall back to the landing zone. The troops were picked up again and reinserted a kilometer and a half south of the 5-60th Mechanized Infantry's firefight in Xom Cau Mat. As the lift ships swung over the hamlet, the troops could see several armored personnel carriers pouring .50-caliber fire into a block of demolished houses. Gunships were firing rockets while jet fighters dropped bombs and napalm; it was a real panorama of battle, and a most unwelcome sight to the grunts looking down from the Hueys.

After getting on the ground, the troops had expected to be directed north into the battle area. Captain Stuart and Alpha Company instead sloshed southwest through the paddies to a specific point along the Rach Xom, a tributary of the Kinh Doi, with orders to search out an enemy command post thought to be in the area. There was a single hootch at the given coordinates. There were also numerous spider holes in the area, and the safety wires from the mortar rounds lobbed that morning into Cholon were found strewn about near a vacated firing position. In addition, medical supplies and seventy mortar rounds were discovered in an underground bunker that had not been camouflaged well enough by the VC. During the search of the area, Specialist Fourth Class Franklin G. Williams, a radioman with the company command group, moved into the underbrush along the stream to investigate some suspicious noises and found himself confronted by a guerrilla armed with an AK-47. The guerrilla pulled the trigger, but the weapon jammed, and Williams cut the VC down in the next instant with his M16.

As dusk approached, Genetti and Stuart, who had been joined by DeLuca and Booras—the battalion reconnaissance platoon provided security for the command group—established night defensive positions in the rice paddies below Xom Cau Mat. Helicopters landed nearby in the meantime, disgorging A/6-31st, B/6-31st, and a platoon from C/6-31st, all of which were placed under the operational control of the 5-60th Mechanized Infantry. After jumping from the slicks, Captain Eckman and Bravo Company moved into position across paddies coated with slimy mud. The grunts, in full combat gear and rucksacks—some even wearing flak jackets, a sign of being new—proceeded step by laborious step, pulling one foot free of the mud at a time. The suction was ferocious. Sergeant Vernon S. Moore, a heavyset fellow, finally bogged down completely, calf deep in the mud and on the verge of passing out with heat exhaustion. Moore was rescued by a helicopter, holding tight to the skid as he was pulled free and set down on a nearby dike where a medic rushed to his assistance.

Reaching a tributary too deep to wade across, Second Lieutenant Nicholas C. Procaccini of the 1st Platoon, B/6-31st, used a sampan to get his people from one side to the other. Procaccini was in the second group, and nearing the opposite bank, he called to Russ Peterson, a soldier in the first group, to grab his CAR-15 and pull the sampan in for a landing. Peterson didn't want to grab a weapon being extended to him muzzle first. Lieutenant Procaccini, a good man and solid platoon leader who, unfortunately, had a snappish temper, shouted at the GI to do as he was told. After some argument, Peterson grabbed the muzzle and the weapon jumped in his hand; against all training and good sense, there had been a round in the chamber, the safety had been off, and Procaccini's finger had been on the trigger. The round unzipped Peterson's forearm before exiting through his elbow, and the trooper dropped to the ground, screaming in agony. Peterson was medevacked, his war over before it had really started, leaving Procaccini sick at what he'd done. It would bother him for the rest of his life. In a black mood, he moved his platoon on to the little cemetery in which the company was to set up for the night, and he tried to ignore the unforgiving glares of some of the troops. After getting the men into position, Procaccini unburdened himself to his sympathetic radioman: "You have to believe it was an accident. I'm really sorry Peterson got hurt!"

That evening, in a prelude to an incident of heart-breaking sickness and waste, Private First Class Michael Monk (the name has been changed), a black soldier with D/6-31st, cleaned his rifle and loaded his ammunition magazines with an intensity that baffled his fellow GIs at Firebase Smoke. His weapon cleaned and oiled, Monk proceeded to sight in on people while boasting, "Now I've got my shit together. I'm ready. I'm a *mean* motherfucker."

Private Monk slipped a flak jacket over his bare chest after nightfall, donned a steel helmet, picked up his rifle, and approached one of the sleeping bunkers near the perimeter berm. Stepping around the sandbagged blast wall protecting the entrance to the bunker, Monk stood unnoticed in the doorway for a moment, then opened fire with his M16. Monk's first shots hit Private First Class Thomas W. Myers, a black infantryman from Company B who happened to be sacking out for the night in Company D's area. Myers was one of many soldiers left behind at Firebase Smoke because there hadn't been enough helicopters available during the afternoon to lift all of Bravo Company to Saigon.

Monk next sprayed the interior of the bunker on automatic, hitting Sergeant Philip L. Culver and Specialist Fourth Class Warren M. Kirsch, two white infantrymen from Company D. Culver was shot in the stomach, Kirsch in the shoulder. The two soldiers at the rear of the bunker, who survived unscathed, assumed that the shadowy figure who disappeared as soon as the firing ended was an enemy sapper who had slipped through the perimeter wire. Meanwhile, two unarmed radar operators sitting atop the bunker jumped to the ground when the shooting started. Emerging from behind the blast wall, Monk fired the last two rounds in his magazine at one of the radar operators at a range of five feet. Missing his target, Monk continued on without breaking stride, disappearing into an unoccupied perimeter bunker where he slapped a fresh magazine into his M16.

Shot in the chest, Myers was choking on his own blood. One of the unscathed troopers from the back of the bunker turned Myers' head to the side to clear his airway, then crawled outside with Culver and Kirsch to shout for a medic. Hearing the cries, Monk opened fire from the bunker in which he had taken refuge. By then, the radar operator who'd almost been shot had ducked behind a cargo trailer, joining a pair of black sergeants, Marvin J. Lewis and John T. Moore—a squad leader and team leader, respectively—who had rushed to the scene from the next bunker to the left. Lewis asked what was going on. "It's just a joke," the radar operator said. "He's firing blanks."

Lewis said that he'd seen tracers, which meant the GI was using live ammunition. "They must be blanks," the radar operator insisted. "He fired at me up close and didn't hit me."

"If this is a practical joke," Lewis shouted, "you had better stop and come out of that bunker—or I'm going to start firing into it!"

Monk came out of the bunker. Instead of surrendering, however, he walked back to the sleeping position where his berserk rampage had begun, and standing over Culver and Kirsch, he pumped rounds into their backs as they lay there helpless. Monk was fumbling for a third magazine when Sergeant Lewis shouldered his own M16 and shot the madman five times on semi-automatic, hitting him in the legs, arm, and neck. "Lewis was shooting to kill," notes Paul J. Fish, a former platoon leader in Delta Company. "Lewis was upset that he'd had to shoot one of our own guys, but he really had no other choice."

John Moore scanned the scene with a starlight scope, confirming that the GI with the M16 was out of action, squirming on the ground, in fact, and groaning in pain. The troops who secured the area then found Phil Culver and Warren Kirsch lying dead beside the blast wall and Tom Myers sprawled lifeless in a pool of blood inside the bunker. Michael Monk lay where he had been shot, too, incoherently mumbling verses from the Bible.

Brigade was contacted and a night medevac dispatched. Culver, Kirsch, and Warren were pronounced dead on arrival at the 9th Medical Battalion at Tan An. Monk was wheeled into surgery and his life saved. Speculation about the shootings buzzed through the 6th of the 31st. It was said—and the rumors were not mutually exclusive—that Monk had been arguing with the men in the bunker before he went for his weapon, that he was stoned out of his mind on marijuana and opium, or that he was a black militant out to kill whitey.

Private Monk was found guilty of murder and attempted murder at his court-martial and sentenced to hard labor for the rest of his natural life. The legal proceedings produced no satisfying answers. When interviewed after the shooting, Monk, speaking in a whisper because of a tracheotomy, described himself as a "morale-booster" in his unit who had no quarrel whatsoever with the men he had murdered. All he could remember of that night, he claimed, was hearing a loud bang while on guard duty. Everything after that was a blank.

The Criminal Investigation Division of the Military Police took no statements from members of Company D to the effect that Monk had a drug problem or had extolled any extreme views on race. The investigation did reveal, however, that Monk had been under psychiatric care before being drafted, leading one to wonder if Monk was simply a dangerously unstable individual who would never have been put into uniform had standards not been lowered to accommodate McNamara's 100,000. The sum of all the speculation and investigation was that three good soldiers had lost their lives "without rhyme or reason," as a baffled Paul Fish puts it. "We were all stunned. No one could believe it happened. No one could make sense of it. It was a completely senseless act for which no rational explanation ever emerged."

Chapter 15

Captain Stuart and Company A, 3rd Battalion, 39th Infantry Regiment, led the way into Xom Cau Mat from the paddies on the morning of May 8. The grunts found the bodies of several guerrillas, and several hapless civilians, while checking the wrecked buildings to either side of the burnt-out personnel carrier sitting on the main street of the hamlet. Stuart's detached platoon, Alpha One, arrived by helicopter during the sweep and, assuming the point position, started east on the canal road and moved into that part of Xom Cau Mat not yet gutted by bombs and rockets. Alpha One soon came under sniper fire and began blasting back with M16s and M60s, while medics treated the three grunts wounded in the initial fusillade.

It took about an hour to eliminate the snipers, or at least drive them from the area. As Stuart paused to medevac his casualties, DeLuca instructed Captain Genetti to leapfrog past with Bravo Company, whose own detached platoon had also been choppered in that morning. After moving past Stuart's position, Genetti's point platoon began kicking in doors and clearing the buildings along the canal road. Genetti noticed movement in the second-floor windows of some of the houses up ahead. As much as he wanted to give the order to open fire, the situation was too ambiguous to actually do so, given the civilians who might not have yet vacated the battle area. The enemy thus got in the first shots, taking the point platoon under fire from somewhere among the block of buildings on the left flank between the canal road and the Kinh Doi.

Genetti immediately received a report that First Lieutenant Joe R. Carrillo of Bravo Two, the point platoon, had been shot by a sniper; the inexperienced platoon leader had apparently darted down an alley to check out something suspicious without first securing the buildings to either side of the narrow passageway.

Carrillo was sprawled in the alley, too badly injured to move. Staff Sergeant William E. Campbell, the platoon sergeant, tried to reach Carrillo only to be shot and seriously wounded by the same hidden sniper.

The company command group, moving quickly to the scene, entered a warehouse adjacent to the alley with several infantrymen. Genetti shouted to Carrillo through a window, asking if he could tell where the fire had come from. In obvious pain, but otherwise keeping his head, Carrillo weakly called back that he didn't know where the shots had come from. This was not surprising given the confusing echoes and ricochets of an automatic-weapon being fired within a block of tightly packed buildings. There was actually little, if any, return fire at that point, as none of the grunts were able to pinpoint the sniper's position. The situation had turned into a trap, with Lieutenant Carrillo serving as bait for the Viet Cong scanning the alleyway through the ring sight of his AK-47.

Captain Genetti returned to the canal road as several tracks from the scout platoon of the 2-47th Mech approached from the Y Bridge, having been dispatched to the scene by DeLuca. Genetti flagged down one of the personnel carriers and pointed out the positions that he wanted the man behind the .50-caliber machine gun to blast on his order. "When you open fire," Genetti explained, "we're going to go out and see if we can't drag our guy back."

The track commander nodded, but Genetti, darting back into the warehouse, was still outlining the scheme to his command group when fire began pouring into the building. Specialist Fourth Class James S. Singletary, the radioman at Genetti's side, was immediately knocked to the floor. Genetti hit the deck, reached for Singletary—a twenty-three-year-old black draftee—and saw that the radioman had been shot through the upper body and assumed that he was killed instantly.

Captain Genetti grabbed the handset to the radio strapped on Singletary's back and called the track commander: "I didn't tell you to fire yet!"

The track commander emphatically replied, "We're not shooting!"

Genetti tried to make himself as small as possible, hands clasped over his helmet. He suddenly felt a sensation as if a long needle had pierced his left forearm; his hand went numb instantly, a bullet having blown a chunk of muscle away, severing the nerves. Genetti couldn't move his fingers.

Finally, realizing that a sniper was firing through the window from a second-story position across the alley, Genetti shouted at everyone to crawl back outside to the canal road. They dragged Singletary with them, as well as the wounded radioman of Lieutenant Bausser, the company's artillery forward observer.

Genetti, on the horn now with DeLuca, realized only belatedly that the new medic who'd rushed up had wrapped a bandage around the wrong arm. Genetti couldn't help but laugh and, trying to keep things light so the overly excited medic wouldn't fumble further, joked that it was his other arm that needed attention: "There's nothing wrong with the one you're bandaging."

A rocket-propelled grenade suddenly slammed into the scout track, causing numerous casualties among the crew and the infantrymen clustered around the vehicle. Someone spotted the back-blast from the launcher in an upper-story window, and finally presented with a target, Carrillo's troops began returning fire. The new medic was one of the wounded, and Lieutenant Bausser bandaged the man amid the exchange of fire. The medic, hit in the neck and arms and bleeding like crazy, frantically cried that Bausser was "using the wrong goddamn dressing." Bausser shouted back, "It's the only fucking one I have!" As the firing continued, Genetti, having been informed that Carrillo had been shot and killed, decided against another attempt to reach the lieutenant before the rest of the company could move up and secure the area. In the meantime, Genetti, who was in great pain once the adrenaline had run its course, expressed regret to DeLuca that he was leaving the job unfinished, and then requested a medevac for himself and five of his GIs.

At the time the request was made, Captains John Harachmak and Frederick R. Grates were piloting a medevac helicopter over an ARVN firefight in the vicinity of Tan An. The South Vietnamese were taking sporadic fire, and Harachmak and Grates orbited at a safe altitude, waiting for the advisor on the ground to pop smoke and bring them in when the enemy fire had been suppressed. As they waited, they overheard a radio transmission to their headquarters to the effect that Savage Trooper—the call sign for DeLuca's battalion—had requested a medevac at a certain coordinate in southern Saigon. "One of the wounded," the voice on the radio crackled, "is Trooper Bravo 6."

The call sign was Genetti's. "That's my buddy," Grates blurted to Harachmak. "Trooper Bravo 6 was my roommate at West Point. We gotta go get him!"

Captain Harachmak, the aircraft commander, requested and received permission from the advisor to respond to the U.S. medevac call before doubling back for the ARVN casualties. With that, Harachmak made contact with a radio-telephone operator in Savage Trooper Bravo. The kid on the radio talked fast, repeating several times that his company commander had been shot. The crack of gunfire was audible in the background of the transmissions. "Calm down," Harachmak said consolingly, coaxing the details he needed out of the shaken radioman. Leaving the paddies behind, the Huey swept in over the southern edge of the city. "Go ahead and pop smoke," Harachmak told the radioman. Moments later, a violet plume rose from the canal road. On the chance the enemy was monitoring the radio, pilots never requested a specific color, lest the VC pop that color themselves as a lure to an ambush. Instead, as Harachmak did now, pilots waited until the infantry tossed out whatever smoke canister was at hand, then identified the color: "Roger, we've got purple smoke."

The radioman confirmed the color. "Where's the last place you took fire from," Harachmak asked, not wanting to overfly an enemy position. "What do you recommend as the best approach?"

Unable to roar in low and drop in fast, Harachmak instead had to come to a fifty-foot hover and lower the aircraft like an elevator to the middle of the canal road. The nose of the medevac was pointed down the road, with the buildings to the left and right not far from the tips of the main rotor.

Grates helped clear Harachmak in, as did the medic and crew chief in the cargo bay: "There's wires on the right side of the street."

"There's wires on the left side, too!"

"Got 'em," Harachmak answered.

The helicopter was a big, lumbering target at that point. Grates' hands were soft on the controls, following Harachmak's movements, ready to take over should the aircraft commander suddenly take a round. The fact that medevacs had no door gunners in keeping with their life-saving role made no difference to the enemy. The standing joke was that the VC used the Red Cross symbol on the nose and the cargo-bay doors of the Hueys as targets.

As soon as the medevac touched down, grunts hustled through the roaring propeller-wash from the right side of the street. The air swirled with smoke, dust, and debris, and with no time to waste, they literally threw the wounded on board. Grates spotted Tom Genetti, head down in the wind storm, his left arm cradled in his right with a soldier helping him along. Reaching through his window, Grates banged on the outside of his door to get Genetti's attention. Genetti looked up, recognized Grates, and broke into a huge grin. Grates gave his buddy the thumbs up, then Genetti disappeared into the cargo bay with the rest of the WIAs.

Instead of the six casualties originally reported, thirteen wounded grunts and scouts crammed into the cargo bay. Had Harachmak been flying an older model Huey with a less-powerful engine, he wouldn't have been able to lift off. As it was, the engine in his top-of-the-line UH-1H Huey groaned, and the chopper shuddered as Harachmak pulled on the collective and hovered back up between the buildings. After a quick flight over Cholon, Harachmak landed at the 3rd Field Hospital outside Tan Son Nhut Airbase.

Captain Genetti was relieved of his weapon, helmet, web gear, and jungle boots in the triage area. There were so many casualties arriving from the various actions in and around the capital that Genetti was not treated in an operating room, for none were available. Instead, he found himself in a little office, sitting shirtless on a chair with his wounded arm lying across a desk. The doctor who went to work after an anesthetic had been administered scalpeled away so much flesh and muscle that Genetti could see the bone in his forearm, and he worriedly asked if they were amputating. No, the doctor replied, he just had to debride the wound, meaning he was cutting away dead tissue to prevent infection. Genetti watched the whole show and then was wheeled to one of the recovery wards. Watching passing gunships from the window and listening to the sounds of nearby battle, Genetti felt naked without his weapon and ridiculous in his army-issue blue pajamas. The out-of-action company commander could only hope that enemy sappers didn't kill the MPs guarding the gate and invade the 3d Field Hospital. .

After the medevac, Platoon Sergeant Stanley E. Thornburgh—a highly respected soldier of twenty-six who had enlisted at the age of fifteen to escape the backwoods of Kentucky—led Bravo One forward to link up with Bravo Two. The snipers were firing again, and the survivors of Carrillo's platoon were hunkered behind cover on the south side of the canal road, blasting back with M16s and M60s.

Thornburgh realized to his dismay that Singletary was lying in the open on the north side of the street. The radioman had not been placed on the medevac because medevacs were only for the wounded. The dead, and Singletary had very much appeared to be dead, only went out after an action on resupply ships. Now, however, Singletary was stirring, if only slightly. It took considerable daring and much cover fire, but Thornburgh's medic and one of his riflemen managed to pull Singletary to cover. "We called in a dust-off," notes Thornburgh. "They didn't want to come in initially, but we assured them that we could suppress the enemy fire. By the time the helicopter landed and we got Singletary over to it, he had died. We made 'em take him out anyway."

As the action continued, Platoon Sergeant Thornburgh was joined by the platoon leader of Bravo One. First Lieutenant Michael K. Polaski (a pseudonym) was in a panic, however, and after making some comment about going back to get help, he left the scene, never to reappear until the shooting had stopped. Polaski was not a young draftee; he was actually a regular, an ex-clerk in the finance corps who had requested OCS in order to accelerate his career, only to end up with a grunt company in Vietnam. "Polaski wasn't a bad guy," notes Thornburgh, "but I think his wife and kids were more on his mind than leading his platoon."

Presently, Thornburgh dashed across the canal road with a four-man fire team from one of his squads to recover the body of Lieutenant Carrillo. Leaning around the side of a building, Thornburgh could see Carrillo lying on his back in the alley where he had been sniped. To Thornburgh's surprise, Carrillo was not dead, as had been reported, but was moaning in pain. "It was the worst sound you could ever hear," recalls Thornburgh. "He was barely living. He couldn't even talk to us. From what I understand, he had tried to move a couple times, and every time he would move, they would shoot him again."

Moving into the building beside the alley, Thornburgh and his team hoped to pull Carrillo inside and back out the way they had come. The team cleared the first room, but the lead man, Private First Class Michael H. Stewart, was just starting into the next room when he saw a Viet Cong crouched in a spider hole by a window, covering the alley with an RPD light machine gun.

Using the platoon sergeant's call sign, Stewart shouted a warning, "One-Five, look out!" as he cut loose from the hip with his M16.

The guerrilla spun in his hole, firing, and Mike Stewart—only eighteen, he was a veteran of six months of combat, a good, solid kid from Wichita, Kansas—was thrown backwards, raked across the chest by the RPD. Thornburgh and the rest of the team threw grenades into the next room, trying unsuccessfully to knock the machine gun out. "There was nothing we could do," recalls Thornburgh. "We couldn't even get Stewart out of that building the fire was so heavy. We were getting hit from several directions." Thornburgh's team backed off, rolling out the door and huddling against the side of the building. "Carrillo was not more than twelve feet away from us in the alley, but if we'd have moved into the open to get him, they would have picked us off one at a time."

Frustrated, the team finally dashed back across the canal road.

DeLuca, orbiting the action in his command ship, was finally forced to call in artillery and gunships. The explosions started fires that leveled the whole complex along the canal where the snipers had been ensconced.

First Lieutenant Jerry A. Thompson of Bravo Three was an ex-collegiate football player who got along well with his men and had all the right moves in combat. Genetti rated him as his best platoon leader, and would have been heartened to learn that Thompson had taken command of Company B. On DeLuca's order, Thompson began moving his people east on the canal road as the gunships rolled in, followed by Captain Stuart and Company A.

Night positions were selected. Company B moved into houses on either side of the canal road after crossing the bridge with the broken water main that spanned the Rach Ong Nho, the tributary snaking south from the Kinh Doi. Company A secured the bridge, leaving a single platoon, Alpha Three, on the west side of the Rach Ong Nho to block any enemy who might approach from the direction of Xom Cau Mat.

The reconnaissance platoon, led by First Lieutenant Joseph L. Rodriquez, continued east on the canal road, all the way to a Buddhist pagoda and Catholic church below the south leg of the Y Bridge. DeLuca disembarked from his command ship in the adjacent field, nicknamed "the green," which was large enough to accommodate several medevac or resupply ships at once. There, Major Booras and the rest of the command group greeted him. After securing permission to use the sacred premises, the battalion command group set up in the pagoda. The roof supported a big plaster dragon. The interior of the little, one-roomed pagoda smelled faintly of incense, was decorated with religious flags, and had a white-and-orange parachute stretched overhead as a kind of false ceiling. The thick altar table supported a lacquered statue of Buddha.

Captain Wilfred A. Geschke, M.D., the battalion surgeon, helicoptered in with a team of medics and established an aid station in the adjacent church, neatly stacking the pews to one side to make room for their stretchers. In a letter home, DeLuca noted the comforting presence of the scout platoon from the 247th Mechanized Infantry, which was led by First Lieutenant Henry L. S. Jezek: "I felt secure in having ten armored personnel carriers on the bridge overlooking my CP[.]"

When the casualty reports were radioed in that evening and entered into the brigade log, what had been a bad day for DeLuca's battalion—and leaving two bodies had stung worst of all—was transformed into a victory. Though few enemy soldiers had actually been seen, Alpha Company supposedly killed ten and Bravo Company an incredible thirty-seven, with the gunships adding another twenty to the official body count. Captain Genetti was subsequently awarded his second Bronze Star, and Lieutenant Carrillo was awarded a posthumous Silver Star. Staff Sergeant Campbell lived to receive his Silver Star. Apparently because the awards section assumed that the senior officer on the scene had taken command when Genetti was wounded, Lieutenant Polaski also won a Bronze Star. The official version aside, "the fight had been pretty chaotic," remembers former lieutenant Bill Bausser. "Everybody was kind of in a state of shock because we had lost so many people so fast."

It was after midnight when mortar rounds began exploding in the dark around the command post and aid station. DeLuca and Booras hit the cement floor of the pagoda with their radiomen, while Geschke and his medics scrambled into a muddy slit trench outside their aid station. Flares popped overhead and mortar rounds thudded in all around, fifty rounds in less than thirty minutes. There followed a lull that lasted nearly an hour and ended when a team of guerrillas, which had worked its way in close, scored a direct hit on the pagoda with an RPG. The enemy also began mortaring the area again and firing automatic-weapons from the houses across the green. For all the fire, there were no serious injuries, and the damage to the command post and aid station was mostly symbolic, as the plaster dragon atop the pagoda had taken hits and the lower half of the cross above the church had been blown away. Before long, a team of gunships came thumping through the night to assist in the defense of the positions at the foot of the Y Bridge.

The rocket fired at the command post—it whooshed in at four in the morning on May 9, 1968—was apparently the signal for other enemy forces to hit the units spread out in the houses along the Kinh Doi. The light jangle of equipment and the crunch of sandals on debris could be heard as enemy soldiers moved around in the dark, and, firing flared in fits and starts all along the line. Meanwhile, multiple rockets sizzled from the paddies to the south toward Captain Stuart's command post and the positions held by Alpha One and Alpha Two. Five grunts were wounded by the RPGs. During the attack, a lone figure, who appeared to be an ARVN, walked down the canal road, calling out, "Hey, GI!" In response, Sergeant Franklin A. Townsend, a shake 'n' bake draftee who had joined Alpha One just days before, stood up from his position only to be instantly cut down and killed when the trickster wheeled on him with an AK-47.

Most of the fire was directed against the bridge over the Rach Ong Nho. The two men positioned on the bridge, Privates First Class Elport Chess and Voltaire J. Soto of Alpha One, kept the enemy at bay with grenades and an M60. For their heroic stand, Chess and Soto both would be decorated with the Silver Star.

Lieutenant Long and the 1st Platoon, C/5-60th Mech, mounted up and headed down the canal road from the mech battalion's position near the Route 5A bridge. As the personnel carriers neared the battle, where artillery was firing and a flareship was up lighting the way, the order was given to sweep both sides of the road with fire to disrupt any ambushers who might be waiting in the shadows. "The tracks fired us up big time as they went by," notes Bill Bausser. "I was on the second-floor of this house, and I could see rounds punching through the walls. We were yelling at them. They didn't realize there were friendlies in the area."

Lieutenant Long was informed that enemy soldiers were in a three-story apartment building on the south side of the canal road. Stopping on the road and wheeling to face the building, his three tracks commenced firing. "We just leveled that building," recalls Jerry Harper. "We were laying down so much fire, palm trees were falling over and everything. If the enemy returned any fire, it wouldn't have been for very long. I think we scared the hell out of 'em, and they just *di-di-mau*'d back into the rice paddies behind the building. We poured thirty-weight motor oil on our .50s to keep the barrels from melting, and just kept blasting away all through the wee hours of the morning until sometime after the break of dawn. These grunts who'd been pinned down came up after we ceased fire. They were so damn happy to see us, they were kissing our tracks."

Each platoon along the canal road secured its position by morning's light. Four enemy bodies were counted in the process.

Captain Eckman and B/6-31st, released from Antila's control early that morning, were transported to DeLuca's command post aboard personnel carriers from the 5-60th. Fires still raged along the canal road, producing corridors of intense heat through which the tracks sped. The tracks also passed a column of ARVN soldiers who were loaded down with pots, pans, and other household items, which they either always carried into combat or, more likely, had just looted from those houses that had not yet gone up in flames.

The enemy fired a rocket-propelled grenade across the green as Captain Eckman walked into DeLuca's command post, so introductions were made while crouching for cover under the thick altar table with the Buddha statue on it. Major Booras asked Eckman, "How many guys you got?"

"I only brought a hundred and fifty."

"Only a hundred and fifty?" snapped an incredulous Booras. "You some kind of smart guy? I've never seen more than eighty guys in a company."

Eckman explained that his unit was new to the war zone and still at full strength. In fact, not enough helicopters had been made available to move Eckman's entire 220-man company to Saigon from Firebase Smoke.

DeLuca wanted Eckman to secure a police outpost that had repelled a ground attack at dawn. To reach the outpost, DeLuca explained, Eckman's company would have to pass under the south leg of the Y Bridge and proceed almost four-hundred meters east on the canal road. Then the company would have to turn right (south) and continue another eight-hundred meters on a side street, which led into an unidentified hamlet occupying the west bank of the Rach Ong Lon, another tributary snaking off the Kinh Doi. The police outpost was inside the unidentified hamlet. Even as Eckman was getting organized to move to the outpost, the defenders reported taking more RPGs. While gunships blasted the houses around the outpost, another helicopter darted in with a resupply of ammunition.

Captain Eckman began moving down the canal road with Second Lieutenant Calton R. Blacker and Bravo Three in the lead. Absent a military-issue map, Eckman peeled a tourist map of Saigon from the wall of one of the buildings cleared by his lead platoon. As the push continued, Eckman flashed back to an afternoon shortly before the battalion had been activated, when Lieutenant Colonel Schmalhorst and his company commanders had toured the training facilities at Fort Lewis in preparation for drafting the unit's training plan. When they stopped at the combat in cities course, Eckman commented that his ARVN troops had fought in a few thatch-roofed villages during his first tour, but never in a city. The other captains, also veterans of previous tours in the war zone, told Schmalhorst the same thing "and collectively," notes Eckman, "we decided we weren't going to waste time training for urban combat. Instead, we'd spend more time getting the troops ready for the rice-paddy war. Fast forward to that day in Saigon, and we're opcon [operational-controlled] to another battalion, we don't have maps, and we're headed for some bigtime combat in cities, whether we'd trained for it or not. It came to my mind that, 'damn, I'm living with a decision that I started!' "

In addition to dispatching Eckman's company to the east to relieve the police compound, DeLuca instructed Thompson's company to advance cautiously to the south, in an effort to catch up with the force that had attacked the command post during the night. Meanwhile, the troops at the command post remained in intermittent battle with a handful of guerrillas holding out in some of the houses around the green. Even as shots were being exchanged, those civilians who had not fled during the first day of the battle, or who had made the mistake of returning to their homes on the second day, streamed over the Y Bridge during this third day of fighting in District 8.

William Tuohy described the scene in the *Los Angeles Times*:

> Under the tropical sun, the refugees carry pigs and cooking pots and small stoves and baby bottles and bags of rice across the bridge. . . . Whole families scurry down the bridge incline, linked hand in

hand. Others push cars and pull wagons filled with their belongings. An old woman jogs along with her traditional carrying pole laden not with produce but a television set and a large radio.

The tracks from Lieutenant Jezek's platoon sat on the bridge amidst the flow of refugees, "their .50-cal machine guns pointed at snipers' lairs 150 yards away," notes Tuohy. Staff Sergeant Robert L. Brantley, the platoon sergeant, told Tuohy how the enemy had reoccupied houses cleared the day before to launch the night attack, then added, "But we don't know what's going on right now. Try the command post. Watch it—Charles has been sniping our tails off." Tuohy's article continues:

"Reaching the command post means a long sprint down the far end of the bridge, leaping the barbed wire at the end, and making another dash over an open field."

Tuohy found DeLuca and Booras monitoring the progress of B/6-31st and B/3-39th over the radios in their command post. DeLuca was candid with Tuohy and the other reporters who congregated in the pagoda, but he was not particularly happy to see any of them. Part of a deeply conservative institution, DeLuca shared the common prejudice among professional military officers that the press corps was an untrustworthy institution motivated by sensationalism and a certain naive sympathy for the communist cause. DeLuca expressed his misgivings in a letter he sent to his wife from Saigon:

Unfortunately, the area that we were sent to is right on the southern edge of the city and across a big Y bridge. The correspondents and reporters have been here everyday in droves—they come up to the bridge in taxis, walk over the bridge and are at our C.P. I've tried to avoid them but they are always there—until 5 PM and then they have their martini parties to go to. I wouldn't put too much stock in what they say because they get such a small picture and play it up big. There have been people here from UPI [United Press International], AP [Associated Press], *Life,* Japan, Germany, Italy, etc.—a real UN group, all with fancy cameras and microphones.

Most reporters actually tried to present a balanced portrayal of events. William Tuohy, for example, quoted a sergeant from DeLuca's battalion who neatly summed up the situation: "This place is really a mess. It seems like one house catches on fire and then whole blocks burn down. But I don't know how else you're going to fight this kind of dirty war."

Some of the grunts instinctively resented the journalists tagging along with them. Others did not. "The reporters didn't get in the way," recalls a former squad leader. "They were doing their jobs, and to me they had a lot of balls."

Danger was indeed part of the job. Tuohy was talking with DeLuca and Booras when a sharp snap sent everyone ducking. "What the hell was that?" asked one of the nervous headquarters personnel. "A bullet, goddamnit!" barked Major Booras. A sergeant pointed out the bullet hole. "Find out where it came from," Booras said, "so we know where the hell the sniper is."

When an enemy soldier was spotted on the top floor of a nearby house, the troops positioned outside the pagoda sent a loud fusillade of fire in his direction. The snipers nevertheless kept popping up. Captain Geschke, the battalion surgeon, was standing outside the command post when the ARVN soldier beside him suddenly jumped, a sniper round having touched his sleeve before burying itself in the door frame behind him. Shortly thereafter, another shot was fired from across the green, and Geschke would never forget the sound of the bullet cracking past his ear.

Tuohy was still on the scene when Lieutenant Jezek's scout platoon radioed that the snipers had finally scored a hit: "We've just had a trooper up here on the bridge take a stomach wound."

Major Booras got on the horn to request "one dust-off for one stomach wound. Litter. U.S. Urgent." The wounded trooper was brought into the pagoda, hastily treated, then rushed to the medevac that landed on the green. General Ewell's helicopter also landed on the green at that time, and the commanding general of the 9th Infantry Division—never shy about dropping into areas where bullets were still buzzing—strode into the pagoda with the division sergeant major. DeLuca provided a hasty briefing, after which Ewell proclaimed to the assembled reporters, "No sweat. We ought to be able to clean this area up by tonight." Ewell gave the impression that the enemy soldiers were on the run: "The main thing we have to do is make sure they don't get out of the city." With that, Ewell, who understood the value of good press relations, cracked a smile and joked with the reporters, "Now I've got to get back to the office."

Gunships began rolling in on the houses across the green following the general's departure, miniguns tearing through walls and rooftops. During the lull that followed, DeLuca offered the reporters a more cautious and realistic appraisal of the situation than Ewell had: "[The enemy soldiers] have the advantage by positioning themselves in houses and shooting at us.

They don't care about the civilians. But we don't want to destroy the city or hurt the civilians, so [clearing the area] is necessarily a slow process."

While DeLuca's battalion was engaged on the east side of the battlefield, Antila's battalion, which had spent the previous day getting resupplied and reorganized, was in position to the west, preparing to conduct a follow-up sweep through Xom Cau Mat in search of any lingering NVA and Viet Cong.

The shooting actually started before the sweep did; Company A of the 5-60th Mech came under fire while lined up on the canal road, waiting for the word to advance. Mark Fenton and a couple of buddies were sitting atop their track with a transistor radio, surreptitiously passing a joint, for as Fenton recalls, "we figured we had it comin', and we weren't expecting anything." Then the enemy snipers opened fire from a nearby building. "All of a sudden, it was bing-bing-bing, and we bailed off the track. I'll never forget it because 'It's a Beautiful Morning' by the Rascals was blaring on the radio, and I thought, 'Beautiful to who?' "

Muzzle flashes were visible from two adjoining windows on the second floor of the building. Intimidated, everyone kept their heads down until one gutsy, or fedup, trooper finally pulled a LAW off the top of the track by its shoulder strap, then exposed himself long enough to take careful aim and send the LAW whooshing toward its target. The rocket impacted between the two windows from which the snipers had been firing, blowing a substantial hole in the side of the building and silencing the VC.

Captain Dobbs—the brand-new, in-over-his-head commander of Company A—appeared then, not to congratulate the GI who had fired the LAW, but to rebuke him: "We're not here to destroy this city."

"And I'm not here to die," the GI shot back.

The dismounted point element of Company A came under more fire upon starting down the main street of Xom Cau Mat. The troops pulled back, and fire was returned. Two frantic children suddenly appeared in the crossfire, and Mark Nauyalis watched amazed as a GI, who had inevitably been nicknamed "Pineapple" as he came from Hawaii, scooped them up, one under each arm, and brought them to safety behind the APCs.

Captain Scarborough's command track and the other fifteen personnel carriers of Company C were parked along the north shoulder of the canal road, facing the Pham The Hien market, a block of two-story buildings at the northeast corner of Xom Cau Mat. Gary Vertrees remembers how he was sipping a beer in the cupola of the deuce track and idly taking photographs of the shops across the street when "all of a sudden, shit started flying, and I dropped down inside the track, then came back up and hit the butterflies on the .50-caliber machine gun."

As fire was returned all along the line, Captain Scarborough sent several three-man teams forward to flush the snipers out. Jerry Harper was sitting on the opened hatch cover in the cupola of his track, feet braced in front of him as he fired the .50, when he noticed Alan Kisling—who had rushed across the street with one of the assault teams—flattened against the building to his front, pitching hand grenades up into a second-floor window. Kisling's third or fourth grenade missed the window and bounced into the street. When the frag exploded, Harper was shocked to catch some of the shrapnel, for he had thought he was safely outside the blast radius, and jumped down behind his track, frantically shouting for a medic. He thought his eye had been blown out, but Doc Birge, checking his injuries, told him he'd been lucky; though a white-hot metal fragment had stung Harper just under the right eye, it had barely broken the skin. Another piece of shrapnel had hit him in the right foot. The end of it was sticking through the tongue of his jungle boot. Harper pulled it out, threw it aside, climbed back aboard his track, and resumed fire.

Captain Scarborough pulled the assault teams back after one of the dismounted troopers was badly wounded in the leg. With the assault teams out of the way, Bandido Charlie poured it on with everything it had—M16s, M60s, M79s, .50-caliber machine guns, and the track-mounted 106mm recoilless rifle—devastating the shops facing the canal road. Whitey Whitehead, the recoilless-rifle gunner, slammed flechette rounds right through the front doors of the shops. Smoke and dust belched from the windows. John Marrs was standing behind a track, leaning past it to fire his machine gun, when he realized his left shoulder was burning. Seeing blood, he called to his buddies to check the injury. It seemed like a wound that could wait; a single piece of shrapnel was buried deep in the muscle of his shoulder. "They asked if I was going to make it," recalls Marrs. "I said, 'Aw, no problem,' and kind of shook it off and kept firing. I have no idea what hit me. We were throwing so much stuff across the street, it could have been a piece of our own shrapnel, for all I know."

John Hohman was peppered in the face, apparently when a shell from the M79 he was firing hit a power line and exploded prematurely. Kisling opened fire from beside a track. The GI standing on the lowered back ramp of the track and firing over the deck was suddenly knocked to the ground, wounded. Doc Birge was treating the man when Kisling suddenly felt as if he'd been stung by hornets in his right knee and groin. He hollered to the medic, thinking himself badly injured. Birge couldn't help but laugh. Kisling had barely been scratched by, apparently, fragments of a bullet that had ricocheted off the track. Birge pulled not a bandage from his aid bag, but band-aids. If the thousand-to-one ratio of outgoing to incoming fire seemed almost hysterical, it served the purpose, notes Birge, of driving some of the enemy soldiers from their cover: "Several VC ran out of the buildings and were immediately killed by our fire."

Gary Vertrees stitched the shops to his front until the heat finally got to be too much and he dropped down inside the track, wringing wet with sweat and feeling as if he were smothering inside his flak jacket. Tomlinson, who had been keeping Vertrees supplied with ammo, asked what was wrong. "I gotta catch my breath," Vertrees gasped. Tomlinson said he would take over the gun. "No, just wait a minute," Vertrees said. "I'll be fine. I'll go back up."

"Nah, take it easy," Jerry Tomlinson said, and with that, he grabbed another box of ammo and climbed up behind the .50. Tomlinson had only fired a few rounds when something zipped painlessly into his left biceps, and he glanced down to see blood pumping from a severed artery in eight-inch spurts. He dropped back inside the vehicle to get out of the fire.

Somebody had shouted for more M60 ammunition, and Vertrees was hauling boxes of the stuff out the back of the track when he realized that Tomlinson wasn't firing the .50 anymore. He turned to find Tomlinson sitting on an ammo crate inside the hull, staring numbly at the blood jetting from his arm. Vertrees shouted to his buddy, but Tomlinson didn't even look up. Tomlinson finally jammed his finger into the wound to stop the bleeding. The medic who scrambled into the track put a compress bandage over the injury. Tomlinson had lost all feeling in his arm, the fragment having severed the nerves as well as the artery. He couldn't lift his arm, couldn't move it at all, "so the medic automatically said I had to go to the hospital and all this stuff," he recalls. "At the time, I wanted to get out of there, but yet I didn't want to go."

Captain Scarborough listened on his radio as Vertrees reported that he had a badly wounded man on his vehicle: "I gotta get him out of here!" In response, Scarborough instructed Vertrees to load all of the company's casualties into his maintenance track and remove them to the battalion command post where a medevac could land. There was no room to maneuver behind the line of personnel carriers, so Vertrees, jumping in the driver's hatch, was forced to roll straight down the canal road between the troops blazing away on the north side and the snipers popping back from the south side. The back ramp was lowered, and six wounded men hurriedly climbed in beside Tomlinson, including Lieutenant Long who had taken shrapnel in his arm. The highly respected platoon leader had argued with Doc Birge that he didn't need to be dusted off, but Captain Scarborough had apparently gotten him on the horn and given him a direct order to present himself at the medevac point.

Gary Vertrees subsequently received the Bronze Star for driving the wounded out under fire. "One of the other guys was kinda upset that I got singled out for a medal. I don't blame him. Sure, okay, in a sense, maybe I took charge, but everybody in the crew should have gotten something, too."

After unloading the wounded, Vertrees and the crew filled their track with ammunition from the stockpiles at the battalion command post, then "turned around and went right back into it again," recounts Vertrees. "We stopped at every track that needed ammo and threw the stuff out. By the time we pulled back into our spot in the line, things were slowing down and guys were kind of milling around, checking the buildings and seeing what kind of damage we had done."

The fronts of the buildings were spattered with ragged holes. Some were on fire, and Vertrees snapped a shot of a grimy, black-faced GI who grinned triumphantly at the camera while the marketplace burned behind him. The Bandidos reported a body count of three. Civilians began to appear, including a hysterical woman who ran to Vertrees with a blood-smeared girl in her arms. The child had a scarf over her head. Vertrees called for a medic, but then the woman pulled the scarf away and he saw that most of the little girl's head was missing.

There were numerous civilian casualties. Vertrees took a photograph of a woman and child lying dead amid the debris in the front room of one of the houses facing the canal road. "We killed people we didn't even know were there," says Vertrees. "War after war, civilians are the ones who catch it, especially when you're fighting in a city. In this case, the enemy used them for cover. They didn't care if the civilians got killed or not. In fact, I think they purposefully opened fire on us so we would hit civilians when we returned fire."

Company A exchanged fire with the snipers in its area for two hours. When the shooting petered out, the teams that moved into the west side of Xom Cau Mat were taking no chances and tossed frags into each house before going through the front door. There was no return fire. The GIs found only an elderly couple hiding in a store and the bodies of four Viet Cong.

Captain Scarborough also dispatched dismounted teams from Company C to clear the north edge of Xom Cau Mat. Scarborough was joined at that time by Lieutenant Garver, whom he had pulled off the line the day before to give him a chance to sleep off a spell of combat fatigue. At that time, Garver had turned the platoon over to Staff Sergeant Bloom. Coming forward again after his rest, Garver had no sooner reached the command track than a heated exchange erupted on the radio between Scarborough and Bloom. No one knew if there were still any enemy soldiers in the houses ahead, but Bloom had no intention of finding out. The young shake 'n' bake sergeant refused to lead his platoon forward.

"You get your ass over to my location right now," Captain Scarborough snapped with uncharacteristic harshness. "I'm going to court-martial you."

"I ain't goin'," Bloom answered, unmoved by the threat of a stint in the infamous Long Binh Jail. "I don't care what you do, I ain't goin'."

Lieutenant Garver rejoined his platoon as Bloom was taken into custody by the first sergeant. After clearing the area without further contact, Garver discovered that some of his Bandidos had confiscated a number of items during the house-to-house sweep, including a little black-and-white television. Garver later took a photo of the television sitting atop a case of Carling Black Label in the back of a personnel carrier; it had been wired into the vehicle's electrical system so the guys could watch the news out in the field, as well as shows like *Combat!*, *Bonanza*, and *Gunsmoke* on the Armed Forces Television Network.

Philip Jones Griffiths, a Welsh photojournalist whose sympathies lay with the National Liberation Front, addresses the issue of looting in his antiwar classic *Vietnam Inc.*:

> The U.S. troops [in District 8, Saigon,] were from the 9th Division and had spent the whole of their tour[s] wading through the mud of the delta. Some GIs were amazed to see multi-story buildings, and many were sobered by the realization that they were now destroying the homes of people who, in some cases, enjoyed a higher standard of material comfort than they themselves did in America. . . . GIs, who'd previously been lucky to find more than a red pepper in deserted homes out in the paddy fields, found themselves with more TV sets, radios, tape recorders and refrigerators than they could carry. . . .

Griffiths charges that U.S. troops "empt[ied] a warehouse full of air-conditioners[.]" His account continues:

The ARVN, who had entered the area first, had taken everything that could be carried by hand. The GIs, with their APCs, were able to take away refrigerators, TV sets, and other heavy items. Each evening they could be seen unloading their vehicles for sleeping. This procedure had been made a rule after two GIs were killed by an enemy mortar round on the first night because their APC was so full they had had to sleep outside.

There is a certain hyperbole in Griffiths' description: no GIs were killed by mortar fire during the battle, and the troops always slept outside their tracks in any event. Most veterans of Mini-Tet consider his charges exaggerated. During the sweep of Xom Cau Mat on day three, "I took a soda from one of the stores that we broke into while checking for enemy soldiers," writes Mark Nauyalis. "Is that considered looting?" Gary Vertrees made souvenirs of several family photographs he found in a house and "saw some cases of soda and beer that walked out of some of the hootches, but that's about it."

If veterans don't recall the kind of systematic looting described by Griffiths, they do admit that not all of their comrades were angels. Specialist Fourth Class Bruce R. Isenhoff of the 2-47th Mech, for example, was astonished to see several GIs loading a refrigerator into a high-backed M577. "The men riding on my track began yelling and laughing at them as we went past," recalls Isenhoff. "They laughed and waved back. That was the only looting I ever saw in Vietnam."

Some troops jokingly flew brassieres from the radio antennas of their tracks. Others picked up umbrellas to shade themselves from the sun. When their officers weren't looking, "a lot of guys looted televisions, anything they could get," says Larry Miller. "Even if they had no use for it, they were just taking it." John Hohman recalls hearing that several safes had been found inside a store after Company C secured the Pham The Hien market: "They were still sitting there when we left, but the doors had been blown off with C4 and the piasters inside had disappeared. They didn't call us the Bandidos for nothing."

At some point during the battle, apparently after the marketplace fight, Miller backed his personnel carrier up to a deserted bar "and we kind of loaded up on provisions. The whole platoon was there. That's the first time I'd ever seen pre-cooked hamburger patties in a can. It was military-issue, but we'd never seen it." Doug Birge notes that the cleaning out of the bar was "the only 'looting' that I saw. I didn't consider this to be looting as we were taking back U.S. military items that had somehow found their way onto the black market."

One of the goals of the second-wave offensive, according to Griffiths, was to disabuse the urban population of any lingering faith that the government could offer protection from the revolutionary forces that dominated the rural areas of Vietnam. The Catholic district of the capital had been specifically targeted for its loyalty to the government. The communists, wrote Griffiths, sent in only a handful of guerrillas, "bank[ing] on an overreaction, blitzkrieg fashion" by U.S. units "untrained and unfamiliar with house-to-house fighting."

While failing to comment on the ruthlessness of such tactics, Griffiths did accurately report that the sledgehammer the U.S. forces applied during the counterattack played into enemy hands, noting with irony that "the roof-bar of the Caravelle offered a grandstand view of the Phantom jets dropping bombs and napalm on the homes of the only pro-American Vietnamese in Saigon."

Such allegiances began to shift as neighborhood after neighborhood was flattened during the battle. While photographing a block of houses still burning from a gunship strike, Griffiths saw a Vietnamese man who was literally shaking with rage as he screamed, "Why Americans crazy? Only four VC! Americans bring many helicopters—destroy everything!"

The anger of the district residents reached critical mass on the third day of the battle when it was learned that, in the course of returning fire on the enemy in the shops along the canal road, Company C of the 5-60th Mech had accidentally shot up a hospital situated behind the snipers who had been firing on the Bandidos. Captain Melvin R. Chatman, a civil-affairs officer, was tasked to investigate the incident after complaints were received from the district chief. Chatman determined that many refugees had congregated on the hospital grounds, where they erected poncho shelters and put up government flags to identity themselves. Twenty-two of these civilians, mostly children and the elderly, had been killed and approximately forty wounded by the fusillades of .50-caliber machine-gun fire that had ripped through the Pham The Hien Market.

Aggrieved survivors told Chatman that no VC had been in the area when an armor column stopped on the canal road and wantonly and indiscriminately opened fire into the marketplace. The survivors—who received fifty dollars for every family member killed—might have been unaware of the enemy snipers in the area. More likely, though, they did not care, for as the residents of District 8 perceived the situation, U.S. units were so preoccupied with minimizing friendly casualties and maximizing those of the enemy that they completely disregarded the innocent

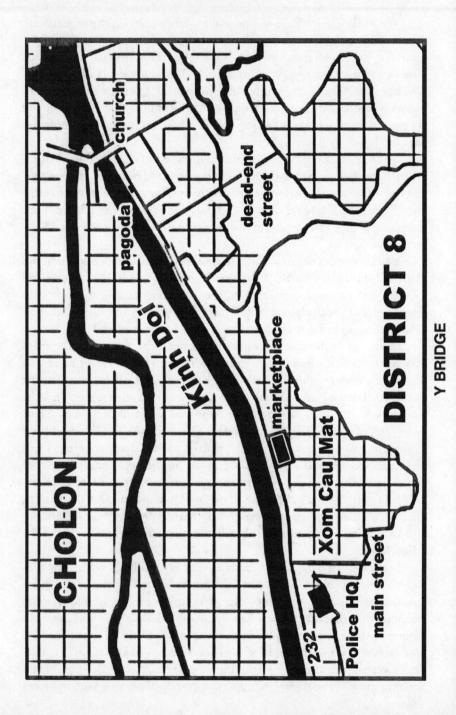

Vietnamese caught in the middle. The perception was not unfounded. Griffiths writes of a captain from the 9th Division who explained to him that "all areas that might be occupied by VC would be destroyed, for this was the most economical way of saving American lives."

However the use of heavy firepower was justified, the results sorely tested the "morale and loyalty of the populace," reports Kevin Buckley of *Newsweek*. "The very sight of U.S. troops now galls many district residents." Buckley spoke with older Vietnamese troubled by the blasé attitude of GIs, who laughed and played softball in the battle's aftermath while refugees picked through the remains of their homes just a few feet away. Younger Vietnamese sneered that U.S. pilots celebrated their victories by pasting little pictures of houses on their aircraft. Buckley also quotes an American social worker who painted a troubling picture: "After Tet, people accepted what had happened and blamed the VC. This time, we're catching it. What happened in District Eight seems to many Vietnamese to support their suspicions about this being a racist war."

The marketplace engagement on the west side of the district had already fizzled out when Captain Eckman and Company B, 6th Battalion, 31st Infantry Regiment, operating on the other side of town, reported coming under sniper fire at approximately two in the afternoon of May 9 while moving to the besieged police outpost along the Rach Ong Lon.

Lieutenant Blacker's point platoon, Bravo Three, had turned off the canal road and was clearing houses to either side of the side street, which led to the police outpost, when the shooting started. Eckman's green troops had never been under direct fire before. "We instantly squatted down," recalls Mark Mudd, "and saw a burst of about seven or eight rounds from an AK-47 hit the cement wall behind us about a foot above our heads." Private First Class Mudd's group ran into a nearby building. "We were trying to figure out what to do when a radioman named Broderick from another platoon ran into the same building. He had been shot in the neck, but was doing okay. I put a bandage on him."

DeLuca informed Eckman that gunships were on the way, then dispatched Company A, 3rd Battalion, 39th Infantry to reinforce his attached company. Captain Eckman, meanwhile, tried to control the action from atop a building. "Dumb move," he notes. "A dud RPG scared me and my RTOs [radio-telephone operators] off the roof."

Sergeant David B. Leader, a squad leader in Bravo Three, took refuge with his men and a diminutive French female photographer who had joined them behind a cement building. They huddled together as they decided what their next move should be. Intending to use his helmet as a seat, Leader took the steel pot off, set it on the ground and was sliding down with his back against the wall into a squatting position when another shot rang out, striking the wall where his head had just been. Leader was unscathed, but one of his team leaders began "hollerin' and rollin' on the ground," recalls Leader, "and the first thing he did was rip his shirt open to see if whatever had hit him in the back had come out his chest." It hadn't. The team leader had caught a small bullet fragment in his back, and "we got him calmed down," notes Leader, "bandaged him up, and got him out of there. He calmed down quickly. He was good. He was trained as an engineer and unhappy about being switched into the infantry, but he was always smiling and making jokes."

Lieutenant Blacker moved down an alley toward the sound of the enemy fire with Leader's squad, and "got a location of the house it was coming from," Leader recounted on a tape he made for his wife after the battle. "[W]e started chucking hand grenades, machine-gun fire, and M79-grenade fire, and small-arms fire, into this house. Oh, by the time we got through shootin' at it, it looked like a piece of Swiss cheese, and we didn't have any more sniper fire."

Thinking the job done, Blacker and Leader were surprised to take fire from another house about a hundred meters away at the far end of the alley. As noted on Leader's tape, the decision was made to pull back to the main street "and shoot down the alley this time instead of being caught *in* the alley, because there were cement houses on both sides." It turned out, however, that yet another sniper was in position in the house facing the mouth of the alley. "He had let us walk by and get down that alley, and then he opened up on us when we started to come out. So, there we were, in the alley, with a sniper at one end and a sniper at the other end."

After a smoke grenade was pitched toward the far end of the alley, Blacker directed a gunship on the sniper firing from that direction. Leader did not mention on the tape he sent home that the gunship flushed a guerrilla into the open. The guerrilla passed directly in front of the sergeant's position as he tried to dash away, and Leader quickly sighted in at a range of less than twenty meters and squeezed the trigger on his M16. The hapless guerrilla cartwheeled when hit and crashed dead into the street. Leader did describe on the tape how the Cobra "pounded all the houses" in the vicinity of the smoke marker with rockets, as well as the minigun and belt-fed grenade launcher in its chin turret, then swung around and "pounded the sniper in the building across the street at the other end of the alley. So, when we stopped receiving fire from there, we chalk[ed] it up as an enemy kill on both ends, and we continued on down the street [toward the police outpost]."

Back in the pagoda command post, DeLuca and Booras were in contact with Eckman on one frequency and Lieutenant Thompson of Company B, 3rd Battalion, 39th Infantry on another. Thompson had reported making contact shortly after Eckman. At the time, Thompson's troops were clearing the houses to either side of a major side street that ran south from the canal road from a point immediately east of the bridge held during the night attack by Alpha Company.

When the shooting started, Lieutenant Thompson darted into a house with Lieutenant Bausser, the forward observer with the command group of Bravo Company. The two peered from the doorway, trying to pinpoint where the fire was coming from. Not wanting to linger in the open, they stepped back after a few moments. Less than a second later, a burst of AK-47 fire stitched the wooden door in front of which they had just been standing. Thompson and Bausser looked at each other and burst out laughing with wild relief. "Wow," Thompson exclaimed, "that's the first time somebody tried to kill me personally!"

Everything slowed down for about thirty minutes as DeLuca and Booras organized gunship support for Thompson; the grunts kept low as the Cobras came in over the roofs, firing rockets. The push had no sooner resumed than more fire was received, and Thompson halted his people while more gunship runs were made on the houses in front of Bravo Company.

The gunships again banked off. The order was once more given to move out. Private First Class Miguel A. Abreu-Batista of New York City—the seasoned veteran walking point for the lead platoon, Bravo One—started across an open intersection to reach the next block of buildings. The snipers had the intersection covered, however, and Abreu-Batista crumpled to the street when a burst of AK-47 fire rang out from a window. Platoon Sergeant Thornburgh, accompanying the squad bringing up the rear, was flabbergasted to see the lead two squads running pell-mell back up the street led by a completely panic-stricken Lieutenant Polaski. Thornburgh grabbed Polaski, attempting to shout some sense into him: "Goddamnit, lieutenant, you're gonna get these people killed!"

Polaski broke away from Thornburgh and tried to dart across to the other side of the street. He didn't make it. "A sniper opened up on his ass,"

Thornburgh would recall with grim satisfaction. "I'll never forget—it was the best thing that could have happened—bup-bup-bup-bup, and he stumbled and fell."

After getting the retreating troops under control, Thornburgh checked on Polaski. The platoon leader had been superficially injured, apparently by gravel or fragments of the rounds that had impacted in the street around him. "Lieutenant, you're hurt," Thornburgh said, making it sound worse than it was. "You need to head back to the battalion aid station."

Polaski departed without hesitation or argument. Meanwhile, the .50 gunner of an armored personnel carrier from the scout platoon of the 2-47th raked the building in which the snipers were concealed, starting a fire that quickly spread to other buildings in the area. Platoon Sergeant Thornburgh and a team of volunteers used the track for cover, as it rolled down the road under continued sniper fire, in order to recover Abreu-Batista's body. The track stopped beside the point man, his body stiff and smoking, his jungle fatigues burned away, and Thornburgh and one of his guys each grabbed an ankle and dragged Abreu-Batista behind the APC. "He was still hot," says a haunted Thornburgh. "I still remember. My hand still burns sometimes."

The company pulled back to get reorganized. Everyone was in a foul mood over the loss of Miguel Abreu-Batista, who was a good soldier and, given his outgoing and cheerful disposition, one of the more popular guys in Bravo Company. Lieutenant Bausser's recon sergeant had been particularly close to Abreu-Batista, and Bausser presently got a call on the radio from Thornburgh, who "asked me to come over to his position because my recon sergeant had just lost it when [Abreu-]Batista got killed and was beating the shit out of a civilian," recalls Bausser. "By the time I got over there, it was all over, and my recon sergeant was sitting against a wall with his head in his arms. [Abreu-]Batista's death really hurt."

A tall, big-boned grunt whom Abreu-Batista had affectionately called "Dum-Dum" became enraged when another of his comrades used the nickname, and said fiercely, "Don't anybody ever call me that anymore!"

They didn't.

Even as Thompson got reorganized, DeLuca and Booras were informed that Stuart's company had linked up with Eckman's and that the combined force had finally reached the besieged police outpost. Enemy snipers had accounted for seven more casualties among Eckman's troops along the way, but the injuries were all relatively superficial. Then the enemy completely faded away as Thompson and Eckman's companies, reinforced by several scout tracks, searched the areas from which the outpost had taken fire. The enemy said goodbye with a few final mortar rounds.

DeLuca instructed Eckman to secure the police outpost and Stuart to return to the command post aboard the scout tracks. Another frustrating day of street fighting was made palatable at that point by radioing in a victorious body count of ten apiece for A/3-39th and B/6-31st, twelve for B/3-39th, and thirty more for the supporting gunships from B/7-1st Cavalry.

Captain Eckman set Bravo Company in defensive positions inside and around the police outpost at dusk; then he had his forward observer call in several hours' worth of artillery fire to prevent the enemy in the area from launching a night attack. The fire landed so close that a chunk of shrapnel ripped through the tin roof of the police barracks and slashed open the arm of one of the grunts sleeping inside. Sergeant Leader was positioned outside, but felt fairly secure behind the fifty-gallon drums that he and his squad had filled with assorted rubble from the half-demolished cinder-block houses across the street from the police outpost.

As the artillery shells exploded in the dark around them, each detonation was followed by a hail of shrapnel. "You'd get under your helmet and hope you didn't get hit," recalls Leader. The shrapnel made a terrifying end-over-end whooshing sound as it rained down, and Leader, crouched behind the barrels, was finally walloped just above the knee by one of the fragments. "It hurt quite a bit, but, luckily, it was a small piece and it hit me flat. It would have done a lot of damage otherwise. When I picked it up, I saw that it was jagged on both ends like knife blades. I carried that piece of shrapnel around for awhile, but someplace or other I finally lost it and didn't get to bring it home as a souvenir."

Lieutenant Polaski rejoined Bravo One within a day or two, his injuries judged too minor at the aid station to rate a ticket out on a medevac. Platoon Sergeant Thornburgh complained to the company executive officer, who had by then replaced Thompson as acting company commander, and said that Polaski had lost the trust of the platoon, but the executive officer opted to give Polaski another chance. "I'll be damned if we didn't get mortared that very night, and Polaski totally broke down," recalls Thornburgh. Polaski shivered and cried inside the position he shared with his platoon sergeant and radioman, on the verge of a nervous breakdown. Thornburgh reported the situation to the acting company commander the next morning, and Polaski quickly disappeared, reassigned to the rear. In the heat of the moment, Thornburgh was absolutely impatient with an officer who behaved under fire as Polaski had. "It's taken me years to realize that it wasn't Polaski's fault that he wasn't equipped for the job he'd been handed," Thornburgh says now. "I don't hold it against him anymore. It could have happened to anybody. It could have happened to any of us at one time or another. If I saw Polaski today, I would shake his hand and hug his neck."

Part Four

OTHER ACTIONS

Chapter 16

Colonel Benson's brigade fought two battles during the offensive. One was in the capital itself. The other was in the countryside south of the city. There, elements of all of Benson's battalions—most notably Lieutenant Colonel Robert L. Adcock's 4th Battalion, 39th Infantry, which was reinforced by C/3-39th and a platoon from A/5-60th—endeavored to prevent additional enemy from joining the fight in Saigon. Benson also tasked Adcock with securing the fuel-tank farm at Nha Be on the Saigon River six kilometers southeast of the capital. Adcock moved a jump command group into Nha Be and weathered several mortar attacks, which ignited spectacular fires among the fuel tanks. Adcock's battalion actually saw its heaviest action not at Nha Be, but in the course of retaking Xom Co Diem, a remote hamlet seven kilometers to the southwest that had been seized by the communists at the beginning of Mini-Tet.

Lieutenant James M. Simmen of the 2nd Platoon, Company A, 5th Battalion (Mechanized), 60th Infantry, was ordered late in the morning on May 8, 1968, to move to the assistance of a South Vietnamese unit that had come under heavy fire while assaulting Xom Co Diem.

Nearing the area, Simmen's platoon halted several hundred meters short of Xom Co Diem on Route 230, which ran due south from Saigon. Up ahead, the ARVN soldiers could be seen pinned down in the flooded paddies to either side of the raised road. It looked to Simmen like they had spread out on line and launched a bold frontal assault, only to be stopped cold at the edge of the village. Casualties were heavy and included both the commander of the South Vietnamese unit and the U.S. major assigned as his advisor. "I made radio contact with the major," recalls Jim Simmen, "and since I had better commo [communication] with our fire support, and he'd just about had it anyway, he turned the show over to me."

Lieutenant Simmen and his shake 'n' bake platoon sergeant, Staff Sergeant Ronald W. Sherfey, set up two squads along the dikes to lay down a base of fire into the village, with the .50 gunners atop the tracks to fire over the heads of the ARVN. Then they continued down Route 230 with the two lead APCs. Simmen kept close behind his track for cover. His radio was inside the hull, with the cord stretched to him through the back door as he brought in a screen of artillery fire to cover the advance, mixing smoke shells with the high explosives.

Drawing abreast of the pinned-down assault line, the tracks halted and dismounted troops crawled through the paddies under the continuing enemy fire to drag the wounded and as many of the dead as could be reached back to the road. "You should have seen my brave men," Simmen wrote to his brother the next day. "They were going after wounded [ARVN] shot right in front of my track whom no one else would go after. I went too. . . . I've never seen such bravery and guts before, and I'm stunned by it."

After the casualties were loaded aboard the tracks, everyone pulled back and a medevac landed on the road. The U.S. advisor and his ARVN counterpart were among the wounded evacuated by the Huey. Airboats arrived on the tributary running under the road where Simmen was positioned, bearing First Lieutenant James W. Kirk's platoon from Company C, 4th Battalion, 39th Infantry Regiment. After conferring with Simmen, Kirk called battalion and recommended that the rest of Charlie Company be dispatched to the scene from Nha Be.

While awaiting the reinforcements, Lieutenant Simmen climbed into the cupola of his track where, on a raised road, the position provided an excellent view and requested another fire mission on Xom Co Diem. The platoon leader had a compass on a cord around his neck, but when he attempted to take a reading, the metal cupola caused the needle to twirl in an endless circle. Simmen was rising up, eyes fixed on the compass in his hand as he waited for the needle to straighten out, when an AK-47 round suddenly struck the cupola, catching him in the stomach. Expecting the worst, Simmen was relieved to see that he been injured only superficially. The bullet had fragmented on impact, and a single piece had zipped across his stomach, leaving a red line. Simmen joked with his guys about getting an easy Purple Heart.

Figures could be seen running around in the hamlet, and some of the troops firing M60s from the dikes reported hitting at least a couple. The prepping of the objective continued throughout. "I controlled two observation helicopters," Simmen wrote his brother, "four gunship helicopters, two jets, and put in over 1,000 rounds of artillery."

Captain Gerald Clark (the name has been changed), the brand-new commanding officer of Charlie Company, assumed control of the operation after arriving on the scene and outlined his plan for taking Xom Co Diem. Two tracks were to advance down the road to shield two squads from Kirk's platoon, which would fan out after entering the village, and blast the enemy soldiers from their holes.

Kirk and Simmen were appalled that Clark planned to bring the tracks within RPG range of Xom Co Diem. "I felt that if we got into close-quarters combat with the enemy," explains Simmen, "they'd blow the lead track, and then chaos would ensue since the tracks had lots of ordnance on board. The captain didn't appreciate the fact that we were sitting ducks for RPGs." Unable to convince Clark to change his plan, Simmen opted to use his command track to lead the attack. "It wasn't a good maneuver to have the platoon leader in front, but I didn't want to send someone else in because I felt what we were doing was going to end badly."

Captain Clark, a brave man whatever his tactical misjudgment, joined Simmen behind the lead vehicle as the two-track assault began. Staff Sergeant Sherfey remained in reserve with the other two personnel carriers. Lieutenant Kirk did likewise with the main body of Charlie Company.

Specialist Fourth Class Danny Avello (not his real name) manned the .50 on the lead track. "He's from California and used to lead the Hell's Angels," Simmen informed his brother. "Now he's leading us."

The driver of the lead track was Sergeant Ralph Richardson, a former police officer and natural-born soldier. "Richardson's a mean bastard," Simmen had written with admiration, adding that "We got killers in our platoon, and if they'd let us fight like we wanted we'd take 'em all on. . . ."

The lead track came to a halt and Lieutenant Simmen lifted the artillery upon reaching the entrance to the village. As the troops spread out along the dikes—they were under fire, plumes of water and mud exploding in the paddies—an enemy soldier materialized on the left flank, having jumped from a spider hole. He was quickly eliminated. "Everyone with a weapon shot at him," notes Simmen. "It was bedlam. I remember thinking, 'Oh, fuck, they're all over the damn place.'"

Avello commenced firing with the .50-caliber machine gun, nailing a VC who popped up with an RPG. Lieutenant Simmen was still behind the lead track when a rocket explosion left him standing in a cloud of smoke and dust, minus his radio handset and M16. Simmen felt no pain, but there was blood on his hands from unseen wounds after he patted himself down. The handset, connected to the radio inside the track by its tightly wound cord, had popped back inside the vehicle through the back door when knocked from Simmen's hand. Simmen climbed through the door to retrieve it and found that his radioman, Private First Class Steven J. Prescott, had taken refuge inside the personnel carrier. Prescott, in-country all of three weeks, looked at his platoon leader with fear-filled eyes, and Simmen quipped, "What do you think of this shit?"

In almost the same instant, there was a brilliant flash of white light inside the track, a rocket having penetrated the front armor. By all rights, Simmen should have been killed. Instead, he was able to dive out the back door and into the roadside ditch, though he was stunned, half-deaf, and splattered with shrapnel. "[T]hree of my men were right there helping me," Simmen wrote home. "I was frightened at the blood, but all the wounds were skin deep. . . . I got some pepper frags in the side and forearms. No sweat—just skinned up. . . . I was lucky. . . ."

Captain Clark caught some shrapnel as he stood at the back door of the track. Richardson was hit in the face, and Danny Avello, whose lower body was inside the hull as he fired the .50, had his leg blown off by the rocket-propelled grenade. "Richardson was temporarily blinded," Simmen wrote, "but he still dragged [Avello] off the track and dragged him off the road. A blind man consoling a man with a lost leg."

Staff Sergeant Sherfey appeared at Simmen's side, having run down the road from the reserve position to the smoldering track. "I always preached to my men about the day I [might] get hit," Simmen wrote. "I wanted my platoon to be able to function without me. They did. Before my track blew they rescued all the injured under heavy fire[.]" Simmen not only told Sherfey to evacuate the wounded, but also to "spread the men out as they were starting to huddle close to me, and there were still rockets going off in the rice paddy alongside us. I was afraid that we were presenting too much of a target. Sherfey took over and did an outstanding job."

Lieutenant Kirk also sprinted forward and, screaming like a berserker, stood in the road, trying to suppress the enemy fire with his CAR-15. The wounded were loaded into the second track, and the whole show was pulling back when Steve Prescott, the new radioman, tumbled out the back door of the lead track, having been overlooked in the chaos. Kirk doubled back to the man with the company artillery spotter and two or three grunts from Charlie Company. "The wounded guy was literally ashen gray," recalls Kirk. "We knew he wasn't going to make it, but what the fuck, it was worth a try and you don't leave anyone behind anyway. Each of us grabbed an arm or leg. The guys on the legs—and I was one of them—turned as we hustled back up the road so we could fire one-handed back into the village."

Back at the reserve position, Lieutenant Kirk's normally shaky medic rushed about, treating the wounded even as enemy fire continued to crack past from Xom Co Diem. "He sucked it up that day," notes Kirk, "and ran out there and did what he had to do. And then he sat there after it was all over and just shook."

Simmen lay on his back inside one of the tracks, too numb to function anymore, dying for a drink of water. No one seemed to have any water left, only beer. Simmen and four of his guys were slated for evacuation, along with Captain Clark and six wounded grunts from Charlie Company. The first Huey took aboard the six most serious casualties—including Steve Prescott, who did not survive—while a second medevac landed thirty minutes later to take out the last six. Simmen wrote that "I [felt] like a crudball leaving my men."

Simmen and Richardson, as well as Kirk and the other men who went back for Steve Prescott, would be awarded the Silver Star. Sherfey and a host of others, including Kirk's shaking medic, would be awarded the Bronze Star. Though the objective had not been secured, the VC had been severely punished: a body count of twelve was claimed by the 4th Battalion, 39th Infantry and another twenty-five by the gunships of Troop D, 3rd Squadron, 5th Cavalry.

Lieutenant Kirk, the acting company commander, marched Company C to a hamlet just west of Route 230. As the troops started up a small hill to set up for the night, villagers ran after them, shouting a warning; the hill was the site of an old French minefield. The villagers showed the GIs the rusting barbed wire and the signs marked "Mine." "They kept us from blundering in there and blowing ourselves up," recalls Kirk. "You can bet we shared our C-rations that night!"

The medevac on which Lieutenant Simmen was riding briefly touched down on a road during the flight to Saigon to pick up a casualty from another unit in another action. Simmen tensed, afraid they were going to be shot down just as he had begun to allow himself to relax. The medevac lifted off again without incident, then landed at the 3rd Field Hospital, where Simmen saw Sergeant Richardson walk blindly away from the Huey with his hands stretched out in front of him. Simmen took him by the arm and led him into the hospital. Richardson sat beside the lieutenant, who told him what was going on to keep him from getting more freaked out than he already was. The trooper on the other side of Simmen sat at attention, a bullet hole through his neck.

Simmen wrote his brother from the hospital that when the medics began cutting his fatigues off, "I caused a small panic here—they had a line of men carrying with both hands the frag grenades, incendiary grenades, white phosphorus [grenades] and flares I had in [the cargo pockets of] my pants." Simmen cautioned his brother not to tell their mother that he had been wounded. "And don't you worry," he added. "I was so damn lucky—no big holes. Somebody up there likes me. . . . They just gave me a local to remove the metal." Unaware of what had happened the day before, Simmen was surprised to find numerous casualties in the wards from Company A's action in southern Saigon. "Half my company is here," he noted. "The 5th/60th is the talk of the hospital again. We're always raising hell."

Lieutenant Kirk made radio contact at daybreak on May 9 with a forward air controller, who reported after buzzing in low over Xom Co Diem that everything looked quiet. It was, in fact, a perfectly beautiful and tranquil morning. To be on the safe side, Kirk nevertheless requested strafing runs on the village and watched as the jet fighters, using the road as a guide, streaked in "right on the deck, twenty mike-mikes [20mm automatic cannons] blazing. One of our guys who had taken his helmet off was hit in the head by a shell casing. There was a thunk, and he was out cold on the road. It was funny as hell, if you can appreciate the context of combat."

After the strafing runs, a large number of villagers proceeded up Route 230 toward Charlie Company. They were led by an old man with two broken legs who sat on the shoulders of a young man. The old man was identified by someone who could speak English as the village chief. "He wanted to thank us for pushing the VC out," recalls Kirk. "It was ironic—we have just shot the shit out of his village, and he's thanking us."

Kirk's troops, along with Captain Latham and C/3-39th, advanced on the objective behind a wall of artillery fire. The village was secured without further contact, and an entry was made in the brigade log which explained the village chief's seemingly inexplicable gratitude: "In the southern portion of the village, 2 families of civilians (6 civilians) were assassinated by the VC. Their hands were tied behind their backs, and they had all been shot in the head."

The enemy mortared Nha Be during the night and launched harassing attacks against the militia outposts in both Can Giuoc and Xom Co Diem. The latter attack was apparently a feint designed to draw attention away from the sampans that moved under cover of darkness through Xom Co Diem on a river leading to Saigon. Unbeknownst to the enemy, C/3-39th had established ambush positions along the river about a kilometer northwest of Xom Co Diem. The grunts fired the sampans up with M16s and M79s, sinking five and damaging one or two more. The ambushers claimed a body count of eight, and as noted in the brigade log, the Tiger Scout who inspected one of the sampans "states that there was enough food stuffs to feed 1 company of VC for 2 days."

Part Five

THE PANTHERS

Chapter 17

Colonel Benson was alerted by division headquarters before dawn on May 9, 1968, that as of eight that morning his brigade would assume responsibility for the easternmost section of District 8, Saigon. Since the beginning of the offensive, the hamlets in the area—part of the village of Ong Doi—had been the scene of heavy fighting between the enemy and an overmatched task force of Vietnamese Marines. Plans were hastily drawn up. With Adcock, Antila, and DeLuca already fully committed, Benson intended to clear Xom Ong Doi with Schmalhorst's battalion and the 2-47th Mechanized Infantry, commanded by Lieutenant Colonel John B. Tower, who was to be attached to the 3rd Brigade after road-marching in from Camp Bearcat. Benson tended to agree with intelligence estimates that two-thousand Viet Cong had occupied southern Saigon. "There was enough contact to justify those estimates," he recalls. "Instead of bringing in another brigade and having a line on the map, it was easier to attach additional battalions to my brigade and put the entire battle under my command."

Lieutenant Colonel Schmalhorst was overhead in his command ship when the slicks bearing Captain Greene and the lead platoon of Company A, 6th Battalion, 31st Infantry, landed on Highway 15 just east of Xom Ong Doi an hour before noon on May 9. The lift ships doubled back to Smoke to pick up the remaining two platoons of Alpha Company. The choppers took heavy fire en route to the landing zone, and when they returned to the firebase a fourth time for Captain Owen and the lead platoon of Company C, the pilots expressed considerable concern about going in again. "In the end, they did, but they changed their approach pattern and speed," recalls Owen. "I've been in a lot of helicopter assaults, but none that ever moved that fast and that low. It was a scary ride, even for us experienced folks. We were so low that if a VC had popped up from a spider hole to fire at the helicopter, the skids would have hit the barrel of his AK-47."

Colonel Benson, airborne in his own command ship, was informed that Companies A and C, minus the latter's detached platoon, were both on the ground as of 12:20 p.m. The 2-47th Mechanized Infantry began rolling out of Bearcat at about the same time. According to the plan, Schmalhorst's force was to proceed east on an unnamed road that ran along the south edge of Xom Ong Doi, a distance of three kilometers. The road linked Highway 15 with Route 230 and defined the western edge of the hamlet along which the Vietnamese Marines were deployed. Schmalhorst was given two hours to get into position. By that time, Tower's column was to have made its way through Saigon, across the Kinh Doi on Highway 15, and turned west onto Route 232. At that point, the column would take up positions along the north edge of Xom Ong Doi. The enemy would thus be boxed in with mechanized infantry to the north, straight-leg grunts to the south, and Vietnamese Marines to the west. For the Viet Cong to escape from the eastern side of the village would mean crossing a wide river, the Rach Bang, and exposing themselves to artillery fire and gunships from the 7th Squadron, 1st Cavalry.

Apparently uninterested in retreat, the enemy fired on the Vietnamese Marines from western Xom Ong Doi. Scout ships spotted a VC platoon moving into position among the houses and vegetation on a tadpole-shaped island at the southern edge of the village. They also spotted machine-gun and recoilless-rifle teams setting up where Route 230 cut south from the canal road at the northwest corner of Xom Ong Doi. A spotter plane buzzing over the area reported Viet Cong soldiers on roof tops and in trees, firing on the Hueys and Cobras. The guerrillas took cover when the gunships rolled in on them. At one point, as recorded in the brigade log, the 7th of the 1st Cav reported to Benson's headquarters that one of its gunships "has reconned by fire [near the junction of Routes 230 and 232] without drawing ground fire. However, [the pilot] feels VC are in area waiting for troops to enter."

Captain Greene and Company A began marching west on the unnamed road that linked Highway 15 with Route 230, followed by Captain Owen and Company C. At 2:15 p.m., Greene, nearing the point where the road terminated against Route 230, reported catching some stray rounds from the ongoing exchange between the VC and the Vietnamese Marines. Pressing on against a stream of fleeing civilians, Greene's company soon came under direct enemy fire from the tadpole-shaped island a hundred meters away on the right flank. The grunts moved off the road and into the grassy wetlands that led to the river along the south edge of the island. They began returning fire into the nippa palm along the opposite shore and the white stucco buildings visible behind the vegetation.

Captain Owen's company also came under fire, and the grunts of Company C, going to the prone or to one knee in the mud and grass along the road, began blazing away across the river. All the while, refugees streamed past, and some were hit by the incoming fire. For dragging the wounded civilians to cover, Private First Class Jeffery J. Quinn of Company A and Staff Sergeant Dennis Meyer, a squad leader in Charlie Hunter Company, were subsequently awarded Army Commendation Medals.

As the exchange dragged on, bullets thumped into one of Owen's riflemen and four of Greene's. The fire from across the river, though accurate, was relatively sporadic; the single shots, punctuated by bursts from a light machine gun, were just enough to keep movement to a minimum. "I'm sure that as excited as we were, our volume of fire actually exceeded the incoming," notes Al Olson. "We could see people running in and around in the buildings across the river. I cannot categorically state that they were enemy soldiers—but we sure thought they were."

Second Lieutenant Anthony Eric Belt, the forward observer, "was the company clown until the situation got serious," notes Owen, "and then he was all business." When the shooting started, Belt had dashed between two of the thatch hootches along the road and on toward the river separating the good guys from the bad guys. "The whole company was in tall grass except for me and my RTO," recalls Belt, who ended up face down in a patch of short grass "in clear view of the enemy with bullets hitting all around us. The VC were entrenched on the other side of the river, and had an especially good machine-gun position out on a tall-grass peninsula that had our men pinned down."

Grabbing the radio handset, Lieutenant Belt tried to call in a fire mission on the machine-gun position, but communication was poor with the firing battery at Smoke. The conversation kept breaking up. "I realized that the fifteen-foot antenna was going to be necessary if I was going to get any fire," recalls Belt. When Belt told his radioman that they were going to have to get up in the fire and switch antennas, "the kid thought I was nuts, but did just as I asked. He sat up and I knelt beside him, unfolded the long antenna [from the canvas utility bag strapped under the radio], and disconnected the short one."

Back at the prone, Lieutenant Belt established good communication with the firing battery and, within a minute, had called in a white-phosphorus marking round, then adjusted a high-explosive round on the peninsula. At that point, Belt "called in a Battery Four, which is four rounds from each of the six guns in the 105 battery coming in as fast as the crews could reload and fire. The first twenty-four rounds hit right on the river bank. Tall pillars of black mud went up thirty feet, and one round hit the VC machine gunner on the peninsula who was keeping everyone pinned down. You could see his body and the machine gun fly up as the round exploded. I kept the fire coming and the entire company looked toward me and cheered."

After the machine gun had been silenced, Captain Owen radioed in a body count of three—his company's first kills since being deployed to the war zone—then resisted battalion's instructions to remain in place. Owen instead secured permission to move Company C past the rear of Company A and, after turning right on Route 230, to proceed over a small bridge that spanned the unnamed river running past the south side of the tadpole-shaped island. There, the company was to get into position to place flanking fire on the Viet Cong in southern Xom Ong Doi.

Once across the bridge, Lieutenant May and the 1st Platoon started down a road into the western side of the village. The platoon almost immediately came under heavy fire and fell back on order to a drainage ditch that was knee-deep with weeds and stagnant water and ran along the road. Lieutenant May called in a team of gunships, but it was difficult to pinpoint where the enemy fire was coming from amid the houses, and the strafing runs seemed to have little effect. Captain Owen finally sent Lieutenant Gale forward, but the 3rd Platoon also came under heavy fire and Gale and his grunts were forced to jump into the drainage ditch with rounds zipping and cracking just overhead. The splashing stirred up a large snake that crawled directly over squad leader Al Olson's lap and on down the line, trying to get away. Terrified that the snake might bite, Olson jumped up and struck at the apparition with his rifle only to be forced back down in the ditch by the incoming fire.

Lieutenant Gale and his platoon were returning fire when the call went up from Lieutenant May's platoon for more ammo. Several of Gale's grunts draped themselves with multiple M16 and M60 bandoliers and started down the drainage ditch on all fours. Privates First Class Leslie J. Haar and James W. Petty were wounded along the way, but continued forward with the other ammo-bearers and were later awarded the Bronze Star to go with their Purple Hearts. The ammo-eating torrent of return fire seemed to have no effect on the enemy, and Owen finally instructed Gale and May to pull back. "We were terribly hot and thirsty by then," notes Al Olson. "Water was needed almost as much as ammunition. Most of us had drained our canteens fighting the heat and excitement."

Getting reorganized, Captain Owen placed Lieutenant May's platoon on line with Lieutenant Gale's in the single row of houses along Route 230. The troops took up positions behind fences and the corners of buildings, machine-gun teams up on rooftops. While Company A maintained its fire on the tadpole-shaped island from the south, Charlie Hunter Company commenced firing from the west with M16s, M60s, and M79s. The enemy positions having been pinpointed by the gunships, the VC soldiers finally began to pull out under the onslaught, but as they came scuttling from their cover, individual grunts were able to line up individual guerrillas in their rifle sights. The firing was not all one way. "I still remember my jaded reaction to having three rounds hit slightly above and to my left while I was leaning against the wall behind my machine-gun team and lighting a cigarette," writes Robert Magdaleno, then a squad leader in Lieutenant May's platoon positioned atop a building. In another instance, Magdaleno ducked behind a large earthen jar filled with rainwater only to get wetted down when a burst of gunfire shattered the jar.

As the exchange continued, Magdaleno was standing next to his M60 team "when I saw a small group of children apparently being shoved out from cover [and used as human shields] by a desperate VC. Because the gunner was aiming at that very building, I kicked the gun to keep him from hitting what I had identified as children but what he might have seen only as targets moving from cover in the heat of the moment. None of the children were hit—at least not at that moment that I was watching them."

Captain Owen moved among the buildings with his command group as he checked with his platoon leaders and made sure everyone was firing in the right direction. Charlie Hunter was credited with fifteen kills by the end of the action. "I was close enough to see a couple of them go down myself," says Owen. The firefight had turned into a slaughter. "It got to the point that I felt truly sorry for the poor bastards. After the action was over, one of my soldiers made the comment that it had been like being back on the rifle range with popup targets."

Chapter 18

The move was organized quickly but efficiently and executed at top speed. Less than an hour elapsed, in fact, between the time Lieutenant Colonel Tower was given his marching orders at division headquarters and when the 2-47th Mechanized Infantry began rolling out of Camp Bearcat, bound for Saigon.

Tower had monitored the column's progress from his helicopter while his operations officer, Major William W. Jones personally led the column in his track, as he would be able to guide the column through Saigon without delay or wrong turns, having traveled the route many times before. Captain James B. Craig followed with Company B. Tower's executive officer, Major William H. Riedl, was next in line with the battalion's support elements, and Captain Harold S. Morgan brought up the rear with Company C. The level of anticipation was terrific, the urgency of the mission was obvious, and the troops riding atop the tracks couldn't help but wonder which of them might shortly end up in a body bag. Their turn had finally come around again, it seemed, for the battalion was normally tasked with securing division headquarters and had seen little combat since the Tet Offensive.

As was to be expected, units operating deep in the delta tended to dismiss Lieutenant Colonel Tower's battalion as a palace-guard outfit. Not exactly. However mundane the battalion's security mission might have been, the pace of operations—mounted and dismounted sweeps, convoy security, night patrols along the roadways to deter mining—was physically demanding. Additionally, the local guerrillas kept nerves on edge by pushing up earthen roadblocks, which were sometimes booby-trapped and sometimes not, and ambushing the occasional roadrunner patrol with AK-47s and RPGs, then vanishing as the night was noisily stitched with return fire and Hueys landed for the casualties.

Tower's was a well-led battalion with solid morale, but the GIs of Companies B and C were naturally grateful when withdrawn to Bearcat for a maintenance standdown on the morning of May 9. "It was our first standdown since Tet," notes Bruce Isenhoff. "We were all looking forward to taking it easy for a few days. We were going to be able to take showers, spend time in the beer garden, and sleep in tents with cots, wooden floors, and mosquito netting."

The standdown had barely begun, however, when the alert siren began howling, the signal to assemble at the motor pool. After being briefed at battalion, Captains Craig and Morgan joined their troops and gave the word to saddle up: the entire battalion—minus Company A, which was securing an engineer unit out in the boondocks—was going to Saigon.

A number of troopers who'd left the battalion area missed the alert. Specialist Fourth Class Jimmy R. Dye, a squad leader in Bravo Company, happened to be ambling back after visiting the Post Exchange when he saw that "all the tracks in the motor pool was up and runnin' and people was jumpin' on 'em. I said, 'What the hell's goin' on?' " Dye rushed to join his squad, but "we left a lot of people in the platoon behind. As a matter of fact, they were grabbin' warm bodies to make up for the people who weren't there. You might have been a cook, but you were going to be a rifleman that day." Dye had a bad case of the flu, but it never occurred to him to go on sick call. The driver of his track, a good trooper named Ronald Bates, didn't object to moving out either, even though he only had three days left on his tour. "He never bitched, never said a word," recalls Dye. "He just cranked it up and moved out with the rest of 'em."

First Lieutenant Guy O. Corry of the 1st Platoon, Company C, told his driver, Bruce Isenhoff, to "Fire it up, Ike," then announced with obvious relish: "We're gonna kill some Charlies today."

As the tracks began rolling out of the motor pool, Corry opened a beer for himself and another for Isenhoff. Exiting the camp gate, Isenhoff asked where they were going, and Lieutenant Corry intoned: "Saigon."

Hoping for the best, Isenhoff—a draftee—asked if they were going to be escorting a convoy. "Nope," Corry answered cryptically, enjoying the mystery, then joked: "You need another beer?"

Lieutenant Corry was short and compact, with the strength and agility of a wrestler, and incredibly gungho. Corry had marked his tracks as Rommel's Fox I, II, III, and IV in honor of Field Marshall Erwin Rommel, and seemed to want to go down in history himself as the greatest combat officer of the Vietnam War. "When I saw the movie *Forrest Gump*, I had to laugh," notes Isenhoff. "Whoever dreamed up the character of Lieutenant Dan must have had Guy Corry in mind. Corry lobbied to have our platoon lead all the maneuvers that we launched as a company. He was usually granted his request. We were the company's lead platoon once again the day we headed for Saigon."

As the lieutenant's driver, Isenhoff was closer to Corry than the other GIs. They talked as friends rather than as commander and subordinate, and Corry tended to use Isenhoff as a sounding board. Corry even asked Isenhoff what the men thought about him personally. In truth, they both respected and resented the platoon leader. "The rest of the guys did not appreciate Lieutenant Corry's lust for the mission," explains Isenhoff. "There seemed to be enough crap coming our way without being volunteered to jump into it with both feet. On the other hand, you could not help but catch the enthusiasm with which Corry attacked everything he did. Corry's drive kept us alert because if a mission was coming down, we knew that we would be involved in it right from the start. This gave us a degree of esprit de corps that elevated our platoon just a little above the rest of Company C—in my mind, anyway."

The road march took about an hour. The radio crackled all the while with instructions about checkpoints, speeds, and intervals as the column proceeded from Bearcat to Long Binh. The column turned onto Route 316, crossed the Nai River, and then, with twenty-five kilometers to go, went to full throttle and thundered down the open road toward Saigon. Upon crossing the Newport Bridge, Major Jones neatly led the battalion through the confusing maze of streets to Highway 15, which followed the inside curves of the Saigon River through bustling downtown Saigon. "MPs and Vietnamese Police stopped traffic and let us speed through," notes Robert A. Dyson, a former track commander in Company B. "We joked that we were going to guard the U.S. Embassy, but deep down we knew we were in for heavy fighting."

Major Riedl had his driver pull over and watched amused as the column roared around a traffic circle in the wrong direction. With so much armor moving so fast through such a crowded part of the city, he was amazed that no cars were flattened or otherwise banged up, and no pedestrians sent to the hospital. When the column rolled past hotels where U.S. support personnel were quartered, "the guys would be out on the balconies," notes Jimmy Dye, "drinking beer and cheering us on: 'Go get 'em!' " In contrast, the Vietnamese on busy sidewalks or zipping past on mopeds didn't give the procession of personnel carriers a second glance. The GIs did, however, garner some lusty waves and shouts from a flock of bar girls. Private First Class John E. Driessler chalked up their enthusiasm to the fact that the offensive and resulting curfew were keeping the garrison troops away from the city's bars and brothels. He jokes that "the sooner the enemy were routed and put on their way, the sooner business could proceed as usual. The incongruity of it all just tickled me."

Four months in command at the time, Lieutenant Colonel Tower had already impressed most of his officers as "one hell of a warrior." Possessing a pugnacious grin, a keen sense of humor, and an aggressive, magnetic personality, John Tower might have come off as an ambitious and decidedly arrogant officer on the fast track. He was also, notes Bill Riedl, "a fiery little guy and an earthy soldier's soldier, certainly not the typical kind of lieutenant colonel who came to get his command ticket punched in Vietnam."

Tower was the son of Canadian immigrants. He lost his father when he was still a child; his widowed mother remarried and moved with her new husband to Dedham, Massachusetts. Tower enlisted after high school on the assumption that he would be drafted anyway. As it happened, he loved the army and, after duty as a paratrooper with the 101st Airborne Division, earned an appointment to OCS in 1953.

As a junior officer, Tower served primarily with infantry and airborne units. Promoted early to major and accumulating an undergraduate and master's degree along the way, he graduated at the top of his class from Command and General Staff College. Tower was subsequently assigned as a foreign exchange officer, and spent 1964–1966 proudly commanding a company in the British Army. Pinning on his silver oak leaves, Tower served next at the Pentagon. Having secured the ultimate assignment for an officer of his rank, Lieutenant Colonel John Tower, age thirty-nine, bid goodbye to his wife and two daughters following his tour at the Pentagon and, fresh off the plane, took command of the 2nd Battalion (Mechanized), 47th Infantry Regiment, 9th Infantry Division at Camp Bearcat, Vietnam, on January 3, 1968.

The new colonel came on strong from the word go. Introducing himself to his officers, Tower told them in his clipped, no-nonsense Massachusetts accent that his job was to find the "Cong" and their job was to kill them, and to rest assured that he *would* find them. The trim vanes of the battalion's personnel carriers sported leaping black panthers. In that spirit, Tower had his radio call sign Panther 6 stenciled on the back of his jeep, along with the slogan he had adopted for his command: Uptight and Ready to Fight.

Lieutenant Colonel Tower was soon put to the test when his Black Panthers were mobilized to defend the Bien Hoa–Long Binh complex on the first morning of the Tet Offensive. Though shot down twice, Tower climbed into a third helicopter and continued to maintain control of his battalion as it fought several simultaneous and fast-paced battles. Major Jones and Company A, for one, linked up with a company from the 199th Light Infantry Brigade and helped destroy a VC battalion that had tried during the night to penetrate the northeast perimeter of Long Binh. Company B (minus one platoon) hunted the sappers who had gotten into the sprawling ammunition storage area on the east side of Long Binh, while Company C engaged snipers and RPG teams in a wild street brawl just outside Bien Hoa Airbase.

Company B's detached platoon, meanwhile, was directed to clean out snipers in a hamlet along the northwest edge of Long Binh. Instead of finding a handful of snipers, the platoon rolled up on a guerrilla battalion poised for a belated sunrise assault across Route 316 into the headquarters of II Field Force. The surprise engagement turned into a murderous, pointblank slugging match. First Lieutenant Brice H. Barnes' battalion scout platoon joined the embattled infantry platoon, at which point both groups of tracks pressed forward on line behind a screen of gunship fire, methodically eliminating the enemy. When the dust settled, three troopers and seventy-seven guerrillas were dead, and several dozen dazed and wounded enemy soldiers had been captured.

Moving on, the scout platoon was ambushed in another roadside hamlet. Four tracks were knocked out by rockets and eleven men were wounded, including Barnes. Staff Sergeant Robert W. Schultz charged headlong into the ambushers and was killed while taking out two machine-gun positions with frags and a captured AK-47. Taking cover in several houses, the scouts furiously returned fire at those buildings in which the enemy was concealed until gunships allowed them to escape the kill zone aboard their four remaining personnel carriers. Barnes, Schultz, and a third scout who had stood in full view of the enemy to fire LAWs, would all receive the Distinguished Service Cross.

As for Tower, he was personally decorated with the Silver Star by General Ewell. Tower had the right stuff indeed in Ewell's book, and his tour with the Panthers would be slightly abbreviated, for Ewell subsequently selected him for the plum position of division G3. "John Tower was a *stud*," declares Gunfighter Emerson. "He was a cocky, flamboyant little guy who could talk the talk and walk the walk—just a magnificent guy."

Tower's reputation at the troop level was more mixed. "The colonel was a little rooster, a little dictator," according to former draftee Richard Uhlich. "You can imagine how us GIs felt about him: we were down on the ground, and the colonel was always up in his little bubble helicopter."

Billy C. Reid, formerly part of the heavy-mortar platoon, remembers the colonel showing a more human face on those occasions when he landed to talk and share a few beers with the GIs. "Incidentally, I had been briefed on the colonel's 'alcohol consumption policy' upon reporting to the battalion," notes Reid. "It went like this: you could drink as much as you wanted, anytime you wanted, as long as it didn't interfere with your duties, but God help you if you were ever too intoxicated to perform when the time came."

Lieutenant Colonel Tower was so blunt and hard-driving that one platoon leader was left with the impression that Panther 6 looked upon his lieutenants as "expendable items." Sergeant First Class William Nelson Butler, on the other hand, considered Tower to be "one of the few battalion commanders who had some actual feelings for the individual soldiers." Butler had been recommended for the Silver Star for Tet. By the time the award was approved, he had been reassigned as an ARVN advisor. Instead of simply having the medal forwarded along, "Tower took the time to sit down and handwrite me a note of apology that he sent along with my Silver Star. He said that he regretted that he could not have awarded it to me personally. I still have the note and the envelope it came in."

Lieutenant Colonel Tower was a commander who believed in fighting hard and playing hard, and he and his officers could get pretty raucous in the rear between operations. Much booze flowed, and old black-and-white stag movies so dated as to be considered hilarious were shown. "Tower was a banty rooster and suffered a bit from the little-man's syndrome," remembers Brice Barnes. "He played volleyball and bridge and war with about the same intensity. The little bastard could jump about eight feet straight up in the air, and would spike the ball from up there, and he'd love to hurt you—as much as you can hurt somebody with a volleyball—if he could spike you. I hated him," continues Barnes, "because he made us work so hard, but at the same time I absolutely loved the man because he was technically and tactically very proficient, and you never doubted his commitment to the troops. He was gutsy, too, and he knew how to fight. He knew how to do war. He had the ability to take people all the way to their limit, and slack off a little bit, then push them hard again. He was a tough, tough commander, but if people are tough and know their jobs— and that describes John Tower—then most soldiers will follow them willingly."

If Tower was the battalion's Dutch uncle, then Major Riedl was its big brother. Cheerful, encouraging, energetic, and handsome, Bill Riedl was from middle-class Worchester, Massachusetts, and was a fraternity member and football player who had married his high-school sweetheart before earning a Reserved Officer Training Corps commission from Norwich University in Vermont. "Major Riedl was a helluva nice guy," recalls Anthony Midkiff, a career soldier who manned the .50 on the executive officer's track. "He was people oriented, a soldier-first kind of officer. His message was always to take care of the soldier."

The battalion operations officer, Major Jones, was a good ol' boy, highly respected and immensely popular. He used to joke that he'd never make colonel because he wouldn't play military politics. Bill Jones had been raised on a tobacco farm in Newport, Tennessee, enlisted out of high school, and had made sergeant before graduating from OCS. Going the airborne-ranger route, Jones earned his combat infantryman badge and became fluent in Vietnamese while commanding a Special Forces A-team on the Cambodian border early in the war. Celebrated for leading from the front, the thirty-year-old major would win three Silver Stars and four Bronze Stars during his second tour in Vietnam. "Jones was crazy," exclaims Jim Craig. "I mean, he was something else!"

Jones was casual and easy-going with his subordinates, and strong-willed when he disagreed with his superiors, which might explain the subtle tension that existed between him and Lieutenant Colonel John Tower. "Old John B. was a man of small stature with a tremendous ego—a Napoleonic complex," according to Jones. "He wanted there to be no doubt that he was the commander, and that he was in charge of everybody and everything that went on. He didn't mince words. He wanted everything to happen exactly when he said it was going to happen, and, of course, things don't always work out that way. For all that," Jones adds, "I thought John was an excellent battalion commander. He was more attuned than most to intelligence, enemy capabilities, and what have you. He was by far the most capable and competent battalion commander that I served under—even if he could be a difficult little shit sometimes."

Exiting the downtown area, the battalion column presently passed through grimy industrial sites and shabby residential neighborhoods. Major Jones led the column over the Kinh Doi near the point where it meets the Saigon River, then turned left onto Route 232 from Highway 15. After Jones crossed a small bridge that spanned a tributary, Tower ordered him to pull into a clearing that was elevated about a foot above the standing water of the adjacent paddies to establish a rally point and field command post. Company B stopped on the road to get organized before pushing on; its mission as the battalion's point element was to make contact with whatever enemy force was down the road in Xom Ong Doi.

Major Riedl and the battalion support elements, as well as Company C, sat idling on the blacktop behind Company B. Tower, Riedl, and Jones had much faith in the two company commanders on the scene. Captain Morgan, a stolid Texan who knew his infantry and looked out for his people, had assumed command of Company C shortly after the Tet Offensive.

Captain Craig of Company B was from Springfield, Massachusetts. The son of a college professor and a woman from a family of old money, rich-kid Jim Craig flunked out of three colleges. "I was only interested in beer and girls," Craig explains. Afterward, his father marched him down to the local recruiting office in an attempt to straighten him out, giving no thought at the time to the distant little war in Vietnam. Loving the excitement and deciding to go career, Craig served two years as a paratrooper before being selected for OCS.

Jim Craig had barely pinned on his bars when he received his orders to Vietnam. His parents were upset, for as intellectuals, they both opposed the war, but he was raring to go. Although he was wounded twice, Craig managed to survive a hair-raising tour as a rifle platoon leader in Gunfighter Emerson's battalion in the 101st Airborne. Newly married to an army nurse and newly promoted, Craig was recruited into the Old Reliables by Emerson. Assigned to the Black Panthers as a staff officer (while his wife was assigned to a nearby evacuation hospital), he immediately let it be known that he wanted a line company. Tower obliged Craig only five days before the road march to Saigon. At first glance, the troops were divided down the middle about Captain Craig, some impressed that he seemed to know his stuff, others put off by what they took to be an arrogant undertone to his personality. For the record, Jones, never one afraid to call a spade a spade, thought Craig "a very competent guy. He was an outgoing, cheerful person, and a good company commander."

Hundreds of terrified townspeople streamed past the tracks on the road, a huge column of black smoke belching from the neighborhood they had fled. "All right, everybody get your shit uptight," Captain Craig intoned over the radio. "Word is that there's a VC company in the area."

Two point men moved well forward of the lead track as the advance began. Only drivers and gunners remained on the personnel carriers. The rest of the troops moved in column along either shoulder of the road, the canal to their right, buildings their left. Specialist Fourth Class Philip Streuding of the 2nd Platoon, Company B, was manning the .50-cal on the lead track. The point team passed an overturned jeep, where two dead policemen sprawled beside the wreck. *This is it,* Streuding thought, but it wasn't—not yet. Bravo Company continued on past several dead civilians and a scattering of slaughtered chickens and ducks, hogs, and water buffaloes. The hamlet had apparently been the scene of some kind of rampage by the Viet Cong. "There was a guy in a ditch who looked like he had been hacked to death with a machete," recalls Jimmy Dye, who would never forget "the stench of rotting bodies and rotting animals."

The enemy was lying in wait a kilometer down the canal road. Those guerrillas in the houses on the left flank of Craig's column held their fire, waiting until the point team had walked into the gun sights of those positioned along Route 230, the roadway running south from Route 232. Upon reaching the intersection at 2:20 p.m., May 9, 1968, the two point men, Private First Class Larry G. Caldwell and Specialist Fourth Class George W. Darnell Jr. were cut down in a sudden fusillade of AK-47 fire.

To face the ambushers directly, the driver of the lead track roared around the corner at a shout from Phil Streuding and jerked to a stop on one side of the street, while the second track in line did the same on the other side. Streuding and the other gunner commenced firing with the .50-cals, stitching every window and door behind which there might be a VC. The wall of the corner house to Streuding's right disintegrated in front of the barrel of his machine gun, revealing a moped and a large drum of gasoline inside the building. Streuding put his next burst into the barrel. "There was a hell of an explosion," he recounts, "but I knew no one would be coming through the flames, and with my flank secure, I was able to concentrate my fire more on what was in front of me."

The ambush having been initiated, the enemy opened fire along the entire column, which immediately stopped, pivoted to face the houses on the left, and began returning fire. "The gooks were right on top of us," recalls Lewis W. Hosler. "You could see them popping up on rooftops to fire down at us." Specialist Fourth Class Hosler, a seasoned veteran on his second tour, fired the machine gun on his track "right over the heads of the guys in the ditch in front of me. We had men pinned down in the drainage ditches on both sides of the road. We had a lot of people just hiding any place they could until we suppressed the fire."

Jimmy Dye crouched beside his track, trying to make himself as small a target as possible as he fired his M16. "You're taught to automatically return fire," says Dye. "You're not thinking, you're just reacting." Specialist Fourth Class Paul J. Ianni pounded away above Dye's head with the .50-cal as Ron Bates, their short-timer driver, kept the ammo coming. Friend and foe were separated by only thirty or forty feet, fighting it out at pointblank range in a flurry of smoke, dust, and ricocheting bullets. The urgent shouts of men could be heard, hollering that they needed more ammunition, had spotted a muzzle flash in a particular window, or a bareheaded figure with an AK-47 rising from the spider holes the enemy had dug in the narrow alleys between the buildings. Says Dye: "It was a madhouse."

Facing an open street near the front of the column, Hosler's track became a prime target. "Hosler received an incredible amount of fire," notes Bob Dyson, who was amazed that no matter how many times Hosler had to duck, he always popped right back up to keep laying down fire with his .50-caliber machine gun. "I did not think he was going to survive." Hosler was wounded near the beginning of the battle by a fragment of unknown origin. "It got me in the forearm," he recalls. "It wasn't but a couple inches deep. No big deal. It just burned like hell." Later, Hosler became the target of a rooftop sniper who emptied the thirty-round magazine in his AK-47 at him in a single burst. One round that went past Hosler's ear "cracked so loud, I thought, 'I'm dead, sure in hell.' But I wasn't, and there wasn't anything to do but get down a little lower and keep firing. We took so much fire that when it was all over with, the front of my track looked like a porcupine from all the rounds sticking in it. They had embedded right in the aluminum armor."

First Lieutenant Paul H. Bowman, the company's forward observer, huddled against the north shoulder of the road with several other men, including a platoon leader who had been shot in the leg. Disregarding the pain of an obviously serious wound, the platoon leader said to the troops who were returning fire, "Give me some magazines. At least I can load 'em."

Finally able to crawl to the command track, Bowman found Captain Craig crouched on what passed for the safe side and requesting permission from battalion to pull back down the street. Bowman recalls asking Craig about the location of other friendly units in the area so he could call in the artillery, but getting no precise answers. It seemed to Bowman that Craig, only five days back in the game, was momentarily dumbfounded by the unrelenting hail of fire.

Frustrated, Lieutenant Bowman crawled on to his own radioman, grabbed the handset, requested a fire mission, and getting a white-phosphorous marking round, he began adjusting the high explosives. To make sure the shells were falling where needed, Bowman darted across the street into a shack from which he could shout adjustments back to his radioman. The shack turned out to be a pig pen, and Bowman took cover behind the cement butcher's platform as an enemy machine gunner to his immediate front fired bursts through the thin walls. Bowman walked shells toward the gun position, the last of which splattered his own position with debris, "provided some relief from the enemy fire hitting the shack," the former artilleryman recalls." I was able to continue calling in artillery, first farther out to the front before sweeping the barrage to the right and clearing the area in front of the lead platoon. I didn't find out till later that I accidentally landed some artillery on Charlie Company."

Having gone to the prone in front of his track, John Driessler lay frozen as rounds gouged out chunks of asphalt only inches away. Driessler then heard his platoon leader shouting at him to return fire, and coming up to one knee, he began firing in the same general direction as everyone else. In short order, a burst of automatic-weapons fire splattered a nearby track, and Driessler caught a spray of little fragments of either the bullets or the aluminum hull in the upper back and along his spine. Though barely breaking the skin, the wounds put the fear in him because he had no idea in the heat of the moment how badly he'd been injured. "If I had any common sense," Driessler recounts, "I would have found some cover at that point, but I was a stupid nineteen-year-old kid and did not want to appear to be a coward, so I kept returning fire."

Others were less concerned with appearances. At one point in the chaos, Driessler saw both his platoon leader and platoon sergeant, who was an older career man, take refuge in the lieutenant's track even as Bob Dyson stood in the command cupola, firing the .50-caliber machine gun. The lieutenant's radioman tried to climb inside, too. Because the whip antenna flapping from the PRC-25 radio on the radioman's back wouldn't work inside the track, the lieutenant physically booted him back out the door, shouting, "I need you out there!"

Disgusted and amused by the spectacle, Driessler burst out laughing. In contrast, Bob Dyson—a former college student from the suburbs of Long Island, New York—respected the platoon leader and saw him as a young officer doing his best under trying circumstances. Dyson recalls the lieutenant getting defensive when Driessler later made a cutting remark about the hiding-in-the-track incident, but cautions that "*everybody* sought cover for a short respite at one time or another during that firefight. The incoming fire was the heaviest I experienced during two tours in Vietnam." The battle was so intense "that gun smoke rose in clouds and made me nauseous," notes Dyson. "I was hit twice, once in the cheek by shrapnel—it was spent, so it caused no injury—and again

in the forearm by flying glass when I was reloading the .50-caliber
machine gun. After I finished reloading, I took a water break inside the
track until the incoming settled down for the moment. It was obvious
that there was more than one VC company in there. Later, we were told
that there was a battalion of NVA."

Captain Craig himself slid under his track during a particularly heavy
salvo of enemy fire. Craig spent most of the battle tucked behind his track
with his ears ringing from the .50 and his forearms blistered from the spent
brass spilling off the deck. Having a handset in each fist, he maintained contact with his platoon leaders, organized the removal of the wounded to the
battalion rally point where medevacs could land, and directed the fire of
gunships that arrived from Troop D, 3rd Squadron, 5th Cavalry.

Notwithstanding the incoming fire, Craig was expected to provide situation reports to the senior officers who were stacked up above the battle in
their command ships. "The battalion commander was in a helicopter,"
recounts Craig. "The brigade commander was in a helicopter. The division
commander was in a helicopter. Word was that there was even somebody
from corps buzzing around the area. And they're all trying to talk to *me*.
They all had my frequency. It was a zoo."

At one point, Company B came under heavy fire from across the Kinh
Doi. As some of the tracks spun around to reply in kind, tracers were soon
flying thickly in both directions over the canal. Lewis Hosler dropped inside
his personnel carrier, grabbed several LAWs, and launched them while kneeling on the lowered back ramp of the APC. His target was a pair of stone
columns. There were any number of figures in olive-drab with weapons
"hustling down toward the river," recounts Hosler. "It looked like they were
taking up positions around those columns. I know I hit in amongst them
with the LAWs."

Captain Craig got a call from Tower, who wanted to know if he was firing across the canal. Craig answered in the affirmative, and Tower ordered
him to cease fire because there were ARVN sweeping the north bank of the
Kinh Doi. The fire from Company B lessened, then rose to full fury again,
there having been no corresponding decrease in the fire being received from
the other side of the canal. It remains unclear if Company B was being shot
at by ARVN who were responding to stray fire zipping across the canal from
the enemy facing the personnel carriers, or if enemy soldiers on the north
side of the canal had slipped between the two forces to provoke just such
an intramural firefight. Several soldiers who appeared to be North
Vietnamese regulars were spotted on a pier jutting into the canal from the
north bank, and a dismounted trooper named Edward Barry raked them

with his M60. One of the soldiers flipped into the canal. Another lay crumpled on the pier as his comrades raced back to shore. Many of the GIs were unconcerned about the possibility that they had fired up their allies. "The ARVN were not our favorite type of people over there," explains Jimmy Dye. "Some of the ARVN, I'd like to shoot them. They'd steal from you. They'd steal the nickels off a dead man."

Specialist Fourth Class Timothy Burke, the forward observer attached to Company B from the battalion's heavy-mortar platoon, had attempted to call for fire when the shooting started. Unable to get through, Burke notes that he "ended up fighting as a rifleman—the only one there who had his own RTO." Burke's radioman was a "little Jamaican named Weir. This was his first action, but he never froze. When I moved, he always moved right with me with his radio and M79."

Having maneuvered to the front of the column, Burke threw several ammo boxes to a machine gunner, who was at the prone on the road and pouring fire into the buildings with his M60. The machine gunner had no cover whatsoever, and Burke motioned for him to join the riflemen firing from the drainage ditch on the north side of the road before clambering into the ditch himself with Weir. The two point men were sprawled on the road beyond the tracks. One was still moving a bit. During a lull in the enemy fire, Specialist Fifth Class Phillip Rogers—a black medic known for his dedication and good cheer—dragged the rifleman to cover in the drainage ditch, "but when we turned him over," recounts Burke, "it was obvious that he was dead, and what we had thought was breathing was just post-mortem spasms." As John Driessler recalls the incident, the point man was still clinging to life, and a litter team started rearward with the casualty. The team took cover along the way beside Driessler, who was down in the roadside ditch, firing his M16. The wounded man was shaking, a bullet having skimmed the top of his head. "I could see cerebral fluid leaking from his skull," notes Driessler. Shouting at several men tucked behind a fence to lay down cover fire, Driessler grabbed one end of the stretcher, while someone else grabbed the other end, and hustled back up the road under heavy fire to where a medic was treating casualties behind an APC. "We had to carry the trooper about the length of a city block," notes Driessler. "It may appear that I was brave to do so. I was not. I was a scared kid in an untenable position and was ecstatic to get the hell out of there by taking the wounded man back." The medic turned his attention to the man on the stretcher, "but said there was nothing he could do. The trooper expired ten or fifteen minutes after we brought him back."

***

Bruce Isenhoff of Company C went cold as he listened to Company B's battle over the radio speaker inside his track. Head down in the driver's hatch, Isenhoff prayed with the fervency of a condemned man that if almighty God would deliver him through this day, he would change his life around and do whatever He asked him to do with it.

Lieutenant Corry slapped the top of Isenhoff's helmet. "Let's go," Corry shouted, and Isenhoff put the track in gear.

Charlie Company was moving out.

Lieutenant Colonel Tower, up in his bubble helicopter, had ordered Captain Morgan and Company C to proceed due south from the rally point and take up firing positions on the west edge of that narrow section of Xom Ong Doi built along the canal road, thus outflanking the enemy engaged with Company B.

The tracks moved down a dirt road that cut across the field adjacent to the rally point. To help coordinate the action, Major Riedl followed aboard his track, which was nicknamed the Pink Pussy Cat. It was easily identifiable because of the 90mm recoilless rifle mounted in the command cupola, its stubby barrel trained through the slot in the gun shield. Expecting Morgan's platoons to be oriented north to south and firing west into the housing along the canal road, Riedl instead found Company C positioned in an east-west line. The tracks were exchanging fire with another enemy force that was located to the south across the Rach Bang Dong in the heart of Xom Ong Doi. Charlie Company did not seem to appreciate that the more immediate problem was not the foe across the river, but the one on its right flank who had Bravo Company pinned down.

Riedl got on the command net to explain the problem. Tower buzzed down for a closer look, and at a word from the colonel, Morgan's tracks began backing up and turning around. To give Morgan the breathing room he needed to reform his line, Riedl plunged to within a hundred meters of the row of hootches at the east end of the hamlet and, ordering his driver to stop, shouted at his crew to open fire. Specialist Fourth Class Roy Derr— the crewcut, stogie-chewing driver—popped away from his hatch with an M16. The battalion chaplain's assistant and several personnel from the battalion's civil-affairs section who had hitchhiked into Saigon aboard the executive officer's track exited through the back door and began firing from behind the APC.

Tony Midkiff, a rugged, old-for-his-rank regular who had reenlisted after a hitch in the peacetime army to get into the war, manned the .50-caliber

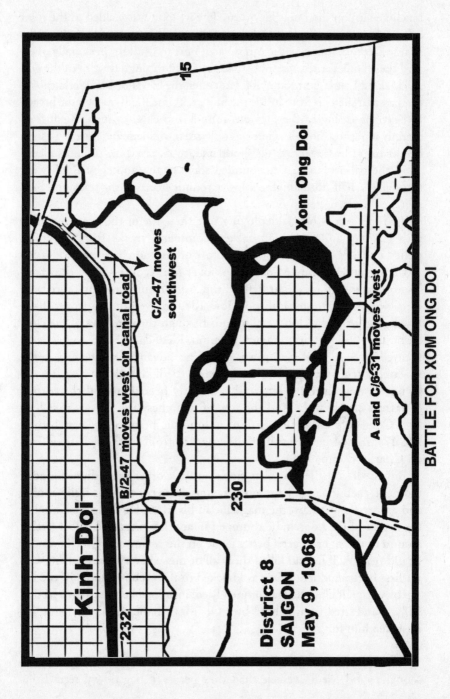

BATTLE FOR XOM ONG DOI

machine gun on the Pink Pussy Cat. The weapon was welded to the right side of the vehicle, displaced by the recoilless rifle in the command cupola. Major Riedl, standing in the cargo hatch next to Midkiff, personally operated the recoilless rifle, its stubby barrel trained through the slot in the gun shield. First Lieutenant Randall J. Lancaster, the battalion's civil-affairs officer, passed a shell up from inside the hull each time Riedl opened the breach to eject the casing of the previous round. Too close to miss, Riedl fired directly into those houses where he could see movement and muzzle flashes, destroying at least three. Walls shuddered, roofs caved in, and fires blazed amid the palm trees that surrounded some of the hootches. Riedl went through the half-dozen high-explosive rounds stored in the track and then switched to flechettes.

The line tracks began deploying to either side of the executive officer's vehicle, and two high-backed command tracks from battalion pulled up from behind. Major Riedl tore off his radio helmet and leaped to the ground as Tony Midkiff took over the recoilless rifle; the chaplain's assistant, in turn, got behind the .50. Meaning to buy more time for Company C to get into position, Riedl moved out in front of the line being formed to lob M79 rounds through the windows of the closest houses. Quickly running out of ammo, Riedl darted back to his track, secured an M16, and, pumping adrenaline, advanced all the way to the row of hootches facing Charlie Company. Riedl kicked down a gate, slid along the hootch to his left, and cautiously peered around the corner. A narrow canal ran behind the row of hootches, and he saw that four Viet Cong soldiers were positioned along the berm of the canal, their AK-47s trained between the two houses in front of them as they fired on Charlie Company.

Bill Riedl and the guerrillas stared at each other for a dumbfounded moment, then the major cut loose, raking the berm without really aiming and emptying in a flash the magazine in his M16. Ducking back around the corner of the hootch, he thumped in another magazine. Riedl circled around to the right to get a better angle on the enemy along the berm, for he didn't know if he had killed them all or missed every one of them with his first burst. Suddenly, he was knocked to the ground, smote in the left hip by what felt like a sledgehammer. Riedl imagined he'd been hit by a dud M79 round fired from behind by a GI from Charlie Company who had mistaken him for a Viet Cong.

Captain Morgan's line began rolling forward, but the tracks had no sooner passed Riedl's vehicle than they began to bog down, terra firma giving way at the edge of the hamlet to marshland. In moments, almost all were hopelessly stuck. The terrain was like a thick mat of grass floating on water, solid enough to walk across but unable to support a twelve-ton armored personnel carrier.

Several tracks were able to back out when the drivers realized what was happening. Most, however, including Captain Morgan's, bottomed out, sunk to the top of their road wheels. No matter. Lieutenant Corry jumped from his track on the left side of the line as his machine gunners laid down cover fire; then he led his dismounted infantrymen toward the first row of hootches. "We finally had to cease firing the .50s as [the assault line] neared the canal [behind the hootches] so that we wouldn't hit our own people," recounts Bruce Isenhoff, who'd scrambled from his driver's hatch to act as assistant gunner on his track. "We sat there and watched helplessly as our friends crossed the canal and disappeared between the houses on the other side."

It was now three in the afternoon. Major Riedl, limping rearward, encountered Corry's platoon sergeant, a black, six-foot-six Regular Army E7 named Clarence Williams. Platoon Sergeant Williams was the heart and soul of Charlie One, the cool head who took care of his men, and the taskmaster who made sure they did their jobs. Williams threw an arm around Riedl and helped him to cover behind the Pink Pussy Cat.

Riedl was aghast. Tower hadn't intended for Morgan to launch a frontal assault into a built-up area occupied by entrenched Viet Cong with a friendly element (Company B) firing into the same area from the flank. The battalion commander had instead wanted Charlie Company to establish a firing line on the east end of the hamlet while Bravo Company continued firing into the north side. The enemy forces would thus be boxed in while their positions were pounded with mortars, artillery, gunships, and the air strikes that Panther 6 was even now urgently requesting as his bubble helicopter orbited Xom Ong Doi.

Though Tower's instructions had been misunderstood, there was little to do but press on. As the dismounted troops fought their way into the hamlet, Captain Morgan's mortar section joined Riedl's group behind the line of stuck-in-the-mud APCs. Riedl was also joined by Captain Louis E. Daughtery, M.D.; the much-admired battalion surgeon was an adventurous young man who usually operated as far forward as possible. In this instance, Doc Daughtery had brought up a team of medics aboard an M577. Major Riedl was conferring with the tough old master sergeant who ran the mortar section when a volley of rocket-propelled grenades began exploding around the command tracks, mortar tracks, and the medical track. The wounded included Riedl, whose thigh was already sore and who now caught some stinging fragments in his left ankle. The enemy followed the rockets with a mortar barrage. "We were lucky because we were in inundated terrain," notes Riedl, "so when RPGs, and even mortar shells, came in, they tended to go plop in the mud and their bursting radius was not very large. They were kind of ineffective."

Second Lieutenant Frederick R. Casper, who had Charlie Three on the right flank, slipped past the marsh and moved into the north edge of the hamlet. Advancing past the hootches and into the first block of two-story buildings on the other side of the canal, Casper's platoon was brought up short by heavy AK-47 fire and two or three RPGs. After the tracks backed up the way they had come, Private First Class Michael H. Jeter leveled his .50 on a bunker to the front and right of his APC. "After a few minutes of steady firing," notes Jeter, "a VC ran from the bunker and disappeared into the canal. After another few minutes of firing, a second VC took off running, again headed for the canal. He didn't get far."

The word was finally passed to pull back. Troops began emerging from the smoke and flames of burning houses, the able-bodied and walking wounded helping the seriously wounded back behind the line of bogged-down personnel carriers. Two men were killed during the withdrawal: Private First Class Kenneth W. Arnold while assisting a casualty, and Private First Class Thomas W. Cranford while lagging behind to provide cover fire with his M16, according to the citations to their posthumous Bronze Stars.

Private First Class Vernon B. Quagon, a track driver, put down his M16 and joined those moving across the marsh to help the casualties get clear of the burning hamlet. Quagon helped one man back behind the tracks, then went back to carry in another one over his shoulder. Making a third dash into the kill zone, he was pulling Ken Arnold's body out of the canal when he was peppered with shrapnel from a nearby explosion and tagged himself as a soon-to-be-medevacked WIA.

Lieutenant Corry returned with several men to collect LAWs, as well as the shoulder-fired 90mm recoilless rifle stored in one of the tracks. There was blood on the left side of Corry's head and a bandage around his forehead. "His eyes were wide open and burning with intensity," recounts Isenhoff. "He was a man on a mission." The group rushed back to the canal and opened fire to cover the last of the troops straggling out of the hamlet. The group was soon raked with automatic-weapons fire. Corry was running back across the marsh to escape the fire when something—probably an RPG—exploded directly behind him, knocking him flat with serious wounds in the lower back and buttocks. Major Riedl, followed by Doc Daughtery and one or two of his medics, dragged Corry behind a track. Isenhoff wasn't able to bid Corry goodbye and good luck before he was loaded onto a medevac. "He never returned, and I never heard from him again. Someone said that he survived and was sent back home."

The gunships continued their runs, flashing over Company C's line, east to west, to unleash their rockets at a frighteningly-low level into buildings less than a hundred meters in front of the tracks. With the dismounted troops out of the way, the gunners and drivers-turned-assistant-gunners atop the personnel carriers began pouring .50-caliber machine-gun fire into the objective again. The troops on the ground joined in with M16s, M60s, M79s, and LAWs as AK-47 fire snapped back from the unseen Viet Cong.

The battalion photographer, a young specialist fourth class named Claude Walker, narrated the scene into his tape recorder:

> We've been fighting on the outskirts of Saigon about an hour and a half now. . . . There's heavy fire from an unknown-sized Viet Cong or NVA regiment—we don't know what size. . . . This is the worst fighting that we've had here . . . the miniguns are coming in—the gunships with their rockets—and the .50-calibers are working, and the 90mm recoilless rifle, the individual weapons of the men. It's been a heroic effort.

The east end of the hamlet was reduced to a shattered, burning mess. "Smoke is spiraling skyward everywhere now," noted Walker, adding: "The fighting really is bad. The villagers are fleeing for their lives—they don't know what it is—what's going on—but the NVA and Viet Cong are hiding behind them."

Walker held his microphone up to a bandaged trooper who identified himself as Private First Class Larry Miller of Indianapolis, Indiana. "What was it like up there?" asked Walker. "Charlie was really shootin' us up," said Miller, who then spoke in a way that defied the stereotype of the cynical grunts of 1968:

> Lot of men tryin' their best to get up and get up into 'em—lot of 'em wounded and a lot of 'em died, but these men are fightin' hard

for their country, for our freedom, and our way of life—and that's what I'm doin' out here, too. The men are doing a tremendous job . . . When one man falls, another one takes his place. It's teamwork, and teamwork is what counts, and that's what these men in the 2nd of the 47th is doin' right now is teamwork—and that's how it is.

First Lieutenant Dennis C. Klingmen, the battalion motor officer, moved forward with a monstrous M88 recovery vehicle to pull Company C's tracks out of the marsh. Working under fire, Klingmen and two mechanics from the company maintenance track were hooking tow cables to one of the bogged-down tracks when a Huey came in low and fast to punch off a salvo of rockets, all of which, save one, sailed past into the enemy-held hamlet. The tailfin of that other rocket snagged as it exited the firing pod and dipped slightly; the 2.75-inch white-phosphorus projectile flashed not into the hootches, but into the back of the very track that Klingmen and crew were preparing to tow behind the M88.

The track was engulfed in white smoke. Troops ran to the scene with fire extinguishers. There were shouts for medics. Specialists Fifth Class Paul R. Standridge and Clarence H. Washington Jr.—both mechanics were career men with eighteen years of service between them—had been killed in the blast, while Lieutenant Klingmen was splattered across his face and down in the groin area with flesh-melting white phosphorus. Unaware that the mishap had not been the result of pilot error, an enraged Captain Morgan informed the gunships that if they came over his position again, he would order his troops to turn their guns on them.

Lieutenant Barnes, then the commanding officer of Headquarters Company—as well as the "shortest" officer in the battalion at the time, due to rotate home within days—jumped in his jeep and raced to the burning M113. One of Lieutenant Klingmen's ears had been burnt off, but he was more concerned with the damage done to his manhood by the white phosphorus. The medics thumped Klingmen with two morphine syrettes. The lieutenant got a happy, drowsy look on his face, but his fears were such that even the morphine could not completely subdue his anxious babbling. Barnes tried to cheer his fellow short-timer by giving him "a large ration of shit for beating me out of the country."

Lieutenant Klingmen was evacuated within fifteen minutes. The medevac had no sooner clattered out than a marking round burst directly above Charlie Company. "As we held our breath, I reasoned that whoever was calling in the artillery would adjust and continue," recounts Isenhoff. "Instead, a few seconds later, artillery rounds started falling directly on our position." Isenhoff and the gunner scrambled inside their track. Captain Morgan screamed at battalion to get the fire shut off, but before the ceasefire was accomplished, a half-dozen rounds had exploded between the tracks, spraying them with mud and water and shrapnel. "The explosions were deafening," notes Isenhoff, "and to this day, it seems incredible to me that no one was killed or injured by those rounds. We learned later that the artillery had been called in by Bravo Company."

Mike Jeter crouched alongside his track, firing into the burning hamlet. During a lull, a guerrilla, naked save for a pair of shorts, popped from a bunker amid the wreckage and raised his arms in surrender, desperately shouting, *"Chieu hoi, chieu hoi!"* Jeter motioned him forward. The man was only twenty or thirty feet away when another GI suddenly came up from behind Jeter and emptied his M16 into the approaching Viet Cong. Jeter spun around, shocked, and the GI blurted, "You aren't going to report me, are you?" Jeter shook his head. "You murdered him," he said. "It'll be on your conscience for the rest of your life—not mine."

Lieutenant Colonel Tower finally got his tactical air support three and a half hours into the action and, in coordination with a forward air controller orbiting the battlefield, began running strikes in support of hard-pressed Company B. The air support came not a moment too soon. The firefight had dragged on so long that some of the troops had run out of ammo, which was almost unheard of given the amounts carried aboard each personnel carrier. Phil Streuding, gunner on the lead track, having used up all twenty cans of .50-caliber ammunition, had grabbed an M60 but the weapon was jammed. While his driver popped away with a grenade launcher, Streuding next found a box of grenades and a rifle and started blindly throwing the frags as far as he could between bursts from the M16.

Targets were marked. After several dummy passes had been conducted to ensure accuracy, Captain Craig gave warning over the radio: "Everybody get your head down, they're comin' in hot!" Then the two Phantoms that had been scrambled took turns roaring in over the rooftops to strafe, bomb, and napalm the houses in front of Bravo Company. "They were so low you could see the pilots wave as they went past," notes Lewis Hosler. "The napalm pulled the air right out of your lungs when the canisters hit. Some guys even got burns on their faces from the intense heat—that's how close it was."

Phil Streuding saw a Vietnamese man emerge from a house with his wife and children, "and having survived us, the enemy, and the air strikes, they made a dash toward us during a very short lull. They made it without getting hurt, which I thought was miraculous."

Unable to stand up to the pounding from above, the enemy began vacating the area. As the enemy's fire tapered off, Jimmy Dye and Platoon Sergeant Lawrence E. Pugh, a highly respected regular, used a stretcher to carry the wounded men who had been pinned down at the front of the column back to the medic who had been treating casualties behind his track. The two had already carried several back and were just starting rearward with the leg-shot lieutenant when caught in the sudden crossfire of a final few guerrillas. Pugh and Dye instinctively dropped the stretcher, and the platoon sergeant kept right on going, racing down the road to find cover, while Dye desperately hugged the ground next to the lieutenant.

The tracks returned the fire, quieting the stay-behind snipers. When Dye attempted to get up, however, the AK-47s began ringing again, and he and the lieutenant were stung by bits of asphalt sent flying by near misses.

Dye went flat again, playing dead as the street reverberated with return fire. Once more, the enemy stopped shooting and didn't open fire again until the lieutenant began thrashing on his stretcher, writhing in agony as he wailed, "We're gonna get killed, we're gonna get killed!"

"If you don't shut up, we are!" Dye snapped. *"Don't move!"*

"Oh, God, I can't help it. Oh, my God, it hurts, it hurts!"

The whole thing lasted twenty or thirty minutes before the snipers were either killed, wounded, or had decided to bug out. A half-hour is a long time for an infantryman who is huddled on the hot asphalt with his head throbbing, adrenaline pounding, and fatigue shirt soaked black with sweat. By the time the situation had been secured, "I was so dried out, I couldn't even spit," recalls Dye. "Some other guys took care of the lieutenant. I was so weak from dehydration, I probably couldn't have picked his stretcher up. Luckily, a track pulled up right about then and threw out a case of beer. They were hot, but I probably drank six of 'em, just one right after the other. Best tasting beer I ever had in my life."

There was no more enemy fire. The wounded were rushed to the rally point, as were a handful of injured civilians who appeared from the wreckage. Bob Dyson was sitting in the cupola of his track near where Doc Rogers was standing and talking to a couple other GIs. The black medic, who had performed so heroically during the battle, suddenly lurched backwards, hit in the shoulder. "Everyone was momentarily stunned because we had heard no incoming fire," recalls Dyson. Nothing further developed, and "Rogers began laughing when he looked at his injury because he knew he would be medevacked. I made a joke that the fight was so bad that the doc was wounded twenty minutes after it was all over. Actually, he was probably wounded by a freak piece of shrapnel from an air strike that was going in about a mile away."

Doc Rogers did not actually have a million-dollar wound, and shortly returned to duty, he was killed while rushing to the aid of a wounded trooper during a firefight outside Saigon.

Chapter 19

Major Jones spent the battle buttoned up in his track at the rally point, waiting for Lieutenant Colonel Tower to send him in to assist one of the line companies. Panther 6 never called. "I was just sitting there, listening to the radio and not really doing much of anything," recalls Jones, dismayed to be left on the sidelines while the battalion commander ran the whole show from his helicopter. "That's just the way Tower was. When a unit made contact he took over, and when he got on the horn, you got off. That was *his* command net. I was upset. I was an infantry soldier, and when my unit was in contact, I was supposed to be up there with them, not sitting to the rear."

The major grew so frustrated that he finally cut in on the command net to request permission to join the battle. "An obvious disagreement ensued," notes Russell Vibberts Jr., the E5 who served as Jones' track commander. "Jones was told to hold his position. In total dismay, he threw the radio handset against the inside of the armored personnel carrier."

The battalion's heavy-mortar platoon was even farther removed from the action, still rumbling through the city on Highway 15 north of the Kinh Doi when contact was made in Xom Ong Doi. The platoon was directed off the road and into an open area where the crews began to set up their 4.2-inch mortars in preparation for a fire mission. "The mission was ready for us before we could get all the guns laid," recalls Bill Reid, then a young sergeant, "and there was a lot of screaming going on to hurry." Reid and his squad had ridden to Saigon aboard the platoon ammunition track, nicknamed the "Camel," as their own track was down with engine trouble at Bearcat. As such, they had to ground mount their mortar tube, and Reid was the last squad leader to indicate that he was ready to fire. "I took a lot of heat from the FDC [fire direction control] track, the platoon leader in particular," notes Reid, "but we got on-line for firing soon enough, and it was pretty much nonstop after that, with only brief pauses to resight until we had fired all the HE [high explosives] and WP [white phosphoros] and there was nothing left in the Camel but CS tear-gas rounds. I think we ended up shooting flares into the ground in an attempt to send *something* to the guys that were calling for support."

The order was given to load up. Reid's men dug their base plate out of the mud and packed everything back into the Camel. Moving on, the platoon finally crossed the Kinh Doi and rendezvoused with the battalion command post. The situation seemed to be under control. People were moving about in the open. The wounded had been dusted off, and the KIAs had been laid out under ponchos. "We were ordered to form a defensive perimeter around the battalion headquarters and get our guns set up," notes Reid. Everyone was bushed from the fire mission, but the troops went to work with no more than the usual grumbling, relieved that an ammo resupply was on the way. "That was good news," explains Reid. "If we had ammo, we would continue to operate as mortarmen. Without ammo, we would be used as infantry."

The resupply had been organized by Tower's supply officer, Captain Leroy L. Brown, a veteran of the 5th Regimental Combat Team, Korea, 1950–1951, who'd been serving as a battalion sergeant major when his reserve commission was activated and he was shipped to Vietnam for his twentieth and final year in the U.S. Army. Captain Brown—a cheerful, can-do, old soldier much admired by Tower, Riedl, and Jones—had rolled into Saigon aboard his M577, pulling a trailer filled with smoke grenades and leading a tracked ammunition carrier and four trucks stacked with even more ammo. Brown's people kept the line platoons supplied with munitions during the ensuing battle and controlled those medevacs that landed at the battalion command post. "The first chopper to appear called for smoke on the LZ [landing zone]," recounts Brown. "Popped smoke, got a 'Roger' [in response]—but no chopper. Called the pilot, and was again told to pop smoke. Popped another smoke and got another 'Roger'—but, still, no chopper. Called the pilot again and asked what the problem was. His response was that the LZ looked hot. 'It *is* hot,' I said, 'but I'm standing in the middle of it, so get your ass down here.' We had no problem with the medevacs after that."

For all the munitions on hand, Brown's supply team ran out of bullets before the line platoons ran out of Viet Cong. Brown requested that Tower declare a tactical emergency. In response, he received a call from a flight leader who had thirteen Huey slicks available to support the 2-47th Mechanized Infantry. Brown asked the pilot if he knew where Camp Bearcat was and, after getting an affirmative, directed that he land his flight at the base camp heliport, where the needed ammunition would be loaded aboard. Brown then used a clear channel to contact the radio tower at Bearcat, and after being connected by landline to Sergeant Whitfield, his supply chief, instructed him to meet the soon-to-arrive slicks with a resupply that included: M16, M60, and .50-caliber ammunition; plus M79 rounds and LAWs; as well as fifty white phosphorus, a hundred illumination, and a hundred high-explosive shells for the heavy-mortar platoon. Each slick had a thousand pounds of ammunition on board when it lifted off and headed for Saigon.

Captain Brown popped smoke at the flight's arrival; to save time and minimize their exposure, the door gunners began pushing the ammo out before the pilots even touched down. The crates splashed into the standing water in the low ground near the tracks. Bill Reid's squad had been assigned to load the KIAs onto the slicks and haul the ammunition off the landing zone. Thinking that the battle was over, the GIs left their weapons behind in order to have both hands free, but had no sooner begun running toward the Hueys when "all hell broke loose," notes Reid. "There was quite a bit of fire coming from the buildings across the [Bang Dong] river, and of course, the guys on the tracks opened up in return with everything they had. The noise was deafening. The choppers took off, and we were caught out in no-man's land without even a rifle to defend ourselves. Some of the guys might have made a dash back to the tracks, but I didn't notice because most everyone out there, myself included, were too busy diving into the mud and water and trying to find something to use for cover."

The only thing that Reid could see that passed for cover was a dead man on a half-submerged litter. Crawling up against the body, Reid saw that the poor guy had been stitched by a VC with an AK-47. There was a line of bullet holes from the dead man's lower stomach straight up through the middle of his chest and face. Reid looked around for something a little more substantial to hide behind. There was an ammunition crate to his left and slightly behind him, and he began sliding through the mud toward it, moving as discreetly as possible given the plumes of water that continued to spurt up in the field from the enemy fire.

Reaching the ammo crate, Reid discovered that Private First Class Julio Gonzalez, the gunner on his mortar team, had gotten there first. Gonzalez screamed in his squad leader's ear over the din, "What are we gonna do, Reid!" "I told him I wasn't sure what *he* was going to do, but that *I* was going to see how low and how fast I could do the army low-crawl back to the higher ground, and then make a break for the tracks," Reid recalls. Reid took off on his belly with Gonzalez right behind him, "and soon I could see the others were following, too. Some decided that the army low-crawl wasn't fast enough, and I remember guys passing us on their hands and knees. I think I may have been the last one back because I wasn't about to stick my ass up there and provide Charlie a better target."

The enemy fire subsided, and the resupply mission continued. Captain Brown imagined that the effect on enemy morale was devastating. "What a thing," he muses. "Thirteen slicks flew in and resupplied us right in sight of the VC, who couldn't get a cup of water without getting shot up."

The forward air controller informed Lieutenant Colonel Tower that a second set of jet fighters was coming on station. Nearly an hour had passed since the initial air strikes had gone in along the canal road, about twenty minutes since the snipers had fired on the resupply helicopters from the housing on the south side of the Rach Bang Dong in the heart of Xom Ong Doi. Targets were marked across the river on Company C's left flank, and Captain Morgan passed the word over the radio: "Charlie, Charlie, Charlie [the chant meant that the message was intended for the entire company], lock down all your victors [vehicles]. We will have an air strike in zero-two minutes."

The strike began at 6:45 p.m. The troops nearest the target area scrambled inside their tracks, closed all hatches as ordered, then peered through the vision blocks (plexiglass panels built into the rims around the drivers' hatches and command cupolas) as the jets swooped in across the river. "What we saw looking through those small windows," recalls Bruce Isenhoff, "was one of the most awesome sights that I have ever witnessed in my life."

The two jet fighters made repeated passes, west to east, reducing several city blocks to flaming wreckage with napalm and automatic cannons that spit out rounds at such a rate that waves of orange fire seemed to race across the tin rooftops. They also cut loose high-drag bombs that nose-dived toward the buildings at an angle, detonated with earth-shaking concussions, and sent up great geysers of smoke and debris. "Each exploding bomb seemed to suck the atmosphere away and then return it in a violent wave of pressure as the jets screamed away," recounts Russ Vibberts. "The pilots told us to be sure to get behind cover when they dropped the hard stuff because they said there would be a lot of shrapnel," adds Bill Reid. "They weren't lying. The shrapnel came by our tracks in almost the same instant the bombs exploded—and it was *screaming*."

Claude Walker's tape recorder picked up the supersonic roar of one of the jet fighters as it dove toward the target, as well as the excited declaration of one of the GIs watching the show: "Goddamn, look at that sucker!"

Somebody else identified the ordnance being released as napalm, and a third GI let out an appreciative whistle when the canister splashed on target. The other jet shrieked past. The bomb that exploded in its wake was

greeted with a rebel yell and more excited patter: "Damn! . . . Wow! . . . We
sure killed a lot of them today! . . ."

After several bomb runs, the forward air controller—Tamale 3-1 in
radioese—informed Captain Morgan that the jets were going to switch
to strafing: "Charlie 6 . . . we'll continue with twenty mike-mike rockets
. . . ." There were more explosions, more excited chatter mixed with laughs,
and the satisfied comment of a GI as the napalm started fires amid the
enemy positions: "Tryin' to burn them motherfuckers out."

The whole thing took about fifteen minutes, then Tamale 3-1
announced: "We're coming in on final pass now." Another direct hit
elicited more applause from the grunts, then the forward air controller
called Tower: "Angry Strike 6, this is Tamale 3-1. That terminates the air
strike."

Colonel Benson came up on the net: "Tamale 3-1, this is Action 6. That
was beautiful. Thank you very much."

"Roger, thank you. Glad we finally got it in for you."

The housing across the river was gutted, silent but for the flames lick-
ing up from the wreckage. It seemed impossible that anyone could have
survived, "but within a short period of time," notes Reid, "we started to
notice people moving out from behind the surviving buildings. They were
carrying some things with them and some were helping others as they
moved very slowly away from the area from which the helicopter resupply
had taken fire. I couldn't help wondering why we didn't open up on them,
as I thought they must have been the enemy for sure. Apparently, someone somewhere had identified them as civilians, and we just watched and
let them go their way."

Everybody didn't get the word to hold their fire. Bruce Isenhoff and
his gunner, back in position atop their track, spotted a dozen women and
children, who had formed what looked like a protective barrier around
a single man, emerge from a building directly across the river. The group
moved east along the river to a canal that led south away from the battle area. By then, the gunner had set the .50 to single shot and fired
sniper-style at the man, punching off several rounds which passed just
over his head as he and his companions crouched down. The guys on the
last track in the line, positioned to the left-rear of Isenhoff's, shouted to
knock it off, that the fire was passing too close to them, then they picked
up where the first gunner had left off. None of their rounds hit home
either, and after several minutes, the strange group edged its way down
the canal and out of sight. In the excitement, Isenhoff had assumed that
their target was a guerrilla using the women and children as human

shields, but on reflection realized that the man might have been a father with his family or a teacher with his class. Better that they had missed.

The radio crackled to life following the air strikes as a trooper on the right flank reported that a man was approaching from the hamlet with hands raised. Isenhoff recalls that the GI asked for instructions, and was told to "Wait one."

There was no further word from the command track, and the GI finally got back on the horn to ask again for instructions. This time, he got a vague response: "We are not taking prisoners."

"What do we do with this one?"

"We are taking no prisoners."

"Please advise. What do we do with this one?"

"Wait one."

Silence, then the GI repeated, "Please advise."

Finally, a definitive answer: "Waste 'im." Moments later, a short burst of .50-cal fire echoed across the otherwise quiet battlefield.

Captain Morgan was forced to establish a night position right where he was in the open field, there being no time to retrieve the tracks that were stuck in the marsh and move to more defensible ground as dusk was approaching. To secure the area, Lieutenant Casper of the 3rd Platoon, Company C, led a foot patrol into the east end of the hamlet. The lieutenant and his radioman moved with the point team of the lead squad. "Casper was gung-ho," recalls Clifford M. Pinkston Jr. "He was ready to go in there and mix it up."

Tall, dark-haired, and athletic in appearance, Fred Casper was twenty-five years old and hailed from Fond du Lac, Wisconsin. "Lieutenant Casper liked being up where the action was," notes former squad leader John Ax. Though wounded in close combat during Tet, Casper, unintimidated, continued to be the kind of platoon leader who "wouldn't ask you to do something he wouldn't do himself," says Ax, "and who would really take up for his people. He was well respected by his men and well liked, too."

Privates First Class Pinkston and James E. Crowston were draftees from Oklahoma and Montana, respectively, who had recently joined the unit as replacements and quickly bonded. They covered a Hawaiian GI who opened the door of a hootch along the road Casper's patrol had taken into the hamlet. There was an enemy soldier hiding inside who cut loose with his AK-47, knocking the Hawaiian GI down. The stunned GI held his hand up. Several fingers had been blown off. "We hit the ground, and the door went back shut," recounts Pinkston. "We popped a trip-flare to set the hootch on fire, and fired into it as we moved away."

Lieutenant Casper took the point himself as the patrol continued down the road, trailed by Private First Class Merrill A. Moser, his radioman, with Jim Crowston falling in behind them. Clifford Pinkston crouched for a moment behind a red Honda parked beside a hootch as the lieutenant approached an open-walled rice-processing plant that was thirty meters away at the end of the road. The interior was stacked with rice bags, from behind which another guerrilla suddenly appeared, head and shoulders visible behind the RPD machine gun lying across the bags. The machine gunner opened up on the most obvious target, the red motorcycle, and the gas tank burst into flames. Even as Pinkston scuttled away, he saw Lieutenant Casper run across his front, trying to get out of the line of fire "and he took direct hits—I seen the flesh coming off his knees and legs, his pants ripping off, and then he fell down into a ditch right there. There was a ditch full of water between the hootches and the rice plant."

Crowston, Moser, and Pinkston, running for their lives, all crowded through the same doorway at the same time. Shutting the door behind them, they hit the deck as the enemy gunner poured rounds through the wooden door and the thatch wall. In moments, a Huey gunship, whose pilot was unaware of the location of the most forward troops, began strafing the rice-processing facility and the hootch in which Crowston, Moser, and Pinkston had sought refuge. Tracer rounds punched through the tin roof to ricochet off the concrete floor.

The crossfire was unbearable. Moser jumped up, shouting, "I can't take it no more! I gotta get outta here! I gotta get outta here!"

Crowston and Pinkston screamed to get down, but Moser yanked the door open, started through, and immediately fell back inside, shot in the chest. Crowston pulled open Moser's blouse to reveal a small blue hole that did not bleed. "I'll believe to my dyin' day that he took friendly fire because it was too small a hole to be an AK-47 or RPD round," says Pinkston. "Someone returning fire from down the street accidentally popped Moser when he ran outside."

Moser took several deep breaths and said, "I'm dyin'."

"No, you're gonna be all right," said Pinkston, who had jerked out a field dressing to cover the wound.

But Merrill Moser, a twenty-year-old married draftee from Alabama, was right. "He took a couple more deep breaths," remembers Pinkston, "and he left. He was dead."

Either Crowston or Pinkston grabbed the handset to Moser's radio and reported the situation. They were instructed to pop smoke outside the door of their hootch to identify their position. They did so, and the gunship adjusted its strafing runs accordingly. The enemy machine gunner was still blazing away from the rice-processing plant, however, and Crowston and Pinkston, who were flat against the floor and unable to return fire, knew they were eventually going to catch some of the rounds cracking over their heads.

Salvation came in the form of a Puerto Rican GI who had already been shot through the thigh, but who nevertheless dragged himself up to their hootch after they popped smoke. "Hang on, hang on," the GI shouted from outside the wall on the side of the hootch opposite the enemy. "I got my knife. I'll cut a hole here!" Crowston and Pinkston crawled through the hole and joined the rest of their squad. In addition to the two dead, five men had also been wounded, and with darkness closing fast and the neighborhood going up in flames, Captain Morgan ordered the patrol to fall back. It was too late in the day to organize an attack on the enemy rearguard.

Pinkston handed his M16 to someone else and helped carry out a dead grunt, probably Tom Cranford, who had been killed in the original assault into the hamlet and left behind in the chaos. The men were troubled that the fire was too heavy to allow them go back to recover Lieutenant Casper and Merrill Moser. "We didn't want to withdraw or leave our KIAs behind," notes Mike Jeter, "but we followed orders."

Captain Craig's people parked their tracks against the same buildings they had riddled with fire during the battle and set up dismounted positions behind the debris. "It looked like we had a long night ahead of us," notes Phil Streuding, who only had four men left in his eight-man squad after the casualties had been medevacked. After wiring some claymores out in front of their position, three of the guys—including one with an M60—set up beside the track while Streuding got on the .50, having scrounged up five or six boxes of machine-gun ammunition. "We stayed awake all night. I just knew the enemy would be coming through us as they tried to escape because we were so understrength."

Though most of Company B was facing south, "we also had some guys on the river bank," notes Lewis Hosler, "watching that sappers didn't come up the canal behind us. They had put the word out that anything out there is fair game. Anything out there that moves, cut it down."

It had just gotten dark when Hosler caught sight of somebody, a silhouette of a man carrying something, moving between the two buildings directly to the front of the personnel carrier. None of the other guys sitting there seemed to notice, and Hosler had no time to give warning as he threw his M16 to his shoulder and emptied his magazine into the black shape. The GIs who checked the area out rushed back with a screaming baby and a wounded man in black pajamas whom they laid on the back ramp of the track while shouting for the medic. The baby had been shot through the stomach and died within moments. Hosler was hysterical, and Captain Craig tried to console the young soldier by telling him that he couldn't blame himself: "Son, don't worry about it. It's war and these kinds of things happen."

Lewis Hosler sat in his track later that night as fires flickered in the wrecked hamlet and gunships continued to work the area over. Punch-drunk from all that had just happened, he wrote an emotional letter to his parents. "It was a goodbye letter, that the next few days would probably be my last, you know. It was tough in there. It was tough. I didn't even know if we were going to be able to fight our way off that canal bank." Hosler stuffed the letter in his pocket, not sure if he should mail it, then, finding himself still alive at the end of the battle, he "folded it up and tucked it in my little Bible. I kept that letter until my parents died years later, and then I threw it away."

Pfc. William L. Sirtola of the 6-31st Infantry, 9th Infantry Division. *Courtesy of William L. Sirtola*

Troops from the 6-31st Infantry disembark from helicopters on Highway 5A immediately south of Saigon on May 10, 1968. *9th Division photo courtesy of Anthony P. DeLuca*

Sgt. Jay T. Crowe of the reconnaissance platoon, 3-39th Infantry, rushes for cover. District 8, Saigon. May 10, 1968. *9th Division photo courtesy of Anthony P. DeLuca*

The reconnaissance platoon, 3-39th Infantry, ducks enemy fire. District 8, Saigon, May 10, 1968. *9th Division photo courtesy of Anthony P. DeLuca*

Above and below: Dismounted troops from Company B of the 2-47th Mechanized Infantry follow an armored personnel carrier down an enemy-held street in District 8, Saigon. May 11, 1968. *Courtesy of Ken Pollard*

A trooper from Company B loses his helmet while dashing for cover under sniper fire. *Courtesy of Ken Pollard*

A medic treats Capt. James B. Craig after the commander of B/2-47th Mechanized Infantry was shot in the chest by a sniper on May 11, 1968.
Courtesy of Ken Pollard

Sp4 Anthony R. Midkiff covers the evacuation of Capt. Craig with the side-mounted .50-caliber machine gun on an armored personnel carrier nicknamed The Pink Pussy Cat. *Courtesy of Ken Pollard*

An armored personnel carrier from B/2-47th Mechanized Infantry moves forward to fire on enemy snipers. *Courtesy of Ken Pollard*

Troops from Company B attempt to flush out the enemy snipers.
Courtesy of Ken Pollard

A soldier from Company B rises up to return fire with his M16. *Courtesy of Ken Pollard*

Capt. Craig is carried to safety past Sp4 Midkiff who peers down from behind the gun shield of The Pink Pussy Cat. *Courtesy of Ken Pollard*

A soldier fans flies away from the face of a captured Viet Cong after B/2-47th Mechanized Infantry secured the enemy-held street on May 11, 1968. *Courtesy of Ken Pollard*

SP4 Ransom C. Cyr pulls Sp5 Ken Pollard to cover after his fellow combat photographer was shot in the leg during a street battle in Saigon. Cyr was killed only moments later by a sniper. *Courtesy of Ken Pollard*

Capt. Wilfred A. Geschke of the 3-39th Infantry on a rooftop near the Y Bridge in District 8, Saigon, following the fighting in May 1968. *Courtesy of Wilfred A. Geschke*

Chapter 20

Lieutenant Colonel Schmalhorst's battalion, supported by gunships and artillery, exchanged fire with snipers until nightfall. By then, a resupply of ammunition had been choppered in, the last of the wounded choppered out, and Companies A and C, 6th Battalion, 31st Infantry, had set up security positions with local militia and ARVN units on and between two small bridges along north-south Route 230, at the southwest corner of Xom Ong Doi.

On the assumption that the enemy would decamp under cover of darkness Captain Owen, acting on orders from battalion, told Lieutenant Gale of the 3rd Platoon, Company C, to deploy a squad-sized ambush on the west side of Xom Ong Doi. Sergeant Olson got the mission, but reaching the northernmost of the two bridges, was offered some emphatic advice by the GIs holding the bridge: "You guys are crazy if you go up that road!"

The grunts explained there were enemy soldiers in the very area that Olson's squad was supposed to pass through on its way to the ambush site. Olson could see shadows flitting across the road, and when offered a look through a starlight scope, the shadows seemed to become identifiable as personnel with weapons. Olson started to call Captain Owen to apprise him of the situation, but then he thought better of it, not wanting to break radio silence and compromise the ambush. "We were all new and green and scared, and some of the guys were getting pretty edgy," recounts Olson. If they continued down the road as ordered, it seemed apparent that the ambush patrol was going to get ambushed itself. "We talked awhile about how we might be able to move through the marsh grass of the fields adjacent to the road and come up on our objective from the rear without being seen. That course of action was rejected as it would not only have left us completely exposed, but also mired in the mud. My guys finally balked on me. They told me they were not going up that road."

The squad wanted Olson to go back and make the case with Captain Owen that their orders should be changed. Olson did, and in so doing, he disappointed himself, wondering if he should have just said "follow me" like in the movies and moved out. Back at the company headquarters, Olson explained the situation to Owen and requested a fire mission on the ambush site and the areas where movement had been detected. Owen said there would be no artillery fire. In the absence of actual contact, the hamlet was a no-fire zone because of the civilians. "I think Owen had made an effort to get artillery, but had been overruled at battalion or higher levels," notes Olson. Denied supporting fires, Olson mustered his courage, for the last thing he wanted to do was defy Charlie Hunter 6, and declared that "I would not take responsibility for walking my men into an ambush. I would take the point and walk the patrol up the road if the order still stood, but I would not *lead* the patrol."

Captain Owen asked the squad leader if he knew what he was saying. Olson said that he did and, expecting the captain's wrath, was surprised when Owen paused, looked evenly at him, and said simply, "Battalion wants that ambush patrol in place. Get moving." That was that. Sergeant Olson made one last appeal for artillery support, and Lieutenant Belt, the forward observer, volunteered to lead the patrol so he would already be on hand if contact developed and a fire mission was approved. "Lieutenant Belt took charge and acted as if it was going to be a walk in the park," recounts Olson. "The guy had guts. The rest of us were scared. We truly thought we were being used as bait and that we were walking straight into an ambush. But I did take point, the men did follow, and we did go up that road and do what we had to do."

The patrol had just crossed the bridge when a grenade exploded in the roadside ditch. Olson's men took cover, but nothing further developed. A suspicion (later confirmed as fact) was voiced that one of the guys had thrown the frag, hoping to get the patrol recalled. No dice, for the squad continued down the road in the darkness. "Civilians gawked at us from various buildings," notes Olson. "We did not get any encouraging or friendly looks." Reaching the ambush site, Olson's squad occupied the top floor of a semi-demolished, two-story house. "Every Vietnamese in town knew we were there. We thought about changing positions after thirty minutes as we had been trained, but decided that there was little use in doing so as we could not have concealed the movement." At one point, Olson "saw and heard four or five people scurry around the rear of the house and braced for an attack. There was no further movement, no action at all, in fact, during the whole nerve-racking night. The enemy never engaged us. I almost wish we had been hit. It's hard to swallow telling your commanding officer that you aren't going to lead a patrol, and then have nothing happen."

At first light, scores of civilians, many of them wounded, emerged from the wrecked hamlet and gathered at Company B's position. Captain Craig sent them down the canal road for medical treatment at the battalion command post.

Soon thereafter, while Captain Morgan's troops winched their bogged-down tracks out of the marsh, Craig dispatched a patrol to recover the two bodies left behind the previous evening by Company C. Lieutenant Casper's body was still intact save for gunshot wounds and a leg blackened by the fire that had burned down the neighborhood in which he had died. The platoon leader's radioman, Merrill Moser, had been so badly burned, reports a member of the patrol, "that the battalion doctor had to identify his remains as human."

Tim Burke asked who the KIAs were when he saw the poncho-covered bodies being carried past on stretchers. "One of 'em's Charlie 3-6," answered a GI. Burke felt as if the wind had been knocked out of him. As a spotter for the mortar platoon, Burke had often been attached to Casper's platoon and had come to know the lieutenant better than any other officer in the battalion. "We had fought our first action together during Tet," notes Burke. "He always took care of me and my RTO, making sure we got our share of whatever was available—chow, Coke, beer, whatever. Not all officers did that. Most watched out for their own troops, and I had to remind them that me and my radioman were in this war, too."

Captain Craig and Company B searched the buildings along the canal road. There was no contact. The enemy had melted away during the night, leaving only those dead who could not be located in the dark, plus an unarmed and thoroughly lost VC soldier who was policed up by Bravo Company in a shot-up house at the intersection of Routes 230 and 232. The prisoner, speaking through Craig's interpreter, said that his company commander was a woman, a fact which the GIs found fascinating. The female officer's weapon had jammed during the firefight, the prisoner explained; she grabbed his AK-47 in exchange, at which point he just crawled into a bunker in the house and hid to escape the air strikes.

Schmalhorst's battalion conducted a simultaneous house-to-house sweep across the tadpole-shaped island on the south side of Xom Ong Doi, gunships swooping in low along potential escape routes. Making no contact, the battalion proceeded north into the heart of the hamlet where Captain Greene of A/6-31st reported finding thirty-six dead civilians in a housing complex used by the families of Vietnamese Marines. The bodies had no sooner been counted than Schmalhorst's people were pulled back, picked up by Hueys on Route 230, and choppered in to reinforce a major action involving the 5-60th Mechanized Infantry just south of Saigon. In the rush, no cause of death was recorded in the battalion log regarding the dead civilians, and there seems to be no way to determine years later whether they were victims of the air strikes called in during the battle or if the military dependents had been systematically murdered by the National Liberation Front. "I didn't personally see the bodies," recalls Greene. "The platoon leader who reported the situation to me thought the killings had been carried out by the enemy."

The battle for Xom Ong Doi was over. The 6-31st Infantry reported taking less than a dozen wounded while accounting for sixteen enemy kills. The 2-47th Mechanized Infantry, reported eight KIA, thirty-six WIAs (the latter figure was low, probably reflecting only those who had been medevacked), and a body count of sixty-one VC and NVA. Typically, the body count was exaggerated, but in this instance, not as badly as it might have been. True, only a dozen bodies were actually found in the wreckage, but the fact that the enemy had been forced to abandon some of his dead and a good number of weapons spoke to the punishment he had received during the battle. There were numerous signs of enemy casualties in the area. John Driessler recalls a GI picking up a wallet "next to a large hole filled with bloody water. We looked through the wallet and found the heroic picture of its owner. It showed him against a faux jungle background, in uniform, with his AK-47. It reminded me of all the hokey pictures taken of ourselves in basic and AIT [advanced individual training]."

Though the hamlet was mostly deserted by the time of the sweep, Company B did find a pregnant woman who had been shot in the stomach but was still alive. At another point, the lifer platoon sergeant of Bravo One saw something move and instinctively opened up with his M16, wounding an old woman. Like the pregnant woman, the old woman was bandaged up and loaded aboard a personnel carrier for transport to the battalion aid station. Meanwhile, hogs that had wandered from smashed pens fed on bullet-riddled water buffalos, and hungry dogs gnawed at human corpses. The dead—animals, civilians, and guerrillas—ripened quickly in the heat, and Lewis Hosler vividly recalls the "bodies in the streets—legs, arms—rotting, covered with flies. The stench is so bad, you burn 'em. You pour diesel fuel on 'em and burn 'em."

Though most of the civilian casualties had been caused by the side with the most firepower, it was the enemy who had set up the situation in which the innocents had been caught in the middle. To quote John Driessler, no believer in the war and no apologist for his fellow GIs: "The communists did not give a shit about the civilians. They used them for cover."

Bravo Company found in one empty building a dead Vietnamese man in monk robes. "Somebody had carved all the flesh from his head so that he had an exposed skull attached to his rotting body," remembers Bob Dyson. "The VC liked killing that way. ARVNs simply shot their victims."

Jimmy Dye's squad, hearing a suspicious noise in the porch area of a house, discovered a teenage girl who had been shot in both knees dragging herself outside at the arrival of the GIs. The platoon medic administered morphine and got the girl ready to be medevacked while the company interpreter asked her what had happened. "She said the VC had shot her to keep her from escaping," recalls Dye. The VC wanted her to remain in the battle area, apparently hoping that her family and neighbors would become inflamed against the foreigners upon finding that she had been killed by American bombs or napalm. Having managed to survive, the girl "eagerly told us how many troops were in the area, or at least how many that she'd seen, and whatever other information she had about the Viet Cong."

During a late-morning break in the sweep, "everybody sort of gathered around, eating Cs [C-rations] and talking," recounts Dye, "and we looked down this road, and here comes a motorcycle, and the driver had a pistol in his hand, waving it." The first to respond was a Regular Army E6 who had volunteered for the infantry and had recently been transferred into Bravo Company from the battalion mess section. The staff sergeant fired a .50 burst, "and the motorcycle went skidding down the street. What we didn't realize was that right behind the driver was the man's father, and sandwiched in between them on the seat was a little girl, maybe a year old," Dye recalls. "They all lived, but the driver was injured, and the little girl had her arm nearly shot off at the elbow. I don't know if she took a solid hit, but her being so small and everything, even a fragment of a .50-caliber shell would just about tear her little arm off."

The staff sergeant was visibly upset. "He wasn't panicking or being stupid when he fired," says Dye. "He was just reacting to the situation, but it really upset him that he had almost killed a child." To make matters worse, the company interpreter told the GIs after speaking with the injured driver that the man wasn't a Viet Cong, but actually an ARVN who had gone into hiding when the enemy occupied the town. The soldier had decided to make a break for it when he saw the personnel carriers on the street. Fearing an unfriendly reception, the government soldier had held his pistol up, meaning to show that he had nothing to hide. Dye was himself shaken by the mishap: "The baby's arm, it was just hanging on by the skin at the elbow, but she never whimpered, never cried, and those big brown eyes were just looking at you." When the medevac landed, somebody tried to hand the infant to Dye, but "I couldn't do it, I couldn't bring myself to touch that baby. The medic took off with her instead and put her on the Huey."

Major Riedl walked over to where Doc Daughtery and his medics had set up a tent at the rear of their track and indicated that his thigh had become terribly sore where he'd been hit during the battle. The major thought a dud M79 round had bounced off his thigh, but upon examining the injury, Daughtery exclaimed, "Hey, you've got a bullet in there!" Daughtery had Riedl lie down on a stretcher, and after he administered morphine, he pushed a stainless steel rod into the entrance wound, made an incision on the other side of the thigh, and popped the bullet out. It had come not from an AK-47 but an M16, and Tower chided Riedl, "No Purple Heart for that. That's a friendly round!"

Doc Daughtery was plucking the rocket shrapnel from Riedl's ankle when a Huey came in to pick up the KIAs lined up under ponchos outside the medical track. "The downwash of the blades blew the ponchos off, uncovering our dead," recounts Bill Riedl. "I will just never forget that sight as long as I live."

The battalion's biggest combat operation since Tet resulted in a plethora of decorations, starting with a pair of Bronze Stars for Lieutenant Colonel Tower and Major Jones for coordinating the battle in Xom Ong Doi. Major Riedl was decorated with both the Silver Star and Purple Heart, and hard-charging Doc Daughtery was pinned with the Silver Star himself for advancing into the battle area with his M577.

Captains Craig and Morgan and most of their platoon leaders were awarded the Silver Star, as was Platoon Sergeant Clarence Williams who had assumed command for the wounded Lieutenant Corry. The dead radioman Merrill Moser was posthumously awarded a Silver Star, while posthumous Bronze Stars and Purple Hearts were presented to the families of Ken Arnold, Tom Cranford, Paul Standridge, and Clarence Washington. According to the citations, Standridge and Washington had been killed by enemy fire, a common enough white lie used when friendly fire incidents occurred as a result of contact with the enemy.

Lieutenant Klingmen, who had been evacuated in a state of panic about his scorched genitals, was pinned with an Army Commendation Medal. Brice Barnes caught up with Klingmen some months later at Brooke Army Medical Center at Fort Sam Houston, Texas. "I saw the wonderful reconstructive work being done there on burn victims," notes Barnes. In

Klingmen's case, "there was no permanent damage below the waist, and his ear had been rebuilt with skin from other parts of his body."

The line troops received a handful of Silver Stars; Paul Ianni was recognized with one, and according to Dyson, Hosler should have been, too. Dozens of Bronze Stars and Army Commendation Medals went to men like Jimmy Dye, Lewis Hosler, Bruce Isenhoff, Mike Jeter, Clifford Pinkston, and Vernon Quagon, who had all seemingly been selected at random to represent the collective heroism of the 2-47th Mechanized Infantry.

There were other, more immediate rewards. Major Riedl, who knew the location of the docks where the big supply ships unloaded, sent the support platoon leader across the Y Bridge with several empty trucks and instructions to "sniff around and make contact with somebody and see if he could get some chow better than C-rations," Riedl recalls. The platoon leader pulled into the compound of a supply unit, whose personnel had been anxiously watching the battle across the Kinh Doi. In gratitude to the infantry, the supply troops filled the lieutenant's trucks with the best rations available in the U.S. Army. "We ate like kings," notes Riedl. "We had mess equipment there with us. The cooks set up mess tents and field stoves, and we had steaks, roasts, pork chops, hamburgers, real mashed potatoes with real gravy—I mean, great chow. We could carry it, too, because we had the tracks, and we had insulated mermite cans, so everybody in the battalion had at least one good hot meal a day for the remainder of the battle, which kept the morale right up there."

Tim Burke remembers one caveat: "There were so many flies, you gave up trying to keep them off your food."

The battalion rearranged its positions before nightfall on order of General Ewell, who had alighted from his command ship to speak with Tower. While Company C remained in the wrecked hamlet, Company B moved down the canal road to the vicinity of the Y Bridge, and the command group set up near the Route 5A bridge to replace the 5-60th Mech. Further battle awaited the Black Panther Battalion in Saigon.

Part Six

ANOTHER TRY

Chapter 21

Lieutenant Colonel DeLuca dispatched Company B, which was still under the acting command of Lieutenant Thompson, west from its position near the pagoda on the morning of May 10, 1968. The company's mission was reconnaissance in force, the area to be searched the hootch-and-nippa-palm fringe of the city just south of the bridge over the Rach Ong Nho.

After sweeping the area from which the enemy had launched an earlier night attack on DeLuca's battalion, Company B was to push west into Xom Cau Mat, which may or may not have been reoccupied. If the enemy was back in position, DeLuca could reinforce B/3-39th with A/3-39th, which was presently securing the bridge over the Rach Ong Nho. He could also, if needed, reinforce the unit with B/6-31st, which was located a kilometer to the east in the police outpost that the attached company had fought its way to the previous evening. If no contact developed, DeLuca's instructions were to turn over the defense of the Y Bridge to Schmalhorst and ready the 3rd Battalion, 39th Infantry, for airmobile operations in pursuit of the retreating Viet Cong.

There had been no enemy withdrawal, however. After turning from the canal road onto a side street running through a residential neighborhood, Bravo Company had no sooner crossed a footbridge that spanned an east-to-west twist in the Rach Ong Nho, and terminated in the rice paddies on the other side, than they came under heavy AK-47 and RPG fire.

Lieutenant Thompson worked the enemy positions with gunships and artillery and requested a medevac for two grunts wounded in the initial fusillade. The guerrillas kept up their fire despite the supporting arms, and DeLuca sent Captain Stuart and Company A into the fray. First Lieutenant Charles D. Gibson's platoon, Alpha Three, led the way and, following Bravo Company's path, was just approaching the north end of the footbridge when five or six bareheaded enemy soldiers in khaki fatigues were spotted on the south side of the tributary. Because the wooden footbridge was arched so that an individual at one end could not see the other end, the VC or NVA were unaware of the reinforcements coming up behind them and were standing in a huddle, AK-47s slung or held loose as they talked amongst themselves.

Platoon Sergeant Ronald N. Klump, a crack shot, hurriedly squared the sights of his M16 on the group, as did radioman Frank Williams and a black squad leader named Davis, another tough Regular Army NCO. The trio opened fire. Klump didn't blaze away on automatic; keeping the muzzle of his weapon down and on target, he squeezed off single shots as quickly as he could pull the trigger, putting at least ten rounds down range before the enemy knew what was happening. Klump knew he had hit the man in his sights, and felt sure that Davis and Williams had done the same, but not one of the enemy soldiers had dropped despite multiple gunshot wounds. Instead, the figures in khaki all dashed for cover on sprinter's legs. Klump, Davis, and Williams, astonished at the turn of events, quickly thumped fresh magazines into their weapons. Nothing moved on the other side of the river. There was no return fire.

Instructed to continue forward, Lieutenant Gibson joined Davis' lead squad as the grunts dashed across the footbridge and into a hail of enemy fire that began as soon as the first man reached the south side of the bridge. The grunt stumbled and fell, apparently wounded, then scrambled to his feet and dove for cover in the drainage ditch running along the left side of the dead-end street. Six feet wide and twenty feet long, the ditch was filled with stagnant rainwater. The rest of the squad and the attached gun team, plus the platoon leader, radioman, and medic, also took refuge in the ditch and began returning fire with M16s, M79s, and the gun team's M60.

Back on the north side of the tributary, Platoon Sergeant Klump put the platoon's other gun team and rifle squad in position to provide fire for Gibson and Davis. Thirteen years in uniform at age thirty, Ron Klump was a powerfully built man whose narrow gaze, square jaw, and cowboy mustache provided him a fierce visage that accurately reflected his attitude about combat if not his fatherly approach to leading GIs.

Commanded by a competent but uncharismatic captain and filled with draftees, shake 'n' bake squad leaders, and brand-new lieutenants, Alpha Company was a good outfit for two reasons. One was its first sergeant, H. D. Johnson, a colorful, cigar-chewing, in-the-field-with-the-troops kind of top beloved for his courage, common sense, and ability to make things happen. The other was Klump. "Johnson and Klump held the company together," according to William B. Spence, formerly the company executive officer. David L. Magnuson, then a rifleman, describes Klump as a leader who was "able to make the right decisions quickly, always looked out for his men, and who you knew you could talk to anytime about anything and know he would give you his honest answer. We all considered ourselves very lucky to have him for a platoon sergeant."

Although there was no cover along the edge of the tributary where Klump positioned his gun team and Specialist Fourth Class Carroll G. Westcott's squad, the enemy had plenty of hiding places behind the berms and buildings on the south side. To open up some fields of fire, Klump tried to burn down the wooden house on the right side of the dead-end street that was opposite Gibson's group in the drainage ditch, as well as a thatch hootch near the south end of the ditch. He ignited trip-flares and heaved them across the tributary toward the structures, but the flares fizzled on impact, doing no good. Klump bellowed for Westcott's men to bring him all their LAWs and ended up with fifteen. Moving along the bank to find good firing positions, Klump sent the LAWs flashing across the tributary into the hootch and the house, plus several other places where he thought the guerrillas might be ensconced. "I fired every damn one of them LAWs," recalls Klump, unconcerned with the ear-ringing backblasts. "You can't even hear 'em go off when your adrenaline is flowing like mine was. I don't know if the enemy was firing on me. Only thing I was concerned about was my men."

Though the enemy had Lieutenant Gibson's group zeroed in and pinned down in a crossfire, grunts continued to pop up at the edge of the drainage ditch to return fire. In doing so, Private First Class Marshall D. Bischoff took a round that punched straight through his steel pot from front to back, grazing his scalp and leaving him dazed, though not so badly that he didn't keep firing his M16.

It was a desultory exchange. An enemy soldier would fire, then a grunt, then another grunt, then another enemy soldier. The grunts were firing at shadows and sounds. The guerrillas were firing at targets, and in short order, the machine gunner and his ammo bearer were both shot, as was Gibson's medic who, despite a severe stomach wound, dragged himself through the muddy ditch with his aid bag and treated his wounded buddies. Staff Sergeant Davis, meanwhile, completely uncowed, heaved grenades, taunting the enemy before each pitch: "You better *chieu hoi!* You better *chieu hoi* before I gitchya!"

Captain Stuart called in gunships and artillery, but neither drove the enemy soldiers from their concealed positions. After an hour and a half of getting nowhere, Stuart called Klump back to his position and said, "I'm thinking about taking the rest of the company across the bridge. What do you think?"

"Sir, let me tell you right now, my advice is don't send nobody else across that damn bridge 'cause you're just gonna get a lot of people killed and a lot of people wounded if you do."

The dilemma was obvious. People had already been wounded. They needed to be medevacked. Charging across the bridge, however, wouldn't force the enemy back, thought Klump, it would just mean giving them more targets. Instead of feeding the whole company into a bad situation, Klump wanted to keep laying down suppressive fire until Gibson's group had a chance to dart back across the footbridge. At best, he suggested to Stuart that he go to Gibson's aid with Westcott's squad. "I'll go across because it's my damn platoon over there," said Klump, "but I advise you not to take the whole company across."

The Alpha Two platoon leader joined the command group at that time, and when queried by Stuart, enthusiastically agreed with the captain's plan. *Young-ass, dumb-ass lieutenant,* thought Klump, who grimaced when Stuart made up his mind then: "Okay, we're goin'."

"All right, sir," said Klump. "I'll get my men lined up."

Ours is not to reason why. . . .

Moments later, Klump was crouched at the north end of the bridge, shielded from the enemy by the arch in the middle with his gun team and Westcott's squad assembled behind him. Letting go a shout, Klump sprang to his feet and, feeling like a target in a shooting gallery, sprinted over the bridge as fast as a guy could go when loaded down with web gear and ammunition bandoliers, and a rifle in one hand, the other holding down his helmet.

Klump's group jumped into the ditch with Lieutenant Gibson. Captain Stuart and only the lead squad of Alpha Two—for enemy fire prevented the rest of the company from crossing the bridge—took cover in a ditch that ran along the south side of the wooden house on the opposite side of the street. Sergeant Howard E. Querry, a twenty-three-year-old shake 'n' bake squad leader who had said goodbye to his wife two months earlier, was dragged into the captain's ditch, having been shot and mortally wounded as he dashed across the footbridge.

Lieutenant Gibson and Staff Sergeant Davis were glad for the help, and the two squads were packed almost shoulder-to-shoulder in the drainage ditch. The additional firepower Klump's group brought to bear, however, had little apparent effect on the enemy. Shots continued to ring out from enemy soldiers who no one could spot. At one point, Klump called to Private First Class David M. Powell for the handset to the radio strapped to his back. Huddled with his face against the side of the ditch, Powell did not respond. Westcott turned Powell around by his shoulders and saw, as did Klump, that the new guy had been shot through the head some moments before, apparently killed instantly.

At another point, one of their veterans, Private First Class Robert M. Jacobs—who wore Coke-bottle glasses and looked the part of the bewildered recruit, but was actually a great soldier—was cut down when he stood up in the ditch to take aim with his M79. Jacobs was also killed instantly. "He was a nice kid," recalls Klump. "I used to call him 'War Machine' because, hell, he wasn't afraid of nothin'."

The enemy soldiers also kept up their fire on Captain Stuart's group, killing both a Tiger Scout and Platoon Sergeant Paul E. Jackson of Alpha Two. Jackson took a bullet fragment or speck of shrapnel through the corner of his eye and into his brain, leaving him unmarked in death, his patented wise-guy grin frozen on his face. Popular, seemingly fearless and a veteran of Tet, Jackson was a dark-haired man of twenty-seven who had a potbelly from drinking army-issue beer for ten years, a German wife, and a young daughter of whom he was immensely proud and whose photographs he liked to share with his grunts and fellow NCOs.

Platoon Sergeant Jackson had gone home on emergency leave a month earlier when his wife had delivered their second child. He had not been the same since, apparently preoccupied with marital problems. "He was always worrying about things, and didn't want to be there anymore," recalls William Spence. "He was still a good man, however, when the chips were down." First Sergeant Johnson would have agreed, writing home that Jackson "was playing John Wayne when he got killed. One squad was already pinned down and he volunteered to go across the bridge to try to get them out. He didn't have to go. He shouldn't even have been in Saigon. He was on a medical appointment when he heard the company was out [and] he hitchhiked back to join them."

With two companies bogged down, DeLuca sent Lieutenant Rodriquez's reconnaissance platoon in from the Y Bridge. Approaching from the east, the platoon made heavy contact a hundred meters short of linking up with Thompson and Stuart. One recon trooper was immediately wounded. While Rodriquez deployed his men, some took up firing positions on the rooftops and a draftee squad leader named Jay T. Crowe moved ahead of the rest of the platoon and sent three LAWs straight into a position from which the enemy had been firing RPGs.

To further reinforce the action, Captain Eckman and Company B, 6th Battalion, 31st Infantry, approached the area on DeLuca's order, moving across the rice paddies from the police outpost in the hamlet to the east. Gunships were rolling in through a criss-crossing network of tracers and smoke-trailing rockets. The grunts of Bravo Company watched amazed as a Cobra pulling out of a strafing run took a hit and, defying all laws of aerodynamics, rolled belly-over-blades to make a complete revolution and right itself just moments before crash-landing into a grassy field on its skids. The canopy flew open, and the two-man crew exited port and starboard. One of the aviators doubled back, apparently to pull the pin on a thermite or white-phosphorus grenade, because the gunship began burning as soon as the man dashed again for cover.

The lead platoon took occasional sniper fire as it advanced through a shabby housing area. Sergeant Richard D. "Rick" Kosar, who ran the lead squad, was on point with his good buddy, Private First Class Lance F. Bergstreser, the squad grenadier. The pair came under heavy fire upon reaching a berm that defined the edge of the backyards of several houses, and along which ran a tall chicken-wire fence. Kosar and Bergstreser were alongside the fence when the enemy opened up, so they hit it right there, using the berm for cover. The rest of the squad sought shelter against the building immediately to the rear of the point team.

Looking back, Bergstreser realized that one of their guys hadn't made it to cover; Private First Class Jose Louis Vieras was lying dead right behind them, apparently killed in the opening fusillade of AK-47 fire.

The point men spotted a bunker to their front and engaged the position. "There was sort of a notch in the berm and a space at the bottom of the chicken-wire fence that you could have almost crawled through," notes Bergstreser, "so Rick and I took turns; one fired through the notch while the other one reloaded. I finally hit the front of the position with an M79 grenade and it got quiet."

Sergeant Kosar went back up for another look and blurted, "Oh, shit!" when he realized that there was a second enemy position beside the first. He just had time to open fire with his M16 before taking a hit and going limp against the berm. "The round entered Rick's right cheek and exited from the middle of the left side of his neck," recounts Bergstreser, willing to return to that day only so that what happened to his friend will not be lost to history. "Rick never regained consciousness. I was not able to stop his bleeding, and he died within a very few minutes. I remained there with him, returning fire occasionally. After awhile, we stopped taking fire, so I figured the NVA had pulled back for whatever reason. I carried Rick back to the rest of the squad, and we got outta there."

Captain Eckman ordered a withdrawal after discussing the situation by radio with DeLuca and reporting that he had taken two dead and nine wounded. The body of Sergeant Kosar was loaded into a poncho litter, while that of Jose Vieras was carried out on a tall louvered window; both dead men were twenty-year-old draftees. Though it seemed that all the civilians had cleared out, a little Vietnamese woman was discovered in one of the houses. "She looked like she was seventy, but she probably wasn't but forty," recalls Vernon Moore, one of two grunts who scooped the woman up under her arms "and toted her back aways to get her out of danger." When they put her down to help carry Vieras, "she took off runnin' and went back, and we couldn't get her 'cause they were shooting at us pretty hard right then."

Moore would learn only later that the Vietnamese woman had dashed back into the battle area to find a loved one: "After we blowed the place apart all night, we went back through and found her layin' there with an individual who I guess was her husband. Both of 'em was dead."

Bravo Company got reorganized, and a personnel carrier arrived to drop off supplies and take out the bodies of Kosar and Vieras. A freelance photographer with a foreign accent was on the scene, and to get more dramatic shots of the dead before they were loaded into the track, he allegedly pulled back the ponchos that had been placed over the KIAs. By some accounts, the photographer was punched in the face for his insensitivity, by others, threatened with summary execution by an outraged grunt with a locked and loaded M16. Dave Leader remembers the incident somewhat less dramatically. According to Leader, Captain Eckman was standing near the bodies when the photographer "tried to sneak in and take his pictures. Eckman went right at him, waving his arms, and shouting at him to get out of there and not take pictures of our dead. Eckman didn't want their families to see their pictures in the papers. He got between the reporter and the bodies and just kept backing the guy up and hollering at him. That was the maddest I've ever seen Eckman."

Eckman recalls that "I confiscated the film and returned the photographer under guard to the battalion command post. I had no problems with other press people."

The stalemate unbroken as dusk approached, DeLuca wanted everybody to pull back so he could bring in air strikes. Ignoring the snipers,

First Lieutenant Richard Bland and Platoon Sergeant Richard B. Regan of Alpha One ranged along the north shore of the tributary as they kept their platoon's suppressive fire going. Several of Bland's grunts brought a sampan across the tributary and took up firing positions as Klump dragged the bodies of Jacobs and Powell to the boat from the ditch where Gibson's group was pinned down. Klump pushed the sampan back to the north shore, hanging on for dear life with one hand as he dog-paddled with the other because he didn't know how to swim. After unloading the dead, Klump made another trip for the wounded. Then he went back a third time to get the rest of his guys, only to discover that everyone had already pulled back across the footbridge, concealed by the smoke pouring from the wooden house nearby that had been set ablaze by an RPG.

Captain Stuart had been forced to leave the bodies of Jackson, Querry, and the Tiger Scout in the ditch in front of the burning building. Hearing that there were still dead on the battlefield, Alpha Two's medic "started back across the bridge," recounts Klump, "but was blowed into the water. He got hit in the shoulder and the impact knocked him off the bridge. He managed to get out of there."

The south side of the tributary was being plastered with artillery when a track from the scout platoon of the 2-47th Mech arrived to evacuate the two bodies that Stuart's men had recovered and the most seriously injured of the two dozen wounded. By the time the track—with weary grunts walking along in column on either side—had rolled back up the side street leading to the canal road and hung a right to return to the Y Bridge, the Phantoms were rolling in behind them. The ground shook as the high-drag bombs went in, shrapnel screaming past, "and, hell," notes Klump, "a bunch of the scouts got wounded on top of that damn APC."

Captain Stuart and Platoon Sergeant Klump were subsequently awarded Silver Stars. Lieutenant Rodriquez, Platoon Sergeant Regan, Sergeants Crowe and Querry, Specialist Fourth Class Westcott, and Privates First Class Jacobs and Powell were among those awarded Bronze Stars. The battalion reported a highly dubious body count of sixty-five. Lieutenant Colonel DeLuca wrote to his wife the next afternoon that May 10 "was the worst day with 6 Killed and 40 wounded. Many of those will be back in a few days so it's not as bad as it looks. I had tears in my eyes yesterday when I was at the helicopter pad seeing some wounded off. One kid was laying on his right side on a stretcher all patched up and still bleeding from neck and shoulder wounds. As I finished talking to him he raised himself up and saluted."

Stuart approached Klump as Alpha Company set up for the night near the command post. "You know, you were right," the captain said, meaning that he shouldn't have ordered the assault across the footbridge.

"You goddamn right I was right," Klump growled.

Captain Eckman returned to the police outpost with two platoons, leaving his forward observer, Second Lieutenant Frederick G. Kaiser, and Lieutenant Blacker's platoon, Bravo Three, outposted a hundred meters away in an abandoned schoolhouse. The schoolhouse was two stories high, a square-shaped building with an open courtyard in the center, and one of the few structures still standing in a neighborhood bordering the rice paddies that had otherwise been shelled into rubble. Blacker's grunts busied themselves as night fell, tearing up concrete slabs from the classroom floors to build bunkers at the gated entranceway to the school grounds. Enough slabs were stacked up that the walls and roofs of the instant bunkers were two and a half feet thick, more than solid enough to withstand the direct hit of a mortar shell or RPG.

In the tape Sergeant Leader sent to his wife after the battle, he noted that "we pounded the enemy all night long with 750-pound bombs, artillery, helicopter gunships—all night long, all through the next morning till daylight."

As the sky lightened, hazy and gray, Lieutenant Blacker and Sergeant Leader "were on watch observing from the second-floor windows of the schoolhouse," the squad leader's tape continued, "and we saw approximately fifty Viet Cong moving in our direction to the left and right. They were planning an assault on the schoolhouse, and [Lieutenant Kaiser] called in 8-inch artillery on 'em, and we caught 'em in the open. They didn't get in soon enough and daylight caught 'em, and we saw 'em, and we got 'em with helicopter gunships, air strikes, and artillery all at the same time. They started to scatter like fleas."

Lieutenant Kaiser, directing the fire from an exposed position, was wounded either by the enemy's sporadic return fire, which included several RPGs, or a piece of shrapnel from the shells he was bringing in danger close. He was subsequently awarded the Silver Star and Purple Heart. The grunts also opened fire with M16s, M60s, and M79s. No body count was recorded, though the VC soldiers were undoubtedly dragging any number of dead and wounded with them as they retreated. Blacker and his grunts were later informed (though it is unclear if the information came from prisoner interrogations or was pure speculation) that the enemy company turned back by Kaiser had planned to overrun their positions in the dark, but had gotten lost on their way to the objective.

Apparently, the scouts who had mapped out the approaches to the schoolhouse had seen the area before it had been blasted apart. When the assault company actually made its approach, the enemy commanders found the buildings they had planned to use as rallying points leveled, and the alleyways down which they had planned to slip through were clotted with rubble. Because of the confusion, recalls Leader, "they didn't get to us in time and got caught in the open at dawn. We were able to put a lot of fire on them. It was a decisive success, and our only casualty was the artillery forward observer."

Captain Stuart's company recrossed the footbridge the next morning and recovered its dead from the muddy ditch. When searching the buildings in the area, the grunts discovered four or five enemy soldiers huddled in one of them. They were all badly wounded and unable to keep up with their comrades who had pulled out during the night. The request was made for a medevac chopper. When it landed, one of the wounded prisoners refused to climb aboard, and terrified, he frantically pushed away the grunts who tried to carry him to the Huey. "The hell with it," Klump finally snapped. "We'll hog-tie the sonuvabitch to a pole and carry him out." The company was moving back across the footbridge when Klump barked at the grunts carrying the pole over their shoulders to dump the prisoner in the water and drown the bastard. "I meant it," recalls Klump. "I had lost two men the day before. That didn't settle too good with me. I would have thrown him in myself, but my men had better heads on their shoulders than me, and they didn't do it."

Part Seven

AMBUSH

Chapter 22

Lieutenant Colonel Antila was instructed late on the morning of May 10, 1968 to proceed with Companies A and C of the 5th Battalion (Mechanized), 60th Infantry—presently in a staging area along Route 5A on the outskirts of the capital—to Xom Tan Liem, a hamlet straddling the slightly elevated dirt highway less than five kilometers south of Saigon. The militia outpost in Xom Tan Liem had come under attack at dawn from the north and west by what the U.S. advisors on the scene estimated to be two companies of Viet Cong.

Antila was up in a helicopter and Captain Dobbs and Company A, followed by Captain Scarborough and Company C, were moving south on Route 5A as of 10:40 p.m. Gunships, meanwhile, rolled in despite the AK-47 and .51-caliber antiaircraft fire zipping past from positions all around Xom Tan Liem.

The tracks came under fire from the first few hootches at the northern fringe of the hamlet. Both companies halted on the highway, which was lined at intervals with palm trees, and cut a straight line across paddies that were mostly flooded. Infantrymen dismounted while gunners returned fire. One of Company A's gunners took a round through the thigh while manning his .50, and one of the dismounted teams fired up the hootch from which the shot had come and reported a dead VC. In the middle of the melee, someone shot a large hog in the stomach. "The hog was running and squalling like mad," recalls Clifford Shields. "City boys don't know that you can't kill a hog by shooting them in the stomach. I shot the animal in the head to end its suffering, and some civilians came out of nowhere and started to dress the hog."

First Lieutenant Carl D. Lange of the 3rd Platoon, Company A—the lead element on the road—had flown out two days earlier to replace Grant Buehrig. The new platoon leader was no novice. Lange, in fact, had reported to OCS as a staff sergeant with nine years of service and had served briefly as a platoon leader before being reassigned as the company executive officer. Sharpe thought Lange an exceptionally fine officer. Even a seasoned soldier like Lange, however, was taken aback by the scene before them now. "We had visual contact with the enemy," he recalls. "You didn't even need binoculars they were so close. They were running around, taking up positions—and we could see that they weren't [all] Viet Cong. There were [also] North Vietnamese in khaki uniforms. It was absolutely shocking because it was the first time we'd ever seen NVA."

Directed to continue the attack, Lieutenant Lange told Sergeant Raggs to get out in front of the lead track in order to protect it from any RPG teams in position down the road. Raggs balked, arguing that his squad should shelter behind the track as it pressed ahead. As the conversation grew heated, the squad leader declared to Lange: "One of *my* men gets shot, you're gonna be the next one."

Unintimidated, Lieutenant Lange started forward to take the point himself and get everyone moving. "He was trying to keep everything cool because he was going to have a mutiny and look bad," according to an unimpressed Howard Ossen. Lange hadn't even cleared the front of the track when a trooper named Fred Tice saw a figure appear from a hootch that sat to the right-front of him and behind a row of palm trees evenly spaced along a berm that bisected the highway. Before Tice could shout a warning, the enemy soldier fired an RPG. The rocket detonated behind the lead track with a red flash that caught everyone but Tice unawares. "I was standing up, then I was on the ground—and I didn't know how I got there," recalls Les Koenig, who put two and two together when he noticed the remains of an RPG lying on the road. He was patting himself down for injuries when he realized that "there were people all over the place, bleedin'."

Koenig had been peppered in the back, Ossen the right leg. The more seriously injured included Shields, Tice, Nauyalis, and Lieutenant Lange, who had been banged up the worst of all with a critical throat wound, not to mention all the other specks of metal that had peppered his buttocks and arm. The seriously wounded, ten in all, were directed to a track that would deliver them to the staging area along the highway where a medevac could land in safety. After helping some of their more seriously wounded buddies to the track, Koenig and Ossen basically hunkered down and let the war proceed without them. "With most of our squad gone," notes Koenig, "we decided that maybe we should hang back toward the rear for awhile."

The medics stripped off Lieutenant Lange's fatigues and bandaged his wounds, wrapping a thick field dressing around his throat. He lay naked on the stretcher when he was loaded aboard the medevac that landed in the staging area. The medevac lifted off and made for the 3rd Field Hospital. Lange would not be back. Howard Ossen, for one, was glad to see the platoon leader get himself shot up and sent home, and would always resent that Lange was subsequently awarded the Silver Star to go with his Purple Heart. "Everyone was exhausted, scared, and agitated, and we simply weren't willing to accept a new guy after losing Lieutenant Buehrig," recalls Mark Fenton, trying to explain the tension that existed between Lange and certain members of the platoon. "We knew that we could count on Buehrig, but all of a sudden, he's hit and gone, and we're supposed to follow this new guy that we know nothing about except that he's gung-ho as hell. Lange probably was a good officer, but he wasn't with us long enough for us to find out."

Captain Dobbs, the incompetent and already shaky new commander of Company A, finally cracked up completely on the road to Xom Tan Liem. John Holder saw Dobbs "running to the rear, looking over his shoulder, almost in tears. He was scared to death. I remember thinking to myself, *Aren't we supposed to shoot those that run away under fire?*"

Captain Scarborough and Company C, having halted several hundred meters behind Company A, exchanged fire with enemy west of the highway. Lieutenant Neild, the artillery spotter, had dismounted with Kisling, his recon sergeant, and radioman Lurch, "and we were moving around on the road, trying to stay out of the way of the bullets," recalls Neild. "Lurch wasn't watching what he was doing, and he walked right in front of a .50-caliber machine gun." The antenna extending from the radio on Hewitt's back was clipped off just above his head, meaning that Neild couldn't call for artillery support "unless I used the radio inside the command track."

Antila directed Scarborough to bypass the enemy on his flank and move forward to reinforce Second Lieutenant Edward B. Gallup, the forward observer who had taken command of Company A when Dobbs fled the scene. At the time, which was around noon, Gallup was pulling back to make room for the fire support, and the next two hours were spent working the area with gunships, artillery, and air strikes.

Antila wanted Scarborough to launch the next attack. Accordingly, Company C squeezed past Company A, and the Bandidos watched the hootches facing them disappear amid the shriek of low-flying jets, bursting napalm canisters, and geysers of smoke, dust, and dirt clouds from the high-drag bombs. Scarborough, meanwhile, walked up to the lead track to confer with Sergeant First Class T. L. Kemper (pseudonym), the platoon-sergeant-turned-acting-platoon-leader of the 1st Platoon. Kemper only had two tracks on the road, the platoon's third operational personnel carrier having been dispatched earlier that morning to escort a fuel carrier that was to take on a load of diesel at Tan Son Nhut.

Sergeant First Class Kemper was a tall and powerfully built man with an accent from the Deep South. Having won his first combat infantry-man's badge in Korea and having spent his entire career in the combat arms, he should have been a great platoon sergeant in Vietnam. Instead, he was despised as an alcoholic who'd "be clear out of his mind drunk every night" according to one of his former GIs. Kemper was also seen as an arrogant, abusive lifer who, his hardcore military bearing aside, says another veteran, was "actually kind of chickenshit about going out on patrols and stuff himself."

Scarborough informed Kemper that his platoon was to speed down the road into the hamlet when the air strike was completed. The rest of the company would follow. Larry Miller, driver of the lead track, was sitting in his hatch when Scarborough turned to him and pointed to a tall, round cement structure with a tin roof, which apparently was a well, on the left side of the road inside the hamlet. Scarborough told Miller that he wanted him to stop fifty meters beyond the well, at which point the infantrymen on the first two tracks would overrun whatever dazed enemy soldiers were still alive in the smoking, blown-to-hell hamlet. "We're gonna charge right into the middle of 'em," Scarborough declared, as energized as any of the troops had ever seen him. "I want you guys to dismount as soon as we stop, run up to the hootches, and just shoot the shit out of everything. We're not gonna wait. We're not gonna give 'em a chance to get reorganized. We're gonna go right at 'em like Bandido Charlies."

Opting to lead from the front, Captain Scarborough had his command track pull in directly behind the lead platoon. One of the company commander's radiomen, a well-liked, nineteen-year-old black private first class named Randolph R. Wilkins, attached grenades to his web belt by their spoons, a ring of them all around his waist. He left his M16 stashed aboard the personnel carrier.

Wilkins happened past Jerry Harper as everyone got ready for the attack. Harper called to him: "Hey, where's your rifle?"

"I don't need it," said Wilkins, who was psyched up and ready to go. "When we get in there, I'm gonna chuck these frags in on 'em."

Captain Scarborough's voice crackled over the radio: "Mount up." Then the air strike ended with a final earth-shaking explosion, and the company commander gave the word: "All right, let's roll."

Miller started forward with Sergeant First Class Kemper sitting behind his hatch and Specialist Fourth Class Edward J. Chaffin's squad riding on the back deck of the APC. Captain Scarborough's track followed the second track, followed, in turn, by the 3d Platoon and the 2d Platoon.

Lieutenant Garver was on the fifth track in line, and he recalls how the north side of the hamlet had been so thoroughly flattened that "we might have been excused for thinking the attack was going to be more like a search-and-clear mission than a full-scale battle."

Lieutenant Garver would later write of "charging down the road with guns ablazing like the cavalry. The charge felt like something right out of a movie. As the tracks neared top speed and as the village came within range, more and more guys started firing." Garver was so caught up in the moment that he pulled his .45 from his shoulder holster and began uselessly firing away with the pistol. The column stopped and the infantrymen on the back decks immediately clambered off to the left side of their tracks.

As the two lead squads rushed the hootches on the flanks, Garver realized that enemy fire was pouring in from the left. The platoon leader and his radioman darted around to the right side of the track, but there was no safety to be found there for fire was pouring in from that direction, too. The air strikes might have done great damage at ground level, but they'd apparently had little effect on the enemy soldiers ensconced in spider holes and the family bunkers found under almost every rural hootch. "Charlie was still there in force," notes Garver. "I'll never forget the helpless feeling as I crouched alongside my track with bullets thudding into the hull and pinging off the treads and road wheels. There was nowhere to hide and no enemy to be seen. They were dug in too well. We were sitting ducks!"

Miller halted fifty meters past the well, as instructed, then he scrambled out of the driver's hatch to keep the gunner in the command cupola supplied with ammo. Chaffin's squad had already dismounted by then and had darted down a berm toward several hootches still standing on the right flank.

As the gunner returned fire on the second track, he was hit in a matter of moments and the driver took his place behind the .50-caliber machine gun. The dismounted troops, meanwhile, sheltered behind whatever meager cover they could find and blasted away, trying to suppress the AK-47 fire that seemed to be snapping in from everywhere. Chaffin bellowed to Jerry Harper, who had the M60: "Fire, Harper! Fire!"

"There's something wrong with the sonuvabitch," Harper shouted back over the din. "It won't shoot!"

Harper popped the feed tray open to make sure that the ammo belt was seated properly. It was, so he recocked the weapon, but nothing happened when he pulled the trigger. Utterly exasperated, he finally called to Chaffin, "This damn thing ain't workin'. I'm gonna have to run back and get an M16."

Harper reached the track in one piece and, quickly pulling the sling off his shoulder, was about to throw the machine gun in the back when he saw that there were three bullet holes in the side of the M60. *Shit, no wonder it ain't workin',* thought Harper, realizing that an enemy marksman had tried to kill him, as machine gunners were always a prime target. The enemy, though, had hit only the weapon and not the man carrying it. Grabbing an M16 and a claymore bag full of magazines, Jerry Harper ran back down the berm to rejoin Ed Chaffin.

Rounds impacted all over the command track as the gunner kept up a steady stream of return fire. "Where the gunner found the nerve to stay on that gun as long as he did, I do not know," notes Kisling, who stood in the cargo hatch behind the command cupola, firing his M16. "It was obvious our return fire was doing the enemy no harm, but I didn't want to un-ass the track and leave the gunner and the driver. I just kept hoping that an RPG wouldn't punch through the side of the track and take off our legs." Either the machine gun jammed or the gunner finally decided to vacate his exposed position; whatever the case, Kisling was glad when the gunner and the driver finally jumped down to the road, allowing him to follow suit without feeling like a deserter. When Kisling caught a glimpse of Lieutenant Neild rushing off the right side of the road, he attempted to fire a covering burst as he followed the forward observer. The M16 jammed. Neild had found sanctuary behind a small concrete culvert running under the highway. Kisling plopped down to Neild's right. "The mud around us," recalls Kisling, "was flying up in the air from all the rounds hitting the paddy."

Captain Scarborough climbed behind the command track with Private First Class David G. Creamer, one of his radiomen. The other radioman, Randolph Wilkins, was about to follow when he suddenly exploded. The young soldier was blown almost completely in half by either a rocket-propelled grenade that caught him in the stomach, or a piece of shrapnel or bullet that detonated one of the hand grenades hooked to his web belt.

Trying to take control of the situation, Scarborough moved to the front of the track with radiomen Creamer and Hewitt, the latter having gotten separated in the pandemonium from Neild and Kisling. The trio was fully exposed to the enemy, who quickly zeroed in on the tall figure, with the silver captain bars on his helmet, holding a radio handset to his ear. Scarborough had earlier instructed Creamer to switch his whip antenna for a fifteen-foot long-range antenna, "and since everybody could see that highboy antenna sticking up," notes a former Bandido, "it was the same as flying a pennant and saying shoot at me."

The enemy did just that, firing an RPG into the middle of the group. Creamer and Hewitt were badly wounded, and Captain Scarborough was killed instantly by a single tiny fragment that zipped through his eye and into his brain. His glasses ended up on the road, one of the lenses shattered. There wasn't a scratch on the company commander's body, and the only evidence of trauma was a small trickle of blood along his neck, apparently from a ruptured eardrum.

The explosion also wounded Millard Goodwin, who had dismounted the track directly behind Scarborough's by scrambling down the front slope. He ended up on his knees in the middle of the road between the two personnel carriers as he returned fire with his M79. Goodwin's target was a hootch to the left-front that seemed to be the source of AK-47 fire; about five minutes into the battle, the RPG that killed Scarborough had, in fact, come sizzling from that hootch. The command track shielded Goodwin from the heart of the blast, but he nonetheless felt something thump into his left leg. "I didn't really pay attention to it. I just kept reloading and firing at that hootch. I must have felt the burning—shrapnel's hot when it hits you—because I finally glanced down and saw a piece about the size of a silver dollar stuck through the trouser leg right above my knee. I reached down and pulled it out, then went back to firing the M79."

Jerry Harper, having secured a rifle, returned to Chaffin's position amid the hootches. Chaffin told him that the captain had been killed. "What the hell!" Harper blurted. "Six is dead?"

"Yeah, he got hit by an RPG back on the road."

"Fuck. . . ."

Larry Miller heard the explosion behind him, but busy securing ammunition for the gunner on the lead track, who was blasting away like a man possessed, he wasn't immediately able to glance back to see if anybody had been hit by the RPG. When he did so, he saw to his dismay that Captain Scarborough was sprawled unmoving on the road with Hewitt and blown-in-half Randolph Wilkins.

An enemy soldier suddenly materialized to the left of the lead track, firing his AK-47 as he rose up from the paddy and emptying the magazine in a single burst. Larry Miller, shot in the upper left arm, was slammed into the gunner in the command cupola with such force as to knock the man away from the .50.

In the next instant, even before the enemy soldier could duck down to switch magazines, the driver-turned-gunner on the second track, Private First Class Robert J. Foris, lowered the barrel of his .50-caliber machine gun on the Viet Cong and fired a burst at pointblank range, knocking him back into the muddy water. Foris was shot in the elbow moments later, and the machine gun on the second track went unmanned for the duration of the battle.

The lead track also fell silent, for the gunner had scrambled from his exposed perch and disappeared from sight. Perhaps he had been unnerved by the relentless hail of fire or had thought himself injured, splattered as he had been by Miller's blood. Possibly, the gunner might simply have been following the lead of Sergeant First Class Kemper, who abandoned the track and raced down the column on foot. Enraged, Larry Miller tried to sight in on the hated lifer's back with his M16. Kemper survived unscathed to take refuge with the last platoon in line. The acting platoon leader spent the rest of the battle huddled inside an APC.

Instead of joining the retreat, Larry Miller climbed behind the .50 and laid down a steady stream of fire to cover Ed Chaffin's squad, which was pulling back. Miller blasted any position in sight that might have been concealing an enemy soldier, alternating between the machine gun and his M16. Miller, a lean, taciturn, hard-eyed country boy, would explain his actions with considerable understatement: "I figured we should keep shooting as long as we could keep shooting."

Miller could lift his wounded left arm, but he had no strength in his hand. As such, he had to change magazines, fit ammo belts into place, and snap back the bolt of his rifle and the cocking handle of the machine gun with his right hand only. Unlike the men farther back in the column, Miller could see enemy soldiers scuttling about between the hootches and popping up to fire from the brush and nippa palm, and he placed his fire directly at these half-glimpsed figures. "I don't like to get into it; but, yeah, I think I saw some of them go down as I fired. They were right there. They were all over us."

Lieutenant Garver and his radioman, a private first class named Jimmy D. Lundberg, who was also the platoon leader's best friend, huddled on their knees beside their track as rounds ricocheted with terrifying frequency off the aluminum armor. Garver had no doubt that they were going to be hit at any moment as he tried to make contact with battalion, having been informed that Captain Scarborough was dead and he was now in charge. Garver eventually realized that he and Lundberg were low enough to the ground and high enough on the slightly raised road to avoid being taken under direct fire by the entrenched NVA and Viet Cong.

The track gunners had no cover. One was soon hit. Specialist Fourth Class William G. Behan pulled the wounded man away in order to take his place behind the .50-caliber machine gun. A twenty-two-year-old married man and draftee, Behan was one of the better soldiers in Garver's platoon, but in short order, he was shot dead. Tom Clemmer, another of Garver's stalwarts, shoved the body out of the way and resumed fire with the .50. Doc Bianco, meanwhile, darted between the personnel carriers to treat the wounded, and when the medic wasn't tying bandages, he was firing an M16.

Lieutenant Garver's three dismounted machine gunners—Flores, Harris, and Helsley—also ignored the incoming rounds as they lay down sheets of fire. Private First Class Richard J. Flores, a nineteen–year-old new guy, was killed—as best can be determined—when raked by a burst of enemy fire while at the prone in the middle of the road, blazing away with his bipod-mounted M60.

Tucked behind the culvert at the bottom of the road, Lieutenant Neild initially was unaware that Scarborough had been killed and his own radioman Lurch Hewitt had been seriously wounded by an RPG. Neild hadn't heard the explosion in the din and didn't know anything was wrong. Kisling, who was unable to make himself heard, though he was shoulder to shoulder with Neild and was shouting in his ear, finally had to physically turn Neild around and point to the bodies up on the road. The sight shocked Neild into action. He knew what he had to do. He had to get some artillery on target, which meant that he had to get to the radio inside the command track. "Oh Christ, I've got to get up there in that track," Neild recalls thinking. "Otherwise, we're stuck; we're going to die here if I don't do something." The idea of breaking from his cover was excruciating, but "as an officer, you're supposed to lead, and I couldn't have stayed behind that culvert forever, anyway. There was no safe choice. If I stayed put, they were eventually going to get me; they were going to get the whole unit. If we didn't get something organized, we were going to be in deeper trouble than we already were. There really wasn't much of an option but to get to that APC."

Kisling watched in awe as Lieutenant Neild jumped up and sprinted to the command track with rounds literally nipping at his heels. Ducking inside through the back, Neild grabbed the handset only to get an earful of static, leaving him to wonder if the enemy was jamming the infantry net. Neild was finally able to establish communication with battalion through the artillery net, but was unsuccessful in obtaining any fire support. "No gunships. No artillery. Things must have been happening so fast that battalion couldn't get the stuff we needed, at least not while we were still in the kill zone. Instead, battalion was telling me to get out of there." Neild later wondered why battalion didn't have the fire support lined up in case heavy contact was made during the attack. "Looking back on it, you think, 'Boy, that's the wrong way to fight a war!' "

The retreat began about thirty minutes into the battle. Garver has a different recollection than Neild about how the decision to pull back was made. "I could not get anyone on the radio," recalls Garver. "Though I heard no one on the radio, that is not to say, however, that no one heard me as I described our situation and requested assistance and advice. After a period of time without radio contact—it seemed like an eternity—I finally decided that even a wrong move was preferable to no move at all. There was just one obvious course of action, and that was to get the hell out of the kill zone as quickly as possible." Garver had his dead and wounded loaded aboard his tracks, but when he gave the order to start backing down the road, "word come back to me that the last track in the column was blocking our escape," having apparently been disabled by a rocket-propelled grenade. "I told them to push it out of the way if necessary, but get past it. They did, and we did."

Chapter 23

The second track, abandoned by its crew, sat in the middle of the road, effectively blocking the lead track because none of the infantrymen up front knew how to drive the thing.

Ed Chaffin, meanwhile, made radio contact with the company first sergeant, who was back at the staging area with the maintenance track and mortar section. Among other things, Chaffin reported that "Six is KIA."

"Say again. Over."

"Six is *Kilo India Alpha*."

The first sergeant shrilly promised that help was on the way. Jerry Harper urged Chaffin: "Tell 'im to send down a driver!"

No driver had appeared by the time the retreat began. Miller was still firing the .50 on the lead track, and Chaffin, Harper, Sam Marr, and Private First Class Donald W. Wendler were still pinned behind a berm in the adjacent paddy while the retreat was taking place. The platoon at the end of the column backed out of the kill zone, followed by Lieutenant Garver's four tracks, plus the company command track, onto which Neild and Kisling had scrambled. In the confusion of the moment, those who pulled back did not seem to realize that they were leaving comrades behind. Hard feelings still exist about this turn of events.

Alone on the lead track, Larry Miller had been so preoccupied with returning fire that the rest of the company was well up the road before he realized that he was stuck on the wrong side of an unmanned track. Marr and Wendler sought cover in the lead track, and Marr took over on the .50 when Miller ducked into the hull to tie a bandage around his bleeding arm. The enemy concentrated their fire on the only two vehicles still in the kill zone. "There was so much incoming, we finally couldn't even stand up to reach the .50," recalls Miller. "I know my shirt was ringing wet with sweat; I didn't figure we'd ever get out of there."

To attempt to reach the second track seemed suicidal, but whatever the risks, someone was going to have to drive it back up the road to clear the way for the lead track. Finally, Sam Marr said he'd give it a try. Leaping from the back door of the lead track, Marr clambered into the driver's hatch of the second track, grabbed the controls, and promptly drove backwards off the road while attempting to turn around. He'd had no training as a driver, so the track had ended up stuck in the rice paddy next to the cement well on the left side of the highway.

It didn't matter. Marr, who rushed back to the lead track, had accomplished the mission: the road was now clear. Miller slipped into the driver's seat and shouted to Marr and Wendler to open the door built into the back ramp so he could see where he was going as he backed up. As soon as the door was opened, however, AK-47 fire stitched the rear of the track and rounds went ricocheting around inside the hull. The door was slammed shut again. Miller managed to get the track turned around on the road then, as he recalls, "hauled ass back to where the rest of the company was regrouping and getting reorganized,"

Ed Chaffin and Jerry Harper sprang up when the track went past, "and we ran alongside of it, one on each side," recalls Harper, "firing our M16s." At that time, the armored personnel carriers of Companies A and C were parked in a long row along the side of the highway, "and I was madder 'n hell," notes Harper, "because they didn't send anybody down to help or nothin'. They all just sat up there watching. There were a lot of tracks sitting there and they didn't do a damn thing. I was yelling at them. I was pretty shook up."

The guys who had earlier escorted the fuel carrier to the airbase returned to the staging area. When informed of the disaster, they raced to rejoin the platoon after loading their track with an ammunition resupply. Miller was sitting at the edge of the road when they arrived, staring dejectedly at the ground. Shutting the track down, Lanny Jones asked Miller what the hell had happened. Miller brightened at the sight of his buddies. "I got shot," he said with a grin, nodding to Doc Birge, "and my damn medic wasn't there to take care of me."

Birge removed the bandage Miller had hastily wrapped around his arm, got the wound properly dressed, then asked if there was anything else he could do.

"Yeah," Miller cracked. "Get me a fucking cold beer."

The lapse in fire support would never be explained. Perhaps jammed or malfunctioning radios were to blame. Maybe one set of gunships had been forced to break station to refuel before another could be made available. Whatever the case, order was soon restored. All available artillery resumed firing at Lieutenant Colonel Antila's command, more gunships rolled in, and jet fighters once again shrieked low over the rice paddies, releasing another cascade of napalm and high-drag bombs into Xom Tan Liem.

Lieutenant Colonel Schmalhorst watched from his own command ship as the helicopters bearing A/6-31st—soon to be followed by C/6-31st—set down on the highway directly behind the 5-60th Mechanized Infantry. An attempt to land nearer the objective had been aborted when .51-caliber fire was received.

The prepatory fires were lifted, and Bandido Charlie advanced again on the hamlet. There was no enemy fire this time; the VC and NVA had melted away. Although they had failed to take the militia outpost, they had wreaked considerable damage on the relief force, which may or may not have been the intention all along.

The track stuck in the mud was towed back onto the road. Captain Scarborough's body was recovered and laid in the narrow space between the front slope of the track and the partially deployed trim vane. Chaffin called to Harper to help him with Wilkins. Grabbing the radioman's arms, they dragged Wilkins' body to the side of the road, and were preparing to wrap the disemboweled corpse—their buddy—in a poncho when Harper began gagging, overcome by the stench. "I can do this," Chaffin said, "go ahead," so Harper turned away, took several steps, fell to his knees, and puked. Sam Marr and Lieutenant Neild went to help Chaffin, "and I remember trying to push the body up behind the trim vane," recounts Neild, "and my hand was right in the middle of the guy's gut. I mean, there was nothing there, there was nothing to push on; he literally had no belly. I had to back off and try to find something more substantial, like his buttocks, to push. I had never seen such gore before."

Twenty-eight wounded troopers were medevacked from the road, including Lurch Hewitt, who lingered for nearly two weeks before succumbing to his injuries and belatedly joining Captain Scarborough and the three troopers—Behan, Flores, and Wilkins—who had been killed instantly during the battle. In exchange, battalion claimed an invented but not improbable body count of twenty Viet Cong.

Surprisingly, a live enemy soldier was pulled from the water and nippa palm along the highway. The prisoner was quickly relieved of his inoperable RPG launcher and stripped to his sopping-wet black shorts, with his arms bound behind his back and a fatigue shirt tied around his face as a blindfold. The prisoner was loaded atop Lieutenant Garver's track to get him back to a helicopter that had landed on the road. Along the way, the gunner swung the barrel of his .50—still hot from the firing that had preceded the final attack—against the VC's neck, making him jerk with pain. Some of the guys laughed. "I don't think it bothered me much at the time," recalls Garver. "I was probably in more of a daze than the prisoner."

Lieutenant Colonel Antila and Lieutenant Franks, his artillery officer, sitting on either side of the pilot flying their bubble helicopter, spotted two more guerrillas from the air. The pair were tight against a paddy dike, trying to avoid detection. The pilot tried without success to slash the nearest guerrilla to death with the main rotor of the helicopter. Franks fired his .45 from the right side of the bubble, grazing the man; then either he or Antila (both would recall being the first out of the chopper) jumped eight feet to the paddy below and advanced on the wounded VC.

Both the wounded man and his nearby compadre instantly surrendered, having already thrown their weapons aside when they realized they'd been spotted. Other less docile enemy could easily be hiding nearby. Thus the man on the ground needed someone to watch his back while he kept his weapon trained on the prisoners. The helicopter swung around and hovered again over the area, allowing the other officer to jump from the skid. It didn't take long before a patrol reached Antila and Franks from the road to collect the prisoners, and the two went airborne again to continue searching for the fleeing Viet Cong.

Brigade decided to replace Antila's battalion with Schmalhorst's, and while A/6-31st moved west in search of the enemy, Captain Owen and C/6-31st marched down the highway with orders to secure the militia outpost in Xom Tan Liem. Along the way, they passed the track on which "bodies were piled in a puzzle of arms and legs," recounts Al Olson, "a couple of ponchos thrown over them as if to hide the truth." There was no communication between the grunts and the Bandidos. "Those guys didn't even make eye contact," notes Olson. "Perhaps they were still in shock. Probably they didn't want us to see the hurt, pain, and loss in their eyes. They apparently thought a great deal of their company commander. You could tell they were upset at his loss."

Lieutenant Belt, forward observer of C/6-31st, tried to get a run down on the situation from a lieutenant he saw on the road, but the guy had nothing coherent to say and was "shaking so bad he couldn't light his cigarette."

Owen's grunts pulled a wounded guerrilla from a caved-in spider hole, the fourth prisoner of the battle. In the meantime, the column of personnel carriers started rearward. "I do not have the ability to describe my emotions while traveling back to the staging area," notes Alan Kisling, who leveled an M60 on a file of civilians moving along the shoulder of the highway. "I wanted so badly to kill every one of them—women, children, whatever. I could have opened up and raked a kilometer of refugees as we went by. No one on the track would have stopped me. Every GI had that same inner feeling, but I didn't do it because there are certain lines you just don't cross."

As dusk approached, Lieutenant Colonel Antila's command group set up beside the highway with Company C, while Company A secured the Route 5A bridge over the Kinh Doi. An emergency resupply of ammunition was delivered by helicopter. The KIAs went out on one of the Hueys.

Les Koenig and Howard Ossen, curled up in ponchos on the cement bridge, were awakened by a single M16 shot and the blood-curdling scream of the GI who had been on guard atop their APC. The guard, a new guy with about a month in the field, had just shot himself in the foot. It was an accident, he claimed; he'd been cleaning his rifle and didn't realize that there was a round in the chamber. Koenig and Ossen thought the act intentional, though the trooper's cries indicated that if such was the case, he'd gotten more than he'd bargained for when he pulled the trigger. "When you put a bullet through your foot," notes Koenig, "I don't think you realize how much it's going to hurt."

Jerry Harper and Sam Marr were also medevacked. Doc Birge would later describe how he had found Marr—who had just lost his best friend and protector, Larry Miller—"sitting by himself, crying softly. His body was trembling. He couldn't talk. He just sat there looking at me." Birge tagged Marr as a combat-fatigue casualty. "No one thought less of the man because of this," writes Birge. "Sam was a good soldier, but had reached his limit. After what he'd been through the last few days, he had every right to cry. Sam was the youngest member of our platoon."

Harper would speak bluntly of the incident. "We cracked up. We were so nervous; every time we heard a pop or something, we jumped up and tried to run. Our nerves were shot." While Birge examined Harper and Marr, Lanny Jones went to find an officer to approve a medevac. By that point, Harper had blanked out. When he came back to reality, he and Marr were back at an aid station. "They sedated us," recalls Harper. "They let us sleep, get cleaned up, get some good hot meals in us, and then we went back out after a few days."

The ambush that ended the battalion's battle in the capital resulted in numerous awards. Lieutenant Colonel Antila and Lieutenant Franks were both pinned with the Air Medal for capturing the two guerrillas on the outskirts of Xom Tan Liem. Franks also won a Bronze Star for calling in fire from the command ship despite the high-caliber enemy weaponry in the area. Lieutenant Neild received a Silver Star that Alan Kisling thought was more than deserved, however ambivalent the forward observer himself felt

about the award. The medal was presented sans the usual descriptive citation. Neild was subsequently instructed to prepare the citation himself.
"They said, 'We don't know what happened, you write it up,' " he recalls,
astonished. It seemed that Neild had been decorated not for his specific
actions, which were unknown to the awards section, but because of the black
bar stitched on his collar, the premise being that any officer on the scene of
a crisis could be assumed to have responded heroically. Neild would have
preferred to have been cited for pulling the wounded radioman out of the
line of fire on the first day of the battle, "but even that would have been
stretching it because we were all just doing our duty."

Lieutenant Garver was not at all ambivalent about the Silver Star
pinned on his own chest. There was no doubt in his mind that he did not
deserve a medal—the heavy enemy fire notwithstanding—for crouching
beside his track, shouting into a radio for help, and getting no answer, finally
opting to sound retreat. "The awards system was an atrocity," declares
Garver. "It was used more as a morale builder and for other political reasons than to reward true valor in combat."

The system was weighted in favor not only of officers, but also senior
NCOs. Thus Larry Miller received nothing for his one-man stand at the
front of the column, and few, if any, of the troops Garver recommended
for decorations—Behan, Bianco, Clemmer, Flores, Harris, Helsley, and
Lundberg—actually received them. Meanwhile, Sergeant First Class Kemper was rewarded with the Silver Star for deserting his platoon.

Antila recommended Captain Edmund B. Scarborough for the Congressional Medal of Honor. It has been suggested that Antila had either been
misinformed about the details of Scarborough's actions or meant to draw
attention away from the disaster that the battle was by casting the dead company commander as an exemplar of combat leadership. "What do you do
when you screw up?" muses Kisling. "You find yourself someone to tag as
a hero." Witness statements were prepared that described how the company
commander had strode fearlessly through the hail of enemy fire, putting
troops into position, pointing out targets, firing his own weapon, and directing gunships and artillery fire before finally falling mortally wounded. The
statements were "bullshit," to quote Kisling; though Scarborough was
indeed a brave officer, he'd had no opportunity to do any of the things that
were written: "The captain got off the track, and, whap! he was killed. It
was just that fast—no heroics, just killed."

Kemper signed one of the statements. Not wanting to make waves,
Garver signed another. Some signatures went uncollected. The company
first sergeant approached three troops, Millard Goodwin among them, who

had repelled an enemy attack on their observation post shortly before the fighting in Saigon. "The first sergeant wanted us to sign these statements about what a war hero Scarborough was," recounts Goodwin; in exchange, the first sergeant promised to put the three GIs up for Silver Stars for the earlier action, "but when we refused to sign the statements, he said no way on the Silver Stars."

As puzzled as anyone by the machinations being carried out to secure for Scarborough the nation's highest honor for battlefield heroism, Lieutenant Neild wondered if Antila felt guilty about putting the captain in a position for which he had proven to be unprepared. Thus, Antila might have wished to make amends with a story of bravery above and beyond the call of duty that might provide some comfort to the dead man's family. Whatever the case, the witness statements and various endorsements were forwarded up the chain of command to the Department of the Army. There, the decision was made to posthumously decorate Captain Scarborough not with the Congressional Medal of Honor but the Distinguished Service Cross.

Talk could be heard about wasting Sergeant First Class Kemper. "We didn't mess around," states Jerry Harper. "Kemper knew the word on him was, 'You're gonna take a round—and maybe not from an AK-47.' "

No one ever pulled the trigger on Kemper. There was no need; the once hard-ass lifer was a broken man after the ambush. When Larry Miller rejoined the platoon from the hospital, Kemper said not a word, but produced his Silver Star the next day and laid it in the ammunition can attached to the .50-cal on their track. "It was like he was throwing it away," says Miller. "He didn't make a big production out of it, but he knew I was there and saw what he was doing."

The medal rode around in the ammo can until the platoon sergeant was reassigned off the line. Jerry Harper tried to give it to Kemper before he left: "Sarge, here's your Silver Star. You can't leave it here."

"I don't want it," said Kemper. "You keep it."

Harper stuffed the medal in his duffel bag as a souvenir.

Captain Dobbs continued to perform poorly as Company A began operating again from Binh Phuoc. The company commander was so befuddled and overwhelmed, that he appeared to be in a fog at times. "Dobbs used to wear a radio helmet," notes former platoon leader Rick Neuman. "The rest of us just wore earphones. It was too damn hot to wear a helmet. Dobbs actually wore the helmet, and I remember the guy jumping down off his personnel carrier one evening and going into a battalion briefing; and the cord connected from the helmet to the radio in the vehicle snapped apart behind him. He walked in and sat down with his helmet on. He'd forgotten he had it on."

The troops took to referring to the hapless company commander as Captain "Dum-Dum" or "Deputy Dawg," in reference to a slow-witted cartoon character. "I mean, guys were getting on the company net and anonymously making cracks to the CO [commanding officer]. That kind of thing was unheard of," says Grant Buehrig, who, like Neuman, had rejoined his platoon after recuperating from wounds he received during Mini-Tet. "There was no respect for the guy, and the battalion commander finally got rid of him several weeks after the battle in Saigon. I hate to talk about it. Dobbs was certainly incompetent, but I don't want to stand in judgment of somebody who should never have been put in command of a combat unit to begin with. More than anything, I felt sorry for Dobbs."

A final postscript about the Bandidos: Jerry Harper was returned to the field after being treated for combat fatigue and soldiered on until September 1968. At that time, the track he was driving rolled over a command-detonated mine buried in a path bulldozed through the jungle in the 1st Infantry Division area of operations. The explosion literally lifted the track off the ground. Regaining his senses, Harper turned to the man who had been crouched behind the driver's hatch, and saw that his buddy's face and chest had been removed.

When Harper tried to climb out, he realized that his right arm had been blown off below the elbow. "I managed to stick my head up a little bit and holler, and Doc Birge came a runnin' from another track in the column." Upon being pulled from his hatch, Harper, who couldn't feel a thing, saw that his right leg was gone just above the knee. Birge applied tourniquets to both stumps and covered Harper to reduce the risk of shock. "Doc's my savior," says Harper. Despite the prompt arrival of a medevac, Harper had lost so much blood by the time he was rushed into surgery in the evacuation hospital that the medical personnel couldn't start an IV in his deflated veins. They finally made an incision in his left ankle, "put a hose into a vein and pushed it open so they could start a transfusion. I knew I'd lost an arm and leg, but I didn't care. I said, 'I'm going back to The World.' That's all I cared about."

Chapter 24

The final act of the drama on the southern outskirts of the capital began to play itself out when Captain Owen and Company C, 6th Battalion, 31st Infantry, hiking past the Bandidos on the highway, reached the militia outpost in Xom Tan Liem as dusk approached on May 10. The lieutenant in command of the outpost was delighted at the company's arrival, as his meagerly equipped militiamen had been fearful of another night attack. The grunts joined the militiamen on the perimeter berm.

Captain Owen's command group set up in a cramped little bunker, sharing what space there was with the wounded guerrilla they'd scooped up on the way in. As a precaution, the senior medic sedated the prisoner after checking his wounds again while he lay on a wooden table in the bunker. It was going on four in the morning and everyone, save the man on radio watch, was conked out when mortar shells began exploding inside the compound. The prisoner sat straight up at the first explosion and dove off the table. Thinking the guerrilla was going for a grenade, Owen and one of his radiomen came flapping out from under their ponchos, simultaneously grabbing their weapons and flipping the safeties off. The medic urgently called them off, exclaiming, "No, no, I got 'im, I got 'im!" The prisoner's only intent was to take cover under a bench. He was so badly injured and heavily sedated that Owen "couldn't believe the guy was capable of moving, let alone protecting himself from the mortar fire. His survival instincts were excellent!"

The mortar barrage was brief; and there were no casualties. No one was hit by the small-arms fire, either, which began snapping in from the darkness beyond the southern perimeter wire. The militiamen on the berm blazed back with their old carbines, M1s, and Browning Automatic Rifles. The militiamen called to the GIs in Vietnamese, pointing to the distant area from which the tracers had originated. In response, "some of us fired a few rounds," notes former squad leader Al Olson. "The entire attack, if you could call it that, lasted only minutes."

Responding to the shouts to cease fire, "we settled back down, and that was it," except, of course, for the counter-mortar fire from the weapons platoon, the gunship runs, and the artillery salvos that lit up the rice paddies to the south. The map indicated a hamlet in the area. Olson would

wonder, in retrospect, if the Viet Cong had intentionally positioned themselves between the outpost and the hamlet, "knowing that we always hit
back hard with everything we had; even as they slipped off, our return fire
would cause civilian casualties and make us the bad guys."

The militia lieutenant thought the attack was a diversion to cover the
movement of the main enemy force out of the area. Captain Owen agreed,
and leaning over a map with the lieutenant—who knew the area inti-
mately—the two of them traced the most likely route the guerrillas would
follow in retreat. Owen next contacted battalion to suggest that Company
C spend the balance of the day in pursuit.

First things first. Captain Owen evacuated his prisoner on a medevac
at daybreak, then he conducted a search of the battle site in Xom Tan Liem.
The troops carried out the search in tense silence, as they were still relatively
green and more than a little spooked by the poncho-covered bodies and
demoralized stares of the day before.

Charlie Hunter Company found a number of abandoned weapons in
the hamlet: an AK-47 here, an RPG launcher there, as well as web gear,
grenades, rockets, and a Chinese-made radio (a real prize). There were also
three bodies. One was that of an old man, and Robert Magdaleno recalls
some of the GIs taking gag photos, using the stiff corpse as a prop. The other
two were VC. "These were the first enemy dead we had seen up close," notes
Olson. "We were told to stay clear of the bodies as they had not as yet been
cleared for booby traps. One corpse held a grenade in a clenched fist, while
the other had an unexploded RPG on the ground next to him." Olson recalls
that documents identified the Viet Cong with the grenade as being "only
fourteen years of age, but already some kind of hero to the other side—well
decorated for killing many Americans."

Captain Greene and Company A, guided by a scout helicopter as they
searched the area from which the night attack had originated, found two
beached sampans strewn with ammo and web gear. The body of another
slain guerrilla lay crumpled in one of the sampans. Colonel Benson and
Lieutenant Colonel Schmalhorst landed in their command ships for a quick
conference at the militia outpost as noon approached. Benson expressed
himself satisfied with Schmalhorst's scheme of maneuver for Da Phuoc,
which Owen had already intended to search. Independently, the village had
just been fingered as an enemy rally point by the prisoner medevacked that
morning. The captured guerrilla informed his interrogators that his dead
and wounded comrades from the battle in Xom Tan Liem had been carried east the previous evening to one of the waterways in the area. From

there, the Viet Cong loaded the wounded and dead into sampans and had then floated them south to Da Phuoc.

With the search of the battle site complete and the captured material evacuated, Schmalhorst lifted Company A to Firebase Smoke, replacing it with Company D. Charlie Hunter Company, meanwhile, proceeded down the highway and turned left off the road three kilometers south of Xom Tan Liem to push on across the paddies to Da Phuoc. Stomachs tightened and fingers rested lightly on triggers. Tempers flared when a trooper accidentally discharged his grenade launcher, sending a round thumping into the ground. Although the round didn't explode because it traveled less than the ten meters required to spin-arm the shell, several stressed-out, sleep-starved GIs turned on the grenadier so voraciously that a staff sergeant had to calm the situation and get everyone moving again. Some switch was flipped as the pursuit continued, notes Olson: "We were no longer quiet. In fact, we were making far more noise than we normally did, certainly more than the captain had drilled into us as being acceptable. We were moving fast. There was a false sense of boldness. The attitude was: 'Come and get us if you dare.' "

The part of Da Phuoc, a klick east of the highway, that Captain Owen and Company C entered was deserted and mostly demolished, blasted out of existence during previous operations. The paddies were pocked with water-filled craters, and the houses were reduced to foundations and crumbling walls. Lieutenant Gale, whose 3rd Platoon was in the lead, reported finding on the main village trail some of the green plastic wrappings that the enemy used to waterproof their mortar shells and RPGs. Moving forward, Owen examined the wrappings himself and saw that the insides still retained an oily film, a fact that set nerves tingling. Such wrappings quickly dried up under the blistering delta sun. That they were still oily meant that the enemy had been in the area within the last hour or so, breaking out ammunition and preparing for battle.

The trail led northeast to an east-west river. A row of partially standing brick and concrete houses faced the near bank. More damaged buildings were visible across the river behind a curtain of heavy brush and nippa palm. Owen instructed Gale to set out flank security, move 3rd Platoon across the stream, and secure the far buildings. The rest of the company would follow.

Lieutenant Gale led the way with Staff Sergeant William Patterson, who had the point squad, and Specialist Fourth Class Gregory A. Russell, the platoon leader's radio-telephone operator. At 3:15 p.m., May 11, 1968, the trio were ten or fifteen feet out in the river, when the Viet Cong soldiers suddenly commenced firing from their unseen spider holes in the nippa palm. The entire far bank exploded with AK-47 and RPD fire and smoke-trailing RPGs.

Greg Russell stumbled as several rounds punched through the radio on his back, but Lieutenant Gale pulled him onto a little island (really an over-grown sandbar) just ahead in the middle of the river. Reaching the island, Gale, Patterson, and Russell went to the prone and began returning fire over the top of the low-lying hump with their M16s.

Behind the point team, those men from the lead squad who had also entered the water were trapped against the near bank, unable to raise their heads or their weapons. The rest of the lead platoon was similarly immo-bilized, pinned down for the moment as the entire area was raked with fire and enemy mortar crews lobbed in rounds from somewhere across the pad-dies to the east. Sergeant Olson had been in the open between the river and the demolished buildings when the ambush began. It was like a sudden storm, he later would describe, one crash of lightning and then a downpour. Hitting the dirt, he scrambled for a log that had once been part of a fence or wall and was not much bigger in diameter than a telephone pole. Three other grunts also headed for the log, and they all hugged the ground behind it, curled up, shoulders touching their helmets, as bullets bit into the ground all around. When one of the guys managed to slip out of his rucksack and throw it over the log in an effort to make more cover, three or four rounds immediately thumped into the pack.

Olson heard an M60 open up from the right flank, and the enemy shoot-ing up the log shifted their fire to deal with the machine gun.

Al Olson gripped his rifle, bracing himself to join the fight.

The gun team on the right flank had been put in position to cover the river crossing. Private First Class Robert York, manning the M60, was one of the first to get his head back up and begin answering the ambushers in kind. The machine gun really got the enemy's attention, but York, unfazed by the slugs whining past, kept up a steady hail of fire across the river.

Lieutenant Gale told Russell to get a new radio so that he could coor-dinate with the platoon sergeant a deployment of the men on line to suppress the enemy fire and, if possible, assault across the river. Captain Owen had always preached that the only way out of an ambush was to gain fire superiority and assault into the enemy, and that was what Gale meant to do now. Gale and Patterson continued blazing away as Russell splashed rearward, secured a working radio, and fearlessly splashed back to the island, somehow passing unscathed through the bullets drawing invisible lines all around him.

No sooner had Gale issued his instructions to the platoon sergeant than Russell informed him that the replacement radio was inoperable, having also taken hits while strapped to the radioman's back. Staff Sergeant Patterson, meanwhile, boldly swam to the far bank, discovering along the way that the current was dangerously swift between the island and the opposing bank. He pitched hand grenades into the nippa palm, trying to knock out the hidden spider holes. Patterson struggled in the current on his way back, and Gale extended his M16 to the squad leader and pulled him ashore.

Moments later, Greg Russell—a bright young man of twenty and one of Gale's best soldiers—was shot through the head and killed instantly as he lay between Gale and Patterson at the edge of the island, firing his M16. It was time to back off. There being no way to get the platoon across the fast-flowing river while under fire, Gale and Patterson—who had been grazed across the face by a bullet—kept up their fire long enough for the men pinned against the river bank behind them to scramble to safety. The two then splashed back across the river, clambered out of the river bed, and plunged on toward the remnants of a destroyed house, twisting around at the waist as they ran to fire back at the enemy with their M16s.

Bob York fired like mad to cover them.

The heat off for the moment, Olson peered over the log sheltering his group and saw Lieutenant Gale, Staff Sergeant Patterson, and a trooper named Pete Murdock emerge from the river bed, running and firing as they headed for the blown-down house about fifty feet to the right of the log. Olson cut loose with his M16. The others behind the log also began laying down cover fire. Gale's group made it to the house, but as the men jumped behind a crumbling wall no more than eight inches high, Olson realized that his friend Greg Russell wasn't with the lieutenant anymore. His heart sank for he knew what that meant. No officer would leave his radioman unless the latter was dead.

Lieutenant Gale got behind a machine gun and began delivering long bursts into those spots within the nippa palm where he had seen movement and muzzle flashes. In return, several rocket-propelled grenades came flashing at the machine gun from across the blue line, as streams were known because of the color of waterways on military-issued maps. One exploded just behind Gale, peppering his back with fragments and knocking the wind out of him. The platoon leader shrugged off his injuries, for the pain barely registered through the adrenaline, and quickly resumed fire with the M60.

Sergeant Olson and his guys, having drawn the enemy's attention when they opened fire, hugged the ground as rounds again thumped into the log and cracked past just inches above their shrunken forms. To rise up with weapon to shoulder was to mean taking one between the running lights, so the four pinned-down grunts took turns blindly pushing their M16s over the log and firing away on automatic.

What was needed was the heavy stuff, and the grunts could have cheered when a puff of white phosphorus—a marking round—burst over the enemy side of the river, followed by the first of many howitzer salvos. Gunships arrived on station not long thereafter, and at some point, Olson saw that Captain Owen and Lieutenant Belt, the forward observer, had moved into position behind the only remaining wall of a bombed-out pagoda just to the rear of Gale and Patterson. "That was as up front as it gets," notes Olson, describing in awe how Charlie Hunter 6 was "pointing, calmly giving orders, talking on different radios, trying to get us better organized, and directing the supporting fires all at the same time."

The firepower had a definite effect. Whereas the enemy fire had been virtually uninterrupted the first ten or fifteen minutes of the engagement, there were now lulls, the enemy soldiers sinking deep in their spider holes amid the incoming. Emboldened, Olson's team, as well as others, began popping up long enough to place aimed bursts across the blue line. Lieutenant Gale, meaning to seize the initiative, scrambled from man to man and group to group, "making sure they had ammo, seeing who had been wounded, and setting them up in the best positions from which to return fire. The 3rd Platoon did not move back an inch, but poured an increasing amount of M16, M60, and M79 fire across the river, plus LAWs, while artillery and gunships pounded the Viet Cong."

The enemy clung tenaciously to their positions, resuming fire after each volley of explosions. Their mortars, in particular, rarely stopped chugging, even though they had been spotted from above in a tree line two klicks away and were being lashed by the gunships, too. Mortar rounds impacted all around the command group and the lead platoon and accounted for a dozen casualties. The damage would have been worse had not at least half of the rounds failed to explode. The ammunition the enemy had on hand either included a lot of duds, or an overly excited crewman was forgetting to pull the safety wires before dropping the rounds down the tube.

As the slugging match dragged on, Sergeant Olson realized that he and his buddies behind the log needed to start conserving ammo, for they had gone through a lot of magazines. In fact, so much carbon had accumulated in the chambers of their rifles, that their M16s were starting to jam. (The battalion was equipped with the notoriously unreliable early model of the weapon.) To Olson's right, Gale, Patterson, Murdock, and York were still "firing up a storm. Somebody had set up another M60, and we were trying to get our machine-gun ammunition to the gunner. Our two machine guns—the second was manned by Tim Hannigan—were really putting down the fire," Olson recounts. The barrel of Hannigan's machine gun glowed red as he consumed ammo belts in uninterrupted bursts. Someone shouted that the barrel was going to burn out. "There was no replacement barrel available," notes Olson, "so Hannigan started to slow his fire to short bursts."

Hannigan and York were finally reduced to a belt or two of ammo, and Olson and his three buddies, each of whom had started the battle with thirty magazines, were down to six or seven apiece. Worse, their fouled and overheated M16s were now jamming every few rounds. Already out of gun oil, Olson's group used their squeeze-bottles of oily insect repellent to keep the carboned-up chambers lubricated, a trick they had learned from training. "We talked about the need to spread out," recalls Olson, "as we were too tightly clumped together in one relatively exposed position behind that log. We knew better, but nobody was moving. It seemed like any movement increased the amount of incoming fire."

Having chanced another quick look through the half-window in the half-demolished wall sheltering the command group, Captain Owen, on his knees, ducked in anticipation of the automatic-weapons fire that greeted him each time he popped into view to appraise the situation. This time, however, the enemy let loose with a rocket-propelled grenade from the other side of the blue line. The projectile slammed into the right side of the window frame, knocking Owen to a sitting position with ringing ears and shrapnel in his upper chest.

Captain Owen's injuries and those of his radiomen, Specialists Fourth Class Douglas Lindner and William McMullen, were superficial, as the main part of the blast passed just over their heads. Several seconds after the explosion, McMullen, whose shirt was unbuttoned, was hit by a chunk of shrapnel that apparently went straight up, then straight down, landing on his solar plexus, as he sat leaning on his rucksack and PRC-25 against the wall, his legs splayed out in front of him.

McMullen quickly brushed the white-hot shrapnel away, but Captain Owen, seeing the burn, said, "There's your Purple Heart."

"No way, sir," McMullen answered, thinking the injury too slight to rate a medal. "My mother would shit when she got the telegram!"

Lieutenant Belt called in the artillery from a doorway in the wall that opened onto a set of steps leading toward the river from the bombed-out pagoda. The grunts were on the gun-target line, meaning they could hear each salvo as it came in overhead toward the opposite shore—a whoosh-rumble caused by the spinning of the shells. Almost inevitably given the close proximity of friend and foe, one round fell short. Luckily, it exploded inside an old crater that absorbed most of the blast. One trooper's finger was sliced off by a piece of shrapnel, however, and Lieutenant Gale, already at a fever-pitch, bellowed at the forward observer: "Belt, I'll shoot you if you kill any of my men!"

Moments later, another RPG whooshed across the blue line and hit the second step below the doorway, detonating before Belt's eyes with a brilliant flash. Knocked unconscious, the lieutenant came to "with my radioman pulling me upside down in a crater twenty feet away from the wall. The kid deserved a medal for dragging me out of the heavy fire and into the crater."

Belt was covered with little brick particles, superficially wounded by both brick and shrapnel, and his ears rang so loudly that he couldn't hear. Shaking off the effects of the blast, Belt kept the artillery coming, writing coordinates and adjustments on his map which his radioman relayed to the 105 battery at Firebase Smoke.

Lieutenant May and the 1st Platoon were firing from positions near the command group. When Gale reported that he was running low on ammo, Owen contacted Second Lieutenant Ronald R. Belloli, who was in reserve with 2nd Platoon. In response, Belloli's platoon sergeant, an exceptionally sharp and distinguished-looking E7 named George A. Segrest, who was the epitome of a professional NCO, brought up a team of men draped with bandoliers of M16 ammunition and belts of M60 ammunition. Segrest had to crawl the last part of the way for he had been shot in the knee when he was advancing, a permanently disabling wound that ended his prewar career with the illustrious 3rd Infantry Regiment. "Segrest came out of the Old Guard that marches at the Tomb of the Unknown Solider," recalls Owen, "and the only thing he was looking forward to was getting the hell out of Vietnam so he could go back to the Old Guard. His wound ended those plans, however. He never marched again."

Lieutenant Colonel Schmalhorst, above the fray in his command ship, had instructed Company D, at Owen's urging, to assume blocking positions north of the enemy force engaged with Company C that would thus trap the Viet Cong against the blue line. Owen was immensely frustrated at his counterpart's slow progress, but at length Company D neared a tree line several hundred meters west of the contact area. Delta Company sloshed across a flooded paddy in the direction of the tree line, with two platoons up and one back. When the company was fifty meters from the tree line, and in the open between two dikes, the guerrillas concealed amid the vegetation unleashed a broadside of AK-47 fire.

Lieutenant Fish's radioman was shot in the leg in the opening salvo, but the platoon leader pulled him to his feet and helped him to the dike to their rear. The rest of the platoon jumped behind the same dike, minus the lead squad, which scrambled for the dike to its front.

The grunts of Delta Company, in their first firefight, began returning fire even as mortar shells and RPGs began plopping into the mud around them. Fish joined in with his M16. When the weapon jammed, he resumed fire with the radioman's rifle, which was full of water and also seized up on him. Furious that they had been issued such a poor excuse of an infantry weapon, Fish picked up a third M16.

Sergeant John Moore was shot through the neck during the exchange, and Lieutenant Fish requested an emergency medevac. It took less than half an hour to get one on station, but by that time Moore was dead. Huey gunships had also been diverted to the scene, and Fish, on the horn with the company commander, explained that he had a squad pinned down along the berm in front of the smoke he had popped to mark his position. Fish's warning must have gotten lost in translation because the lead gunship opened up too soon during its initial pass. The curtain of paddy water thrown up by its machine guns extended through the lead squad and on into the tree line. Remarkably, there were no friendly casualties, and after the gunships were reoriented, the grunts settled against the dikes and watched the Hueys take turns working the tree line with machine guns and salvos of rockets. Now spectators of their own battle, one squad leader began filming the show with the home-movie camera he had brought with him from the United States.

As dusk fell, one of Olson's buddies behind the log finally took off to find more ammunition. Olson himself scuttled over to Lieutenant Gale behind the crumbled wall. The platoon leader was shouting orders and ripping off bursts, as was Staff Sergeant Patterson and Bob York, who had also been injured but nevertheless continued to blaze away across the blue line with his M60.

Gale confirmed that Russell was dead. He pointed to the island in the river. Olson blurted that he was going to get the body and the radio. It wasn't a rational declaration; Olson, however, was not only upset but guilt-stricken, too. Having served as the lieutenant's original radioman during training, Olson knew that had he not been reassigned as a team leader, and then a squad leader, he might himself be dead and the man who replaced him still very much alive.

Al Olson stood up to dash to the river, but there was the flash of an explosion at that instant, and the sergeant was suddenly flat on his back, struggling to catch his breath. He was numb all over, his ears ringing and his head throbbing from a concussion. Tasting blood, he spit out a mouthful, unsure what had happened to him. When the roaring in his ears subsided, Olson yelled for a medic. The one who appeared ignored the relatively superficial wounds on Olson's shoulder, chest, and side, and instead secured a bandage around Olson's neck, which had been slashed by a big chunk of shrapnel and bits of brick. Next, someone—maybe the medic, maybe another grunt, it was all a blur—helped Olson rearward past riflemen who were rushing forward with ammunition that had just been unloaded from a resupply Huey.

Captain Owen had decided to risk bringing in resupply ships after an air strike went in across the blue line. Lieutenant Belloli secured a landing zone, which was basically a wet paddy field back up the village trail, and got on the aviation frequency to control the helicopters. The air strike had not knocked the enemy into submission, however, and just about every one of the incoming choppers took AK-47 fire as it flared to land where smoke had been popped. The last helicopter into the landing zone was a medevac. Several seriously wounded men were helped into the cargo bay, including Al Olson and the platoon's Tiger Scout. Lieutenant Gale was furious when he realized that a not-so-seriously wounded GI, one of their McNamara's 100,000, had also climbed aboard, apparently under the impression that a cut finger rated a ride out aboard the Huey.

The medevac had just lifted off, nose down as the pilot picked up initial forward speed, when a RPG came sizzling toward it from across the blue line; flew in one side of the cargo bay; somehow missed everyone and everything inside (a pristine intersection of two moving objects); and sailed out the other side to plummet spent into the rice paddies below. "I could not believe my eyes," recalls Owen. "We stood there in absolute awe." Owen could hear Belloli on the radio, asking the pilot with wonder in his voice if he realized a rocket had just passed harmlessly through his helicopter. "Ron couldn't believe it, either. If the rocket had hit anything, we would have lost the chopper, the crew, and all the wounded. Miracles do happen!"

Captain Owen was informed that the battalion's direct-support battery was going to cease fire. In its stead, 155mm howitzers would commence firing. "They changed guns in mid-mission," recalls Owen, "because we'd had the 105s firing so long that they had to cool the tubes down." The first round from the heavy battery could be heard tearing through the sky on its way in, but the pitch was all wrong. Sensing trouble, Captain Owen and Lieutenant Belt, who had been peering over their wall watching for the expected explosion, had just enough time to duck before the 155mm projectile slammed into the left of their position. The deafening, earth-shaking blast injured several men, including Owen, who caught several half-inch steel splinters in his thigh and groin. The fire was quickly adjusted and the bombardment resumed. No one had been killed or even seriously wounded, notes Owen, "because the shell landed in a wet, soggy area, and most of the blast was absorbed by the mud. We were really lucky."

The wet terrain protected the enemy, too. Though some of the guerrillas crouching in their muddy spider holes in the nippa palm must have been killed by direct hits, most survived the gunships, the artillery, and, concussions and ruptured eardrums aside, even the high-drag bombs delivered at intervals by the jet fighters. The battle continued after sundown, red tracers slicing one way over the river, lime-green tracers the other, and gunships rolling in on targets that glowed white in a sea of black, thanks to the illumination rounds slowly floating down on the north side of the blue line. As the enemy fire finally began to taper off, Captain Owen consolidated his positions in the dark; the grunts, unable to dig in because of the high water table, set up for the night among clumps of palm trees and behind the walls of blown-down houses.

Lieutenant Belloli used a strobe light to bring in a resupply slick loaded with ammunition for the mortar platoon. It was almost midnight when a final air strike went in across the river. After having the artillery register defensive concentrations around his perimeter, Owen began placing fire from the 105s and 155s and his own 81mm mortars along the likely avenues of enemy withdrawal. "We knew they were going to sneak out on us," says Owen, "especially with Company D having failed to get into position to block anything."

High above in the night sky, one Spooky gunship droned in lazy circles above Charlie Hunter's position and jettisoned flares, while a second did the same for Delta Company. A small patrol, meanwhile, slipped into the river and, reaching the island in the middle without drawing fire, quickly returned with the body of Greg Russell, plus his rifle and radio. Gale had wanted to accompany the patrol, but Owen had instructed the exhausted platoon leader to stay with the main body of his platoon, explaining that sometimes a lieutenant needs to let the sergeants do their work. Much later, almost three in the morning, the enemy fired a last rocket-propelled grenade across the blue line. Helicopters equipped with night scopes orbited the battlefield, trying to spot the enemy soldiers as they slipped away, and it was nearly dawn when one of them spotted fifteen figures moving across the rice paddies several hundred meters east of Charlie Hunter Company. Artillery fire was shifted onto the Viet Cong.

Come morning Captain Owen was psyched to move across the river and see what damage had been done, but Schmalhorst, concerned that the enemy had rigged the area with booby traps before withdrawing, said no. Instead, resupply was carried out, then Company C combat-assaulted south of Da Phuoc and Company D west of Xom Tan Liem in the ongoing hunt for the enemy in the area. Company C had suffered one dead and seventeen wounded, Company D one dead and three wounded. In exchange, the 6th of the 31st, being new to the war zone and not yet appreciating the rules of the game, reported an absolutely accurate body count of zero at the end of the battle for Da Phuoc.

By happenstance, Company C hop-scotched back into Da Phuoc some days later, allowing finally for a reckoning of the enemy's losses. The grunts found bloody bandages and several dead guerrillas. "I only saw two or three bodies," notes Owen. "I wouldn't think there were many more than that."

Schmalhorst wrote home after the battle that "Capt. Owen and his boys did a wonderful job—I've recommended Bill for a Silver Star—he was a real cool customer." In another letter, Schmalhorst noted that "I got the Bronze Star for riding in my helicopter during the Saigon war—ha!"

Captain Owen received the Silver Star, as did Lieutenant Gale, Staff Sergeant Patterson, and machine gunner Bob York. Among others, Lieutenant Belt and Platoon Sergeant Segrest were pinned with the Bronze Star, and on Gale's recommendation, Specialist Fourth Class Gregory A. Russell was posthumously awarded the Distinguished Service Cross. There was a certain purity to these awards in a system gone corrupt: almost all were accompanied by a Purple Heart.

Charlie Hunter Company, still a bit green when it went into Da Phuoc, emerged fully blooded and sure of itself. The bond between Captain Owen and his troops, already strong, became unbreakable after Da Phuoc. "If you wanted to find Owen," notes Olson, "you only had to look toward the loudest part of the engagement. It didn't matter who you were or where you were, if you were under fire, Owen was just over your shoulder. He was always calm when everything else was going crazy. In many ways, he was our courage. For the guys in the platoons, Captain Owen was our faith and trust. He never let us down."

Part Eight
AN END TO IT

Chapter 25

First Lieutenant Hildebrando "Mad" Madrigal had served seven months in combat, mostly with the battalion reconnaissance platoon, before being pulled off the line to a staff position. When the battalion air-assaulted into the capital less than a week later, he was tasked with keeping the supplies flowing from the battalion helipad. The jovial Mexican-American college-student-turned-volunteer requested permission to join the fight, as he felt he owed it to DeLuca, but Major Booras gave him the thumbs down. After listening to the battle over the tactical net for three days, Madrigal could stand no more. He turned the resupply point over to a lieutenant who'd been sent back with light wounds, and the next morning, he climbed aboard one of the ammo-laden Hueys headed for Saigon.

Not sure where to go upon disembarking, Madrigal headed for the nearest building, the pagoda serving as DeLuca's command post. When stepping through the front door, he ran smack into Major Booras. Brusque even on his good days, Booras chewed Madrigal out in style, threatening to court-martial his ass should he ever again disobey orders, and instructing him to turn right around and catch the next chopper headed back to Rach Kien.

Lieutenant Colonel DeLuca fortuitously appeared then, and beaming at the sight of his old recon platoon leader, said, "Hi, Mad, you ready to go to work?"

"Yes, sir!" Madrigal answered, glancing over to Booras.

DeLuca turned to Booras: "Get Madrigal oriented. Get him a map and get him down to Bravo Company."

Lieutenant Madrigal was transported by armored personnel carrier to the company's present position at the top of the dead-end street along which the outfit had taken casualties two days before. As it happened, the company executive officer, First Lieutenant Ken Foster (a pseudonym) had come forward that same morning of May 11, 1968, to replace Jerry Thompson as commanding officer of Company B, 3rd Battalion, 39th Infantry. Foster asked Madrigal to take over Bravo Two and lead the push down the dead-end street to the enemy-occupied militia outpost at the bottom. "Hold on a minute," Madrigal protested. "Let me get my feet wet a little bit. Let me get a feel for this city stuff before I take over the lead."

Foster agreed, and Lieutenant Thompson, back with his old Bravo Three, led the way, with Lieutenant Madrigal following with Bravo Two. The grunts leapfrogged past each other from the doorway of one demolished building to the next. Enemy fire began ringing out less than a hundred meters down the road. Darting forward, Lieutenant Thompson faltered in mid-stride and hopped to cover, desperately shouting that he had been shot in the balls. Dropping his trousers before being medevacked, the platoon leader saw to his immense relief that he had only been grazed across the bottom of his sack.

Platoon Sergeant Thornburgh led Bravo One, the trail platoon, behind the buildings along the dead-end street in an attempt to outflank the snipers firing on Bravo Two and Three. Thornburgh's grunts came under fire while crossing a marshy area divided by canals, and Private First Class Richard E. Grossa was hit as he rushed from one canal to another, firing his M60 on the run. Thornburgh dragged the machine gunner back into the canal from which he had just emerged. Grossa was incoherent, as his scalp had been laid open by the bullet that had blown his helmet off. Thornburgh got a bandage around his head and carried him back to the medics. "I did my job," reflects Thornburgh, who was awarded the Silver Star for Saigon. "I worked hard, but I don't think I did anything beyond what any other NCO would have done with the same background and training."

To Thornburgh, the real heroes of the battle were the grunts. "Those young kids were wonderful soldiers. I loved 'em because they always did what I asked 'em to do. Most of them were draftees, but they would always come through. If anybody in the platoon would have been a hippie back home, Grossa would have been the one. He was kind of nonchalant about everything, but he was an extremely good machine gunner. I saw him again after I came back from Vietnam. He lived in Detroit. My dad was living there too at the time, and when I went up to visit my dad, I had a chance to stop in with Grossa. It was just a wonderful reunion."

Lieutenant Madrigal positioned a gun team at the window of a little house to cover the rescue of a member of the point team who had been shot in the gut. The grunt lay in a roadside ditch, moaning in pain as a couple buddies bandaged his wounds. The situation was stalemated. Unable to spot the snipers, everyone hunkered down, returning fire as best he could but unwilling to risk a bullet in the back by trying to carry the wounded man back up the street.

Spotting movement across a debris-strewn clearing, Madrigal had the M60 gunner rake the area with fire. Darting outside and crouching beside the courtyard gate, he peeped over the wall and shouted directions to the gun team: "Okay, a little to the left . . . a little more! Okay, right there!"

Taking another look, Madrigal ducked back down and turned his head to shout something to the machine gunner, only to have a chunk of plaster explode from the wall a scant few inches from his head. *Wow, what the hell are they firing,* he wondered, *that they can put rounds through concrete?*

But there was no hole in the wall, Madrigal now saw, only the pockmark of an AK-47 round, meaning the shot had come not from the front, but from a sniper positioned somewhere behind and above him. Madrigal scrambled inside the house. "That shot had been meant for my head," reflects Madrigal. "I think the sniper had me in his sights, and only because I turned at that instant did I cheat death. I made everybody aware that we had a sniper behind us somewhere. We had to focus some attention on that, lay down some fire on the two-story buildings behind us, and I didn't have any more problems from that area. I can't say that we got him. Maybe he just took a pot shot and left."

Madrigal worked some artillery on the buildings across the clearing, and he recalls how "that calmed the enemy fire down, and we were able to get our wounded guy. We got him out of there, and then we all pulled back up the street to get reorganized."

While Foster fought toward the militia outpost from the north, Captain Eckman and Company B, 6th Battalion, 31st Infantry, pressed in east-to-west from the police compound in the hamlet along the Rach Ong Lon. Making contact almost immediately, Eckman received a call from the command post of the 3-39th Infantry: "What's your body count?"

"I don't know. I've got a couple out here."

"Two-zero!" came the enthusiastic response from a field-grade officer intent on making a good report better.

"Negative, negative," said Eckman. "Negative two-zero. I have one, two confirmed, maybe one, two, three probables—but no blood trails."

The field-grade officer was having none of it. "Roger your two-zero," he said, repeating the figure that would, in fact, go down in the battalion log.

More contacts soon followed. Captain Eckman's command group was moving down a wide boulevard with Lieutenant Procaccini of Bravo One when a group of enemy soldiers a block or two ahead took notice of all the radio antennas and let loose an RPG. Procaccini's radioman, Private First Class David E. Gray, actually saw the projectile coming at them, spiraling like a football and trailing a ribbon of white smoke, but there was no chance to react before it exploded dead ahead in the middle of the street. Gray, who had been superficially wounded the day before, remained standing, too stunned to realize that he'd been hit again until someone pushed him down and pointed out the blood on his trouser leg. A medic treated the slice on Gray's inner thigh with iodine and a band-aid—his second Purple Heart.

Lieutenant Procaccini led an attack toward the rocket team. Procaccini was viewed skeptically by some, but Gray always respected the platoon leader. "He was a brave guy. At times, he was more gung-ho than I liked. When we were fighting between those buildings, he would run out, guns blazing, and shout, 'Follow me, Dave!' That was a little bit more than I had in mind!"

In a similar vein, the bond between the grunts and Captain Eckman, already strong from training, was cemented in Saigon. "Captain Eckman would not crouch down or hide when the snipers fired at us," recalls Mark Mudd, who ended up carrying the artillery radio in the company command group. "Many times during the battle, I would tell him we had to take cover. If he did take cover, he did so reluctantly, and a few times I even grabbed him by his shirt and pulled him back. He was fearless. I don't know how he could remain so calm, but it definitely helped us rookies get through."

It was not as if the snipers couldn't hit what they were aiming at. Mudd was on a rooftop when Private First Class Michael Nicholin was suddenly shot in the chest and knocked on his ass. Nicholin's compadres rushed to him, thinking he must be seriously wounded, if not dead, and were stunned when he sat up and said he was okay. Nicholin had two bandoliers criss-crossed over his chest and the round had been stopped by the ammo magazine over his heart.

Sergeant Leader of Bravo Three came around the corner of a house at another point during the chaotic, running firefight and realized with a start that there was a GI standing twenty feet away with a LAW over his shoulder. "The back of the rocket was looking right at me," recalls Leader, who "did an about face and beat it back around the corner as fast as I could go. He touched off the rocket before I completely cleared the corner. I was far enough away that the back-blast didn't kill me. The roar did deafen me, however. People would move their mouths, but I couldn't hear a thing. My hearing finally returned, but it was scary to be in the middle of a battle and not be able to hear what was going on."

Sergeant Vernon Moore, a spotter from the mortar platoon, was inside a house with several riflemen from Bravo Three. There were little, two-inch-square ventilation holes in the walls about two feet up from the floor formed by the arrangement of the bricks of the house. Enemy fire thumped into the house, some of the rounds blasting through the wall in unnerving sprays of plaster. Peering through a ventilation hole during a lull, Moore "spotted the sniper—the only live one I seen during the battle—about a hundred feet away on the other side of a canal. He was in a hole under a trash pile. He had a piece of tin over his position. He'd raise that piece of tin up and shoot his AK-47. He'd been wounded or something because I could see a bandage around his head."

It was impossible to zero in on the sniper from inside the room, the ventilation holes being too small to accommodate the sights on their rifles. Private First Class Larry J. Marchal—a slow-talking farm boy and natural soldier—entered the room then, and listened impassively as the situation with the sniper was explained to him. "Well, I can get him," Marchal drawled, trading his machine gun for a grenade launcher. "You all just stick your rifles through them holes and shoot at him, keep him down while I get a bead on him." With that, Marchal slipped out the back door and took up a position behind a large clay jug positioned against the house to catch rainwater, exposing just enough of himself to sight in on the sniper's position. "When we quit shooting," recounts Moore, "that piece of tin flew up and the sniper popped up to fire another burst, but Marchal fired first, and the top of the sniper's head came off. The sniper wasn't very far away, and Marchal direct-fired right into him with the M79. Marchal was like that. He was country, you know. He'd just do whatever had to be done."

Before resuming the attack down the dead-end street, Lieutenant Madrigal told Lieutenant Foster that he wanted to recon an alley that he thought might offer a more surreptitious approach to the area from which the enemy had been firing. Madrigal remembers that he reached the end of the alley without incident, "but they were just waiting for me to get all the way down there, and then they opened fire with a fuckin' machine gun. I had nowhere to go, so I turned around and was running, zig-zagging, as bullets kicked up dirt around me and hit the wall on my right. I could see dust and stucco flying off the wall. I thought I was dead for sure."

Somehow passing unscathed through the fire, Madrigal turned and dove when he hit the top of the alley. Foster, Madrigal, and Bausser, the artillery spotter, crouched at the top of the alley then, "trying to figure out what the hell to do," recounts Madrigal. "I said, let me take another shot at it, that machine gun's got to be in this particular area, but I don't want to take the whole platoon down there, it's too many people, too much confusion."

Instead, Madrigal wanted to make his approach with a single rifleman. "I asked for a volunteer to come with me. The guys didn't know me and nobody really wanted to move into that area. Every time you'd go down there, same thing would happen, but one of them finally volunteered to go. He was a black kid. Nice kid, sharp kid. I never knew his name. I just said, 'Let's move out; we're gonna go around here, and we're gonna get that sonuvabitch.'"

The pair wound their way through a number of buildings and were crawling along a ditch to come up on the flank of the machine gun when someone opened fire from another unseen position. Madrigal ducked behind a fifty-five-gallon drum sitting beside a house, the rifleman leapfrogging over him to take shelter behind another drum. Had the drums been full of rainwater as Madrigal assumed they were, they would have been good protection from the enemy fire, but they were empty and "a bullet went through the drum the black kid was behind. He got hit right below the eye. He grabbed his head and was writhing in pain. He got to his feet and I got him out of there. I'm still pissed at myself for having dragged that kid down there with me and getting him shot, but that's just the nature of the business, I guess."

DeLuca wanted another attempt made to knock out the machine gun that was holding up the attack, and with Madrigal's platoon in the lead, Bravo Company began moving through the backyards of the first row of buildings facing the dead-end street. The area was swamped, a narrow walkway made of boards providing the only quick and dry way across. Madrigal sent one guy across at a time, and the walkway sagged underwater at the weight. The machine gun took the movement under fire, and an army photographer tagging along with the grunts fell into the water while hurrying across the slippery walkway. The photographer lunged on to safety. "We all laughed and were very happy to see him get himself out of there so we wouldn't have to go back in and rescue him," recalls Madrigal. "We finally got everybody across. Nobody got hurt."

The platoon assembled on a side street. Before advancing again, Madrigal had several grunts use their LAWs. "We fired into some buildings to our front. We didn't know if we were doing any good or not. We found out we weren't because every time we tried to move, we took fire just as heavy as before. Our return fire wasn't doing any good at all. We were really befuddled."

DeLuca finally instructed Foster to pull back in order to give the gunships a free hand. Bravo Company was nearing the end of its tether by then. "I was so damn tired, I didn't know where I was half the time," recalls Thornburgh. Lieutenant Bausser saw any number of frustrated grunts wreck the houses through which Bravo Company maneuvered. "There was a lot of rage," he explains. "You got a bunch of young people armed to the hilt. They're pissed off, and if you saw a nice piece of furniture or something like that, it wasn't uncommon to shoot it up. We were in almost constant contact. It was very chaotic. We were getting shot at from all sides, and we weren't getting much direction or support from above. We were pretty much operating on our own."

Snipers could appear anywhere, for the guerrillas knocked holes in the walls between buildings so as to be able to slip unnoticed between them. There seemed no way to come to grips with such an enemy, no way to inflict casualties upon its soldiers except to level the neighborhoods they had infested. "They were positioned so they could cover what were for us two key streets," notes Madrigal. "They were very well disciplined and very well hidden, and they controlled the area. There weren't that many of 'em, but we couldn't progress beyond a certain point." There was no center of mass at which the grunts could strike. "You were getting sniped at; you were getting hit from different areas; you were taking casualties; and you just couldn't figure out where the hell the fire was coming from," recalls Madrigal. "No matter which way we moved, we took fire. We didn't know if our own fire was effective or not. You had to test it. How do you test it? You get up and move forward. And when you take more fire, you realize, 'Well, holy shit, we didn't get 'em after all.' " Only when the battle was over did Madrigal realize how truly clever the enemy's tactics had been. "The punchline was that they ended up being underground. We were firing at windows and doors, and it turned out that their main machine-gun position was in a slit trench under some corrugated tin. The trench was in a courtyard covered with litter, so the tin sheets just looked like more junk lying out there."

DeLuca and Booras monitored several overlapping firefights. In addition to Foster's blunted efforts and Eckman's ongoing push toward the enemy-occupied militia outpost, Captain Stuart and A/3-39th made contact in a bunker complex in an area of hootches and rice paddies between Xom Cau Mat and the Rach Ong Nho. An air strike was organized, and the scout platoon of the 2-47th Mech dispatched to take up blocking positions north of the battle area. The air strike, which came in at noon, drove a number of the enemy soldiers into the scout platoon, which opened fire, .50-caliber machine guns against AK-47s and RPGs.

Captain Latham and C/3-39th landed in the paddies a klick and a half south of the militia outpost. Moving north, Latham's company soon came under fire, and the grunts returned fire as gunships fell upon the VC.

DeLuca, meanwhile, instructed Captain Craig of B/2-47th, which had been attached to his battalion, to launch an attack down the dead-end street, hoping the armored personnel carriers had the punch needed to dislodge the enemy. Craig had had a premonition the night before that something very bad was going to happen to him. He'd been preparing to eat at the time. "Whenever you could take a few minutes to sit down, relax, and open up a can of C-rations at the end of the day," he recalls, "it was just Shangri-La time, but that night a little voice inside me said, 'Don't eat because you don't want anything on your stomach if you end up in the hospital.' I didn't eat. I drank water instead, and then the next morning, the same thing. I had the same feeling and didn't eat again."

Major Riedl, the hard-charging battalion executive officer, arrived aboard his track with the recoilless rifle and side-mounted machine gun, intending to accompany Bravo Company in the attack. Specialist Fifth Class Pollard, the combat photographer stationed with the 221st Signal Company at Tan Son Nhut, also hooked up with Company B. Pollard had spotted the personnel carriers by happenstance from the jeep that his buddy—who will be called Rick Laurent here—was driving. Pollard and Laurent had just arrived to document the street battle on the south side of the Kinh Doi. "Civilian traffic was normal until we arrived at a sort of cut-off point where there was massive damage to the buildings on the main east-west street," recounts Pollard. "Everything south of this street seemed to be a dead zone— no civilians, no movement. We parked the jeep on the street and joined a mechanized unit from the 9th Division."

A twenty-two-year-old former newspaper and television-news stringer, Ken Pollard had joined up to be a combat correspondent and was halfway through his second tour in Vietnam. Buttoned up in helmet and flak jacket, with a holster on his hip and two cameras around his neck, the bespectacled Pollard looked the part of an official army photographer. His partner, Rick Laurent, a young black man with intense eyes and dark, narrow features who sported tiger-stripe utilities and a cut-down bush hat, did not. There was a reason. Laurent was not really a photographer, but an absent-without-leave (AWOL) paratrooper from the 101st Airborne. Laurent told Pollard that he had experienced much racial prejudice in his unit, and that when he was sent to Saigon to sign divorce papers, he decided not to go back. Instead, he went underground. One day, Laurent showed up at the 221st Signal Company's compound with a unit member he had befriended, and from then on he began tagging along with the combat photographers, equipped with a camera and sidearm as camouflage. "He enjoyed going with us," recalls Pollard. "He also liked the fact that we could go anywhere with no questions asked. He was safe from the military police with us. I liked having him around because he drove the jeep and had an M16."

Tripping on the war in his own way at his own speed, Laurent spent his days in combat and his nights in the warrens of Soul Alley. "Rick was definitely street smart," notes Pollard. Unlike many of his brothers in the underground, Laurent gave no indication of being a drug addict or black militant. "He seemed like a regular guy, really. He was rather quiet and friendly with us. We got along well, and I absolutely trusted him in the field."

The sweep began at two in the afternoon. Captain Craig, taking his premonition seriously, pinned his bars on the inside of his collar and hoped that no sniper would notice the antennas that marked him as he walked alongside his track with his radiomen. The gunners on the lead tracks reconned by fire as the column advanced down the dead-end street. Enemy fire was almost immediately returned, but "once we started, there was no turning back," reports Pollard who, along with Laurent, accompanied the dismounted troops moving with the personnel carriers.

The sustained roar of automatic weapons and machine guns was trapped and amplified between the gutted buildings, making it impossible to distinguish the incoming from the outgoing. Pollard slid into a wall next to another soldier, "and a burnt-up corpse rolled out of the debris on top of me. I started to scramble away in horror, but bullets hit nearby and I moved back behind the wall." Pollard was finally able to dart forward again. The machine gunner to the front of Pollard's new position took a graze across the neck, but he ignored the injury and kept his weapon in action. Somewhere in there, Pollard caught sight of several bareheaded enemy soldiers in khaki uniforms—regulars, he presumed—darting from one building to another, assault rifles in hand. "I don't know if they made it, or if they were cut down. Since I had my eye to the camera most of the time, it was hard to see what was going on around me. More than one trooper told me I was crazy to be there taking pictures."

Perhaps meaning to clear away potential booby traps, the gunner on the lead track fired into several fifty-five-gallon drums sitting on the right side of the road. One drum exploded; as it turned out, it was filled with gasoline. The lead track rumbled past the blaze, followed by the second track in the column. The flames spread to a little Renault on the left side of the road that also exploded, forcing the dismounted infantrymen to dash through a curtain of fire. "The flames were over our heads," notes Bob Dyson. "The VC got on the rooftops and tried to shoot us as we ran through the flames. The .50 gunners shot them off the roofs."

When the gunners on the lead tracks ran low on ammo, Dyson and several other troops went back up the street to secure more from the tracks bringing up the rear. The group returned to find the lead tracks well forward of the dismounted element and was told that there were hot power lines down on the road. "I figured that if the lead tracks had gotten through, so could I," recounts Dyson, who thought the personnel carriers would have been forced to halt had there been much voltage left in the power lines. He sprinted toward the track. It suddenly dawned on him that vehicles with rubber-cleated treads don't conduct electricity. That they had rolled over the power lines without effect meant nothing. "I slowed down then, looking for the wires. By now, the VC had seen me and began shooting. The rounds struck behind me. I ran faster, hoping to throw off their aim before they could adjust their fire. When I reached the tracks, I threw my ammunition to the gunner of the lead vehicle, then turned and saw that I was the only one who'd made the run. Moments later, my squad, carrying the rest of the ammunition, started running down the street, too, with [Private First Class] Gann—from Alabama—in the lead. Resupplied and reorganized, we continued our advance."

Captain Craig was walking in a half-crouch several feet to the left of his slowly advancing track, with his handset to his ear and his radiomen trailing behind, when he was suddenly knocked off his feet by what felt like a sledgehammer being swung into his right shoulder. The senior company medic pulled Craig to cover in the little hollow between two mounds of dirt, a building to one side, a halted personnel carrier to the other. Dismounted infantrymen blasted the alley from which the burst of enemy fire had come. One soldier reared up to fling hand grenades, while the nearest machine gunners stitched the walls to either side of the narrow passageway with a barrage of .50-caliber fire from their APCs.

As the medic began working on the company commander, Craig mumbled a message to pass command to the 1st Platoon leader and keep the attack going. "Captain Craig was coherent," recalls Jimmy Dye. "In fact, he was still trying to direct fire and everything. Troops were left there to take care of him and cover him, and we just kept moving. We didn't stop."

Ken Pollard photographed the huddle around the company commander while lying on his back amid the continuing fire. Captain Craig, his helmet still on and shirt pulled open, grimaced as the senior company medic, Specialist Fifth Class Michael A. Sailers, got a pressure bandage in place over the sucking chest wound. Sailers, who would later be awarded the Silver Star, provided an expert description of the wound to the medevac speeding to the scene. In sum, an AK-47 round that had struck the hull of Craig's track had ricocheted into the captain at a downward angle, piercing his chest just below the joint of his right shoulder and exiting his back below his shoulder blade. The bullet had punctured the pleura (the membrane around the chest cavity), decompressing the right lung. Craig was in bad shape, but lucky in the sense that the bullet was almost spent when it hit him and both the entrance and exit wounds were small. If evacuated quickly, he would survive.

Sailers rolled the captain onto his right side to keep pressure on the wound. Craig's face rested against the ground, his helmet having rolled away. He felt as if he had seven martinis in his system. "Don't go into shock," he mumbled, forcing himself awake. Having seen enough seriously wounded men in his time, he knew that shock was the big killer on the battlefield. "Don't go into shock, don't go into shock, don't go into shock. . . ."

Sailers and two other troops carried Craig like a log past Major Riedl and the Pink Pussy Cat. Riedl ordered his driver forward, intent on pushing on, for the medevac pilot had radioed that he would be unable to land until the area had been secured. Enemy soldiers were still firing at the lead platoon. "All of us were hugging the floor because rounds were going through the plaster walls above us," recounts Phil Streuding, who had become pinned down with several other GIs inside a building at the front of the attack. "I remember one soldier sticking his M16 around the corner of the front door with only his hands showing and firing short bursts, and he got shot in the wrist just like that."

Major Riedl's track came to a stop at the end of the street, and Pollard took more photos as the gunner, Tony Midkiff, stitched the buildings with the .50-caliber machine gun. The enemy fire petered out. Riedl broke out his binoculars and, while scanning an open area across which the enemy had probably withdrawn, caught sight of an individual moving unhurriedly from one building to another. The man was carrying something. Riedl was unsure if he had spotted a farmer with a hoe or a guerrilla with a weapon and debated whether or not he should have Midkiff cut the guy in half. "I finally decided to withhold fire," says Riedl, who doubted the wisdom of that choice as the unidentified figure disappeared from view. "On the one hand, I knew this was a civilian area, but on the other, there were no civilians there anymore. They had all evacuated the area—meaning this guy had to be a VC carrying an AK-47."

***

The medevac landed on the street. Captain Craig was loaded into the cargo bay, and the pilot immediately pulled pitch. The medic on board got an IV going and, kneeling beside his only patient, held Craig's hand in a reassuring grip and shouted into his ear over the throb of the engine and the roar of the wind: "It's gonna be all right, you're gonna be fine. . . . Hang in there, hang in there. . . . You're gonna be fine, you're gonna be fine. . . ."

Craig was still mumbling his own mantra to himself: "Don't go into shock, don't go into shock, don't go into shock. . . ."

The flight took only minutes. The personnel at the 3rd Field Hospital helipad were waiting with a stretcher, and Craig was carried into a triage area where blood was drawn and a plastic identification band was secured to his wrist. A doctor checked the wristband and smiled: "Mike, you're going to be all right."

"Not Mike," Craig croaked. "Not Mike. . . ."

"You're not Mike Dunaway?"

"No. . . . James Craig. . . ."

The doctor flew into a rage, shouting at the triage medics about getting the wristbands mixed up. The doctor ordered Craig's blood work to be done again on the double. Later, the doctor told him, "We've got to get the bullet out."

Craig was frantic; there was no bullet to dig out, for the round had already exited below his shoulder blade. No longer able to speak, he violently shook his head. "What are you trying to tell me?" the doctor asked. Finally catching Craig's meaning, the doctor called to a medic: "Turn him over!"

The doctor saw the exit wound and also saw that it had been leaking blood all along. The middle of the stretcher was soaked, as were the seat of Craig's trousers where the captain had mistakenly thought he'd pissed himself. The doctor rushed Craig into surgery and, preparing to insert a chest tube, he had a medic grab each of Craig's arms and legs while a nurse straddled his stomach, pinning him down. Craig knew what was coming. It was going to be bad, but he also knew they had to do it; he had to get it over with. (Morphine was not allowed during the procedure for it would further depress the patient's breathing.) The doctor made his incision—the pain was excruciating—then he slipped a thin tube into Craig's chest cavity, allowing the fluids to drain into a glass jar sitting on the floor beside the operating table. Craig's deflated lung began pumping itself back up. He could finally breathe again. He knew he was going to make it. The situation only got better when Craig's wife, an in-country army nurse, was dispatched to attend to his injuries while he recuperated at the 3d Field Hospital.

Near the end of the firefight, a haggard young staff sergeant with bandaged arms ran over to Major Riedl's track to report something. Riedl was in the middle of some business on the radio, so Midkiff, the gunner, said to the staff sergeant, "Here, hold this first," and handed him an ice-cold beer from the ice-filled cooler inside the track. "He looked like he needed a beer to me," recalls Midkiff. "He was about half-dead. When I handed him the beer, his eyes lit up like two Christmas trees. I don't know if he drank, but he did that day!"

Following the medevac, Pollard photographed the jet that screamed in right over the rooftops, dropping the napalm canisters that finally and completely ended the battle for the dead-end street. Pollard next trained his camera on an enemy soldier who had been policed up in the debris. The prisoner's head was swathed in bloody bandages, and he lay in a makeshift litter fashioned from a rug rolled around two long wooden slats. His hands, one of which was wrapped with gauze, were curled like claws and pressed against his face. The man looked hardly alive, and it was Pollard's impression that he had been wounded some days earlier and carried along by comrades who then had become casualties themselves, or had been chased away during this latest action. The litter was placed on the lowered back ramp of a personnel carrier. One of the soldiers sitting inside the hull—an older-looking regular in helmet and flak jacket—fanned the flies away from the prisoner's face with his map, a small gesture of compassion that surprised Pollard, given the pitiless indifference with which the grunts usually treated captured VC and NVA.

Pollard and Laurent returned to where they had left their jeep on the canal road, only to find that the vehicle was missing. They spotted a jeep a block away and, hurrying over, found that it was indeed theirs. Several grunts had borrowed the jeep, and having shot off the front-door lock of a liquor store, they were in the process of loading the vehicle with bottles of Jack Daniel's and Johnny Walker. The grunts apologized for taking the jeep, but Pollard told them not to worry about it, climbed behind the wheel, and asked where they wanted all their liberated booze dropped off. The grunts pointed to the house where they were bivouacked, then walked alongside the overloaded jeep as Pollard drove to the position, helped unload the liquor, then anxious to get back to his compound before dark, finally hit the road for Tan Son Nhut.

Private First Class William L. Sirtola of the Mortar Platoon, B/6-31st, which was dug in near the command post of the 3-39th Infantry, saw the driver and commander of a personnel carrier drinking cans of "33," a locally brewed beer. Sirtola asked where they'd gotten the beer, and they described a warehouse about two blocks from the Y Bridge. They also warned Sirtola to be careful if he planned to secure some for himself because there were snipers in the area. "I got five guys who were standing around from different units," recounts Sirtola, "and we decided to make two forays. Three guys would be armed to protect the unarmed, who could carry more beer, and the armed and unarmed would switch for the second foray."

The group found cases of both beer and soda in the warehouse, as well as blocks of ice in a refrigeration unit. Sirtola climbed aboard a Honda 90 that was parked inside the warehouse on a flat tire. "I'd had a Honda Scrambler at Michigan State, and had even carried a pony keg on it, so I figured I'd have no trouble even with the flat. I kicked it a few times, but it refused to start. That's when I noticed the bullet hole in the gas tank." One of the grunts found a rickshaw whose two front wheels were spaced to accommodate a large basket. Like the moped, the rear tire of the rickshaw was also flat, but Sirtola said he would push if the grunt would pedal, and they loaded the basket with two blocks of ice, a couple cases of soda, and five or six cases of beer. "About six feet down the road, we hit a big pothole and our rig stopped. I can still see this picture of the other GI standing on the right pedal with all his weight on his right foot, bouncing, trying to get it going." The GI finally jumped off, helped Sirtola push the rickshaw out of the pothole, then "he jumped back on, and with him pedaling and me pushing, we made it out of there. In retrospect, it would have been pretty damn silly if any of us had lost our lives for a few cans of beer."

By late afternoon, Captain Eckman and Company B, 6th Battalion, 31st Infantry, had reached a large paddy situated on the east side of the militia outpost at the bottom of the dead-end street. Lieutenant Blacker's platoon advanced on the outpost, leaving the concealment of the thatch-and-stucco hootches, behind which the rest of the company took cover, and trotting single-file along one of the east-west dikes cutting across the flooded paddy. The platoon ran into a wall of fire a hundred meters from the objective. Taking cover in the mud behind an intersecting north-south dike, the grunts furiously returned fire and pitched grenades.

Eckman requested gunships. A pair soon arrived, and smoke grenades were thrown to mark the enemy positions. Sergeant Leader, in a good position to adjust the gun runs, got a confirmation about the color of the smoke from the flight leader: "I see the enemy. I see your smoke. We're comin' in hot."

Leader rolled onto his back behind the dike to watch the lead gunship as it came in low from the east from the rear of the platoon, the minigun in the chin turret trained on the target. The target was no longer clear, however, as some of the smoke had blown back over the platoon, and the gunner in the cockpit pressed the firing button a moment too soon. During the most terrifying few seconds of his life, Leader grabbed his handset as the minigun began blazing at four-thousand rounds a minute—a spray of water advancing directly at his squad—and shouted to cease fire as the burst tore over the dike, catching the grunt to his left. One of the minigun rounds had struck the pistol-grip of the M16 the grunt was holding and, mushrooming, it removed the heel of the man's hand, as well as his pinkie and ring finger. Leader secured a bandage around the gory mess, amazed that he hadn't lost more men and thankful that the gunship had not been firing rockets. The squad leader almost felt a pang of sympathy for what the enemy endured at the receiving end of all their firepower.

The gunships rolled in until out of ammunition, then turned the job over to a set of jet fighters. "We thought they were in the buildings, so we leveled about a whole city block of cement houses between air strikes and helicopter gunships and M72 LAWs we were carrying," Leader informed his wife in the tape he mailed home after the battle. "We leveled every house within sight right to the ground, and we started to get up [to resume the attack], thinking we had it made—and we started gettin' just as much fire as we did the first time." The grunts again took cover behind the dike. "[W]e couldn't move either way. They had us pinned down . . . and we couldn't tell where those shots we're coming from, all we could hear was the cracking of the AK-47s over our head."

As the exchange continued, Leader actually saw one of the guerrillas as he popped up to let loose another AK-47 burst. *My God, there they are,* Leader thought, shocked, for the enemy soldier was not back among the buildings into which the platoon was firing, but was dug into the berm at the end of the paddy not more than fifty meters away. Captain Eckman ordered Lieutenant Blacker to pull back so that supporting arms could be brought to bear along the berm. The only way out was atop the dikes, for a grunt could sink to his armpits in the paddies. To rush straight back, however, on the east-west dike along which the platoon had originally advanced would only get a lot of guys shot in the back. Better to get out from under the muzzles of the enemy's weapons by moving north along the intersecting north-south dike behind which the platoon was sheltered, then dart rearward atop the next east-west dike bisecting the field.

Blacker told Leader to move to the elbow where the two dikes met and lay down a base of fire to cover the withdrawal. Leader called to Larry Marchal, the machine gunner attached to his squad. The two crawled along the north-south dike while the rest of the platoon kept up its fire, then upon reaching the elbow, they commenced firing. Marchal was behind the M60 and Leader, kneeling to his left, fed ammunition belts into the machine gun with one hand and fired his M16 on full automatic with the other. Leader bellowed at the grunts to come on, but none could hear him over the din. He finally started using hand signals, waving the men his way and then pointing rearward down the dike that lead back to the thatch-and-stucco hootches.

Firing without respite, Marchal had gone through eight or nine ammo belts when the machine gun jammed. Leader helped him replace the burned-out barrel, and Marchal resumed fire until the last member of the platoon had rushed past on his way to safety. With that, Leader shouted at Marchal to take off too, then fell in behind him, walking backwards while continuing to blast away with his M16. "I guess that's why they're going to give me a medal of some kind," said Leader on the tape he sent home, explaining that he had been recommended for a valor award for providing cover fire during the retreat. He didn't think he deserved a medal. "I mean, I can't see it because there was no other way to get off the dike."

Captain Eckman plastered the area with artillery, more gunships, and more jet fighters, which delivered both napalm and high-drag bombs, then resumed the attack. "[T]he other two platoons were just going into the area to take a body count," Leader explained on his tape. "We were so certain that [the enemy] had gone, and those air strikes had really torn 'em up and taken care of 'em."

The optimism was misplaced. The enemy might have been hurt by the firepower, but there were still enough of them holding out in water-filled bunkers, layered with palm logs and earth, to halt Bravo Company again. The grunts later found aiming stakes in the bunkers which trained the enemy's AK-47 directly on the dike in front of the berm. "They were already pre-tested and pre-sighted," Leader said on the tape. "They waited until the two platoons got on the dike in the right impact area, and then they fired. They had their weapons zeroed right on the top of the dike. . . . Anytime we'd rise up, they'd just pull the trigger and the rounds would hit right along the top of the dike."

The grunts took ten casualties. "Some of 'em were fingers shot off, some of 'em were in the stomach, chest, legs," Leader continued on the tape. The gunships, meanwhile, made possible a second retreat: "They'd fire into the enemy, keeping 'em pinned down long enough so that [the] two platoons could withdraw."

The worst of the casualties was Specialist Fourth Class Fred G. Losel Jr., the radioman with the spotter team attached to Bravo Company. Though quickly medevacked from the scene, Losel died in the evacuation hospital, and was posthumously awarded the Silver Star to go with his Purple Heart. In addition to coordinating supporting fires during the action, Losel had acted as a rifleman to cover the withdrawal from the rice paddy. Vernon Moore understood that Losel had been very close with Lieutenant Kaiser, who had been medevacked that morning and, upset at losing his team leader, he "more or less went crazy that day, started doin' crazy things. There were a lot of grass houses there. Hell, bullets would come right through 'em, but he was standing behind one of 'em, sticking his rifle around the side of it and shootin'. Somebody told me he grabbed a machine gun, too, and run out, firing it from the hip. He was doin' John Wayne stuff, and I remember us talkin' about it at the time: 'There ain't no live John Waynes over here.' "

The grunts were getting reorganized when a track pulled up; the uptight crewmen hurriedly unloaded a stack of ammunition crates, then departed at top speed, anxious to make it back to the battalion command post before nightfall. The grunts needed the ammo. They needed water blivets, too, but for the second day in a row none were delivered. No rations had been delivered either, but that didn't matter because appetites had shriveled and most of the troops hadn't even finished the C-rations that they'd stuffed in their pockets when they originally choppered into Saigon. Throats were parched now, tongues swelled. "We were doing so much running around in the heat, popping salt pills to keep from passing out, that we desperately needed water," notes Leader, "but with so much of the city destroyed, there wasn't any water to be had." Large earthenware jars were normally positioned under the down spouts at the corners of each house to collect rainwater, but as the houses had been destroyed, so too had the jars. As luck would have it, several of Sergeant Leader's men stumbled upon an intact jar sitting beside a partially demolished house. It was a big one, about four feet high and three feet in diameter, with a cloth covering. "When we took the cover off, we could see that the water was full of mosquito larvae. I can remember just plunging my head down in that jug and drinking, wigglers and all."

Chapter 26

One of the slicks resupplying DeLuca's battalion at dusk took hits and was forced to make an emergency landing. At that time, DeLuca and Booras were setting up a new command post at the top of the dead-end street, the area having become the focus of the battle. The command group of the 2-47th Mech replaced them in the pagoda under the Y Bridge.

Night positions were organized, and the day's box score was reported to brigade: fourteen U.S. soldiers medevacked against a body count of ninety-eight VC.

The letter Tony DeLuca penned to his wife that night noted that:

> The noise level has been tremendous with a constant stream of air and artillery support. These troops are great—for 4 days we have been pounding a [VC] battalion that is holding an area [on the] south [side] of the city. We have gone a total of 800 meters—pushing, taking casualties, and pushing back. So far we have accounted for over 200 VC but we have paid for it. . . . [T]oday in the aid station everyone was looking glum except one soldier & he smiled as I came up to talk to him; yep, he was the wounded one, with a bad head wound. It tears you up [to see injured American soldiers] but [their uncomplaining attitude] gives you the charge you need to keep pushing.

DeLuca addressed his touchy relationship with Ewell in his letter: "I'm sure the General isn't happy. [Two] days ago he said [the area] would be cleaned up by 4 p.m. [that same day] and he was wrong. He accuses us of a lack of aggression but he doesn't understand the war. Colonel Benson is in my corner and that's all I care about." Benson wryly informed DeLuca that Ewell kept asking him, "Why doesn't DeLuca finish it up?" In that, DeLuca wrote home that the division commander "reminded me of the Pope in *The Agony and the Ecstasy*, always asking Michelangelo [during the painting of the Sistine Chapel] 'when will it be done?' His answer was mine: 'when it is finished.' "

Colonel Benson spent the battle bouncing between the command posts of the five line battalions attached to his brigade, in order to speak directly with DeLuca, Adcock, Antila, Tower, and Schmalhorst to understand better what they were facing and organize the support they needed. "It was a basic, clean-cut infantry battle," Benson says, shrugging off as what colonels get paid for both his role in coordinating the action and the automatic-weapons fire he occasionally took up in his Huey. "No big deal. I didn't even know we were getting shot at half the time. You'd come back at the end of the day, and the pilots would say, 'We took six hits today, colonel.' I'd say, 'Well, good luck!' "

Ewell subsequently awarded Benson the Silver Star for his role in the defense of Saigon. Captain Geschke, the surgeon attached to the 3-39th Infantry, was involved in an incident that spoke to the brigade commander's leadership and understated courage. Benson happened to be standing with Geschke at the doorway of the battalion aid station one day during the battle, watching a jet fighter make a bomb run, when a foot-and-a-half-long piece of "Made in the U.S.A." shrapnel suddenly ripped through the corrugated tin roof and slammed with killing force into the floor a few feet away. "I was very frightened," recalls Geschke, a draftee and married man who had no interest whatsoever in dying in Vietnam. "I immediately hit the floor, but then nothing else happened and I got up. It was obvious that I was a little shaken, and this big, tall bird colonel who was there wanted to encourage me, and said, 'Well, we never really get used to this type of thing.' You could tell that the colonel was a compassionate individual, and his comment made me feel a bit better. He gave me the courage I needed at that time."

The people caught in the middle of the battle saw the soldiers clearing the area not as heroes but as madmen. Charles Sweet of the U.S. Embassy discovered as much when he drove his scout to District 8 on the afternoon of May 11.

Sweet entered the district headquarters during a meeting being held by members of the New Life Construction Project, the community-development organization that had been doing good works in the area since 1965. Though Sweet had worked closely with these men all that time, they greeted his arrival with icy stares. A thirty-year-old lawyer named Doan Thanh Liem, whose family had fled the north after the communist takeover and who was then a project manager in Cholon and District 8, finally broke the silence with an anguished reference to all the bombs being dropped in residential neighborhoods whose inhabitants were loyal to the government. "When you must use these tactics," he said quietly, "I know we are losing the war."

During Tet, the ARVN rangers sent in to reclaim the district had relied on local police to pinpoint enemy positions before calling in artillery fire and Skyraiders from the Vietnamese Air Force. The battle had resulted in a fair share of property damage, but little resentment from residents who appreciated the care taken by the rangers. The situation had changed dramatically during the second urban offensive, Liem presently informed Sweet. The people were outraged. Though the enemy had attacked in smaller numbers this time, the Americans had responded with a tsunami of firepower that dwarfed what had been used by the rangers three months earlier. The result: considerably more civilian casualties and wrecked houses, but far fewer dead Viet Cong.

No one could make sense of the fact that three years of progress was being wiped away because seventy or eighty guerrillas had slipped into the district. There were actually more, but in his anger, Liem was apparently providing Sweet with the lowest number he had heard from residents. Irregardless, there was no doubt that U.S. units led with firepower and were more than willing to bring down a neighborhood to eliminate a handful of snipers rather than lose people in house-to-house combat. Though Liem was again low balling the numbers when he told Sweet that only twenty VC had been killed for all the bombing, the project manager's estimate of enemy casualties was more realistic than the padded body counts being claimed by the 9th Division. According to Liem, the Americans had killed two hundred residents of the district thus far, wounded another thousand, and demolished four thousand homes: "Two hundred houses are being destroyed for every Viet Cong killed!"

"Enough talk," Liem snapped. He wanted Sweet to see for himself what was happening. Liem insisted on putting a sign marked *bao chi* on the windshield of Sweet's scout so to protect themselves not from the enemy, he explained, but from enraged residents who might react violently at the sight of someone from the U.S. Embassy. Liem and Sweet drove through Xom Cau Mat, the most damaged hamlet in the district and, turning onto the canal road, passed thousands of refugees encamped in makeshift shelters along the Kinh Doi. Liem pointed out the gutted Pham The Hien market where sixty civilians had been killed and wounded two days before when a mechanized unit responded with what the residents viewed as hysterical overkill to a few sniper shots.

Liem argued that instead of blowing the place down, U.S. officers should have used the project manager's cadre to pinpoint enemy positions identified by the locals, at which point exit routes could have been blocked and tear-gas could have been employed to flush the enemy into the open. The guerrillas, after all, were operating in small teams, equipped only with

AK-47s and RPGs. To respond to snipers with air strikes was to play directly into the communists' hands. The communists wanted the bombs to fall. They wanted to embitter the people against the Americans.

Reaching the point where the battle for the dead-end street was then raging, Liem and Sweet were forced to turn around in the face of the gunships and jet fighters working the area over. Proceeding back the way they had come and then over the Kinh Doi into Cholon, they drove past block upon block of flattened buildings. The destruction was more widespread than anything Sweet had seen during Tet, and he and Liem, parking the scout, spent some time walking along rubbled streets, sensing the fear of the people who lived there. Over three hundred civilians had been killed in Cholon, Liem said. At the end of their trip, Liem asked Sweet to bring what he had seen to the attention of his superiors, adding that "someone should be tried for this murder and destruction."

Sweet prepared a written report the next day which ultimately led to an official MACV investigation of the 9th Infantry Division.

DeLuca's command group came under recoilless-rifle fire, twenty-three rounds in all, in the hours before dawn on May 12, 1968.

The enemy also subjected Tower's new command post, where Bill Sirtola was dug in beside the pagoda with his mortar team from B/6-31st, to some harassing fire. Sirtola and his buddies sat on the sandbags of their mortar pit, spectators to an exchange of fire between an enemy rocket team on the top floor of a three-story building and the tracks on the Y Bridge. In short order, a jeep pulled up to the building. A tough, phlegmatic old major in the passenger seat trained a searchlight on the enemy position, then turned on a bullhorn. "Don't shoot," the major's voice boomed through the night. "I'm going to try and take some prisoners."

The major turned toward the enemy-held building with his bullhorn and began speaking in Vietnamese. He'd only gotten a few sentences out when the crew of a recoilless rifle mounted on one of the tracks on the Y Bridge punched off a round at the perfectly illuminated target, a direct hit which ended all debate and discussion. Though the major hadn't been expecting the shot, he hadn't flinched, which amazed Sirtola. "We could see the silhouette of the gutsy major standing on the jeep," Sirtola writes, "bullhorn still to his lips, against a background of expanding dust illuminated by the searchlight. He held the position for a few more seconds, then we heard the bullhorn crackle off, saw the searchlight turned off, and heard the putt-putt of the jeep backing away. We roared. What a performance!"

***

While DeLuca's troops began fighting their way through the streets again during the late morning, B/2-47th, which was still attached, swept the more open areas to the south. It was almost noon when the 1st Platoon, moving on foot, approached a cluster of hootches that sat on the other side of a deep canal. Bob Dyson, on point, paused uneasily at the rickety footbridge spanning the canal. He sensed trouble. The hamlets on the outskirts of the city occupied widened dikes separated by rice paddies that had become open sewers. Movement through the muck was too slow and exposed to be safe, forcing units to channel their movements down the widened dikes.

Perhaps not understanding why Dyson had stopped, one of the men in column—a private named Larious—sprinted past and onto the footbridge. He was about halfway across when the enemy machine gunner who had been waiting in ambush on the other side suddenly commenced firing. Though wounded, Larious made it to the far side and hit the dirt, only to realize that he had taken cover next to a spider hole occupied by a VC with an AK-47.

Larious played dead. Dyson, meanwhile, saw two rounds kick up dirt in front of him. He dropped and rolled, let loose an angry shout at the enemy gunner, and lifted his head so he could see what he was shooting at as he shouldered his M16. By doing so, he made himself a target; a bullet cracked past his ear and two more zipped over his back so close he could feel them. Several men shouted at him to join them behind a nearby hootch. Dyson had no sooner crawled to them than the thatch burst into flames, the incoming fire having apparently ignited a container of cooking oil. Dyson and his buddies escaped the burning hootch by crawling backwards into one of the stagnant, muddy, waste-filled paddies.

John Driessler also found sanctuary in the reeking paddy, having survived at the beginning of the ambush a burst of fire that had impacted just in front of his face and slapped mud against his forehead with such force that he thought he'd been hit. The platoon leader, crouching nearby, spotted an enemy soldier in a spider hole across the canal and pitched a grenade at him. The frag fell short, but the unlucky Viet Cong popped up at that instant to fire another AK-47 burst and was killed by the explosion.

Major Riedl was parked along a canal on the flank of the engaged platoon and, while scanning the hamlet with his binoculars, could see several figures moving about in the vicinity of what looked like a bunker. Riedl and his gunner, Tony Midkiff, fired on the position with the 90mm recoilless rifle mounted in the command cupola of their track. Midkiff then grabbed an M79 and lobbed smoke shells toward a number of muzzle flashes he could see, pinpointing the spider holes for the .50-caliber gunners on several nearby APCs.

The enemy returned the favor, several rounds suddenly clanging across the gun shield behind which Riedl and Midkiff were crouched; the former peering around the left side with his binoculars, the latter firing from the right side with his grenade launcher. Tony Midkiff was knocked backwards into the cargo hatch. Feeling nothing, he imagined that a ricochet had glanced off his flak jacket. He reached for his M79, but something was wrong, he couldn't pick it up—his hand wasn't working. Then he saw that his right arm was missing a chunk of flesh at the elbow and blood was jetting from a severed artery.

After a medic secured a tourniquet around Midkiff's arm, Riedl shouted at his driver, Roy Derr, to haul ass for the medevac point under the Y Bridge. Reaching the green, the track stopped, the back ramp was lowered, and Midkiff, who was drifting in and out of consciousness, was laid on a stretcher. A medevac landed within moments. Somebody shouted that the wounded man needed a flak jacket, and Midkiff realized that he was no longer wearing his armored vest. The medic had apparently stripped it off to check for additional wounds, but now there was a demand that he have one on lest the medevac take ground fire on its way out. Riedl threw his own flak jacket over Midkiff, and the stretcher was hurriedly loaded into the Huey. The evacuation process was handled so quickly that Midkiff's life was saved, as was his arm. Riedl, however, would always feel guilty about how, in his enthusiasm for going to the sound of the guns, he had turned the job of crewman on the executive officer's track—normally one of the safest assignments in a mechanized-infantry battalion—into a near death trip for tough, loyal Tony Midkiff.

First Lieutenant Jerome Johnson, the executive officer and acting commander of B/2-47th, had placed the 3rd Platoon in a blocking position near the hamlet that the 1st Platoon had been approaching when ambushed. The tracks, positioned along a trail, began taking some fire of their own from across the paddy on that side of the enemy-held hamlet.

Paul Ianni called to his squad leader, Jimmy Dye, and told him that he had spotted a muzzle flash. "I'll mark it," he shouted, training the .50-caliber machine gun on the target. "I'll try to mark it with a tracer."

Dye prepared a LAW and, following Ianni's tracer—the red needle zipped into a dike—pushed the firing button and sent the projectile across the paddies to impact within feet of the spider hole that had been marked.

The explosion didn't kill the occupant, but it did send him scurrying for better cover. He never made it. The enemy soldier was moving slow, waist-deep in paddy muck, recalls Dye, "and that's when Ianni dusted him with the .50."

Paul Ianni was one of the most popular guys in the platoon, a little five-foot-two Italian from New York with an upbeat attitude and the courage of a lion as vividly demonstrated by his willingness to serve as the platoon tunnel rat. A good son, he had a friend at Bearcat type his letters home, the better to fool his parents into believing his story of being a clerk in a support base. What none of Ianni's buddies knew was that he was homosexual and his bravery, in part, was a response to this hidden part of his life. Ianni almost wanted to die in combat, a heroic soldier respected by his buddies. "I was so ashamed of being gay, I figured that getting killed was the best way to get out of it."*

The battle continued. Bob Dyson of the 1st Platoon darted to a small brick house from behind which several troops were firing. One of them sent an M79 round into a hootch across the canal, then shouted that he'd seen two or three VC run out of the back after the explosion. It was at that time, about an hour into the action, when the enemy finally began to slip away. As the enemy fire petered out, the platoon sergeant—who had earned the scorn of his troops by diving into the lieutenant's track on the first day of the battle—changed a lot of minds by boldly crawling out ahead of everyone else to lay down the suppressive fire needed for Larious to swim back to safety from the enemy side of the canal. Larious' wounds turned out to be relatively minor thanks to the machine-gun ammo criss-crossed across his chest that had deflected the rounds that should have killed or seriously wounded him. Superficial or not, the wounds were bad enough to warrant a trip out on a medevac, and Larious couldn't help but laugh with relief when so informed by the platoon medic.

Meanwhile, several of the retreating enemy soldiers were being cut down as they tried to slosh across the open paddies. The official body count was ten.

Lieutenants Madrigal and Bausser of Company B, 3rd Battalion, 39th Infantry, along with their two radiomen and a rifleman, crawled down a

---

* Older and wiser now, Ianni speaks of his disappointment in a society that gave him medals "for killing other men at my country's direction" even while offering only "discrimination and hatred for loving another man."

drainage ditch, which ran north-to-south between two buildings, and led into an open area approximately the size of a football field. The group took up a position inside a two-walled house at the northwest corner of the clearing, ready to call down fire on any enemy soldiers who might be flushed out by the troops sweeping the buildings situated along the dead-end street to the east. Madrigal positioned the rifleman, a new guy, at a window and told him to keep his eyes peeled. The new guy did just that, blurting out only moments later, "Jesus, I can see 'em runnin' around!"

Madrigal saw a figure with a weapon hustling across the south end of the clearing. The new guy, a Kentuckian, licked his thumb, rubbed the front sight, shouldered the M16, sighted in, and with a single squeeze of the trigger, dropped a running target at a hundred meters. "Got 'im!"

"Good job!" Lieutenant Madrigal exclaimed. "Now keep watching, and if you see anybody else going across there, you kill 'im, too."

The new guy repeated the performance as a second and then a third VC tried to reposition from one building to another, unaware that there were Americans watching from the top of the clearing. "He popped three guys back-to-back," says Madrigal. "Instead of just cutting loose on automatic, this kid took his time. He licked his thumb each time, rubbed his front sight, took careful aim, and fired. It was awesome. It was really cool. If killing somebody can be cool, that was."

Someone on the far side of the clearing finally took notice of the shots coming from the two-walled house, and AK-47 fire started to pour in. "Chunks of plaster were flying all over," notes Bausser. "Madrigal and I looked at each other, and we both said, 'Let's get the fuck out of here.' We retreated. I mean, we ran out of there." During the dash to safety, Sergeant Henry—the recon sergeant was carrying the radio in the absence of the team's wounded radioman—suddenly stumbled, but Lieutenant Bausser grabbed his harness on the run and helped him back to his feet. "You could hear the crack of AK fire and the whistle as the rounds went by," remembers Bausser. "When we got back to the street corner where we had set up our headquarters, I tried to make a call on the radio but it didn't work. Henry removed the radio from his back, and we noticed a bullet had embedded in the battery. I guess the impact was what had thrown Henry forward. We got another battery and were back in business shortly."

DeLuca wanted another attack. "Nobody wanted to go back," notes Bausser, "but the colonel thought it was important."

Bringing more riflemen the second time, Lieutenants Madrigal and Bausser crawled once more into the two-sided house, which was in the enemy's sights, to be sure, but offered a good place from which to direct fire. It was going on six o'clock by then. At that time, having pulled back from the tiny hamlet on the edge of the city, B/2-47th was deployed along the dead-end street less than a hundred meters to the east, on the other side of a single block of buildings.

Lieutenant Johnson, the acting company commander, had positioned his tracks at intervals along the cluttered roadway, noses pushed up against the smashed fences and mounds of dirt in front of the houses. The troops had spent the last thirty minutes buttoned up inside their vehicles while Lieutenant Bowman—the forward observer of the company and the only one in the open besides his recon sergeant—directed artillery fire onto a house from which fire had been received, carefully adjusting the barrage to within thirty meters of the APCs.

Bowman had no sooner ended the fire mission than Lieutenant Madrigal's group came under fire again from a half-smashed building thirty meters south of their position. Overhead in his command ship, DeLuca wanted Bausser to have the battery supporting his battalion place one more round on Bowman's target, then adjust the fire from there onto the snipers in the half-smashed building. Bausser tried to warn Bowman that another howitzer shell would be fired into his area, but could not make contact with his counterpart due to all the traffic on the radio. Given the urgency of the situation, DeLuca instructed Bausser to go ahead and fire. Bausser reluctantly did so. The firing battery gave Bausser a countdown to the splash, but when he peeked his head up, he saw no explosion; the round had overshot the target to impact out of sight on the other side of the buildings along the dead-end street. Bausser's stomach dropped as he heard Bowman shouting urgently over the radio: "Check fire, check fire, check fire!"

Lieutenant Johnson's troops had just emerged from their tracks and were assembling to assault the house Bowman had blasted when the long round hurtled in without warning. The shell exploded in the center of the street. Specialist Fourth Class Anthony P. Palumbo—a black-haired, olive-skinned draftee, age twenty, from Buffalo, New York—was struck in the head by a chunk of shrapnel and killed instantly. Though a veteran of nearly eight months in combat, he still possessed a perpetual smile and dealt with his comrades with a warmth and sincerity not to be found in the average GI. Earlier that day, in fact, John Driessler and another trooper, both of whom were out of water, had asked Palumbo if he had any left. In response, Palumbo had handed his last half-filled canteen to his parched buddies, telling them to finish it even though there was no way of knowing when they might get a water resupply.

Of the wounded, Private First Class Philip M. Wooten, who was only recently assigned to the company maintenance track, was in the worst shape. Bob Dyson heard that the injured man's brother, also in-country, had visited him earlier that very day. The brother, reports Dyson, "helped carry Wooten to the clearing used for the medevac, where he died."

Driessler helped one of the wounded to the medevac, "and I almost cried when he thanked me. He'd lost a lot of blood and half my uniform was soaked in it."

The cause of the accident which snuffed out two lives so capriciously was never determined. Upon receiving the check-fire, the battery commander had immediately reviewed the firing data at his fire direction center and at the howitzers themselves. All the data was correct. In addition, the probable circle of error for the charge and range used was fifteen meters, meaning that when the round overshot the target, it should have detonated in front of the tracks. Instead, the round went long by a full thirty meters to impact behind the tracks. The officer who investigated the incident speculated that because ten minutes had elapsed between the original half-hour barrage and that single errant round, the cooling of the tube involved might have affected its ballistic characteristics.

Such explanations would have meant little to the despondent, tight-mouthed medic photographed by Philip Jones Griffiths as he stood behind his personnel carrier, one arm resting on the aid bag slung over his shoulder, a cigarette in his other hand. The body of Anthony Palumbo was lying on its back to the side of the track, with a large towel draped over the face and upper body, his arms crossed atop his stomach. The posture was that of a man sleeping. "If there was a Vietcong sniper around," Griffiths wrote, "he missed a lot of easy targets, for after the artillery stopped, the GIs stood in exposed groups, utterly dejected, telling each other what awful torture they had planned for the artillery officers back at their camp."

The lieutenant running Palumbo's platoon wanted one last look at this soldier to whom he was deeply attached, but by then a heavy trail of blood was running from the towel covering the dead man's head and a GI stopped him with the comment: "You don't want to look at him, lieutenant."

Once the situation had stabilized, DeLuca, who still had a battle to fight, told Bausser to bring in the artillery on the snipers firing on Madrigal's group. Bausser tried to beg off, arguing that it was unsafe to continue firing when he couldn't see the other friendly units in the area or get through to them by radio. DeLuca pressed Bausser to carry out his orders and get the artillery cranked up again. Bausser, getting emotional, finally told

DeLuca to go to hell even as his friend Madrigal tried to snatch the radio handset from him. DeLuca snapped back that the artillery lieutenant should consider himself relieved of his duties as of that moment. The issue became moot, as the unrelenting enemy fire prompted another withdrawal down the drainage ditch soon thereafter. Platoon Sergeant Thornburgh handed Bausser a bottle of Johnny Walker that he had liberated in the rubbled house where his reserve platoon had taken shelter. The alcohol must have had an effect, because Madrigal later saw Bausser sitting "with his head buried in his hands, just weeping. He just broke down. He was very upset."

Whatever was said in the heat of the moment, DeLuca did not remove Bausser from Bravo Company. "When it was all over, and we were back at Rach Kien," notes Bausser, "and I was in what was called the Officers Club, DeLuca came in there and we sort of glared at each other, but we never had any words about the incident. He never brought it up, and life went on."

Chapter 27

The heaviest contact of the day was made when Captain Eckman and Company B, 6th Battalion, 31st Infantry, in coordination with Company C, 3rd Battalion, 39th Infantry, attempted again to dislodge the enemy who had occupied the abandoned militia outpost. The troops were rankled that the previous day's attack had been repulsed. Sergeant Leader caught the mood in the tape he sent home when he described how after the way had been paved with artillery, "we moved on to the objective itself, this time determined to take it."

There was a feeling of resolve among the men. There were other emotions, too, as David Gray noted in a letter he wrote his parents before shouldering his radio, picking up his rifle, and moving out that morning: "I'm really scared."

The shooting started almost immediately. Lieutenant Procaccini's platoon was in the lead when the point squad, led by Sergeant Kenneth R. Davis, came under fire while moving down the street that led to the militia outpost. When several rounds snapped over Davis' head, he sensed the direction from which they came and managed to spot the sniper, or at least the silhouette of his upper body. The sniper was darting from one end of a back porch to the other, laying down AK-47 bursts almost in cadence. Davis, who was exactly where he wanted to be—in the infantry and in combat—worked his way toward the porch, finally taking up a position behind a concrete light pole. The silhouette stopped in the middle of the porch then, a stationary target, and Davis notes how he saw his chance, "pulled the safety off a LAW, gauged the distance, set the sight, and stuck it too him chest high. He could not have survived."

Nearing the militia outpost and still in the lead, Sergeant Davis' squad took fire from a thatched hut that, save for a dead dog laying on the dirt floor, proved empty when Davis and two of his team leaders approached while covering each other. They checked the walls and the overhead, finding nothing. Davis was convinced that the clay stove inside the hootch concealed the entrance of a tunnel. What else could explain how the sniper had been there one moment and gone the next?

Davis and his team leaders were starting back to rejoin the squad when, infuriatingly, another sniper's round snapped through the hootch. There was no opportunity to respond. Lieutenant Procaccini had passed the word that Captain Eckman wanted the point platoon to clear a string of thatch hootches that ran in a relatively straight line to the rice paddy around the militia outpost. Some of these hootches were still intact, others reduced to ash and debris. There was, behind the hootches, a retaining berm about three feet high that held back a rancid accumulation of garbage and stagnant rain water.

As enemy fire came zipping their way, Sergeant Davis and most of his squad scrambled through what had once been a front door to take shelter inside a semi-demolished hootch. Staff Sergeant Rexford Humes, who ran the platoon's weapons squad, took up a position at an outside corner of the hootch with Private First Class Percy Horton, who was soon laying down a sheet of return fire with his M60.

With the machine gun blazing, Davis grabbed his two team leaders again, and duck-walking to stay below the windows, he crept out the back door to a brick wall that ran parallel to the retaining berm behind the hootches. Davis peered around the edge of the wall, watching for shots, and was startled when they came not from some relatively distant location, but from a spider hole dug into the retaining berm not ten feet from where he was squatting. The hole was camouflaged with palm fronds, and smoke leaked out as the Viet Cong inside squeezed off four or five quick shots at intervals from his AK-47.

Sergeant Davis wanted to put a grenade-launcher round into the spider hole, but did not call for his grenadier. He didn't really have one. The GI who carried the squad's M79 was one of several unreliable soldiers in the squad—guys only concerned with saving their own skins and blank-eyed members of McNamara's 100,000. Davis used these unreliable men as pack mules to carry extra ammunition and extra weapons, like the pump shotgun he liked having on hand, given the propensity for their rifles to jam. "If you can't do anything else," Davis had instructed these duds, "just bring the weapons and ammo up to me and the team leaders when we need 'em."

The grenade launcher was passed to Davis, who fired a beehive round into the spider hole. The guerrilla flew up against the retaining berm, then slowly slid back into his hole. "The position was hot again within five minutes," notes Davis, unsure if there had been a second guerrilla in the spider hole all along or if the enemy positions were interconnected with tunnels.

As the exchange continued, Percy Horton's machine gun took a round that sent a piece of the sight flying, opening up a slice along his cheekbone.

Horton hung tight behind the M60, covering Davis as he pulled his squad back in the face of increasing enemy fire from the flank. Looking back after reaching cover, Davis could see rounds smacking into a hootch the enemy did not realize had just been vacated. Staff Sergeant Humes' gun team came out last. "Humes, Horton, and their ammo bearers all stick out in my mind as gritty soldiers," recalls Davis. Humes was a white guy, a regular, and Horton a black draftee in his early twenties. The team's ammo bearers were also black and had gravitated into a job that kept them close to Horton. At a time when the unit was fairly new in-country, and "so many of the men were acting like they were still back on the block," notes Davis, "Percy acted like a soldier. He was a fellow warrior. He had the spirit of an older, wiser man, and knew how to encourage the men working with him and Humes. Percy Horton also had enthusiasm, a winner's attitude, and a desire to live to go home. He wasn't about to become a statistic without a fight."

First Lieutenant Michael J. Canney of C/3-39th, which was deployed in a blocking position south of the militia outpost, thought the rounds zipping overhead sounded more like friendly fire than enemy. Charlie Company was apparently catching some stray stuff from Bravo Company, but the fire ceased after smoke grenades were popped to mark positions and company commander Latham got on the horn with company commander Eckman.

Latham instructed Canney to link up with Bravo Company. The only way forward was through a small opening over a moat. Wondering if a sniper was watching the opening, Lieutenant Canney went first, thinking it best to lead from the front in such a situation. There was no fire, and Canney's radioman followed. Specialist Fourth Class Jaime A. Rivera-Lopez, who normally walked point, went next only to sink knee-deep in the moat. Several grunts from Bravo Company, clustered behind some nearby hootches, pulled Rivera-Lopez from the mud, at which point he was shot in the head and killed instantly. Canney had been right; a sniper was covering the opening. Canney would never know if Rivera-Lopez had ended up in the sniper's sights because he became an easy target when he got stuck, or because he had followed the radioman through the opening, giving the impression that he was the platoon leader. "Because of the unusual positioning of personnel," reflects Canney, "[Rivera-]Lopez may well have gotten the fate intended for me."

David Gray, radioman for the 1st Platoon, B/6-31st, was shot by the sniper an instant after Rivera-Lopez, whom he had been helping pull from the mud. Knocked backwards onto his radio, Gray tried to roll to cover, only to be hit again and again as the sniper mercilessly tracked him in the sights of his AK-47. Shot thirteen times in both legs, Gray felt no pain, only a peaceful numbness. Then strong hands fastened upon his wrists and web gear, jolting him back to reality and pulling him behind a hootch. Staff Sergeant Terry Dotson, a black squad leader on his second tour, was one of those who had rushed out into the fire to rescue the wounded radioman. Gray also recognized Mark Mudd and a draftee team leader named Sam Flores. He would never forget these men and the risk they took to save his life.

Several grunts laid Gray on a door, then hustled him rearward to Captain Eckman's location where the senior company medic checked his injuries. Both femoral arteries were gushing blood, his left ankle and kneecap were shattered, and chunks of muscle were missing from the exit wounds in his upper right thigh. The medic secured tourniquets and hooked up an IV. The tourniquets weren't enough to stop the flow. Gray felt himself fading away again, but a medevac barreled in then and he was hurriedly loaded aboard. Gray stared up at the diamond-shaped pattern stitched into the padded ceiling of the cargo bay. The dust-off medic crouched beside him, shouting to hang on, and within minutes, the Huey was touching down at the 3rd Field Hospital.

Lifted onto a gurney, Gray was wheeled into a triage area. As he was covered in mud, a pair of medics wearing green rubber gloves and green rubber butcher's aprons prepared him for surgery by washing him down with a hose. The shock of the water on his gaping wounds was unbearable. He shrieked in pain.

In moments, Gray was in surgery. He must have asked what condition he was in because one of the doctors told him honestly that they might have to amputate his left leg. "Don't do it," Gray begged. "Please, please, whatever you do, don't take my leg off!"

Gray was told to open his mouth, and a tube was slipped down his throat. He was put under then, and the surgery began.

When Gray awoke, he still had his leg.

The snipers were not invincible. Lieutenant Procaccini's platoon eliminated one who was perched in a palm tree and another who was firing from a house. The latter was reduced to hamburger when Sergeant Davis crawled out in front of his squad with a DayGlo orange marking panel and brought in a jet fighter. (Davis was awarded the Silver Star for his aggressive leadership that day.) The Phantom passed overhead so closely that he could read the markings on its underside, and it placed with perfect precision a high-drag bomb into the sniper's hiding place.

Sergeant Davis moved on to a little sheet-metal shed after the air strike. Leaving his men outside, the better to maintain the element of surprise, Davis ducked inside through an empty door frame and started over the bags of rice strewn across the floor. Spotting movement inside a white house visible through the opposite doorway, Davis pulled the pins on two grenades. Before he could throw them, he realized that there was a hole in the earthen floor of the shed and rice bags were arranged to conceal what was the entrance to an underground bunker.

In the same instant that someone opened fire on the shed with an AK-47, something exploded beneath Davis. He later surmised that the enemy had probably detonated a charge in the underground bunker. Feeling as if electrocuted, he let go of the two fragmentation grenades gripped in his fists. The spoons popped off.

Dazed but not incoherent with his helmet slammed down across his nose, Sergeant Davis spotted one of the grenades, snatched it up, and threw it down the hole in the floor. Davis found the other grenade—the metal egg seemed burning hot—with his left hand and frantically flung the frag toward the opening he was facing, but the thing explode in his face not three feet from his fingertips. That he was not killed instantly was miraculous. Instead, he survived with ringing ears, fragment wounds in his shoulder and chest, and the vivid memory of a brilliant white and yellow flash with a black center. Partially flashblinded and unsure of how badly he had been injured, Davis called on the name of the Lord.

Lieutenant Procaccini was stunned when he caught a glimpse of Private First Class Lyle W. Hansen, radioman for Davis' squad, sprinting across a patch of open ground, firing his M16 from the hip. Hansen, a humorous kid who did his job but had never before been anybody's idea of a super soldier, made it to the shed in which Davis lay wounded, then laid his rifle aside and shrugged out of his radio harness, the better to drag his squad leader out of harm's way. Scrambling over the bags of rice, Hansen crouched above Davis to ask, "Sarge, are you okay?"

As Davis started to answer, Lyle Hansen was shot twice in the face, and collapsed heavily across his squad leader, killed instantly. Working his way out from under the body of his dead radioman, Davis crawled over the bags of rice, hoping not to get shot himself in the process, and made it back through the opening in the shed to rejoin his squad. Davis told his guys to make sure they got Hansen out of there. They promised they would, then one of them wrapped an arm around Sergeant Davis and helped him rearward so that he could be medevacked. Hansen would be awarded a posthumous Silver Star.

The grunts of the lead platoon, down in drainage ditches and scattered behind hootches and palm trees, faced the paddy encircling the little island on which the enemy-occupied militia outpost was situated. Some of the grunts poured fire with a gusto into the houses on the other side of the paddy. Others held their weapons above them, firing blindly. Still others had gone heads-down for the duration. Lieutenant Procaccini himself blasted away with his CAR-15 when not shouting directions or talking on the horn with Captain Eckman, who was linked via his other radio with DeLuca.

Eckman sent Sergeant Leader's squad to reinforce Procaccini, and Specialist Fourth Class Dennis K. Jones—attached to Leader as a spotter only the day before from the battalion heavy-mortar platoon—moved freely through the enemy fire as he helped coordinate the artillery fire and gunships pummeling the other side of the rice paddy. Jones finally took cover behind the cement wall of the porch of a little cinder-block house; raising up to fire quick bursts with his M16, he was too excited to pay attention to the grunts who shouted at him to fire and move so the enemy couldn't get a fix on his position. In short order, Dennis Jones paid for his bravery and inexperience with a bullet to the head. Leader dragged Jones into the cinder-block house. Part of the man's skull had been blown away. Blood poured from his head and nose. Leader couldn't believe that the human body contained so much blood. It lay thick on the floor like Jell-O.

Instructed to fall back and secure a landing zone, Leader helped carry the door being used as a stretcher for Dennis Jones, his eyes fixed on the gray matter hanging grotesquely over the side from the unconscious and mortally wounded man's head, which bounced as they ran. The litter team made it to a clearing beside a hootch where the company first sergeant had collected the wounded for the medevac that was inbound. The first attempt to land was greeted with automatic-weapons fire, and the pilot pulled up and swung away from the clearing. Leader fanned his troops out. They didn't spot the sniper, but there was no more fire, and when the pilot, circling overhead, asked if the landing zone was secure, Leader answered that it seemed to be. Actually, it wasn't. Another attempted landing was again broken off under fire.

On the third attempt, Leader intently scanned the area and noticed movement behind a palm tree fifty meters away on the other side of an open and marshy paddy field he hadn't wanted to send his men across. All

he could see of the sniper kneeling behind the tree was one of the sneak-
ers the man was wearing. The front of the tennis shoe was sticking out in
plain view. Leader shouldered his M16 even as the medevac flared to land,
hurriedly sighted in, and squeezed off a single shot before the sniper swung
his own weapon around the side of the tree and opened fire again. The
sniper jerked his foot back, obviously injured. Leader reckoned the surprise of getting a bullet in his foot would keep the enemy soldier
preoccupied long enough to get the casualties loaded aboard the medevac
and the pilot to pull pitch, and this time he was right. The sniper remained
silent throughout the evacuation process, and when it was over, Leader and
his squad rejoined the battle.

Dennis Jones received a posthumous Distinguished Service Cross.

As the firefight dragged on, there came a point when either DeLuca
or Eckman determined that the only way to retake the militia outpost
was to make an old-fashioned fire-and-maneuver rush on the position
and knock the spider holes and bunkers out with fragmentation
grenades. "I have a memory of someone wanting my platoon to assist
in an attack across a difficult area," notes Canney, "but that idea was
nixed by Captain Latham."

Lieutenant Procaccini, ordered by Eckman to conduct the assault, also
tried to nix the idea, explaining to the company commander that "we can't
see anyone. They're close, but we don't know exactly where they are. I've
got a bunch of chicken-wire in front of me," Procaccini continued, "and
then a rice paddy. I don't think I can get my people through the chicken-
wire and across the open paddy without getting everybody wiped out in the
process."

According to Procaccini, Eckman snapped impatiently that the platoon
leader had his orders and to get on with it. Procaccini moved over to Staff
Sergeant Dotson, whom he had always leaned on, given the squad leader's
previous combat tour, and shouted to him over the gunfire, "We gotta get
the men on line! We're making an assault!"

"You're crazy," Dotson shouted back. "There's no way we can get across
there and do anything and be effective."

"It's a direct order from the captain."

"Ain't no way," Dotson said firmly. He wasn't going, and he wasn't ordering his squad to go, either.

Procaccini's heart was pounding. The young lieutenant wasn't sure
what to do next, but on the premise that doing something was better
than doing nothing, he cradled his CAR-15, slipped under the chicken-

wire fence, and low-crawled through the muck of the paddy until he was up against he berm on the enemy side. Procaccini started screaming for the others to come on, but his radioman hollered back that the assault had been called off. Instead, more jets were on the way, and everyone was supposed to pull back. The air strike would be coming in danger close.

Desperate to rejoin the platoon lest he be left behind, Procaccini lobbed grenades into the nippa palm, then slid back into the paddy on his belly. Dotson laid down a continuous barrage of cover fire over him with an M60. Making it back safely, Procaccini joined the retreat, furious that Eckman had been willing to send his platoon on what seemed a completely suicidal venture. "There was no way we were going to lose the battle," explains Procaccini. "Why sacrifice American boys to try to win it more swiftly? Thank God the men did not move forward because we would have had a lot of dead soldiers if they had."

When the lead platoon had pulled back a safe distance, Eckman turned off the arty he had been firing to cover the withdrawal and began bringing in the bombs and napalm. Procaccini came up on the radio at that time to report that one of his men, Hansen, was missing and believed dead. "Confirm it," Eckman snapped. "Is he dead or is he alive?" Procaccini soon reported that the missing man had definitely been killed. "Well, if he's dead," Eckman sighed, "we can get him in the morning. There's no use getting anybody else killed today."

At some point during the night, Captain Eckman was informed that the man on radio watch in Procaccini's platoon had failed to answer the call for a situation report. Eckman trooped over to Procaccini's position with his first sergeant to find the whole platoon conked out. The first sergeant woke the troops as he and Eckman went down the line, finally finding Lieutenant Procaccini curled up in his poncho liner. Eckman began raising hell. In response, Procaccini defended his guys, trying to explain that they'd been in combat for days on end and were physically wrecked. Eckman saw red. "You don't argue, discuss, or rationalize at a time like that," Eckman says. "You don't alibi your troops. I came unglued. Nick tried to tell me that the men should be sleeping because they were tired—and I smacked him. I shouldn't have, but I did. I mean, there are just things you don't do in combat, and one of 'em is you don't let all your people go to sleep. Sure the guys were tired, but you're not operating under union rules in a battle situation. You push as hard as you can in order to stay alive, and in a situation like that, we damn well needed every other man awake and alert."

In the end, Procaccini, who had intended to stay in the army, received a medal for his personal heroism and a career-busting efficiency report for his lack of leadership. Eckman recalls "being questioned up to brigade level as to why I had crucified this lieutenant. I told 'em. Nick was a brave young man and a capable lieutenant as far as tactics and handling troops, but he made some stupid judgment calls and he was too soft on his men."

Chapter 28

Generals Ewell and Roseborough choppered in for a quick briefing during the late afternoon, after which the division commander pinned the Silver Star on DeLuca. "It was a surprise and not deserved," DeLuca wrote his wife that night. "It's 10:30 PM and we are still resupplying our companies in the field," the letter continued. "At just about dark our A company ran into a hornet's nest and things have just settled down. This was not the best day because it cost us 5 killed and 25 wounded at a cost to the VC of 85."

Noting the dramatic publicity the battle was receiving, DeLuca added, "Don't worry[,] doll—we are a damn good battalion and we're tough."

Captain Stuart and A/3-39th had indeed made heavy contact shortly before sundown when they stumbled into a bunker complex less than a kilometer south of the canal road in the rice paddies along the Rach Ong Nho. The enemy soldiers were dug into the dikes, and the grunts ended up pinned down in the open fields, a number of them passing out from heat exhaustion. Those who still had the energy to fight did so, including a rifleman named Gunnerson and grenadier Willo T. Naramore Jr., who spotted a spider hole from which a sniper was firing on Alpha One. Naramore blew open the top of the spider hole with his M79. The sniper inside was not silenced, however, and all the hand grenades that Naramore and Gunnerson threw didn't do the job, either. Out of frags, the two grunts worked their way to the spider hole, but before Gunnerson could fire his M16 down into the opening, the Viet Cong stuck the barrel of his AK-47 up into view and shot the grunt three or four times across the stomach.

Dropping flat, Naramore was unable to fire the single shell he had left; it had to travel ten meters to spin enough to arm. Naramore was too close. Luckily, Staff Sergeant Robert D. Long, a young black regular, scrambled forward and knocked the spider hole out once and for all with a single well-placed grenade. Long would be decorated with the Silver Star, Gunnerson and Naramore with Bronze Stars.

Platoon Sergeant Klump of Alpha Three had jumped into a water-filled ditch next to a burial mound when the shooting started and "wallowed around in there like an old hog to cool down." Klump gathered the platoon's canteens and crawled to a nearby thatch hootch with one of his grunts. They filled the canteens from the rain-filled drums beside the hootch. The grunt was injured in the process when a near-miss sent a clod of dirt into his side, producing a ferocious purple bruise. The two then crawled back to distribute the badly-needed water. Klump requested a medevac for two heat casualties in his platoon. "The chopper came in," he recounts. "Now I got to get up and take these two dudes over to it, and the enemy's shootin' and I'm scared, but we got 'em on the chopper."

The entrenched enemy maintained their fire as the sun sank. Rather than risk having a unit mired in a paddy in the dark with enemy soldiers all around, DeLuca opted to help Stuart break contact with some tactical air support to be delivered danger close. "The next thing I know," recalls Klump, "here comes a FAC [forward air controller], and he shoots a smoke rocket to mark the target. The sonuvabitch hit within three feet of me." Dusted with the colored powder inside the marking round, Klump "looked up, and I seen this fighter coming in low and dropping his bomb. Hell, I couldn't do anything. I just lay down as low as I could get. I thought, 'I'm dead,' and the bomb went over about fifty feet or so and landed in the stream—and it was a dud."

The spotter plane was piloted by Flight Lieutenant Garry G. Cooper of the Royal Australian Air Force. Cooper was a brash, thirty-year-old exchange officer only recently attached to the 19th Tactical Air Support Squadron, U.S. Air Force, at Dong Tam. Cooper was subsequently awarded the Silver Star for braving heavy ground fire to precisely mark the targets and then bring the jets in along a narrow corridor between the supporting mortar and artillery fire and a skyful of gunships, command ships, and resupply ships. Cooper's efforts allowed B/6-31st, A/3-39th, and C/3-39th to pull back and regroup, and all the elements on the battlefield to get resupplied.

Cooper's commanding officer wrote that because some of the ground units did not have smoke grenades, "Flight Lieutenant Cooper flew low over the area in order to establish the position of all the friendly troops. Due to his low altitude and turning within such a small area, he was extremely vulnerable to the hostile fire and was immediately drawing intense [.51] caliber machine gun fire. With complete disregard to his own safety he continued to evaluate the situation[,] weaving all the time to evade the hail of ground fire." Once the disposition of the enemy and friendly units had been clarified, Cooper "dived low at the [first] target to obtain an accurate mark for the fighters," and was "immediately met by a deadly crossfire and could hear the rounds going past his windshield. With the first marker right on target, he brought the fighters in but they were distracted by the ground fire and were a little inaccurate."

Cooper turned on his navigation lights and rotating beacon and instructed the fighter pilots to turn theirs off. (It was almost dark by then.) After marking the target again, he circled low over the spot to draw the enemy fire to his own aircraft and then slowly glided from the area, being chased by tracers that otherwise would have been heading for the fighters that were rolling in on the enemy position. The target was destroyed. Cooper used his spotter plane as bait five more times. While observing the damage that had been done, Cooper took fire from yet another enemy position, whereupon "he did a wing over and dived right at this position[,] putting his last rocket in accurately."

Darkness had completely engulfed the battlefield by then, and the ground commanders had not wanted to fire illumination as they established their night defensive positions, lest the enemy be drawn to them. "By this time the fighters were turning final with lights out, and Flight Lieutenant Cooper only had their exhaust flames to see them by," continued the statement from the commanding officer. Out of rockets, Cooper marked additional targets with smoke and white-phosphorus grenades dropped from his window. To prevent the fighter pilots from losing sight of the smoke, Cooper "circled low over the smoke with navigation lights on and had the fighters use him as a reference. All the time he was receiving intense ground fire which also gave the fighters a good target reference." With the bombs exploding close enough to shake his aircraft, "Flight Lieutenant Cooper remained in the target area directing artillery onto likely enemy retreat areas until he was forced to leave due to low fuel."

Cooper had been airborne for three hours. Upon returning to Dong Tam, he was surprised to find only minor battle damage to his spotter plane. The enemy was afforded the chance to further ventilate the aircraft when word was received a half hour before midnight that DeLuca's command post was taking AK-47 and RPG fire, and with his spotter plane refueled and rearmed, Cooper headed back through the night for Saigon. Cooper put in three more air strikes and the attack fizzled.

DeLuca had been informed sometime during the early evening that a prisoner scooped up in the area by the Vietnamese National Police had identified himself as a squad leader in one of the enemy's more celebrated units.

"We found out today that we have been facing the Phu Loi II Battalion, one of the best in Vietnam," DeLuca told his wife in the letter he wrote home that night, adding that other units had been unsuccessful in coming to grips with these veteran guerrilla fighters. "They [have] the reputation of being a phantom battalion."

These facts came into play when Lieutenant Foster, the acting commander of B/3-39th, contacted DeLuca the next morning, May 13, 1968, as the battalion prepared to once again move on its objectives. DeLuca described the conversation in a letter he wrote a week later:

> Pete [Booras] told me today that one speech I gave to a Company Commander over the radio during the Saigon battle brought tears to his eyes. It was a tough time in the battle, and [Lieutenant Foster] had been trying for almost three days to crack a VC position and he was about to give up and requested some other officer who could accomplish the mission be sent down. I don't remember exactly what I said except to express my admiration for the outstanding job that he and the company were doing against the best VC battalion in Vietnam, and [my] confidence that they would stick with it. They did, and they cracked the position.

The final act for Foster's company was actually anticlimactic. The troops secured the area without a shot being fired in anger, finding two dead enemy soldiers under a scorched piece of corrugated tin. "I saw the bodies," recalls Mad Madrigal. "They were crispy critters. The napalm had got 'em."

Similar reports reached DeLuca's command post from all of his companies. Objectives were being secured without contact; what was left of the enemy assault force had melted away under cover of darkness after six days of intense fighting. It was an old story. The communists usually started battles and usually ended them, too. Only two live guerrillas were encountered during the day—one who was already wounded was captured by B/2-47th, the other was killed by B/6-31st—as wrecked homes were searched, empty spider holes fragged, enemy weapons collected, and the bodies of enemy soldiers counted, forty-five in all according to the reports forwarded up the chain of command. Jack Brunet, a medic with the 3rd of the 39th, accompanied a patrol from the recon platoon the day the shooting stopped. "We were making a last house-to-house search," recalls Brunet. "One house we went into, we pushed the door open—it was open some, but we pushed it all the way open—and behind the door, in the corner, there was a mother who had been breast-feeding her baby, and she was crouched down, trying to protect the child as much as she could with her body. They'd both been hit anyway. They were both dead."

Lieutenant Procaccini's platoon from B/6-31st secured the militia outpost, recovering the body of Lyle Hansen in the process, and found that the enemy had turned the compound into a strongpoint with spider holes and bunkers covered with palm logs and mud. "It was all sort of surrealistic," recalls Procaccini. "There was smoke and fire and bodies strewn about, bloated, disgusting." The grunts knew that the battle must really be over when the civilians began reappearing. "They were walking around, looking at their destroyed property," notes Procaccini. "Lot of old people. Lot of crying. It was really sad."

The press described the battle as a Pyrrhic victory. With the enemy gone, Captain Stuart and A/3-39th were choppered back to the French Fort before nightfall on May 13. First Sergeant Johnson wrote his wife that the return trip was worse than the battle itself: "I hitched a ride with a recon ship [pilot] who was looking for the enemy that was left. He flew all the way back about 15 feet above ground at 105 knots. I've never been so shook up in my life."

DeLuca and his command group, plus the reconnaissance platoon, B/3-39th, and C/3-39th were shuttled by helicopter back to Rach Kien on the morning of May 14, while B/6-31st returned to Firebase Smoke. Many of the grunts shed their filthy fatigues before departing and showered under a cracked water pipe running along the south leg of the Y Bridge, a scene recorded for posterity by numerous reporters. "We're back home and it's a good feeling," DeLuca wrote his wife that evening. "The troop morale is high. . . . The 3rd Brigade is being recommended for a Presidential Unit Citation for its part in the action, and plenty of my people are receiving Silver Stars and Bronze Stars. There were so many heroes that it makes you want to burst with pride. They are really the greatest. Today they went right to work getting weapons cleaned, shaving, getting their haircuts, etc. At chapel services in the field yesterday they were apologizing for not being shaven!"

First Sergeant Johnson reported in a letter written three days after the return to the French Fort that Alpha Company "is ready to go again. After the war stories and rest everyone is Gung ho again." The company supply sergeant scrounged up several dozen cases of beer and soda for a party held on the evening of May 16. "We let the troops relax and have a big party,"

First Sergeant Johnson wrote home. "They sure had fun. First free time they've had since I've been here. You'd never know we'd just had a big shoot out. Everybody was happy. We've got some real good guitar players here and they played and some of the troops sang. It was a real riot." With the street battle over, the old paddy war beckoned. There was an awards ceremony the morning after the party. "Before it was over," Johnson's letter continued, "the troops were alerted and moved out. They killed 5 VC and captured 3 before they were out an hour. One of the prisoners is a company commander. . . ."

Lieutenant Colonel Tower and the 2-47th Mech, reinforced by C/6-31st, continued to secure the Y Bridge and patrol the area as engineer units began clearing away the rubble. Medical units also arrived to treat civilians for wounds and the diseases breaking out because of the crowded and unsanitary living conditions among those who had lost their homes. There was a final bit of action when the enemy mortared the Y Bridge from the distant rice paddies on the evening of May 14–15, scoring two direct hits, but there were no casualties. The only risks the troops ran at the end of the operation were dying of boredom, waking up with hangovers from all the beer that was available, or contracting venereal disease from the prostitutes who set up shop inside the shells of battle-damaged buildings as soon as the shooting stopped.

The operation folded up completely on May 20 when C/6-31st was lifted out by helicopter, and Tower's battalion crossed the Y Bridge in column, rumbled through the city, passed over the Newport Bridge, and road-marched back to Camp Bearcat. At that point, security for District 8, Saigon, reverted to the ARVN and the National Police. Before departing, the Black Panther Battalion provided security to the Vietnamese relief workers who were removing the dead civilians from the wreckage and evacuating them in red pickup trucks. GIs found many of them in a schoolhouse. "There were probably thirty or forty people that had been rounded up in there and executed by the VC," states Jimmy Dye, who'd been among the first to stumble upon the bloody mess in the schoolhouse. "There were bodies on top of bodies. We called in the ARVNs, and the relief workers began carrying the bodies out, and every one of 'em—men, women, and children—had been shot in the head."

The Panthers had previously found government officials who had been shot in the head by the communists, their bodies dumped in the rice paddies around Bearcat. The schoolhouse massacre in Saigon was a psychotic

escalation of the enemy policy of selective assassination, "like a scene out of the Holocaust," according to Dye. "The bodies had been in there for several days, decomposing in the heat. The stench was unbearable. The relief workers all had gas masks on or rags tied over their mouth and nose. The bodies were literally falling apart. I remember this one litter coming out, and it probably had two or three bodies on it, and this arm was dangling over the side, and all of a sudden it just fell off."

Closing the loop on combat photographer Ken Pollard and his AWOL Screaming Eagle buddy Rick Laurent takes us to May 28, 1968. Pollard, Laurent, and Specialist Fourth Class Ransom C. Cyr, another combat photographer, were accompanying a Vietnamese Marine unit during a third-wave of enemy attacks in Cholon. Pollard was shot through his left thigh while crossing an alley. The round severed the femoral artery. Cyr pulled him out of the line of fire and secured a tourniquet to stop the blood jetting from the wound. In this action, he was acting as a soldier not a friend, for Pollard and Cyr were not on good terms. Then Cyr was shot and killed while rushing to find a medic for Pollard.

Rick Laurent came to the rescue, shouting and waving his .45 as he led two Vietnamese Marines forward with a stretcher. Pollard was loaded into an ARVN ambulance, which departed the scene with siren wailing and Laurent perched on the running board. The ambulance pulled into the driveway of the 3rd Field Hospital. The MP at the gate, apparently under instructions not to allow Vietnamese casualties inside the compound and unaware that there was actually a GI inside the ARVN ambulance, objected, "You can't bring that ambulance in here." Laurent snapped in reply, "Open the gate or I'll blow your fucking head off!"

That did the trick, and Pollard received the emergency treatment he needed to save his leg and his life. Laurent later returned to the contact area to help recover Cyr's body. In thanks, the commanding officer of the 221st Signal Company arranged for the AWOL paratrooper to return without court-martial to the 101st Airborne. As it turned out, Laurent came home from the war unscathed, but barely survived the World. During a 1970 reunion, Laurent showed Pollard the gunshot wounds he had received following a card game gone wrong in Detroit. Laurent dropped in on Pollard again while passing through the Sacramento area with his girlfriend in 1978. They were on the run. "The FBI's after me. Let me show you why," Laurent said, as he started to open the briefcase he was carrying. "No, don't show me," Pollard blurted. "If they come around asking questions, I don't want to be able to tell 'em anything." Pollard never saw Laurent again.

Epilogue
RECRIMINATIONS

General Ewell presided over an awards ceremony held on the green beneath the Y Bridge on the last day of the operation. There were flags, speeches, various generals, colonels, and members of the press seated in folding chairs on a makeshift reviewing stand and, finally, a medal and a handshake from General Palmer for each of the nearly one hundred officers and men drawn up at attention who represented each of the units that had fought in Saigon.

Standing behind a microphone, Ewell noted the division had lost 39 KIA and 265 WIA in the battle for Saigon: there had been 7 fatalities in the 5-60th Mechanized Infantry, 10 in the 3-39th Infantry, 10 in the 2-47th Infantry, and 12 in the 6-31st Infantry.

In exchange, declared Ewell, the Old Reliables had accounted for 976 Viet Cong and North Vietnamese; thus the communist offensive had been transformed into "one of the biggest allied victories of the war."

DeLuca received a note soon thereafter from a lieutenant colonel serving at division headquarters. "Congratulations to you and the 3/39 for the tremendous job this last week," the message read. DeLuca's friend, however, cautioned that speeches and ceremonies aside, Ewell was actually displeased that the Saigon laurels hadn't been won by his hand-picked subordinates: "[T]he splendid success of the 3rd Brigade has curdled Gen Ewell's stomach (and Emerson's). General E's bias is plainly apparent and all of us are most upset." Disgusted that Benson never transformed into another super-aggressive Gunfighter Emerson, Ewell had the final word, derailing Benson's career with his end-of-tour efficiency report. Such evaluations were so inflated that Ewell did not have to explicitly criticize Benson, but merely to use midrange adjectives instead of the superlatives that won stars for favored brigade commanders. "I reviewed my ER [efficiency report] with my old buddy Bill Knowlton before I left," recalls Benson, "and he said, 'Well, he kinda killed you with kindness.' I never did make BG [brigadier general]."

It has been suggested that a bit of George Benson went into the character of George Robertson, the wronged brigade commander who serves as the moral center of *The Lionheads,* Josiah Bunting's thinly-disguised novel about General Ewell.

The victory was not applauded by all. "[S]ome Embassy civilian finks are upset about all the damage that was caused by us in Saigon and the MACV IG [inspector general] will be investigating it," DeLuca wrote home. "We are lining up our ducks and have no doubt that we did only minimum essential damage. That's something though!"

The embassy officials in question were Charles Sweet and his immediate superior, General Edward G. Lansdale, U.S. Air Force, Retired, then serving as a special assistant to Ellsworth Bunker. On May 12, Lansdale had sent to Ambassador Bunker, General Westmoreland, and other key members of the U.S. Mission the two-page memo written by Sweet following his visit to Cholon and District 8. Lansdale referred to the memo as "sobering" in his cover letter, adding that when he saw Sweet after his inspection of the battle area, "he was shaken by the deep anger against all Americans shown by Vietnamese with whom he had been close friends until the actions in the urban areas these past few days. I asked him to write a report, so that I could share it with you."

General Westmoreland instructed Colonel Robert M. Cook, the MACV IG, to conduct a "priority investigation" into the matter. Colonel Cook did a group interview with, among others, General Roseborough, Colonel Benson, the G3 of II Field Force, and the deputy senior advisor for the Capital Military District. In addition, Colonel Robert W. Marshall, chief of the MACV IG's Investigations Division, headed a team that studied after-action reports and aerial photographs while also collecting sworn testimony from gunship pilots, advisors, battalion commanders, and staff officers at the battalion, brigade, and division level. "I spent a couple of hours this afternoon waiting to be interrogated by [a lieutenant colonel from] the MACV IG," DeLuca wrote his wife on May 22. "There's a team investigating allegations of unnecessary damage and they are talking to everybody. I concluded our talk with the statement that if I had to do it again it would be the same way, and with the same degree of force. They asked me what would have happened if we didn't use air strikes, artillery, and gunships—my answer was a lot more casualties and a lot longer battle with much more troops required. I told Col Benson I'll be the scapegoat if it will get me home early—no such luck—he has first crack at that deal!"

No scapegoats were required. Colonel Marshall's report thoroughly exonerated the 9th Division units that had fought in District 8. Accepting all witness testimony at face value, Marshall wrote that Benson's brigade had faced a "VC/NVA force composed of elements of seven battalions with an estimated strength of 2200 effectives." There were among the enemy "an unusually high proportion of NVA," and prisoners "stated that their instructions were to fight to the death." Faced with a resolute foe who offered "a stubborn house-to-house defense employing strongpoints and bunkers," the battalion commanders tasked with clearing the district had been forced to employ artillery, helicopter gunships, and tactical air support. The rules of engagement had been followed. Clearances to employ supporting arms had been obtained from the proper authorities. Civilians had been warned to leave targeted areas, and "US commanders on the scene demonstrated a high degree of concern both for civilian casualties and property destruction. . . . In the judgment of commanders on the scene, extensive fire support was essential to the timely destruction of the enemy force and significantly reduced the number of friendly casualties suffered."

The idea that the communists might have accomplished their mission by forcing the allies to destroy a pro-government district was addressed indirectly, and dismissed, in the report:

> Information gained from enemy POWs [prisoners of war] reveals that the mission of the enemy force was apparently that of seizing the Y Bridge in order to gain access to Saigon for the accomplishment of further assigned missions. The aggressive action by the 3rd Brigade, 9th Division successfully secured the bridges over the canal, contained the enemy in a peripheral area of Saigon and systematically destroyed his force. . . . [T]he enemy was prevented from entering the heart of Saigon where combat action to dislodge him would predictably have resulted in far greater damage and casualties, both military and civilian.

Colonel Marshall concluded that Liem had exaggerated the number of civilian casualties and the amount of property damage when speaking with Sweet, then gave the back of his hand to Sweet:

> The most serious distortion contained in Mr. Sweet's report was the implied lack of appreciation for the seriousness of the VC/NVA threat in the 6th and 8th Precincts, and the level of sustained combat

required to dislodge the enemy in these areas. While Mr. Sweet's report was based upon the understandably emotional reaction of Mr. Doan Thanh Liem, who was highly instrumental in the civic programs of these two precincts, it, nevertheless, represents a totally unbalanced view that the destruction resulted from massive US firepower directed against a mere handful of enemy personnel. In fact, the destruction resulted from two intense combat actions which effectively prevented the penetration of the enemy into areas of metropolitan Saigon where greater damage predictably would have ensued. It is unfortunate that Mr. Sweet, a representative of the US Government, did not see fit to explain to Mr. Liem the restraint which has consistently governed the employment of US firepower in RVN, and that its use within the city of Saigon was subject to either the request or approval of appropriate Vietnamese military and political authorities.

Despite official exonerations and the effort by public spokesmen to draw attention to the enemy's overarching complicity in the destruction, the ranks had not completely closed on the issue. Colonel Nguyen Van Luan, the Saigon chief of police—soon to be accidentally killed by a U.S. gunship during a brief third-wave of attacks in the capital—commented bitterly to news reporters that "the Viet Cong has no air force of his own, so he uses ours." The U.S. Embassy sent a cable to the State Department, noting that "if the enemy continues to create refugees, to destroy and damage houses and industrial plants, and to impose on friendly forces the need to use air and artillery in a built-up area with resultant civilian casualties . . . the question is how long this can be endured without threatening all that has been achieved here."

Upon succeeding Westmoreland as theater commander, General Creighton W. Abrams banned the use of supporting arms in Saigon without his personal approval. As the communists made no serious incursions into the capital during Abrams' watch, it remains unknown how he would have dealt with a battle within the city limits. It is clear, however, that Abrams understood the political damage the communists were inflicting even as their assault troops were decimated in the streets. Following a briefing by General Weyand at Long Binh about II Field Force's successful defense of the Saigon area during the May Offensive, a dejected Abrams told his staff that "as I rode back in my helicopter after hearing how well we were doing, smoke was billowing up in Saigon, flames shooting up in the air. I have estimated that we can successfully defend seven more times, and then we're going to be faced with the embarrassment that there's no city left. And I don't know how the hell we're going to explain these nine successful defenses of Saigon—but no goddamn city!"

The question remains: How large a force did the enemy deploy in District 8, Saigon? A platoon, according to Griffiths. A company, according to Liem. Two regiments, according to MACV. When journalist Frank Palmos returned to Vietnam twenty years after he narrowly escaped being slaughtered by the VC in Cholon, he arranged an interview with a retired general who had commanded the forces that fought in District 8. According to the retired general, two battalions of liberation fighters had infiltrated the district, which sounds about right given the level of resistance encountered by the 9th Division. "It was a terrible battle," said the general. "The Americans fought courageously against us at the important Y Bridge. Both sides lost many good men in that week." According to the general, one full battalion occupied the housing at the southern approach to the bridge. The battle for the bridge became a "duel" between the guerrilla battalion and a battalion of American infantry, said the general, a mostly honest old soldier who couldn't help but remember the outcome through a gauze of revolutionary fervor: "By the end of the fighting this battalion had been awarded, not once, but thrice, Heroes of Vietnam honors. . . . The Americans threw everything at us from the air and the ground. But we were well entrenched. Finally, our battalion won. It was a rare phenomenon in any war for one battalion to liquidate another one entirely."

Lieutenant Colonel DeLuca continued operations in the Rach Kien area until the second week of June 1968, when General Ewell moved Emerson's brigade into Benson's area of operations and Benson's brigade into Emerson's former area of operations.

Ewell would have argued that Emerson was better suited than Benson to destroy the enemy in what was the division's most active sector. DeLuca, however, was appalled by the switch, which he viewed as a political move designed to garner Ewell's favorite brigade commander further glory by giving him a crack at a guerrilla beehive; never mind that Benson and his battalion commanders had already been operating quite successfully in the area. Neither Ewell nor Emerson had much use for civic action, and DeLuca saw his good works at Rach Kien squandered when the 3rd of the 39th was replaced by one of the Gunfighter's battalions. DeLuca wrote home in frustration after the switch that the new battalion had already "antagonized the people by divorcing themselves from them, refusing them medical treatment[,] and making plans to remove their homes so the perimeter will be clear of obstructions."

Pushed deeper into the delta and away from the capital, DeLuca's battalion ended up securing a stretch of Highway 4. On July 8, while Benson was on leave, the division G3, a lieutenant colonel then serving as acting brigade commander discussed with DeLuca a one-company operation he wanted the 3d of the 39th to launch the next morning into the Plain of Reeds. Intelligence indicated a large enemy force had recently moved into the marshy wasteland. Given the heavy casualties suffered by other units that had ventured into the enemy sanctuary, DeLuca asked, "Well, if you know that they're there, why don't you send the B-52s over and just bomb the hell out of 'em?"

The acting brigade commander was of the opinion that an infantry operation would be more successful in finding and destroying the enemy. In that case, noting that the next day's forecast called for bad weather that would ground their tactical air support and leave them dependent on gunships, DeLuca said he would need to move his attached artillery battery within range of the Plain of Reeds. "Oh, no, no, we're not going to do that," the acting brigade commander said. DeLuca asked why not. "Because," he was told, "every time we move artillery, the enemy knows that the range is thirteen kilometers and they immediately move beyond that circle."

Denied artillery, DeLuca, on solid ground in that the acting brigade commander did not outrank him, declared, "I'm not taking this battalion in there."

The acting brigade commander came up with a way around DeLuca's refusal, by instructing DeLuca to place Captain Stuart and Alpha Company under operational control of brigade headquarters. DeLuca had thus been cut out of the loop when Stuart radioed in on the morning of July 9 to inform the battalion commander that brigade had just tasked him with launching an air assault. Unfortunately, noted Stuart, only three slicks had been dispatched to his pickup zone instead of the fifteen required to move a rifle company. The three slicks could only accommodate eighteen infantrymen. Monitoring the radio, DeLuca realized that this three-ship assault was headed for the previously discussed target area in the Plain of Reeds.

The first load came under heavy fire upon disembarking into the knee-deep muck of a paddy. The three Hueys returned to the pickup zone for the next eighteen men, including Captain Stuart, and dropped them with the first group. All three helicopters were shot up in the process. By then, DeLuca was screaming on the radio for a command ship so that he could get to the battle area. Finally provided a bubble helicopter, he climbed aboard with his artillery liaison officer. DeLuca arrived on the scene to find that neither the acting brigade commander nor anyone else was overhead to coordinate the action, that a third load of troops had been inserted a thousand meters from the ongoing battle, and that three men had been killed, three seriously wounded, and many more less severely injured among the thirty-six soldiers pinned down on the original landing zone.

DeLuca wanted the two groups to link up and form a perimeter, and instructed his pilot to drop to six-hundred feet and provide a guide by flying a path from one group to the other while he leaned out the door to give hand-and-arm signals to the troops below. At one point, the pilot slowed the bubble helicopter into a hover, perhaps meaning to give DeLuca more time to signal the troops. Not wanting to be turned into a stationary target, DeLuca drove his elbow into the pilot, shouting to "get the hell out of here!" Before the pilot could react, the little chopper was riddled by a .51-caliber machine gun. DeLuca caught fragments in the back of his head. The pilot took a round in the temple and was killed instantly, slumped over the controls, sending the chopper into a sharp descent that ended a terrifying moment later in the rice paddy.

DeLuca realized he was still alive, but that the machine gun was firing on the downed helicopter. He scrambled out, sloshed around to the other door to pull his injured liaison officer from his seat, then dragged him to cover behind the wreck. Gunships had been scrambled and, informed by Stuart of the battalion commander's demise, proceeded to saturate the crash site with machine-gun and rocket fire in order to catch any VC who might be approaching with the idea of salvaging radios, maps, and weapons from the helicopter. DeLuca crawled back to the helicopter to retrieve the single smoke grenade inside, which he then lobbed toward the raised edge of the paddy, the only dry ground he could see. To his horror, he missed. Thankfully, green smoke rose from the muddy water where the grenade had disappeared, and the gunship pilots got the message and ceased their fire. In short order, a Huey arrived. DeLuca loaded the liaison officer on board, but kept the man's M16.

Fire was still pouring in as DeLuca low-crawled toward his grunts, dragging his commandeered rifle by its sling. When a round suddenly snapped past his ear, he thought it was all over, that a sniper had him in his sights. Then he realized that he had almost blown his own head off: the M16 he was dragging was loaded, the safety was off, and long, thick grass had wrapped around the trigger.

DeLuca finally found Stuart, and they began pulling everyone together into a tight little perimeter. The gunships were unable to suppress the enemy fire, and the wounded and dead had to be dragged through the mud and water and weeds, everyone keeping low for all the rounds cracking just overhead. DeLuca saw one grunt with bloody legs pulling himself along with his hands. It was well after sundown before the perimeter was in place. *At least we'll be in this mess together,* DeLuca thought. He was sitting up to his waist in water, which suddenly turned warm around him; he realized he was so exhausted he was pissing himself.

The slicks that attempted to extract DeLuca's group were driven back by enemy fire, and the decision was finally made to try again in the morning. All was not lost, however, because DeLuca's artillery battery had been hastily moved overland from its firebase to a position within range of the battle and it began to deliver fire. DeLuca instructed the battery commander to bring his fires in closer. The captain was reluctant to do so until DeLuca explained that unless his troops could actually feel the shrapnel going past, they probably would not survive the night. The captain said that he understood and proceeded to put a ring of fire around the last-stand perimeter, twenty-two hundred rounds in all that prevented the enemy from overrunning the position.

The rest of the battalion assaulted into the area the next morning, and DeLuca's morale soared when he heard Benson's voice on the command net. The real brigade commander was back. Ewell landed at DeLuca's position during the extraction and said with a grimace, "I don't know what took you so long to get those troops together last night."

"Because there were bad guys shooting real bullets," DeLuca snapped back.

Despite the hard words, Ewell decorated DeLuca with another Silver Star.

In August 1968, DeLuca turned the battalion colors over to his replacement and stopped by General Ewell's office at the new division headquarters in Dong Tam for a courtesy exit visit. Ewell began to speak to DeLuca of what a great job his battalion had done. DeLuca stopped him. "General, I really don't want to hear it," he said, so disenchanted with the senior leadership he had seen in Vietnam that he was no longer interested in being respectful. "Not one time during the seven months I had that battalion did you have a good thing to say. Not once did you take the time to send any praise—but any way you want to measure results, that battalion performed as well or better than any battalion you got." And, with that, DeLuca saluted, turned on his heel, and left.

Among the items Tony DeLuca packed for the trip home was a plaque Captain Stuart's boys had presented to him after the debacle in the Plain of Reeds. At the top, there was a plexiglass-covered section from a topographical map with a symbol depicting where the colonel's helicopter had been shot down, and beneath the map an engraved plate:

Know ye by these presents that
Lieutenant Colonel Anthony P. DeLuca
is an official member of the paddy crawlers and bullet dodgers
association of
Alpha Company, 3d Battalion 39th Infantry Regiment
9th Infantry Division.
Having earned his baptism under fire in the rice paddies of Dinh
Tuong Province, Republic of Vietnam on the ninth day of July
1968 in witness whereof he is hereby authorized to drink hot beer
and eat cold "C" rations with the members of Alpha Company
wherever and whenever his chopper may come to rest.
"DROP IN ANY TIME"
LOYALLY
COMPANY "A"

General Ewell was to win a third star at the end of his command tour for his magnificent successes with the 9th Division. Ewell had said he wanted to produce dead guerrillas with the efficiency of an assembly line and had accomplished as much. Ewell had taken the war to the enemy and hurt him in a real way, making inconsequential, at least in the eyes of higher command, the stories his subordinates could tell about inflated body counts, fake body counts, and all the luckless villagers included in the tabulation of enemy dead.

Following his promotion, Ewell took over II Field Force and continued to pursue the enemy with maximum aggression. General Abrams often remarked that Ewell was his finest corps commander. Abrams might have been a proponent of pacification, but for pacification to work, the enemy's conventional forces had to be destroyed. Ewell was Abrams' man for that job, and after Ewell's second command tour was completed, he was rewarded with another prestige assignment, though one that struck some as the ultimate in bitter irony: military advisor to the U.S. Delegation at the Paris Peace Talks.

A final note about Ewell: there is a rumor, impossible to verify, that it has been made known to the former division commander that he would be unwelcome at the reunions held by those who served in Vietnam with the Old Reliables.

Appendix
KNOWN FATALITIES—SAIGON, MAY 5–12, 1968

May 5, 1968
Specialist Fourth Class Arnold L. Stewart (Company D, 6th Battalion, 31st Infantry)
Hasso Rudt von Collenberg (First Secretary, West German Embassy)
Michael Y. Birch (Australian Associated Press)
John L. Cantwell (*Time* Magazine)
Ronald B. Laramy (*Reuters*)
Bruce S. Piggott (*Reuters*)

May 6, 1968
Private First Class Bobby R. Childs (Company A, 6th Battalion, 31st Infantry)
Staff Sergeant Jimmy Bedgood (Company C, 52nd Infantry)
Charles R. Eggleston (United Press International)
Colonel Luu Kim Cuong (33rd Air Wing, Vietnamese Air Force)

May 7, 1968
Sergeant Philip L. Culver (Company D, 6th Battalion, 31st Infantry)
Specialist Fourth Class Warren M. Kirsch (Company D, 6th Battalion, 31st Infantry)
Private First Class Thomas W. Myers (Company B, 6th Battalion, 31st Infantry)
Specialist Fourth Class Harry G. Koyl (Medic attached to Company A, 5th Battalion [Mechanized], 60th Infantry)
Private First Class Dalton H. McWaters (Company A, 5th Battalion [Mechanized], 60th Infantry)

May 8, 1968
First Lieutenant Joe R. Carrillo Jr. (Company B, 3rd Battalion, 39th Infantry)
Specialist Fourth Class James S. Singletary (Company B, 3rd Battalion, 39th Infantry)
Private First Class Michael H. Stewart (Company B, 3rd Battalion, 39th Infantry)

Private First Class Steven J. Prescott (Company A, 5th Battalion [Mechanized] 60th Infantry)

May 9, 1968

Sergeant Franklin A. Townsend (Company A, 3rd Battalion, 39th Infantry)

Private First Class Miguel A. Abreu-Batista (Company B, 3rd Battalion, 39th Infantry)

Second Lieutenant Frederick R. Casper (Company C, 2nd Battalion [Mechanized], 47th Infantry)

Specialist Fifth Class Paul R. Standridge (Company C, 2nd Battalion [Mechanized], 47th Infantry)

Specialist Fifth Class Clarence H. Washington Jr. (Company C, 2nd Battalion [Mechanized], 47th Infantry)

Specialist Fourth Class George W. Darnell Jr. (Company B, 2 Battalion [Mechanized], 47th Infantry)

Private First Class Kenneth W. Arnold (Company C, 2nd Battalion [Mechanized] -47th Infantry)

Private First Class Larry G. Caldwell (Company B, 2nd Battalion [Mechanized], 47th Infantry)

Private First Class Thomas W. Cranford (Company C, 2nd Battalion [Mechanized], 47th Infantry)

Private First Class Merrill A. Moser (Company C, 2nd Battalion [Mechanized], 47th Infantry)

May 10, 1968

Sergeant Richard D. "Rick" Kosar (Company B, 6th Battalion, 31st Infantry)

Private First Class Jose L. Vieras (Company B, 6th Battalion, 31st Infantry)

Platoon Sergeant Paul E. Jackson (Company A, 3rd Battalion, 39th Infantry)

Sergeant Howard E. Querry (Company A, 3rd Battalion, 39th Infantry)

Private First Class Robert M. Jacobs (Company A, 3rd Battalion, 39th Infantry)

Private First Class David M. Powell (Company A, 3rd Battalion, 39th Infantry)

Captain Edmund B. Scarborough (Company C, 5th Battalion [Mechanized], 60th Infantry)

Specialist Fourth Class William G. Behan (Company C, 5th Battalion [Mechanized], 60th Infantry)

Private First Class Richard J. Flores (Company C, 5th Battalion [Mechanized], 60th Infantry)

Private First Class James J. "Lurch" Hewitt (pseudonym)(Forward Observer Team, 2nd Battalion,4th Artillery, attached to Company C, 5th Battalion [Mechanized], 60th Infantry)(Died of Wounds, May 21)

Private First Class Randolph R. Wilkins (Company C, 5th Battalion [Mechanized] 60th Infantry)

May 11, 1968

Sergeant John T. Moore (Company D, 6th Battalion, 31st Infantry)

Specialist Fourth Class Fred G. Losel Jr. (Company B, 6th Battalion, 31st Infantry)(Died of Wounds, May 12)

Specialist Fourth Class Gregory A. Russell (Company C, 6th Battalion, 31st Infantry)

May 12, 1968

Specialist Fourth Class Dennis K. Jones (Company B, 6th Battalion, 31st Infantry)

Private First Class Lyle W. Hansen (Company B, 6th Battalion, 31st Infantry)

Specialist Fourth Class Jaime A. Rivera-Lopez (Company C, 3rd Battalion, 39th Infantry)

Specialist Fourth Class Anthony P. Palumbo (Company B, 2nd Battalion [Mechanized], 47th Infantry)

Private First Class Philip M. Wooten (Company B, 2nd Battalion [Mechanized], 47th Infantry)

Glossary

AK-47 standard communist 7.62mm assault rifle
APC armored personnel carrier
ARVN Army of the Republic of Vietnam
AWOL absent without leave
Beehives nickname for flechette rounds
Big Red One nickname for 1st Infantry Division
Birddog nickname for the single-engine OV-1 scout plane
Blue line nickname for a stream
C4 white, clay-like plastic explosives
CAR-15 standard U.S. 5.56mm submachine gun
Chinook nickname for the CH47 cargo helicopter
Cobra nickname for the AH1G helicopter gunship
Dragonfly nickname for the jet-engine A-37 fighter-bomber
Dust-off nickname for medical evacuation helicopters and units
Frags short for fragmentation grenades
H23 small helicopter with bubble-encased cockpit
Hootch name for living quarters in Vietnam
HQ headquarters
Huey nickname for the UH1 series of helicopter
IG inspector general
KIA killed in action
Klicks short for kilometers
LAW standard U.S. 66mm light-anti-tank weapon (a shoulder-fired rocket in a disposable one-shot fiberglass tube)
M14 standard U.S. 7.62mm automatic rifle
M16 standard U.S. 5.56mm automatic rifle
M60 standard U.S. 7.62mm light machine gun
M79 standard U.S. 40mm grenade launcher
M113 standard U.S. armored personnel carrier
M577 armored personnel carrier modified into a command vehicle with a higher hull to accommodate radios and other equipment
MACV Military Assistance Command, Vietnam
Medevac medical evacuation
Mike-mike millimeter

MP military police
NCO noncommissioned officer
NVA North Vietnamese Army
OCS officer candidate school
Old Reliables nickname for 9th Infantry Division
Phantom nickname for the F4 series of jet-engine fighter-bombers
RPD communist light machine gun
RPG communist rocket-propelled grenade
ROTC reserve officer training corps
RTO radio-telephone operator
Sapper Viet Cong demolitionist
Shake 'n' bakes nickname for sergeants who earned their stripes at the Non-commissioned Officers Candidate School
Short-timer a soldier whose Vietnam tour was almost finished
Skyraider nickname for the single-engine A1E fighter-bomber
Slicks nickname for Huey helicopters used to transport troops instead of being outfitted as gunships
Straight-leg a unit that uses leg power to travel
The World anyplace but Vietnam
Tiger Scout a Viet Cong defector assigned to a U.S. unit as a scout and interpreter
Track nickname for an armored personnel carrier
VC Viet Cong
WIA wounded in action
XM148 an M16 modified with a grenade launcher

Selected Bibliography

Several researchers and writers assisted with this book, to include Colonel Karl Lowe, U.S. Army (Retired), who provided much information about operatings in the Mekong Delta, where he served as both an ARVN advisor and a company commander with the 9th Division; Courtney L. Frobenius, a former 9th Division platoon leader who had much to impart about grunt morale under the reign of the Butcher of the Delta; Bruce Swander, a Vietnam-veteran-turned-researcher-extraordinaire who unearthed official documentation related to the murders at Firebase Smoke; Brian Tate, a former Australian army artilleryman who had much information about Garry Cooper, the Royal Australian Air Force pilot who flew in support of the 9th Division; George Lepre, a former army infantryman who is now writing a book about fragging and who shared what information he had in his files about the 9th Division; and, of course, Captain Stan Sirmans, U.S. Navy (Retired), who hunkered down for me at the National Archives, photocopying unit records, digging up the MACV IG investigation, and culling through the general orders file of the 9th Division for citations relevant to the action in Saigon. Finally, many thanks are due my agent, E. J. McCarthy, for his key role in making this book happen.

Books
Numerous histories and references books were consulted. Those of particular value include:

Braestrup, Peter. *Big Story: How the American Press and Television Reported and Interpreted the Crisis of Tet 1968 in Vietnam and Washington.* New Haven: Yale University Press, 1983.

Edelman, Bernard, ed. *Dear America: Letters Home from Vietnam.* New York: W. W. Norton & Company, 1985.

Griffiths, Philip Jones. *Vietnam Inc.* New York: Collier Books, 1971.

Hackworth, David H. and Julie Sherman. *About Face: Odyssey of an American Warrior.* New York: Simon and Schuster, 1989.

Hammond, William M. *Public Affairs: The Military and the Media, 1962–1968.* Washington, D.C.: Center of Military History, United States Army, 1988.

————. *Public Affairs: The Military and the Media, 1968–1973.* Washington, D.C.: Center of Military History, United States Army, 1996.

Herr, Michael. *Dispatches.* New York: Alfred A. Knopf, 1977.

Johnson, James D. *Combat Chaplain: A 30-Year Vietnam Battle.* Denton, Texas: University of North Texas Press, 2001.

Krepinevich, Andrew F., Jr. *The Army and Vietnam.* Baltimore: The John Hopkins University Press, 1986.

Palmer, Laura. *Shrapnel in the Heart: Letters and Remembrances from the Vietnam Veterans Memorial.* New York: Random House, 1987.

Palmos, Frank. *Ridding the Devils.* London: Arrow Books, 1991.

Spector, Ronald H. *After Tet: The Bloodiest Year in Vietnam.* New York: The Free Press, 1993.

Periodicals

Contemporary newspaper and magazine accounts were reviewed. Two particularly good articles from more recent publications were: "River Rats to the Rescue at Ben Tre," by Wynn A. Goldsmith (*Vietnam*, February 1998); and "A Friendship Forged in Danger" by Wallace Terry (*Parade Magazine*, July 1, 1990)

Documents

"Daily Staff Journal [or] Duty Officer's Log: 6th Battalion 31st Infantry." April and May 1968.

"Daily Staff Journal or Duty Officers [*sic*] Log: S-3 3/39th Infantry." May 1968.

"Daily Staff Journal or Duty Officer's Log: 2nd Bn (M) 47th Inf." May 1968.

"Daily Staff Journal or Duty Officer's Log: Headquarters 716th Military Police Battalion (S2)." May 1968.

"Department of the Army, 3d Brigade, 9th Infantry Division, APO San Francisco 96373. Subject: Combat Operations After Action Report (MACV/RCS/J3/32)(U), 11 August 1968."

"Department of the Army, Headquarters, 5th Battalion (M), 60th Infantry, APO San Francisco 96307: Combat After Action Report (FS/PB Jager [sic])."

"Headquarters, United States Military Assistance Command, Vietnam, APO San Francisco 96222, Office of the Inspector General. Subject: Report of Investigation Concerning Destruction Resulting from the VC Offensive of 5–13 May 1968 (U), 2 June 1968."

"History of 377th Security Police Squadron April–June 1968."

"Task Force Hay (Hurricane Forward) After Action Report 05–16 May 1968."

Interviews

Most interviews were conducted by phone, letter, and email, mostly between 2000 and 2003; only a small number were conducted in person. Quotes from interviews were often edited for clarity and conciseness; everyone involved had the opportunity to review the book manuscript for accuracy before publication. The following veterans, divided by unit, participated in the interviews and/or the review process:

MACV, U.S. Army Vietnam, II Field Force Vietnam, and 9th Infantry Division: General William A. Knowlton (Retired); General James J. Lindsay (Retired); Lieutenant General Henry E. "Hank" Emerson (Retired); Brigadier General Donald D. Dunlop (Retired); Brigadier General Douglas Kinnard (Retired); Colonel George C. Benson (Retired); Colonel John Haseman (Retired); Colonel William Locke Hauser (Retired); Colonel John B. Keeley (Retired); Colonel William T. Leggett Jr. (Retired); Colonel Karl Lowe (Retired); and David Cargill

6th Battalion, 31st Infantry: Colonel William J. Owen (Retired); Lieutenant Colonel Philip L. Eckman (Retired); Lieutenant Colonel Channing M. Greene (Retired); Lieutenant Colonel David P. Wilson (Retired); Major John E. DeVore (Retired); Anthony Eric Belt; Lance F. Bergstreser; Kenneth R. Davis; Paul J. Fish; Charles W. "Bill" Gale; David E. Gray; Jon R. Jones; David B. Leader; William McMullen; Robert Magdaleno; Vernon S. Moore; Mark Mudd; Ralph A. "Al" Olson; Jerry Pickens; Nicholas C. Procaccini; Richard Rebischke; and William L. Sirtola

3rd Battalion, 39th Infantry: Colonel Anthony P. DeLuca (Retired); Colonel Thomas R. Genetti (Retired); Command Sergeant Major Stanley E. Thornburgh (Retired); First Sergeant Herchel D. Johnson (Retired); First Sergeant Ronald N. Klump (Retired); William Bausser; Jack A. Brunet; Michael J. Canney; Gary Feicke; Wilfred A. Geschke, M.D.; George Franklin Humphreys II; Hildebrando "Mad" Madrigal; Willo T. Naramore Jr.; William B. Spence; and James Tunney

4th Battalion, 39th Infantry: Tony Keberlein; James W. Kirk; and Russell Pollard

2nd Battalion (Mechanized), 47th Infantry: Colonel Brice H. Barnes, U.S. Army Reserve (Retired); Colonel Henry L. S. Jezek, U.S. Army National Guard; Colonel William W. Jones (Retired); Colonel William H. Riedl (Retired); Lieutenant Colonel James B. Craig (Retired); Captain Leroy L. Brown (Retired); First Sergeant Anthony R. Midkiff (Retired); Platoon Sergeant William N. Butler (Retired); John Ax; Paul H. Bowman; Timothy Burke; John E. Driessler; Jimmy R. Dye; Robert A. Dyson; Robert Elston; Philip T. Grignon; Tom Hagel; Lewis W. Hosler; Tony M. Hughes; Paul J. Ianni; Bruce R. Isenhoff; Michael H. Jeter; Frank W. McIntosh; Harold Peterson Clifford M. Pinkston Jr.; Robert Pries; Vernon B. Quagon; Billy C. Reid; Phil Streuding; Richard Uhlich; and Russell E. Vibberts Jr.

5th Battalion (Mechanized), 60th Infantry: Colonel Wendelin Winslow (Retired); Lieutenant Colonel Eric F. Antila (Retired); Lieutenant Colonel Tim Koeneman, U.S. Army National Guard; Major Carl D. Lange (Retired); Major Theodore R. Moen, Michigan National Guard; Sergeant First Class Charles Baker (Retired); Lee B. Alley; Douglas G. Birge; Grant S. Buehrig; Edward J. Chaffin; Ron Cunningham; Ronnie T. Everidge; Mark D. Fenton; Dawin G. "Buddy" Gault; Ronald P. Garver; Millard R. Goodwin; Jearold L. Harper; James F. Harrier; Curtis Hatterman; Greg Hawkins; John H. Hohman; John Holder; Lanny E. Jones; Alan D. Kisling; Leslie F. Koenig; Larry A. Lamonica; Samuel E. Marr; John E. Marrs; William Paul Metzler; William R. Milano; Larry D. Miller; Robert Mark Nauyalis; Frank R. Neild, M.D.; Richard F. Neuman; Howard A. Ossen; Wayne Parrish; David Rohe; Merle James "Jim" Sharpe; Clifford E. Shields; James M. Simmen; John R. Sweet; Charles E. Taylor; Jerrold J. Tomlinson; and Gary P. Vertrees

Aviation Units: Colonel Richard L. Sneary, U.S. Air Force (Retired); Garry G. Cooper; and Frederick R. Grates

18th Military Police Brigade: Lieutenant Colonel Steve Senkovich (Retired); Lieutenant Colonel Gary Whitaker (Retired); Walter R. Foster; Robert Ghirlanda; Kirk L. Pagel; and Tom Watson

U.S. Air Force, Tan Son Nhut Airbase: Colonel Melvin G. Grover (Retired); Lieutenant Colonel Carl R. Bender (Retired); Lieutenant Colonel John H. Manley (Ret.); Master Sergeant William J. McKissick (Retired); Master Sergeant Robert S. Need (Retired); Charles Beatie;

Frank Bracken; William M. Burckhalter; Dannie Davis; Renato P. "Ron" DellaPorta; David M. Dowdell; Jerald E. Fish; Leo Goozey; Gene Harris; David E. Koopman; Daniel F. McKegney; Johnny A. Martin; Charles E. Penley; Richard Quintana-Sena; James A. Stewart; and David C. Wollstadt

Military Correspondents: James Fitzpatrick; Bruce A. McIlhaney; John S. Olson; and C. Ken Pollard

Civilian Correspondents: Joseph L. Galloway and Zalin B. "Zip" Grant

Family Members: Kevin Bedgood, son of Staff Sergeant Jimmy Bedgood, killed in action; Janet S. Schmalhorst and Joseph M. Schmalhorst, widow and son, respectively, of Colonel Joseph H. Schmalhorst (Retired), now deceased; Rita E. Tower, widow of Colonel John B. Tower (Retired), now deceased

Index